The World of Small States

Volume 8

Small states differ considerably in their geography, history, political structures, legal systems and wealth. Nevertheless, because of their size, small states face a set of common challenges including vulnerability to external economic impacts such as changing trade regimes and limited ability to diversify economic activity; limited public and private sector capacity, including the legal and judicial infrastructure. A number of small states have experienced colonization and must accommodate the legacy of one or more forms of colonial law alongside the customary law of the indigenous people. Many small states are islands. These are particularly susceptible to environmental impacts such as natural disasters and climate change. Small states can also be flexible, adaptable, sites of social development and innovation, and have an influence in the world disproportionate to their size.

The importance of research into small states is increasingly recognised by the global legal community . Small states are microcosms which allow us to study and gain insight into the challenges of big states. Their small size makes research easier and the testing of solutions more easily. Small states, however, also have unique problems for which unique solutions must be designed. For example, in a small state with a correspondingly-sized legal profession, ethical guidelines in regard to the appointment of judges have to take into account to the small size of the profession.

The aim of this exciting and unique series is to be the essential compendium for every legal researcher interested in small states but also for practitioners and policy makers working in small state.

More information about this series at http://www.springer.com/series/15142

Danny Pieters

Social Security Law in Small Jurisdictions

Springer

Danny Pieters
Department of Law
KU Leuven
Leuven, Belgium

ISSN 2627-5996 ISSN 2627-6003 (electronic)
The World of Small States
ISBN 978-3-030-78246-7 ISBN 978-3-030-78247-4 (eBook)
https://doi.org/10.1007/978-3-030-78247-4

This Springer imprint is published by the registered company Springer Nature Switzerland AG.
The registered company address is: Gewerbestrasse 11, 6330 Cham, Switzerland

Preface

This book examines the following key question: are small jurisdictions (states) confronted with specific issues/problems providing social security and how to deal with these issues/problems? How is social security law impacted by the smallness of the jurisdiction?

In order to address these questions, we examine in a first chapter the key concepts of 'small jurisdiction' and 'social security' as we understand them in the current literature. Next, we pay some attention to the relation between social security and social security law and subsequently make an excursion to explore the notion of legal transplants. In a second chapter, we examine the main features that characterise small states according to the general literature on small states, naturally focusing on these features that may be relevant to social security. We also include an overview of the (limited) literature dealing with the specific social security issues small jurisdictions have to deal with. In Part II of the book, we look at the social security systems of 20 selected small jurisdictions. We do this in a uniform scheme to facilitate their comparison. In Part III, we compare the social security systems of the 20 small jurisdictions. This allows us not only to draw some conclusions about our main question but also to test the validity of the current literature on the topic as described in Chap. 2 of Part I. In the concluding part of the book, we formulate some suggestions for the benefit of the social security systems of the small jurisdictions, based on our research.

The book reflects information and literature available up to May 2020. However, at the time of writing, a pandemic hit the world and made it necessary during the writing of Part II to rely primarily on information accessible on the web as well as on the assistance of people from the concerned jurisdiction.

As always, a monograph is not really the book of only one person. In writing this work, I could count on the collaboration of many. For the information on the social security systems of the selected small jurisdictions, the collection of materials, and the help with the redaction of the country reports, we would like to express our gratitude to Leroy Adolphus, Dennis Arrindell, Cheryl Joy Augustine-Kanu, Julia Axelsson, Joelle Barnes, Antonella Benedettini, Carlos Bollen, Sieglien Burleson, Pema Choden, Colin Connelly, Daniel D'Amato, Sangay Dorjee, Milika Feaomoemanu Tuita, Marcello Forcellini, Christian Frommelt, Mahesh Gajmer, Glenda Gil, João Gabriel Gonçalves, Flora Goudappel, Joyce Grech, David Hales, Regin Djurhuus Hammer, Richard Herr, Mininnguaq Kleist, Bárður Larsen, Philip Martis, Elin Mortensen, Kirsten Olesen, Elia Panayiotis, Paul Patron, Michael Peil, Rachel Perri, Nicholas Richardson, Patricia Schiess, Shaista Shameem, Jan Sjóstein, Hassan Sobir, Hildur Sverrisdóttir Röed, Adi Talanaivini Mafi, Pem Thinley, Lisa Tomassini, Marisol Tromp, and Nicolas Vantomme, all in their respective capacities and with their respective titles. I would also like to thank for their precious help in the various stages of the research project: Gerard Everaet, Patrik Jaspers, Thijs Keersmaekers, Niel Laenen, Eric Mijts, and Elzaan Rossouw. A special word of thanks goes to our colleagues Dr. Caroline Morris, Director of the Centre for Small States at Queen Mary University London, Prof. Peter Edge of Oxford Brookes University, as well as our colleagues at KU Leuven Prof. Paul Schoukens and Prof. Bert Demarsin, as they showed interest in the project from its very start and were a great support throughout the writing of this book. Finally, I would like to mention the Institute for Comparative Law of the KU Leuven and especially its Small Jurisdictions Research Group: here I found the best environment to do this research. May many other research projects and publications on small jurisdictions follow!

Leuven, Belgium
Spring 2021

Danny Pieters

Contents

Part I
Small Jurisdictions and Social Security: State of the Art

In this part, we first examine the key concepts 'small jurisdiction' and 'social security' as we understand them. Next, we pay some attention to the relation between social security and social security law and subsequently make an excursion to explore the notion of legal transplants. In a second chapter a state of the art of the literature on small jurisdictions is provided, focusing on the features most relevant to social security, such as: the impact of economic and environmental shocks; scale disadvantages and flexibility; the limited human resources and infrastructure; the training needs; the limited number of people covered by social security; the importance of migration; and the strong ties with other states. Issues related to homogeneity and proximity, to the unity of administration and the lack thereof in the benefit schemes, and financial issues will be discussed. In this chapter, we also give an overview of the existing literature dealing with the common features of small jurisdictions, focusing on the features relevant to social security. As such, this part gives a *status quaestionis* concerning our central theme: are small jurisdictions confronted with specific issues or problems when dealing with social security?

Chapter 1
Conceptual Framework

1.1 Small Jurisdictions

We will examine the social security systems of small jurisdictions. Our understand ing of jurisdictions includes states as well as semi-sovereign entities that enjoy full autonomy as far as social security is concerned. As such, our study will complement the emerging literature on small states/small jurisdictions.[1]

Various authors have deplored that scientific interest in small states has been limited in the past; an evolution that, as a consequence of the competitive, career and economic pressures on the scientific world, seems to rather worsen than ameliorate.[2] Nevertheless, it is interesting to study small states, not only for the sake of these states, but also because they can be perceived as laboratories, the results of which can also be relevant for larger countries.[3]

Bogdan wrote in this respect:

> Among the many interesting research problems of a general nature found within the area of comparative law, two complex issues are particularly fascinating . . .: the problem of mixed (hybrid) legal systems and the problem of the so-called "small jurisdictions".[4]

But how do we define 'small jurisdictions' as a category?

Simply put: small jurisdictions are jurisdictions that are small. They consist of states, i.e. politically and legally speaking sovereign countries. In this way, sovereignty can be used as a blunt criterion, as could be the membership of the United Nations. For many purposes more or less independent territories (such as the British) or confederated or federated entities with elements of sovereignty may present

[1]Unless otherwise mentioned, we shall use the terms small state and small jurisdiction in an interchangeable way.

[2]Kirt and Waschkuhn (2001); Wolf (2016), p. 1.

[3]Wolf (2016), p. vi (nr. 35) and p. 2.

[4]Bogdan (1989), as quoted by Donlan et al. (2017), p. 191.

D. Pieters, *Social Security Law in Small Jurisdictions*, The World of Small States 8,
https://doi.org/10.1007/978-3-030-78247-4_1

similar features for concrete legal research.[5] In our research, we decided to include in our study the small states, members of the United Nations Organisation, with some territories enjoying partial independence and full autonomy in the area of interest to us, social security.

The other element to be defined is 'small'. Small states are not characterised by having fewer tasks to fulfil than larger states, but they are different on the basis of specific qualitative or quantitative criteria. The criteria chosen to identify small states will depend on the context.[6] For instance, in economics, the Gross Domestic Product (GDP) may be a useful criterion. Nevertheless, the World Bank prefers the criterion of population size. A general abstract definition of 'the small state' is thus not present.[7] Criteria most used to define a small state are the superficies of the territory and the number of the population.[8] These criteria not only appear most pragmatic, but are also appropriate, as the specificity of the concerned states often depends on their limited human resources and, although to a lesser extent, the limited space they cover. Sometimes one will even distinguish between small states and very small states or microstates, although that distinction is often disputed.[9]

In general, small states are thus usually defined by their population of up to 1½ million people, a criterion first used by the Commonwealth and then adopted by the World Bank (although not as a formal category).[10] We shall follow this approach, as we find that the number of inhabitants of the state is indeed the most relevant factor as far as social security is concerned.

Whatever definition is used of small states, it is clear that there is a high degree of variability among these states. Small states are spread across five continents. Jeanne Hey (2003) groups the small states into three groups: the insular microstates of the Caribbean, the Pacific and along the African coast; the European small and microstates; and African states and former colonies.

Many small states belong to a category that has a "high vulnerability", i.e. being among the poorest countries in the world. Very often, literature on small states and on developing countries tends to coincide, although there are clearly many small states that are more developed. In fact, some small countries are among the richest in the world, as defined by GDP per capita.

From a research standpoint, yet another distinction can be made between the small states: between the Anglophone small states, which are more frequently the

[5]Wolf (2016), p. 3.

[6]Ibid.

[7]Maass (2009), p. 75.

[8]*Ibidem.*

[9]Geser (2001), p. 92; Gstöhl (2001), pp. 123–124; Wolf (2016), p. 4.

[10]One has to be cautious when browsing literature, as sometimes also countries like Belgium, Norway etc. are called 'small countries', see e.g. Katzenstein's comparative study *Small states in world markets* explaining why, during the 1980s, standards of living were higher in the 'smallest' European states. With 'small states' he meant countries like Austria, Belgium, Denmark, the Netherlands, Norway, Sweden, and Switzerland, none of which qualify as a 'small state' as we understand it (Irving 2011, p. 230).

subject of comparative research, and the small states using other languages, such as Dutch or Portuguese.[11]

Small jurisdictions are many and diverse; over sixty small jurisdictions can be found all over the world. Given the above variety of small jurisdictions, we selected the following twenty as a representative sample: in Europe, the states Cyprus, Iceland, Liechtenstein, Malta and San Marino, and the semi-independent territories Gibraltar, Faroe Islands and Greenland; in South America: Suriname and Guyana; in the Caribbean: the states Trinidad and Tobago and Grenada, and the countries of the Kingdom of the Netherlands: Curaçao, Aruba and Sint-Maarten; in the Pacific the states Fiji and Tonga; in Asia: Bhutan and the Maldives; and in Africa: the Seychelles. We have a combination of member states of the UNO and of territories with a link to Britain, The Netherlands and Denmark. We have small countries with a population above half a million (Cyprus, Suriname, Guyana, Fiji, Bhutan and the Maldives) and microstates (or territories with 100,000 or less population (San Marino, Liechtenstein, Gibraltar, Greenland, Aruba, Sint Maarten, Tonga and Seychelles). Two thirds are small island states. Some of the small states have a large territories (e.g. Greenland), while others are very small (such as Gibraltar or Aruba). Some states have a very high GDP per capita, such as Liechtenstein and Iceland (world top 10) or a low GDP per capita such as Guyana or Tonga. Some of the small states listed have very low poverty rates, such as Liechtenstein, while the percentage of the population in poverty is high in others, such as Suriname or Fiji. Some of the selected small jurisdictions can be considered common law countries, other civil law countries or even belonging to other hybrid legal systems.

We realise that we have chosen about one third of the small jurisdictions of the world and that others would make other choices, but we believe that our selection makes sense as it tries to reflect a wide diversity.

The following scheme is intended only to give an idea of the diversity of the twenty selected countries; the figures are not suitable for genuine comparison as they are taken from a various sources at various points in time.

[11] Veenendaal and Wolf (2016).

	Region of the world	Pop. (* by 100,000)[a]	GDP per cap. Int $[b]	Poverty % pop living below national poverty line[c]	% of pop. Daily Income <5.5 $[d]
Liechtenstein (LI)	Europe	0.4	*139*	NA	NA
Malta (MT)	Europe	4.6	43	16	0
Iceland (IS)	Europe	3.4	57	NA	0
Cyprus (CY)	Europe	8.5 (12.7)[e]	36	NA	0
San Marino (SM)	Europe	0.3	*59*	NA	NA
Gibraltar (GI)	Europe	0.3	*62*	NA	NA
Faroe Islands (FO)	Europe	0.5	*40*	10	NA
Greenland (GL)	Europe	0.6	*42*	16	NA
Suriname (SR)	South America	6.1	16	70	56
Guyana (GY)	South America	7.5	9	35	56
Trinidad and Tobago (TT)	Caribbean	12	32	20	33
Granada (GD)	Caribbean	1.1	16	38	NA
Aruba (AW)	Caribbean	1.2	25	NA	NA
Curaçao (CW)	Caribbean	1.5	*15*	NA	NA
Sint Maarten (SX)	Caribbean	0.4	67	NA	NA
Fiji (FJ)	Pacific	9.3	11	31	49
Tonga (TO)	Pacific	1	6	23	28
Bhutan (BT)	Asia	7.8	11	12	39
Maldives (MV)	Asia	4 (5.4)[f]	15	15	54
Seychelles (SC)	Africa	1	31	39	7

[a]Rounded figures, based on 2020 United Nations Population Division estimates and our own country reports of Part III. See Worldometer (2020)

[b]Rounded figures for 2018 of the World Bank estimates. See World Development Indicators Database (2018a). The figures in italic are rounded figures from the World Factbook of the Central Intelligence Agency. See World Factbook (2020)

[c]Rounded figures from the World Factbook of the Central Intelligence Agency. See World Factbook (2020)

[d]Rounded figures from The World Databank of The World Bank. See World Development Indicators Database (2018b)

[e]The total population of the island of Cyprus is approximately 1,270,000, but only 855,000 are living under the jurisdiction of the Republic of Cyprus

[f]According to the above mentioned Worldometer (2020): 5.4; according to countrymeters (https://countrymeters.info/en/Maldives) and sources consulted when drafting the Maldives report: 4, a figure most likely considering the 2014 census reported 3.4 Maldivians

1.2 Social Security

Social security can be defined in very general terms as the body of arrangements shaping the solidarity with people facing (the threat of) a lack of earnings (i.e. income from paid labour) or particular costs, and this in the case of recognised 'social risks'. Social security can take the form of social insurances or social assistance.[12] The goal of social security arrangements is usually defined in a double way: the fight against poverty or social exclusion, and the provision of income replacement or financial support in the case of certain eventualities, called 'social risks'. The first objective is most often associated with social assistance, the second with social insurances, although social insurances are increasingly also perceived in the perspective of combatting poverty.[13]

Social assistance can take the form of money transfers or the form of the provision of goods and services in kind. Regardless of the names given to the arrangements, nearly all countries have one or more such arrangements aimed at alleviating the burden of poverty and social exclusion for the poorest sections of the population. Legislation defines who qualifies as belonging to these poorest sections.

Social insurances usually cover one or more of the social risks enumerated in the ILO Convention no. 102 on the minimum norms in social security: schemes covering medical care, sickness, unemployment, old age, industrial injury and industrial illness, family, maternity, invalidity and survivor's benefits. In this sense, it does not normally include social assistance. The social insurances cover all or some groups of workers and/or all or some groups of the population. Yet not all states have expanded their social insurance schemes to all workers or to the entire population; it seems that social insurance is rather the privilege of some stronger groups in some more vulnerable economies.[14] Again, legislation determines which workers/inhabitants qualify for the personal scope of the most important social insurance schemes.

It will not always be easy to draw the line between social insurance and social assistance schemes, e.g. when a means tested benefit is targeted to the poorest sections of the population. Moreover, the terminology that states use to qualify the benefit schemes may sometimes be confusing. It may also sometimes be difficult to distinguish social security schemes from other social protection programmes. To avoid most of these problems and to maintain a sufficient degree of comparability, we have opted to limit our research to public cash transfer schemes that provide an income or compensate for certain costs, in the case of old age, survivorship, incapacity to work (sickness or invalidity, both in general or related to professional risks), unemployment, need for medical care, family burden or poverty. We shall not include social services; health care will only be included as far as the coverage of health care costs are concerned; the provision of health care by the state will in

[12] Pieters (2006), pp. 1–8.

[13] Pieters (2009), pp. 21–25.

[14] Pieters and Schoukens (2012), p. 10.

principle not be examined. We shall also not deal with other social programmes, such as the ones relating to education or food. We are aware that this relatively narrows the perspective we have chosen and may pass by some important social policy issues, but we want to focus on what is traditionally viewed as one, valuable, social policy instrument, i.e. social security.

While social security, both social assistance and social insurances, have been the subject of much research, also legal and comparative research,[15] attention to the social security arrangements of small states has remained limited.[16] Moreover, the research very often focussed on regional issues, such as in the Caribbean or Pacific regions, which while certainly relevant to the small states concerned, are not necessarily linked to the fact that these jurisdictions were small (but e.g. rather linked to the high unemployment or poor demographic situation). We will explore whether the fact that a jurisdiction as such is small impacts its social security legislation and the way the social security system functions.

1.3 Social Security and the Law

Having defined the two crucial concepts of our research, i.e. small jurisdictions and social security, it is now important to clarify our research question. As we mentioned earlier, we would like to find out whether the fact that a state/jurisdiction as such is small has an impact on both the contents of the social security system and the way the social security law has been developed.

As for the impact of smallness on the social security system, it will be important to distinguish features of the social security systems of small jurisdictions that are not related to their limited population (but related to other features) and those directly connected to the limited population covered. Here, at first glance, some older studies related to small social security systems of larger countries may also seem to be relevant: when, for instance, in a country like Italy, self-employed architects have their own social security arrangements, these are small in terms of covered population, although Italy is not a small state. Small states' social security systems are small by definition, but in larger states, small social security systems may also exist. However interesting it may be to draw a comparison between small social security

[15]See e.g. the research mentioned in Pennings (2006) and Pennings and Vonk (2015).

[16]Exceptions being e.g. UNRISD (2009). A worldwide overview of the main social insurance schemes, including also smaller states, is to be found in Social Security Programs Throughout the World (2020), in (the older) International Social Security Association (1980) or International Social Security Association (1994).

The renowned Commonwealth Small States Centre of Excellence in Malta focuses on public debt management, natural disaster management and mitigation, broadband internet connectivity, diplomatic training, women and enterprises and ocean governance; thus no social topics are included (see Commonwealth Small States Centre of Excellence 2020).

arrangements of bigger states and social security arrangements of small states,[17] it makes sense to focus here only on the social security systems of small jurisdictions: only they lack the administrative, financial, etc. backing of a large state; their lawyers and legislators who can deal with the social security law are limited (unlike in larger countries).

We shall not describe the social security systems of the 20 small jurisdictions under examination in detail, but rather explore the impact of their small population on these contents. Where possible, in our conclusions we shall not only identify some common features and challenges the social security systems of small jurisdictions face, but also suggest some paths to address these.

With regard to the impact of smallness upon social security law and its implementation, we shall naturally have to deal with a number of issues that are typically related to law and small states, such as the capacity of legislators (parliaments, governments, but also judges and administrators) to produce good law, more precisely good social security law. Special attention will be paid to the question where these legislators get their inspiration: is there an important phenomenon of legal transplants that must also be identified in social security law of small states? And if legal transplants have been used in some way, can they be considered to have been successful?

An extensive literature on legal transplants already exists, but it does not engage with the area of social security law. Considering the importance of elaborating the comparative legal theory on legal transplants, also in the area of social security law, we expand on the state of the art as far as legal transplants are concerned. Our study of the social security law of the twenty small jurisdictions will enable us to start verifying the general theory, doing so for an atypical sample of countries and an area of law that is often considered peripheral in comparative law.

As access to social assistance (under whatever name and form) and access (of some workers/inhabitants) to social insurance are quintessential for attaining the first of the sustainable development goals defined by the United Nations,[18] i.e. the fight against poverty, we will focus on the way the laws of social security of small states have defined that access.

Researching the impact of smallness on both the contents of the social security systems of small states and on the law governing these, can be distinguished, but in practice both aspects will often show to be strongly intertwined. This may already be exemplified by our special focus on the access-issue.

---

[17] As was the case in International Social Security Association (1980). International Social Security Association (1994).

[18] See: United Nations (2020).

1.4 An Excursion: Legal Transplants

No legal order has developed completely independently from all other legal orders. All legal orders were influenced to a larger or lesser extent by foreign law. Each legal order consists of a unique mix of innovative law-making and borrowing of law.

In the case of a legal order, part thereof or an isolated legal norm or institution being taken over by domestic law from foreign law, we are dealing with a legal transplant or legal transfer. Some authors prefer to use other terminology, such as a 'transposition of law',[19] 'the circulation of legal models'[20] or even 'legal irritants'.[21] We use the terms most commonly used in the literature, 'legal transplant' and 'legal transfer'.

At this stage, it is already important to see that, notwithstanding the value of the concept of legal transfer or legal transplant, we are not confronted with a monolithic phenomenon, but rather with a spectrum that goes from influence to reception. Legal transplants or transfers will usually not be an exact copy of the foreign example. There is usually a translation: a linguistic translation and a translation into the legal language of the recipient legal order. Other adaptations may also be made to fit the recipient country's legal order to coordinate with other legislation of the recipient country or simply to introduce local preferences etc. Of course, the more adaptations made, the greater the distance between the transferring and the recipient pieces of law will grow. Let us also observe in this context that it may not always be opportune for a recipient legal order to be open about the presence of a foreign influence or a transplant; as a consequence, legal transplants often go 'undercover' and are 'disguised' as genuine domestic law.[22]

Comparative law 'discovered' the issue of legal transplants in the 1970s with the pioneering work of Alan Watson.[23] In subsequent years, important literature on the topic was produced. Some have opposed the idea of legal transplants being possible altogether,[24] but the mainstream literature accepted the concept and focused not so much on the 'if', but rather on the 'how' of legal transplants.

Legal transplants can operate through case law, jurisprudence and legislation. Mainly legal transplants via legislation, new statutes or regulations, attracted most scientific interest,[25] but transplants have also been addressed through court decisions. We will also concentrate on transfers operated through legislation, when a lawmaker more or less takes over statutes or regulations developed elsewhere; some call it cases of 'happy plagiarism' by the lawmakers. This preference for statutory or regulatory transplants is related to the legal area. Social security law, which we are

[19] Örücü (2004).
[20] Sacco (1990).
[21] Teubner (1998).
[22] Fedtke (2012), p. 552.
[23] Watson (1974).
[24] See: Legrand (1997).
[25] Barak-Erez (2014), p. 17.

considering examining, is usually dominated by statutes and regulations, also in common law countries.

As mentioned, the literature on legal transplants has so far shown particular interest in other areas of law, such as private law in general, commercial law, investment law, financial and banking law etc. It has also focused a great deal on transfers of law from Western European or US law to the law of other parts of the world. According to Jörg Fedtke,

> borrowing is easier in areas of the law which could be described as more 'technical' in nature [. . .], whereas the outcome of a legal transplant becomes far less predictable when policy considerations and fundamental values such as human rights come into play.[26]

A similar distinction between 'organic matters' and more mechanical ones had already been made by Otto Kahn-Freund.[27]

The comparatist is interested in the phenomenon of legal transplants as such, but even more so in questions such as the factors determining a successful legal transfer. Also, the choice of the source legal order and the evaluation of the (dis)advantages of legal transfers as opposed to those of 'home grown' legislation, will fascinate the comparatist.

The reasons why a lawmaker, say a parliament or a government, will adopt pieces of legislation from another country can be very diverse. It can be for very pragmatic reasons: importing foreign law can simply save time and money compared to what one would have to spend writing new legislation oneself. This may be especially true when countries need to legislate in rather important areas of law in a very short space of time, as is the case after a substantial regime change (e.g. independence; end of communism; fall of a dictatorship). It may also be related to the need to respond to technological innovations and the possible moral dilemmas associated with these innovations.[28]

It is also possible that the transplant is motivated by the will to enjoy (at least part of) the prestige or credibility of the legal order one copies. A country may copy legislation of another country with a good reputation to promote foreign investment. The recipient country may also simply want to refer to another country whose prestige is important, even without consideration of a specific legal issue. The transplant may also occur because of popular pressure, be it ideological, political or religious preferences. For example, the impact of Soviet law on countries adopting Communism or, more recently, the pressure to incorporate parts of Sharia Law into domestic law in some countries.

Michele Graziadei observes that the role of university teaching and education, and that of private actors, such as global law firms, should also not be underestimated.[29] When most of your judges, practising lawyers, members of

---

[26]Fedtke (2012), p. 552.

[27]Kahn-Freund (1974), pp. 1–17.

[28]Barak-Erez (2014), p. 19.

[29]Graziadei (2006), p. 473.

Parliament and other actors received their education in a specific country (the former colonial power, the US or the Soviet-Union, for instance) it is likely that the legal orders of these countries will continue to have an impact on them when active in the small state.

Transplants may also occur under some form of external pressure. In its milder form, a country may be invited or advised by other countries or international institutions to adapt certain pieces of domestic legislation. The pressure will of course increase if there are financial consequences for accepting a legal transfer. Here we can refer to all kinds of 'recommendations' from international lenders or international institutions. In an extreme form of pressure, the transplant will simply be imposed upon the recipient country by an occupying force or a colonial power. In such cases, the transplant is carried out *manu militari*, by force and without much of a say for the recipient country.

Finally, the transplant may be due to the adoption of international institutions establishing model laws. In such cases, the parties to the treaty are supposed to introduce domestic legislation more or less identical to the model law.

In the case of small states adopting foreign legislation, any of the reasons mentioned above for the use of legal transfers may be present, although some reasons may be more important for smaller states than for larger ones. For instance, the lack of personnel and resources is more likely to force small states to borrow from other states. There may also be a conflicting stance on the takeover of the legal system of the former colonial power: motives of prestige and reliability may encourage the adoption of laws from former colonial rulers, whereas this same historical relationship may discourage adoption if independence was gained as a result of conflict.

It is also important to look at the success of transplants, because developing a system to make better use of them would greatly benefit smaller states. As Barak-Erez puts it: "[r]ather than resisting transplantation, the focus should be on bettering its quality. In other words, the concern should be, to a large extent, regarding the quality of the transplants and the mechanisms that facilitate them".[30] In the literature, much attention has also been paid to the conditions that are more likely to lead to a successful legal transfer. These include the social, economic, cultural, ideological and religious environment in which the legal transplant will have to function, as well as the suitability of the foreign law to be incorporated in the recipient legal order. The flexibility of the transplant to adapt to a new legal environment and the political acceptation of foreign influence or pressure can be mentioned here too.

Finally, coming back to our starting point, because every legal order is a mix of domestic innovative law-making and legal transplants, we could say that the measure of success of a legal transplant could be compared to the (hypothetical) success of an equivalent domestic law-making process. It is, however, remarkable that until recently relatively little attention has been paid to directly comparing legal transplantation to its alternative; domestic law-making. An exception is the research by

[30]Barak-Erez (2014), p. 25.

Grajzl and Dimitrova-Grajzl (2009), who explored the trade-off between the promulgation costs of a novel, home grown set of laws and the adjustment costs associated with subsequent amendments of transferred law. They conclude that transplantation saves on initial drafting and administrative costs compared to domestic law-making. On the other hand, when initial rules are transplanted, the need for subsequent adjustment, which is costly, may be greater. In their conclusions, they find that the factors that determine the choice to be made include the degree of heterogeneity of interests, the extent to which law reform caters to political elites, the attained level of legal maturity in a jurisdiction, the perceived match of the law considered for transplantation to local reality, and the degree of adaptability of the legal system.

Focusing on the specificities of small states, we believe we might find quasi-laboratory situations where the comparison between the "cost" of using a legal transplant and the "cost" of developing a home grown law may be easier to make. This could be the case for some small island states of the same region of the world, with similar legal systems and histories, some having chosen to develop legislation on a given topic themselves, whereas others have implemented it with a legal transplant. In our future research, we hope to be able to identify those cases which, for the theory of legal transplants, could prove to be extremely valuable. This could also illustrate the value of borrowing from other small states, rather than always looking to larger, often former colonial, jurisdictions.

References

Barak-Erez D (2014) Legislation as transplantation. In: Lupo N, Scaffardi L (eds) Comparative law in legislative drafting: the increasing importance of dialogue amongst parliaments. Eleven International Publishing, Den Haag, pp 17–26

Bogdan M (1989) The law of Mauritius and Seychelles: a study of two small mixed legal systems. Juristförlaget i Lund, Lund

Commonwealth Small States Centre of Excellence. 2020. Commonwealth Small States Centre of Excellence in Malta. https://thecommonwealth.org/small-states-centre-excellence. Accessed 7 Feb 2020

Donlan et al (2017) Legal education and the profession in three mixed/micro jurisdictions: Malta, Jersey, and Seychelles. In: Butler P, Morris C (eds) Small States in a legal world. Springer, Cham, pp 191–212

Fedtke J (2012) Legal Transplants. In: Smits JM (ed) Elgar Encyclopedia of comparative law. Edward Elgar, Cheltenham, pp 550–554

Geser H (2001) Was ist eigentlich ein Kleinstaat? In: Kirt R, Waschkuhn A (eds) Kleinstaaten-Kontinent Europa. Probleme und Perspektiven. Nomos, Baden-Baden, pp 89–100

Graziadei M (2006) Comparative law as the study of transplants and receptions. In: Reimann M, Zimmermann R (eds) The Oxford handbook of comparative law. Oxford University Press, Oxford, pp 441–475

Grajzl P, Dimitrova-Grajzl V (2009) The Choice in the lawmaking process: legal transplants vs. Indigenous law. De Gruyter. https://doi.org/10.2202/1555-5879.1402

Gstöhl S (2001) Der Mikrostaat als Variante des Kleinstaats? Erfahrungen mit UNO und EU. In: Kirt R, Waschkuhn A (eds) Kleinstaaten-Kontinent Europa. Probleme und Perspektiven. Nomos, Baden-Baden, pp 101–125

Hey J (2003) Small States in World politics. Lynne Rienner, Boulder

International Social Security Association (1980) Small social security schemes and their problems. International Social Security Association, Geneva

International Social Security Association (1994) Small schemes in today's social security. International Social Security Association, Geneva

Irving Z (2011) Curious cases: small island states' exceptionalism and its contribution to comparative welfare theory. Editorial Board Sociol Rev 2011:227–245

Kahn-Freund O (1974) On uses and misuses of comparative law. Mod Law Rev 37:1–17

Kirt R, Waschkuhn A (2001) Was ist und zu welchem Zwecke betreibt man Kleinstaaten-Forschung? Ein Plädoyer für die wissenschaftliche Beschäftigung mit kleinen Nationen. In: Kirt R, Waschkuhn A (eds) Kleinstaaten-Kontinent Europa. Probleme und Perspektiven. Nomos, Baden-Baden, pp 23–46

Legrand P (1997) The impossibility of 'legal transplants'. Maastricht J Eur Comp Law 4:111–124

Maass M (2009) The elusive definition of the small state. Int Polit 46:65–83

Örücü E (2004) The Enigma of comparative law: variations on a theme for the twenty-first century. Martinus Nijhoff Publishers, Leiden/Boston

Pennings FJL (2006) Social security. In: Smits JM (ed) Elgar Encyclopedia of comparative law. Edward Elgar Publishing, Cheltenham, pp 654–667

Pennings FJL, Vonk G (2015) Research handbook on European social security law. Edward Elgar Publishing, Cheltenham

Pieters D (2006) Social security: an introduction to the basic principles. Kluwer Law International, Alphen aan den Rijn

Pieters D (2009) Onze sociale zekerheid: anders en beter. Pelckmans, Kapellen

Pieters D, Schoukens P (2012) Social security in the BRIC countries. IBM Center for the BRIC Countries, Washington

Sacco RG (1990) La circulation des modèles juridiques. In: Rapports généraux au XIIIe Congrès International de Droit Comparé (ed) Académie internationale de droit comparé. Les éditions Yvon Blais, Cowansville, pp 1–20

Teubner G (1998) Legal irritants: good faith in British law or how unifying law ends up in new divergences. Mod Law Rev 61:11–32

United Nations (2020) Sustainable Development Goals. https://www.un.org/sustainabledevelopment/. Accessed 7 Feb 2020

UNRISD (2009) Social policies in small states. http://www.unrisd.org/research/spd/smallstates. Accessed 20 Feb 2020

Veenendaal W, Wolf S (2016) Concluding remarks: achievements, challenges, and opportunities of small state research. In: Wolf S (ed) State Size Matters. Politik und Recht im Kontext von Kleinstaatslichkeit und Monarchie. Springer Fachmedien, Wiesbaden, pp 277–284

Watson A (1974) Legal transplants: an approach to comparative law. Scottish Academic Press/University Press of Virginia, Edinburgh/Charlottesville

Wolf S (2016) Die Erforschung von Politik und Recht in Kleinstaat und Monarchie. Eine konzeptionelle Einführung. In: Wolf S (ed) State Size Matters. Politik und Recht im Kontext von Kleinstaatslichkeit und Monarchie. Springer Fachmedien, Wiesbaden, pp 1–12. Recht im Kontext von Kleinstaatslichkeit und Monarchie, In: Wolf S (ed) Springer Fachmedien, Wiesbaden, pp 277–284

World Development Indicators Database (2018a) The World Bank. http://data.worldbank.org/indicator/NY.GDP.PCAP.PP.CD?view=chart).data.worldbank.org. Accessed 7 Jan 2020

World Development Indicators Database (2018b) The World Bank. https://data.worldbank.org/indicator/SI.POV.UMIC?locations=CO&view=map&year%20high%20desc=true). Accessed 12 Feb 2020

World Factbook (2020) Central Intelligence Agency. https://www.cia.gov/library/publications/the-world-factbook/rankorder/2004rank.html). Accessed 12 Feb 2020

Worldometer (2020) Countries in the world by population. https://www.worldometers.info/world-population/population-by-country/. Accessed 12 Feb 2020

Chapter 2
Small Jurisdictions; Their Common Features, in General and as Far as Social Security Is Concerned

In this chapter a state of the art of the literature on small jurisdictions is provided, focusing on the features most relevant to social security, such as: the impact of economic and environmental shocks; scale disadvantages and flexibility; the limited human resources and infrastructure; the training needs; the limited number of people covered by social security; the importance of migration; and the strong ties with other states. Also, issues related to homogeneity and proximity, to the unity of administration and the lack thereof in the benefit schemes, and financial issues will be discussed.

In this chapter, we give an overview of the existing literature dealing with the common features of small jurisdictions, focusing on the features relevant to social security. As such, this part gives a *status quaestionis* concerning our central theme: are small jurisdictions confronted with specific issues or problems when dealing with social security?

Some authors believe that, "whatever criterion is adopted, small states form too broad a category for purposes of analysis".[1] There would be no such thing as 'small states interests', as their interests vary considerably amongst them.[2]

Specifically with relation to social security, the question is raised as to whether it makes sense to deal with social security issues of 'small states' and whether other approaches such as social security in developing countries, social security in the South etc. would not be more fruitful.[3]

Still, the majority of authors generally believe that it is possible to "identify a common small state behavior in relation to certain situations, some issue areas,

[1]Baehr (1976), pp. 163 ff.

[2]Panke (2010), quoted by Thorhallsson (2017), p. 40.

[3]Mumford asks a similar question in relation with taxation, suggesting that perhaps taxation can better be considered from the perspective of the globalised South or from the perspective of developing countries (Mumford 2017, pp. 96 ff).

D. Pieters, *Social Security Law in Small Jurisdictions*, The World of Small States 8,
https://doi.org/10.1007/978-3-030-78247-4_2

certain interests";[4] and also specifically for social security, the significance of dealing with the specificities of the social security systems and law of small jurisdictions has been recognised.[5]

Bertram (2011) suggests in this context that small welfare states may be qualitatively different from larger welfare states. He emphasises that small states (under 1.5 million) have been ignored in much of the literature on the welfare regime, and that, when small size is considered, focus is given to larger small states (5–10 million).[6] Irving adds

> While the size of states and the significance of 'islandness' have been of mild interest within the comparative study of politics and economics, the theoretical frameworks that operate within contemporary comparative analyses of welfare and social policy rest upon a large unremarked assumption that population size does not matter.[7]

It may be noted here that when Srebrnik[8] examines jurisdiction (or even sovereignty) of the small countries as a resource and enumerates the manifestations of such resourcefulness, no reference is made to the control of social security. This reflects the general poor attention social security receives in the literature concerning small jurisdictions.

Let us reiterate here from the outset that we shall not discuss social security issues that may affect small jurisdictions, and may affect them greatly, but are in no way to be related to the smallness of the state. As examples of such issues, we could mention:

- The need to limit social security expenditure and promote the protection against poverty, as was mentioned by the Conference of the presidents of the parliaments of small states of Europe in their joint declaration of 26 September 2014;[9]
- The containment of informal economic activity in the small island states of the Pacific or e.g. in Guyana;[10] or
- A better targeting through social cash transfer programmes of the most vulnerable and poor, fighting unemployment or responding to the impending ageing in the Caribbean.[11]

---

[4]Christmas-Møller (1983), p. 46.

[5]Moitrier (1980), pp. 77–78, adding that this is true even if in theory first thoughts would lead to the opposite conclusion that as regards both objectives and manner of execution no such specific distinction exists: from the point of view of objectives, whatever its size may be, a social security system fulfils the same needs and ensures the same objectives; and from the point of view of its manner of execution, it could be considered that a social security system does not depend upon the number of beneficiaries it may have.

[6]Bertram (2011), p. 1.

[7]Irving (2011), p. 227.

[8]Srebrnik (2004), pp. 329–341.

[9]Consell General (2014), p. 10.

[10]Williams et al. (2013), p. 15.

[11]Henry (2013), pp. 32–33 and 37; Williams et al. (2013), p. 2.

Although not yet a common feature of small jurisdictions relevant to social security, one recent evolution requires our special attention: the use of the Internet for international sourcing and marketing and the supply of outsourced business services. The emergence of platform work, the gig economy and so on are universal phenomena, but it is likely that small jurisdictions will try to conquer niches based on the latest technological evolutions.[12] This could have an important impact on social security, as the location of work, the identification of the worker, the link of subordination of the home workers and such like will be less easy to establish.

The common features of small jurisdictions relevant to social security have been grouped under the following twelve headings:

- Economic and environmental shocks;
- Scale disadvantage and flexibility;
- Limited human resources and limited infrastructure;
- Training needs;
- Limited number of people covered by social security;
- Importance of migration;
  Strong ties with other states;
- Homogeneity, social cohesion and democracy;
- Proximity;
- Unified administration and fragmentation;
- Financial issues; and
- Legal and social security transplants.

2.1 Economic and Environmental Shocks

Most small states have an economy based on a very limited range of areas of activity: this can be the monoculture, often introduced by the former colonial power, oil or phosphate, iron and steel, or financial and other services; very often tourism will be important too.[13] Due to the very small domestic markets, small states have no choice but to rely on international trade and are thus more exposed to international economic trends.[14] This applies not only to the export side, but the small state, which often has limited natural resources, will also have to rely on import for essential commodities (food products; industrial supplies, fuel and the like) that are not present in the country.[15]

All of this makes the small states very vulnerable to economic shocks, such as fluctuations in commodity prices, shrinking demands for certain products or

[12] Encouraging small jurisdictions to do so is e.g. Bernal (2018), pp. 98–99.

[13] Butler and Morris (2017), p. v; Williams et al. (2013), p. 9; Castro-Guttiérrez (2008), p. 2; International Social Security Association (1980a), p. 14.

[14] International Social Security Association (1980a), pp. 13–14.

[15] International Social Security Association (1980a), pp. 13–14.

services, changes in preferences on the world markets, economic restrictions imposed by other states.[16] Inflation may also be imported from important trade partners.[17] Vulnerability is even seen as a characteristic feature of small states.[18] Some add that economic resilience, i.e. the capacity to resist or reverse the negative effects of economic vulnerability, would also be a feature of the more successful small jurisdictions.[19]

Many small states, especially but not only small island states, are also confronted with the danger of environmental shocks.[20] The impact of natural disasters, such as hurricanes, earthquakes, floods and alike has been enormous for some small island states.[21] Climate change is even threatening the very existence of many small island states. Also, for non-island small states, the impact of a natural disaster can be expected to be more significant than in a larger state, where, by hypothesis, only part of the country is likely to be hit by the natural disaster.

The economic and environmental shocks may have an immediate impact on employment in the small jurisdiction and thus on the (equilibrium) of its social security.[22] After a natural catastrophe, the entire state may face huge reconstruction challenges and the fact that many people have lost everything they possessed.

Increasing the state's responsiveness to economic and environmental shocks is therefore considered to be one of the most important challenges for any small jurisdiction.[23]

In theory, social security helps provide security and acts as a stabilising factor in times of crisis. Social protection will be seen as a buffer in the face of economic (and environmental) shocks, but as the impact of such shock in the small state may be so drastic and all-encompassing, it seems difficult to expect from the small state's social security to fully absorb these shocks.

Some have therefore promoted the idea that small states, and especially their social security systems, should constitute special reserves[24] in order to cope with exceptional raises in benefits recipients (of social assistance, health care, work incapacity and unemployment benefits, survivor benefits) as a consequence of the occurrence of a major environmental or economic shock. It was stated that the reserve should be proportionally more important, the smaller the country is.[25] It

[16] Brown (2010), p. 58.

[17] International Social Security Association (1980a), p. 13.

[18] On this, see Briguglio (2018).

[19] See also Briguglio (2018), p. 88.

[20] Brown (2010), p. 58; see also Bernal (2018), pp. 95–96.

[21] An island like Granada was nearly completely destroyed by hurricane Ivan in 2004; many more other examples could be given.

[22] Castro-Guttiérrez (2008), p. 2.

[23] Williams et al. (2013), p. 2.

[24] Williams et al. (2013), p. 52; Castro-Guttiérrez (2008), p. 2; International Social Security Association (1980a), p. 13.

[25] International Social Security Association (1980a), p. 13.

has also been observed that, if such reserves funds are set up, they should also be readily transformable into cash, without upsetting the small jurisdiction's money markets or the overall finances of the social security scheme.[26] The reserve fund could also be used in a broader perspective than social security alone, enabling the development of a more diversified economy or the promoting a better protection against natural disasters.[27] The more this is the case, the less social security will directly benefit, to meet increased cash transfer demands.

Let us observe in this context, that at a macro level, small island states of the Caribbean have benefited from the Caribbean Catastrophe Insurance Facility (CCIF), which pooled risks to mitigate the financial impact of hurricanes, earthquakes and excessive rainfall at the 'lowest possible pricing'. The CCIF quickly disburses liquidity to the states concerned when faced with such an environmental shock. The facility is available to governments when the country endures an environmental hazard.[28]

2.2 Scale Disadvantage and Flexibility

Small jurisdictions are small and can thus be expected to lack scale advantages compared to larger entities. This applies to their administration in general and social security administration in particular. Most public infrastructure, goods and services are characterised by their inherent indivisibility, i.e. the relative cost of producing them is the same regardless of the size of the population. Hence, small jurisdictions will be characterised by a diseconomy of scale.[29]

It is however debated whether the scale disadvantage of the small jurisdiction is as important as what could be expected. According to Muriel Bouchet, whilst comparing the public expenditure per capita between European countries, you cannot see small states spending more than larger states; this contradicts what you would expect as a consequence of scale disadvantages.[30] This is again contradicted by other authors.[31]

The scale disadvantage supposedly presented by small jurisdictions and their social security is often set-off against the greater flexibility that would characterise the small jurisdictions. Small jurisdictions would have more flexibility to swiftly respond to new challenges, because of their smallness and the related proximity

[26]Castro-Guttiérrez (2008), p. 2.

[27]International Social Security Association (1980a), p. 14.

[28]Williams et al. (2013), p. 52.

[29]Prasad et al. (2013), p. 8; Brown (2010), pp. 51–52; Osborne (2012), p. 3; Caruana and Kalweit (2019), pp. 13–14; Williams et al. (2013), p. 29.

[30]Bouchet (2019), p. 6.

[31]Prasad et al. (2013), p. 8; Brown (2010), pp. 51–52.

between citizens, political actors and the administration.[32] But even this feature attributed to small jurisdictions is being contested, as small states appear rather reluctant to seriously consider structural reforms.[33]

2.3 Limited Human Resources and Limited Infrastructure

Small jurisdictions have limited human resources,[34] even the relatively rich and better organised ones.[35] Their administrations in the broad sense (Parliament, Government, Agencies, and the Judiciary) have a limited capacity. Although tasks similar to those of a larger state must be performed, this has to be done by a far more restricted number of people. This is not in contradiction with the finding that the number of people working in public service and thus also in the social security administrations, in relation to the population served, will often be quite important. The latter is related to the fact that public sector employment in several small states has been an important means of sustaining livelihoods of many people through wages.[36] A direct consequence of a limited number of staff is that the absence of a few collaborators can have an impact on the proper functioning of an entire administration.[37]

Small states have difficulties finding the right professionals for their administration. As the population of the small state is, by definition, limited, this makes the pool of appropriate skilled personnel rather shallow.[38] The problem becomes even bigger when some public functions are reserved to the nationals of the small jurisdiction.[39]

The public service of the small jurisdiction is often also less competitive vis-à-vis compensation in the private sector or opportunities abroad. As far as the Caribbean region is concerned, Brown observes:

> even though public-sector employment was historically attractive to qualified job-seekers because it offered stability, prospects for training, pensions and some benefits, the wages in themselves are not attractive to the best and brightest. Research has shown that public sector compensation tends to be higher than in the private sector at lower levels but lower at higher-skilled technical, professional and managerial levels (Kitchen 1994). The decline in the

[32]Butler and Morris (2017); Caruana and Kalweit (2019), pp. 13–14.

[33]Osborne (2012), p. 3; see also Bouchet (2019), p. 7.

[34]Henry (2013), pp. 32–33; Castro-Guttiérrez (2008), p. 2.

[35]Grön Caroline, as quoted in Thorhallsson (2017), p. 40.

[36]Prasad et al. (2013), p. 34, referring to Bertram (2011); the Seychelles and Malta being given as examples.

[37]International Social Security Association (1980b), p. 40.

[38]Williams et al. (2013), p. 9; Brown (2010), p. 56.

[39]International Social Security Association (1980b), p. 40.

> caliber of persons entering the public service today when compared with the immediate post-independence period in the 1960s is palpable.[40]

Emigration and the consequent brain drain is often referred to as one of the major handicaps faced by many small jurisdictions.[41] In addition to financial reasons, poor working conditions; lack of career prospects; underuse of skills; insufficient training and opportunities for career progression would explain emigration.[42] It should also be taken into account that the absence of specialised educational and training institutions in the small state[43] will not only create a (financial and emotional) burden to overcome for locals to get the relevant knowledge and skills abroad, but will increase the chance that these locals will stay outside the country after obtaining the education or training abroad.

According to the World Bank, the shortage of qualified applicants would cause some high-level positions to be filled by inadequately qualified or inexperienced individuals.[44]

Sometimes the administrations of small jurisdictions will (be compelled to) call upon foreign experts to fulfil specialised tasks. This can occur occasionally or take the form of initiatives such as the 'strategic gap-filling' developed by the Common wealth Secretariat. This approach essentially consists in

> the filling of line positions in government ministries/departments with expatriate experts on the assumption that a national will be appointed as a 'counterpart' to understudy the expert, thereby enabling the counterpart to assume full responsibility at the expiration of the expert's tour of duty.[45]

However, according to Brown,

> the evidence suggests that counterparts are seldom identified and appointed in a timely manner, if at all, raising the issue of sustainability which is always salient in the case of small states. There is an obvious risk that countries will use the gap-filling to avoid dealing with some of the more difficult issues discussed above, such as low salaries, poor conditions of service and other constraints. Gap-filling of this type could actually push out nationals who become de-motivated by salary inequities so that, in the long run, the provision of outsiders under the banner of institutional development could actually undermine capacity rather than build it.[46]

---

[40] Brown (2010), pp. 51–52; see also International Social Security Association (1980b), p. 40.

[41] Brown (2010, p. 56), referring to Baker (1992) making the point that "in case of small states, only a few brains need be drained before a serious systemic crisis occurs." A report from the OECD on the characteristics of the populations of 28 OECD countries around the year 2000 found that the Caribbean region loses between 25 and 47% of its nationals with higher education through emigration each year.

[42] X (Latin American Economic Outlook) (2019a), pp. 193–194; also Mortimer (1980), p. 83.

[43] Wettenhall (1992) as referred to in Brown (2010), p. 56.

[44] Brown (2010), p. 56.

[45] Brown (2010), p. 61.

[46] Brown (2010), p. 61.

Let us also recall that many small jurisdictions will not have their own higher education institutions, which means that even nationals will have to obtain their professional qualification in another country. This also influences the way in which these professionals, especially law professionals, will function in the context of the small jurisdiction. The distance to the specificity of the small jurisdiction will probably be even more considerable when foreigners are called upon. When we focus on the legal profession, we may observe that judges, practicing lawyers (advocates, etc.) in small states may, and often will, come from another legal background or at least not be nationals of the small state. For instance, in Seychelles many judges are drawn from the Bench of other Commonwealth countries. Such judges arguably have a broader perspective, greater objectivity, or special experience that local jurists in a small jurisdiction might not have. There may, however, be a problem when the expatriate judge does not understand the (legal) language and specificities of the (often mixed legal tradition) of the small state.[47]

Since a limited number of people have to perform a whole variety of tasks, they will have to be multifunctional. As Brown puts it:

> Unlike larger countries, small states do not have the luxury of differentiating between specialists and generalists. Officials are expected, for the most part, to be reasonably flexible, adaptable, knowledgeable generalists who could be called upon to cover many issues and perform a broad range of functions all at once. Very often, there are a few key people whose advice is sought on almost every significant policy decision or who are entrusted with overseeing the implementation of almost every important policy, programme or project.[48]

Some authors propose to deal with the limited human and financial resources, and often expertise capacities, of social security systems of small jurisdictions by pooling their human resources management, as well as their personnel qualified to train the personnel.[49] We will address training in more depth in the next chapter.

We have already dealt with the often lacking educational and training infrastructure,[50] as well as the sometimes incomplete legal infrastructure;[51] let us also examine some other infrastructural weaknesses, especially relevant to social security.

Small states will usually not offer all necessary specialised medical care, as the necessary care providers and specialised hospitals are not present in the country.[52]

---

[47]Donlan et al. (2017), pp. 207–208.

[48]Brown (2010), p. 57; in the same sense International Social Security Association (1980b), p. 40 and Moitrier (1980), p. 83.

[49]Castro-Guttiérrez (2008), p. 5.

The heads of the CARICOM Social Security Organisations meeting in 2019 asked for special attention for the modernisation of the social security schemes, the use of ICT, as well as for training and research (X. (CARICOM. Social security schemes urged to modernize) 2019b). Also the year before the Governor of the Eastern Caribbean Central Bank called for a more functional cooperation among social security schemes in areas such as corporate governance, research and development and investment (SKNIS 2018).

[50]Brown (2010), p. 56.

[51]Butler and Morris (2017), p. 5.

[52]On these issues, see: Azzopardi Muscat and Camilleri (2018).

Patients who require such specialised care will thus have to travel abroad to get the necessary care. This may sometimes imply considerable travel costs.[53] If the national health system or social insurance of the small jurisdiction wants to include health care abroad in its package, how can a good coverage of health care costs be provided while these costs are generated in another country, possibly with a higher standard of living and thus less accessible tariffs? Agreements with neighbouring countries or medical hospitals outside the small jurisdiction may offer a solution, but may be rather costly for the social security of the small state.

Given their size, small social security schemes are also often confronted with difficult problems of cost and return on investment when introducing, maintaining and constantly up-dating modern information technology.[54] The limited or inadequate monitoring and evaluation systems and the limited data collection facilities of the social security administrations (in the wider sense) of small states are often perceived as a serious handicap.[55] This is perhaps more so in the eyes of foreign experts than for the own social security people, who have close contact with local reality. According to some authors, the limited human resources available to the small jurisdictions and their (social security) administrations may indeed also present some advantages, such as the lack of the need to coordinate between many services and persons,[56] the direct communication lines between international representation and the domestic sector;[57] or the polyvalence of individual staff members that makes it possible to practically reply to all the queries of the population.[58] We shall deal with the proximity element later in this text.

2.4 Training Needs

Given the lack of human resources characterising small jurisdictions, as we described in the previous chapter, it is evident that small states will show a particular interest in training people who work in their (social security) administrations. Small states also often ask for specific support to meet their training needs.

However, since educational and training facilities are often not present in the country, this means either sending trainees out of the country or importing training programmes and staff. A combination of both is also possible.

However, sending trainees abroad for longer periods might increase the risk of them staying abroad.[59] On the other hand, it may be attractive to encourage persons

[53]Bertram (2011), p. 13.

[54]International Social Security Association (1994), p. 2; Hartley Lees (1994), p. 8.

[55]Henry (2013), pp. 33 and 51; Williams et al. (2013), pp. 2, 49 and 56.

[56]Gales (1994), p. 64.

[57]Thorhallsson (2017), pp. 41–42.

[58]International Social Security Association (1980b), p. 40.

[59]Prasad et al. (2013), p. 5.

who left the small jurisdiction, received a good education or training abroad, and have spent a longer period abroad to return home and to let the small state benefit from their experience.[60]

It may also be problematic to involve (social security) administrative staff, or for that matter policy makers or lawyers in substantive training programmes abroad or in the country. In other words, the capacity to absorb training may appear to be limited.

> The limited number of trainable personnel available means that the same small group continuously benefits from training opportunities, especially where these involve foreign travel. Similarly, small size makes it very difficult to release staff to attend training programmes for any length of time.[61]

We have seen in the previous chapter, that also *in-situ* training, such as the coaching and mentoring initiatives of the 'strategic gap-filling' strategy, developed by the Commonwealth Secretariat, apparently do not always succeed in their training purpose.[62]

Considering these points, it is not surprising that on-line educational and training initiatives appear increasingly attractive,[63] although they will often lack to take into consideration the reality of small states.

It is also important to reflect upon the real educational and training needs of the (social security) administrations (in the broad sense) of small states. Given the limited human resource pool and the need for administrators with broad expertise and who are multifunctional, it is important to educate and train staff in broad areas of public administration.[64] For those involved in social security policy making and administration, this implies giving them a 'helicopter view' rather than training them in highly specialised and internationally 'fashionable' issues. Also, providing regular information on recent findings and trends, e.g. in social security, will be useful; it will be even more useful if that information is subsequently discussed within, and translated to, a small states context.

However, it may also be that a small state administration needs highly qualified personnel at some point to improve its functioning. This may for social security, for example, be linked to the introduction or the improvement of its IT system or to the investment of the funds of the social security.[65] Of course, it is possible that the necessary capacity is present in the concerned administration, but this will often not be the case. Training existing staff to handle the specialized tasks may be highly problematic, as would be the hiring of additional staff. In such case it may be useful to consider outsourcing the task to another administration or even to a private company or a foreign administration. The possibility of pooling highly specialised personnel between various small states of the region is an approach that needs to be

[60] Prasad et al. (2013), p. 5.

[61] Brown (2010), p. 60.

[62] See also Brown (2010), p. 56 in favour of in situ training.

[63] Brown (2010), p. 61.

[64] Brown (2010), p. 61.

[65] Castro-Guttiérrez (2008), p. 6.

considered more frequently, as it has the advantage of fully taking into account the specificity of both social security and the small jurisdiction's reality.

Social Security Training Centres Across the World

A broad basic training and education on social security is being provided by the Executive Summer School and Master in European Social Security that are offered at the KU Leuven university in Belgium. The programme provides in an in-depth study of social security and social protection from a legal, economical, sociological, administrative and philosophical perspective. In addition to being multidisciplinary, the programme also contains strong comparative and multinational aspects, as it focuses on the provision of social protection rights across Europe and outside Europe. The educational programmes combine a limited number of residential weeks with on-line teaching. Let us observe that the Centre for the Law of Small Jurisdictions is also situated at the same Faculty, with which the Social Security Institute actively co-operates. See www.law.kuleuven.be/EMSS/emss

The International Social Security Association (ISSA) in Geneva aims to strengthen the capacity of social security administration in order to respond to the needs of its members. In the particular case of small jurisdictions, the ISSA sees its role as promoting and providing means of action, knowledge acquisition and transfer and facilitating exchange of expertise and guidance.[66] The International Training Centre for the International Labour Organisation (ITCILO) may also provide interesting programmes. See www.issa.int and www.itcilo.org

For French-speaking countries in Africa, social security promotion and human resources development activities, which include the organisation of training, are provided by the '*Conférence Interafricaine de la Prévoyance Sociale*' (CIPRES, the Inter-African Conference on Social Security). See www.lacipres.org. The French '*Ecole Nationale Supérieure de Sécurité Sociale*' (EN3S, the National School of Higher Social Security Studies), is the French, European and international reference centre for the training of French speaking social security managers. See www.en3s.fr

For Spanish-speaking and English-speaking countries in Latin America and the Caribbean, the "*Centro Interamericano de Estudios de Seguridad Social*"

(continued)

[66]Castro-Guttiérrez (2008), p. 6.

(CIESS, the Inter-American Centre for Social Security Studies), and the '*Organización Iberoamericana de Seguridad Social*' (OISS, the Ibero-American Organisation for Social Security), provide basic and specialised training for social security organisations.[67] See www.ciess.org and www.oiss.org

2.5 Limited Number of People Covered by Social Security

Small jurisdictions have been defined as countries with a population of less than 1 ½ million people. Social security schemes in the small state will thus, by definition, cover a limited number of people. Of course, people living outside the country may also be socially insured in the country as frontier workers or posted workers—more about the impact of migration later—but, on the other hand, social insurance schemes will not necessarily be universal (i.e. covering the whole population). They may and often do restrict their personal scope to the working population, the wage-earners and sometimes the self-employed too. In this context, it should be mentioned that in a considerable number of (developing) small states there may also be an important informal sector that escapes social insurance affiliation.

So social security systems of small jurisdictions have a limited personal scope. Whether there is a minimal or an optimal number of socially insured persons *in abstracto* is debated,[68] but it seems to be answered negatively as long as there is the backing of a public authority (state or alike).[69] *In concreto* we can observe that some small to very small social security systems may perform well, others not, whereas the same could be said about large to very large social insurance arrangements.

However, the small number of participants in a social insurance arrangement has its consequences. The demographic composition of the insured group may be very specific and deviate from what is usually present in larger states. This will often be related to the high importance of migration in many small jurisdictions. Earlier we addressed the impact economic and environmental shocks may have on the (social security of) small states. But even apart from these shocks, one has to agree that

> the smaller the number of persons exposed to the risk, the more probable it is to encounter fluctuations in the experience of the risk, which implies the use of very specialised management techniques, in particular reserves against fluctuations. The smaller the financial base of a scheme, the greater the occurrence of certain exceptional risks requires the accumulation of extensive reserves compared to the total amount of benefits normally granted by a scheme.[70]

[67] Castro-Guttiérrez (2008), pp. 8–9.

[68] See e.g. International Social Security Association (1980b), p. 42 and Moitrier (1980), p. 81.

[69] International Social Security Association (1980d), pp. 93–94.

[70] International Social Security Association (1980d), p. 94; Castro-Guttiérrez (2008), p. 2.

> The cost of the creation and the administration of such reserves is obviously high and the effects of inflation may be expected to play a greater role, the more important these reserves are in relation to the financial resources of the scheme or even the country itself.[71]

Small jurisdictions and their limited number of inhabitants, may also face specific health care related problems, as their population may, more than that of larger countries, be confronted with small genetic pools, leading to specific genetic disorders.[72] For the social coverage of the health care costs, this may present a non-negligible additional cost.

2.6 Importance of Migration

Depending on their economic performance and some other factors, some small jurisdictions may attract a large amount of people coming to work and live in the country, whereas in others, many people may emigrate or at least temporarily seek employment outside the small jurisdiction. Some small jurisdictions will combine important emigration and immigration flows. Migration seems to be a very relevant factor to nearly all[73] small jurisdictions. The mobility may be within the immediate neighbourhood of the small country or may mainly be between the small country and some preferred larger states further away, not seldom the previous colonial powers.[74]

In case of important temporary or permanent immigration, this will result in social security administrations of the small jurisdiction facing a high number of non-nationals, and eventually even non-residents, being socially insured in the country.[75] This has important consequences: social security files with a foreign component are often more complex than purely national files and require more work to handle.[76] When the group of persons who participate in the social security system and the group of persons who have political (voting) rights differ

[71]International Social Security Association (1980d), p. 94.

[72]On health in small states, see: Azzopardi Muscat and Camilleri (2018).

[73]International Social Security Association (1980c), p. 56. Iceland would be one of the few exceptions. For the Caribbean small states emigration and to a lesser extent immigration is very important (Williams et al. 2013, p. 16).

[74]Sometimes the emigration of larger amounts of people from one larger state to the small country reflects particular historic coincidences; we can refer e.g. to the important Portuguese migration to small states like Andorra or Luxembourg.

[75]For some small countries the number of foreigners resident in the country outnumbers the nationals (sometimes up to 2 foreigners to 1 national) (Moitrier 1980, p. 82). See also Bartumeu (1994, p. 76 or 56); Ewen (1994, p. 91) and International Social Security Association (1980c, pp. 56–57).

[76]The processing of a pension application for a migrant worker was often considerably lengthier than if he/she had worked in only one country. From 10–12 October 1979 the ISSA held a regional European meeting in London on the problems of speeding up the processing of migrant workers' benefit claims, a brief record of which appeared in No. 4/79 of the International Social Security Review. See also International Social Security Association (1980c), pp. 56–57.

considerably, the danger also exists of a conflict of interests between the nationals and the socially insured foreigners. Many temporary foreign workers, especially seasonal workers or frontier workers, will also call for complex solutions; the number of 'dormant' social insured persons may be important and the 'turn-over' of insured persons considerable.[77]

A special kind of very temporal movement into the country consists of tourists visiting the country; although they are mostly outside the scope of social security schemes in general, they may present special challenges, especially to the health care system.[78]

In case of important emigration flows, this can be a blessing or a curse for the small jurisdiction. It will be beneficial as the emigrants will possibly send money back home; in some small jurisdictions foreign remittances indeed account for a non-negligible part of the income of a substantial number of residents.[79] The emigrants may also keep close ties with the country of origin and let that country benefit from their activities in the larger state.

The emigration may often also cause the most attractive, best educated work force to leave the small jurisdiction to make a career in the larger state; a career and the professional income associated with it, that he or she would have difficulties realising in the small state. Some authors like Baldacchino[80] oppose the danger of brain drain, a concept of brain/brawn rotation and circulation, where the small state capitalises on the skills of its diaspora.[81]

A side-effect of the brain drain may however be that, in order to keep professionals in the small state, some salaries in the small state are pushed up to levels not corresponding to what the (economy of the) small state normally is able to bear. This might also be true for those active in the law making, policy making, government, legal system and such like. More generally speaking, we can say that the labour cost in small jurisdictions will often be largely determined by factors external to the country.

---

[77]Castro-Guttiérrez (2008), p. 2; also Moitrier (1980), p. 82.

[78]International Social Security Association (1980c, pp. 56–57): The participants also devoted special attention to the question of movements of tourists; each year streams of temporary migrants, sometimes of considerable intensity, passed through many of the small states represented at the meeting. "This could not fail to influence the operation of social security". See also with relation to health care: International Social Security Association (1980c), p. 58.

[79]Prasad et al. (2013), p. 34. On the issue of remittances in the small Commonwealth states, see: Cover-Kus et al. (2018), here pp. 11–12.

An interesting social security issue with relation to remittances, consist in the question whether these remittances should be included in the income of the recipients of income tested social security benefits.

[80]Baldacchino (2011).

[81]Prasad et al. (2013), p. 31.

As a consequence of migration, the demographic transitions experienced by small jurisdictions may be accelerated or delayed, compared to the evolution that could be expected when migration would not occur.[82]

An important phenomenon to take into consideration, especially also in relation to its social security implications, is the fact that people may have emigrated from the small state and return after some years or at the end of their active career. Other persons may have immigrated and subsequently left the small state, losing all or most ties with the country. In both cases, one can ask the question, what is the social responsibility of the small state? Is the small state obliged to provide good social protection to those who have worked most of their lives abroad?[83] If they worked legally abroad, they will probably have constituted social security entitlements in that other country, but is the small state aware of this? If they worked in the informal sector or illegally abroad, they will have no social entitlements in their back-pack, but is it then up to the country they did not actively contribute to (in work, in taxes or social security contributions) to provide them adequate social protection? Should the small state keep in contact with people who have only been active in the country for a restricted period of time? Should the state make considerable expenses for the administrative delivery of very small benefits to these former workers? And related to all these issues, the question remains whether nationality should play a role: is there a special duty to care for people with the nationality of the small state, even if their bond with the country is weak, if not absent?[84]

Migration may also result in the social status of a person being defined by the social security systems of more than one country, e.g. that of the country of residence and that of the country where most of the active life is spent and where pension and other social entitlements are built up.[85] In order to address some of the social security issues resulting from international mobility, states have concluded social security coordination agreements between them, and this on a bilateral or multilateral basis. We shall deal with the international social security co-ordination in a following chapter.

---

[82]On this issue, see: Von Brockdorff and Vella (2018).

[83]On this issue, see Bertram (2011, p. 12), where we read: "So long as diaspora members retain their citizenship and the right of return, they are effectively part of the set of individuals and groups to whom social policy applies. Social policy is here understood as policy that shapes the long-term structure and functioning of all social groups for which the small state is their economic, cultural and political 'home' and source of identity."

[84]See also Moitrier (1980), p. 82.

[85]Bertram (2011), p. 20.

2.7 Strong Ties with Other States

Small states are essentially more dependent on the input of human resources and the import of goods from abroad, the trade with foreign countries etc. In other words, a small jurisdiction is bound to have strong economic ties with other states.

Sometimes small states associate with one another, as is the case in the Caribbean region in an effort to create an economic union with free movement of, amongst other things, labour; in social security this translates into multilateral coordination instruments. Sometimes small states are part of an economic or even political union; the most prominent example of this is Malta and Cyprus being members of the European Union. Two more small states, Iceland and Liechtenstein, have joined the EU multilateral coordination mechanism as members of the European Trade Association (EFTA).

An Example of Regional Social Security Coordination: Coordination in the Caribbean[86]

The two social security coordination instruments concluded between small jurisdictions of the Caribbean, deserve some special attention: the CARICOM Agreement on Social Security (CASS) of 1996 and the OECS Convention on Social Security of 1991.

The Organisation of Eastern Caribbean States (OECS) is a group of 7 small jurisdictions: Antigua and Barbuda, Dominica, Grenada, St Kitts and Nevis, St. Lucia, St. Vincent and Grenadines, and Montserrat. The Caribbean Community (CARICOM) brings together the OECS jurisdictions plus Barbados, the Bahamas, Belize, Guyana, Jamaica, Haiti, Suriname, and Trinidad and Tobago.

CASS has been concluded between all CARICOM states except Haiti and Suriname, the latter country having a too different social security system. It came into effect as of the 1st of April 1997. CASS protects nationals of the member states belonging to the following groups of workers: workers in transnational enterprises, workers in international transport and on ships, workers in diplomatic missions, consulates and international organisations, self-employed workers and itinerant workers (i.e. working in more than one member state) as well as eventually their dependant family members. To be covered by CASS, the worker needs to move to work or to have worked in two or more member states. CASS only includes in its material scope (contributory) pensions in case of invalidity, disablement, old age and retirement,

(continued)

[86]Forteza (2008); Organisation of American States and Inter-American Council for Integral Development (2015), pp. 8–9; X (*Projects of the Caribbean Community*); Williams et al. (2013), pp. 18, 33 and 54.

survivor's benefits and death benefits. CASS contains a non-discrimination based on the nationality clause. CASS ensures that workers who have not made enough contributions to obtain an independent pension from a state's social security system, enjoy a totalisation with contributions in other member states; the worker will in such case get an apportioned pension in the first state. CASS leaves untouched pensions, which are acquired solely based on the social security of one's member state. Furthermore, CASS contains rules for the posting of workers of international enterprises (in principle up to 2 years) and contains rules assigning the competent country (or countries) for the other groups of workers.

The impact of CASS appeared to remain below expectations: the number of applications to benefit from CASS remained low. This was explained by a low awareness of the agreement in the general public and some interpretation issues. Other explanations refer to the importance of the informal sector and the all in all limited labour mobility within the region.[87]

The OECS Convention has a broader scope than CASS, as it covers also short-term benefits such as maternity and illness-related benefits. Yet it covers only 7 small jurisdictions, many of which have not ratified the Convention. The OECS Convention has received far less attention than CASS.

The small state will very often have preferential relations with one or more larger countries. This is evident for small jurisdictions whose external relations are not their own competence, but that of e.g. the United Kingdom or the Netherlands, as is the case for Gibraltar, and Aruba, Curaçao and Sint Maarten respectively. For the coordination of their social security systems with those of other countries, this means they will depend on the goodwill of their 'mother' state when the latter negotiates coordination agreements with other states. This may lead to agreements in which the specificities of the small jurisdiction's social security will not fully be taken into account. On the other hand, the more important negotiating power of the 'mother' state may lead to the conclusion of coordination agreements with third countries, which the small jurisdiction itself would not have been able to conclude.[88]

Also, fully sovereign small states will often have one or two privileged partners, including not infrequently the former colonial power, as is the case for many independent small Commonwealth states. It is important for (the social security of) the small state to be able to at least conclude bilateral coordination instruments with these most important countries of emigration and/or immigration. A concern in this respect may be the considerable asymmetry between the negotiating power (both in

[87]Forteza (2008), pp. 25–26; Organisation of American States and Inter-American Council for Integral Development (2015), p. 9.

[88]See e.g. for Jersey: Gales (1994), p. 62.

terms of personnel, skills, financial means) of the large partner and that of the small jurisdiction.[89]

Coordination[90] agreements usually include principles such as non-discrimination on the basis of nationality, exportability of acquired rights, administrative co-operation; possibly also the aggregation of periods and rules concerning the assignment of the competence to socially insure the person concerned. Rules to avoid double payments may also be included. Usually, the coordination agreements do not apply to second or third pillar pension arrangements.

More generally, one should take in consideration that larger partners of the small jurisdiction, as well as international agencies, may exert considerable pressure on the small states, economically, financially, politically and, exceptionally even, militarily. This pressure may take hard forms, but may also take the gentle form of allocating (or not) grants for initiatives in the small states, thereby making subsidies to the small jurisdiction conditional.[91] But even without foreign partners pressuring the small state, the latter will often undergo important external influences, as the socially insured or the citizens and administrations of the small jurisdiction will be influenced by what they see in the neighbouring or larger partner states.[92]

2.8 Homogeneity, Social Cohesion and Democracy

Some have argued that 'small is harmonious' and thus small jurisdictions would be characterised by a high degree of cultural homogeneity.[93] Upon closer examination, it is learned that this view is distorted, often a 'romanticised view' of the small states by people from larger states.[94] Indeed, many small jurisdictions are "quite heterogeneous, divided along ethnic, linguistic or religious lines (for example Fiji, Vanuatu, and Trinidad and Tobago, respectively). Even some homogenous societies are politically polarised, such as Malta."[95] The diversity may be linked to the colonial legacy, past and present immigration, or the huge distances between islands

---

[89] See also Hartley Lees (1994), p. 8.

[90] It is remarkable that in some literature, especially relating to the Caribbean coordination agreements, there seems to be a confusion between the concepts 'harmonisation' and 'coordination', using the first concept when the latter is meant. See e.g. Williams et al. (2013), pp. 18 and 54.

[91] External financing is important for many small states. More specifically, foreign assistance and concessionary loans have often played an important role in subsidizing development and the welfare et al. 2013, p. 34).

[92] Bertram (2011), p. 12; Prasad et al. (2013), pp. 33–34 referring to Baldacchino (2011).

[93] Prasad et al. (2013), p. 28 referring to Bertram (2011) for a summary.

[94] Brown (2010), pp. 46–47.

[95] Prasad et al. (2013), pp. iii and 28–29.

composing the small jurisdiction. Furthermore, some small states will show an important divide between rural and urban areas.[96]

The diversity met in many small states calls for appropriate social policies to promote social cohesion and inclusion within the state. On the other hand, "social cohesion at the group level may lead to divisive polities based on interest group influences instead of national interests, as is arguably the case in the Fiji".[97]

The lack of homogeneity of many small state societies need not contradict the fact that there may be a common disposition characterising people who live in small states, especially small island states. Professor Baldacchino, well known for his studies of small (island) states, for instance "associates the economic success of many small island states with the resourcefulness, flexibility, street wisdom and 'economies of scope' practiced by islanders and small state citizens".[98]

Traditionally it has also been claimed that small size is the ideal condition for democracy. Most small jurisdictions are indeed political democracies, be it in different degrees.[99] It is interesting to see in this context that all but one of the twenty smallest member states of the United Nations hold democratic elections.[100] Some democratic small jurisdictions however also show sharply partisan features and intolerance of dissent.[101]

2.9 Proximity

As we have defined the small jurisdictions by the number of its inhabitants being less than 1 ½ million, one can expect a greater proximity between policy makers, members of parliament and social security administrators, on the one hand, and the citizen on the other hand. We shall see that such proximity presents both positive and negative aspects, in general and more specifically in relation to social security. Before dealing with these positive and negative aspects, let us relativise the proximity that would characterise small jurisdictions.

We have seen that homogeneity and a high degree of social cohesion are not necessarily linked to the smallness of a state. Small states are small in terms of their population, but may be rather big or extended geographically. Sometimes the small jurisdictions will be island groups with considerable distances between the various islands. Sometimes large parts of the 'small state' will be poorly populated or not at

[96]Prasad et al. (2013), p. 29 referring to for instance Grenada and Trinidad and Tobago.

[97]Prasad et al. (2013), p. 29.

[98]Caruana and Kalweit (2019), p. 13.

[99]Prasad et al. (2013), p. 8 referring to the studies of Anckar (2002, 2004) and Srebrnik (2004); Prasad et al. (2013), p. 30 referring to Hintjens (2012), who points out that small size certainly does not necessarily translate into more democracy.

[100]Veenendaal (2013), p. 245.

[101]Brown (2010), p. 48, referring to Collings and Warrington (1997).

all; some small states are situated in mountainous regions, with rather difficult access. All of this means that the contact between the citizen (or social insured) situated in remote and difficult accessible locations, and the administration, which is often concentrated in the capital, may encounter a number of physical obstacles.

The proximity argument may also sometimes be questioned, for instance, as a consequence of linguistic policy, the language(s) spoken by the majority of the population, and especially the weaker sectors, do(es) sometimes not correspond with the language of the law and administration of the small jurisdiction.[102] For matters relating to the protection of the weakest, such as social security, this is problematic.

On the positive side of proximity, it is stated that small states would "provide more opportunity for citizens to participate effectively in decisions".[103] Brown gives a good summary (and subsequently criticises it):[104]

> Smallness also allows for a closer relationship between the state and its citizens; easy access to key decision-makers allows for a more consultative policy process and thereby yields policies that are founded on broad-based consensus. In terms of the public service, smallness is thought to render hierarchical structure irrelevant and to make service delivery decentralized almost by definition. In a nutshell, according to this school of thought, smallness just makes the job of the public servant a great deal easier.[105]

Many authors however also suggest negative aspects of the proximity. Let us summarise the most important.

- "Where political differences exist in small states, they tend to be more personal, more intense and more emotionally charged, often leading to deep divisions and cleavages that undermine any suggestion of social cohesion";[106]
- The leadership may be easily accessible, but often behaves in a paternalistic if not authoritarian way;[107]
- Organisational structures that are hierarchical, bureaucratic, rigid and inflexible;[108]
- Management unresponsive to client needs and who serve themselves or their organisations rather than their clients;[109]

[102] This can be the consequence of legally relevant texts being in the older national language (e.g. Italian in Malta) or the continued use of the language of the former colonisator, which often is then even elevated to the rank of official language of the state (exclusively or in combination with the broadly spoken national language, as with Papiamento in Aruba).

[103] Dahl and Tufte (1973), p. 13; Butler and Morris (2017), p. vii.

[104] Brown is hard in its critics: "These are seductive arguments – usually put forward by analysts whose life experiences are almost exclusively in large countries – that distort and romanticize the observed reality of small states. It is a 'big country' view of small states" (Brown 2010, pp. 47–48).

[105] Brown (2010), pp. 46–47.

[106] Brown (2010), pp. 46–48; also Veenendaal (2013), p. 247.

[107] Brown (2010), pp. 46–48 referring to Collins and Warrington (1997).

[108] Brown (2010), pp. 46–48.

[109] Brown (2010), pp. 46–48.

- Difficulties for all concerned to distinguish between the duty to the public interest and claims of kinship[110] affinity or personal relations, that may lead to conflicts of interests, if not nepotism or corruption,[111] of which major public scandals are often the result;[112] and
- "Face-to-face injustices may be hard to swallow, and few exit strategies exist for small state citizens. Smaller distances do not necessarily translate into more political engagement, and tight elite circles may actually be more exclusionary".[113]

More generally speaking, small jurisdictions often struggle with integrity problems and the distance between 'law in the books' and 'law in action' may be considerable. The latter phenomenon may also be linked to the inappropriate use of legal transplants, as will be dealt with further.

It is remarkable that, with relation to social security and its administration, the positive aspects of proximity are mostly highlighted and that little attention is paid to the negative aspects.[114] This might be explained by the fact that the comments on the relevance of proximity were usually made by people of the social security administrations themselves. The advantages of small states' social security systems and their administrations can be summarised as follows:

- A global, holistic approach to basic problems; the social security administration has easy access to relevant data and statistics and is therefore able to plan and implement suitable reforms.[115]
- An individual management approach. Castro-Guttiérrez formulates it as follows:

> Because the number of active insured persons and beneficiaries is small, income and expenditure data are readily available; financial administration is easily managed. In principle, small schemes can be handled on a day-to-day basis.[116]

---

[110]Sometimes this is even reflecting custom. Mrs Kuautonga, a young Solomon Islands lawyer reports: "[...] there is a custom called the wantok system that is very common in Solomon Islands, whereby the position as public servant is used to serve the benefit of relatives, family members and friends. It is a form of corruption that has been imprinted in the minds of the general public. As long as one is public servant, you have to serve your wantoks despire the fact that you have certain codes of conduct to abide by. So it's a conflict between performing to the expected standard and using the office for the best interest of wantoks..." (Caruana and Kalweit 2019, pp. 13–14).

[111]That corruption was a problem needing further examination in small jurisdictions was recognised by the meeting of law ministers and attorneys general of all commonwealth jurisdictions. See: The Commonwealth (2018).

[112]Veenendaal (2013), p. 247; Brown (2010), pp. 46–48 referring also to Collins and Warrington (1997).

[113]Prasad et al. (2013), p. 30.

[114]An exception, being Osborne writing: "Most programs, however, are plagued by varying degrees of political interference" (Osborne 2012, p. 3).

[115]Castro-Guttiérrez (2008), p. 1; also International Social Security Association (1980b), p. 41 and Moitrier (1980), pp. 79–80.

[116]Castro-Guttiérrez (2008), p. 1; also Moitrier (1980), pp. 79–80.

As others formulate it: there is a possibility of management at sight.[117]

– An administration that is close to the beneficiaries. There is often a direct human contact between the social security administration and the social security contributors or beneficiaries.[118] An administrator commented:

> Close contact between the population and the administrators meant that the latter had to be in a position to inform each insured person of his rights at any time, in full and without delay, since insured persons were able to get in direct touch with administrators, often knowing their names, faces, and even their private telephone numbers, to demand information to which they considered themselves entitled. This public pressure thus had a highly favourable effect in that it obliged the institutions to be more efficient and to improve the quality of their service.[119]

The easy, personal access to the social security administration is not only a self-evident human advantage for the insured people, but is also seen as positive by the social security administrations, as it would allow them to detect problems and objections in the public early on, allowing them to eventually adapt their decisions or rules.[120]

It was also mentioned that the participation of politicians in the administration boards of social security institutions contributes to a better understanding of the social security challenges by both administrators and politicians.[121]

Finally, let us observe that related to, but distinct from, the proximity argument, we find the argument in a number of small states that social security needs not to be fully developed as in larger states, because in the small jurisdiction informal support mechanisms, churches, local community, family or clan will care for the people and that the impersonal social security should not interfere.[122] Without denying the importance of the informal support mechanisms, especially in remote communities or in times of natural disasters,[123] it remains important to recall that, as was the case in large countries, the transformation from dependency upon the goodwill of others to social security rights as a worker, resident or citizen, has been a landmark in the constitution of really democratic societies, respecting the human rights of all, including those who do not conform to the expectations of the family, clan or church.

[117] Moitrier (1980), p. 81.

[118] Castro-Guttiérrez (2008), p. 2.

[119] International Social Security Association (1980b), p. 41.

[120] Moitrier (1980), p. 81.

[121] International Social Security Association (1980b), p. 41.

[122] See Bertram (2011), pp. 13–14.

[123] Prasad et al. (2013), p. 27.

2.10 Unified Administration and Fragmentation

Social security in small jurisdictions would more easily operate unified administrations and even unified schemes. Whereas the administration of social security schemes in small states is indeed often concentrated in one specialised institution[124] or one larger branch of government (e.g. together with taxation),[125] we find less evidence that there would be less fragmentation in the structure of social security (many social schemes coexist) within the small state.[126] In fact, quite a few small jurisdictions, especially of the Commonwealth, count a large variety of social security schemes and different benefits, just like in the United Kingdom. It was also mentioned that in some countries social security schemes developed systematically to deal with specific issues or groups, resulting sometimes in a mixture of social security programmes. A consequence was a waste of resources, as the variety of non-co-ordinated schemes resulted in benefits being abused by some, and not being taken up by others.[127] The lack of integrated standards to identify the most vulnerable and the poor is considered to be especially detrimental.[128] As a result, many plead for consolidating the social protection programmes in order to improve efficiency.[129]

2.11 Financial Issues

Social security systems around the world seem to constantly struggle with their financing. Small jurisdictions are no exceptions in that respect. Although specific social insurance schemes may be in financial trouble, the state remains the final guarantor of people's social security rights, this is also universal. What may however be specific to some small jurisdictions, is that the financial solidity of the small state may be less reassuring. Many small states have a relatively weak internal tax base and rely largely on 'border taxes'.[130] Whereas it is difficult to imagine a larger state going bankrupt, this seems less unthinkable for smaller jurisdictions.

---

[124]Castro-Guttiérrez (2008), p. 3.

[125]This integration in broader institutions is seen by some as problematic: see Hartley Lees (1994), p. 8.

[126]The lesser fragmentation of schemes was seen as an advantage of the social security of smaller jurisdiction; see: Moitrier (1980), p. 80.

[127]Henry (2013), p. 31.

[128]Henry (2013), p. 32–33 and 39; Williams et al. (2013), p. 33.

[129]Williams et al. (2013), pp. 54–55.

[130]Especially small island developing states have a weak internal tax base and rely on 'border taxes' (Williams et al. 2013, p. 35); see also Bertram (2011), pp. 15–16. By border taxes we understand trade taxes collected by customs, which in some small states may account for a disproportionately large share of total revenues vis-à-vis personal/corporate income or property taxes (Brown 2010, p. 53).

Another aspect of the financing of social security schemes in small jurisdictions also requires our attention. When schemes, especially pension schemes, rely on capitalisation, it is of the highest importance that the funds are invested appropriately. This is of course also the case for larger funds, but small jurisdictions often lack highly professional, independent public investor capacities, and the political authorities may often be interested in acquiring financial means through investment of the funds in domestic projects or even state bonds. There may even be a good case to make for investing in one's own country, but one has to keep in mind the economic and environmental shocks many small states may be exposed to: in such case, they risk eroding the pension funds completely![131] One should also avoid the risk of provoking a disastrous overheating of the economy by indiscriminate investment of reserves in local industries.[132] On the other hand, investing in international markets may also bear risks, especially if done without the needed high financial and investment skills required to play on the international markets. Whereas outsourcing the investment policy of social security to professional private agents, may also entail considerable risks that a pension scheme is not able or ready to take. Moneys invested abroad should also retain sufficient liquidity to enable them to be rapidly repatriated in case of need.[133] Either way, it appears that investment portfolios are poorly diversified in a number of small states.

When the small state has a repartition based (PAYG) financing of social security, it may also be important to mention that in recently independent or autonomous small jurisdictions, the schemes in operation are relatively young and possibly not yet matured.[134] As we know from older social security systems of large countries, at the moment of the maturation of the system, i.e. when one starts to pay out benefits based on a full social security career, one may be confronted with unreasonable promises made in the past.

We can also observe that in some small jurisdictions external financing/grants were a non-negligible source of income for social protection programmes.[135] In these countries, foreign assistance and concessionary loans played an important role in subsidising development and the welfare state.[136]

[131]Paddison (2006), p. 20.

[132]International Social Security Association (1980a), p. 14.

[133]International Social Security Association (1980a), p. 14.

[134]Williams et al. (2013), p. 28.

[135]Williams et al. (2013), pp. 44–45.

[136]Prasad et al. (2013), p. 34.

2.12 Legal and Social Security Transplants

Due to the limitation in both quantity and quality of the human resources available for policy development, law making, administrative regulation and implementation, and judicial decision-making, the actors concerned and especially the small jurisdiction's lawyers will often seek inspiration abroad, very often to the former colonial power or the country in which they received their education. This means that small jurisdictions will use 'legal transplants' more often than larger states.[137] However, as Veenendaal and Wolf observe: "[w]hile small states often adopt legal regulations of larger neighbouring states, the smallness entails that the practical functioning of such rules may be markedly different, and that regulations are often adapted to better suit the small-scale context".[138]

This 'copying' phenomenon is not only limited to law, but also social security solutions as such are sometimes taken over from large states, although these solutions are sometimes less suited to the smaller state. When Luxembourg, for example, developed its social insurances, it looked to the German system and took over its complexity based on different social insurance schemes for the various professional groups.[139] The Andorran social security system was strongly inspired by the then existing French complementary social insurances.[140]

References

Anckar D (2002) Why are small island states democracies? Round Table 365:375–390

Anckar D (2004) Direct democracy in microstates and small island states. World Dev 32:379–390

Azzopardi Muscat N, Camilleri C (2018) Challenges and opportunities for the health sector in small states. In: Briguglio L (ed) Handbook of small states. Economic, social and environmental issues. Routledge, London, pp 445–774

Baehr PR (1976) The perennial problem of small states: a survey of research efforts. Coop Conflict 11(2):163–182

Baker R (1992) Scale and administrative performance: the governance of small states and microstates. In: Baker R (ed) Public administration in small and Island states. Kumarian Press, West Hartford, pp 5–25

Baldacchino G (2011) The power of Jurisdiction in promoting social policies in small states. UNRISD. www.unrisd.org/publications/pp-baldacchino. Accessed 8 Feb 2020

Bartumeu E (1994) Social security for migrant and cross-frontier workers in Andorra. In: International Social Security Association (ed) Small schemes in today's social security. International Social Security Association, Geneva, pp 73–90

Bernal RL (2018) Small states in the global geopolitical landscape. In: Commonwealth Secretariat (ed) Small States. Economic Review and Basic Statistics. Commonwealth Secretariat, London, pp 93–100

[137]Wolf (2016), p. 7.

[138]Veenendaal and Wolf (2016), p. 281.

[139]International Social Security Association (1980b), p. 40.

[140]Bartumeu (1994), p. 75.

Bertram G (2011) Assessing the structure of small welfare states. Social policies in smalls states series. Commonwealth Secretariat and United Nations Research Institute for Social Development, London

Bouchet M (2019) Déconstruisons le concept de "petite nation": le cas du Luxembourg. Idea Fondation. https://www.fondation-idea.lu/2019/04/25/deconstruisons-le-concept-de-petite-nation-le-cas-du-luxembourg/. Accessed 1 June 2020

Briguglio L (2018) The vulnerability of small states. In: Commonwealth Secretariat (ed) Small states. Economic review and basic statistics. Commonwealth Secretariat, London, pp 85–92

Brown DE (2010) Institutional development in small states: evidence from the commonwealth Caribbean. Halduskultuur – Adm Cult 11(1):44–65

Butler P, Morris C (2017) Preface. In: Butler P, Morris C (eds) Small states in a legal world. Springer, Cham, pp v–viii

Caruana J, Kalweit D (2019) The Islands and Small States Institute: from a programme to a centre of excellence. In: 30th Anniversary Commemorative Publication. University of Malta, Valletta

Castro-Guttiérrez A (2008) Pooling administrative resources. Human resources management: improving personal qualifications and training. Presented at the International conference for social security schemes in small countries, Libreville, Gabon

Christmas-Møller W (1983) Some thoughts on the scientific applicability of the small state concept: a research history and a discussion. In: Höll O (ed) Small states in Europe and dependence. Wilhelm Braumüller, Wien, pp 35–53

Collins P, Warrington E (1997) The new public administration: lessons from the experiences of small and Island states. CAPAM/IASIA, Mahé

Consell General (2014) Déclaration Commune des Présidents de Parlement des Petits États d'Europe. Actes i Exposicions. http://www.consellgeneral.ad/ca/actes-i-exposicions/9-conferencia-de-presidents-de-parlament-dels-petits-estats-d2019europa/declaration-commune-des-presidents-de-parlement-des-petits-etats-d2019europe-a-l2019occasion-de-la-conference-organisee-a-andorre-en-date-du-26-septembre-2014. Accessed 7 Feb 2020

Cover-Kus H, Zaman S, Hope Khonje W, Ebrahim Z (2018) Small states in the global economy – a look at the past 25 years. In: Commonwealth Secretariat (ed) Small states. Economic review and basic statistics. Commonwealth Secretariat, London, pp 3–33

Dahl R, Tufte E (1973) Size and democracy. Stanford University Press, Stanford

Donlan SP et al (2017) Legal education and the profession in three mixed/micro jurisdictions: Malta, Jersey, and Seychelles. In: Butler P, Morris C (eds) Small states in a legal world. Springer, Cham, pp 191–212

Ewen C (1994) Social security for migrant and cross-frontier workers in Luxembourg. In: Small Schemes in Today's Social Security (ed) International Social Security Association, pp 91–104

Forteza A (2008) The portability of pension rights: general principals and the Caribbean case. The World Bank, Washington, DC

Gales T (1994) Social security for migrant workers in Jersey. In: International Social Security Association (ed) Small schemes in today's social security. International Social Security Association, Geneva, pp 57–72

Hartley Lees J (1994) Small social security schemes: problems and perspectives. In: International Social Security Association (ed) Small schemes in today's social security. International Social Security Association, Geneva, pp 3–10

Henry R (2013) Caribbean development report: macroeconomic policy for structural transformation and social protection in small states. Economic Commission for Latin America and the Caribbean, Port of Spain

Hintjens H (2012) Consensual and participatory forms of democracy. Unpublished. Paper prepared for UNRISD – Commonwealth Secretariat project on Social Policy in Small States

International Social Security Association (1980a) Particular problems of small social security schemes: summary of the discussions. In: International Social Security Association (ed) Small social security schemes and their problems. European Series No. 3. International Social Security Association, Geneva, pp 12–14

International Social Security Association (1980b) Organisation and management of small social security schemes: summary of the discussions. In: International Social Security Association (ed) Small social security schemes and their problems. European Series No. 3. International Social Security Association, Geneva, pp 40–42

International Social Security Association (1980c) Problems arising from the relative scale of migratory movements: summary of the discussions. In: International Social Security Association (ed) Small social security schemes and their problems. European Series No. 3. International Social Security Association, Geneva, pp 56–58

International Social Security Association (1980d) Annex II: viability of social security schemes with a small number of participants. In: International Social Security Association (ed) Small social security schemes and their problems. European Series No. 3. International Social Security Association, Geneva, pp 93–94

International Social Security Association (1994) Small schemes in today's social security. International Social Security Association, Geneva

Irving Z (2011) Curious cases: small island states' exceptionalism and its contribution to comparative welfare theory. Editorial Board Sociol Rev 2011:227–245

Moitrier J (1980) Conclusions of the general reporter. In: International Social Security Association (ed) Small social security schemes and their problems. European Series No. 3. International Social Security Association, Geneva, pp 77–84

Mumford A (2017) The taxation of small states and the challenge of commonality. In: Butler P, Morris C (eds) Small states in a legal world. Springer, Cham, pp 87–99

Organisation of American States and Inter-American Council for Integral Development (2015) Analysis of bilateral and multilateral social security security agreement as they relate to pensions. Presented during the Second Meetings of the Working Groups of the XVIII Inter-American Conference of Ministers of Labor.

Osborne D (2012) The impact of economic conditions on the financial sustainability of social security schemes. The global economic crisis was not all bad for the financial sustainability of Caribbean social security schemes. Presented at the International Conference of Social Security Actuaries and Statisticians, Berlin, Germany

Paddison O (2006) Social security in the English-speaking Caribbean. United Nations, Santiago

Panke D (2010) Small states in the European Union. Coping with structural disadvantages. Routledge, London

Prasad N, Hypher N, Gerecke M (2013) Seeing big. Transformative social policies in small states (Research paper 2013-3). UNRISD, Geneva

SKNIS (2018) CARICOM heads of social security meeting. www.sknis.kn/29th-caricom-heads-of-social-security-meeting/. Accessed 1 June 2020

Srebrnik HF (2004) Small Island Nations and democratic values. World Dev 32:329–341

The Commonwealth (2018) Commonwealth Small States Centre for Excellence in Malta. https://thecommonwealth.org/small-states-centre-excellence. Accessed on 1 June 2020

Thorhallsson B (2017) Small states in the UNSC and the EU: structural weaknesses and ability to influence. In: Butler P, Morris C (eds) Small states in a legal world. Springer, Cham, pp 35–64

Veenendaal W (2013) Size and personalistic politics: characteristics of political competition in four microstates. Round Table – Commonw J Int Aff 102:245–257

Von Brockdorff P, Vella M (2018) Demographic transition and population ageing in small states. In: Briguglio L (ed) Handbook of small states. Economic, social and environmental issues. Routledge, New York, pp 475–490

Wettenhall R (1992) Small states: some machinery-of-government considerations. In: Baker R (ed) Public administration in small and Island States. Kumarian Press, West Hartford, pp 49–68

Williams A, Cheston T, Coudouel A, Subran L (2013) Tailoring social protection to Small Island developing states. Lessons Learned from the Caribbean (Discussion paper Social Protection & Labor, no. 1306). The World Bank, Washington, DC

Wolf S (2016) Die Erforschung von Politik und Recht in Kleinstaat und Monarchie. Eine konzeptionelle Einführung. In: State Size Matters. Politik und Recht im Kontext von Kleinstaatslichkeit und Monarchie, Sebastian Wolf (ed) Springer Fachmedien, Wiesbaden, pp 1–12; Recht im Kontext von Kleinstaatslichkeit und Monarchie, Sebastian Wolf (ed) Springer Fachmedien, Wiesbaden, pp 277–284

X (2019a) Chapter 6. Special feature: the Caribbean small states. In: OECD (ed) Latin American economic outlook. OECD, Paris, pp 185–199

X (2019b) CARICOM social security schemes urged to modernize. https://guyanachronicle.com/2019/07/17/caricom-social-security-schemes-urged-to-modernise. Accessed 1 June 2020

X, Projects of the Caribbean Community, https://en.wikipedia.org/wiki/Projects_of_the_Caribbean_Community

Part II
Country Studies: Social Security in Twenty Small Jurisdictions

In this part, we examine 20 small jurisdictions and their social security, according to a uniform pattern. First, we provide a context and the legal framework of the rights to social security (constitutional context and social security legislation and structure), after which we deal with the population of the small jurisdiction and the personal scope of its social security schemes. The administration of social security and the coordination arrangements that apply to the small jurisdiction are discussed and we conclude by adding some other relevant information. The countries we report upon are: Aruba, Bhutan, Curaçao, Cyprus, the Faroe Islands, Fiji, Gibraltar, Greenland, Grenada, Guyana, Iceland, Liechtenstein, Maldives, Malta, San Marino, Seychelles, Sint Maarten, Suriname, Tonga and Trinidad and Tobago.

It is important to recall here that we do not intend to present a full picture of the social security schemes in each country, with all the benefits, their amounts and the social contributions and levies associated with it. Rather, we wanted to outline those aspects of the social security systems that may be relevant to the central question of this book: is there a specificity of the features and issues of social security (law) arrangements of small jurisdictions? Likewise, we shall not go into the problems that all social security systems are confronted with, such as ageing or financing, which are of course also relevant to the social security systems of small jurisdictions. Only when such general problems and issues present specific aspects in the case of small countries, shall we include information on these problems and issues.

For each of the examined countries, we start by outlining the general context. Under this item we provide general facts on the country and the decision-making structures in the small jurisdiction. What are the main political forces in the country? Do specific social, cultural and religious actors play an important role? In this item we also examine whether the country has special bonds with some other countries.

Secondly, we deal with the legal framework of the rights to social security. Here we will first look at the constitutional context. The main statutes on social security and the basic structure of the social security system are also presented. The procedures to be followed in case of discontent with social security decisions receive some attention too. Finally, we ask: is social security, as outlined in legal instruments, providing the main social protection or are other, more informal mechanisms more important?

Thirdly, we pay special attention to the composition of the population and the personal scope of the social security schemes. Some general data on the population of the country are first provided. Thereafter we focus on the legal definition of the personal scope of social insurance and social assistance schemes.

Fourthly, the administrative structure of social security is highlighted. Who is responsible for the social policy? What are the departments, institutions and agencies collecting contributions and/or distributing benefits? How are these institutions governed? These, and similar questions, are discussed here.

Fifthly, the coordination of the national social security schemes with foreign schemes is examined. More generally we ask ourselves how migration impacts the way social security is organised. We focus on the specific issue of the social coverage of health care provided outside the small jurisdiction.

Sixthly, we add some relevant information concerning features usually associated with 'smallstateness', such as the impact of economic and environmental shocks or integrity issues.

The difference in the length of the country reports may be explained by the complex information to be provided, as well as the volume of available information. In general, we have preferred to deal more extensively with countries whose social security systems are less well known.

For data and comparable figures on all twenty countries, we consulted the following:

- The country reports of the International Social Security Association;[1] and
- The *World Factbook* of the United States of America Central Intelligence Agency (the country reports and more specifically the information under 'people and society', 'Government' and 'economy').[2]

We do not repeat the references to these sources in each country report.

In line with the *World Factbook* we use in our country reports, unless mentioned otherwise, the following definitions:

- Net migration rate: the difference between the number of persons entering and leaving a country during the year per 1000 persons (based on midyear population). An excess of persons entering the country is referred to as net immigration; an excess of persons leaving the country as net emigration. The net migration rate does not distinguish between economic migrants, refugees, and other types of migrants nor does it distinguish between lawful migrants and undocumented migrants;

[1]Country Profiles. 2020. International Social Security Association, https://www.issa.int/en_GB/country-profiles. Accessed 12 Feb 2020.

[2]World Factbook. 2020. Central Intelligence Agency. https://www.cia.gov/library/publications/resources/the-world-factbook/. Accessed 12 Feb 2020.

- Youth unemployment ratio: the percent of the total labour force ages 15–24 unemployed during a specified year; and
- Population below the poverty line: national estimates based on surveys of sub-groups, with the results weighted by the number of people in each group. Definitions of poverty vary considerably among countries.

Other concepts are defined as we indicated in Part I, or as these concepts are commonly defined.

All websites referred to in the country reports were last accessed on June 1st, 2020.

Chapter 3
Aruba

3.1 Context

Aruba[1] is an island in the South Caribbean Sea, situated about 30 km north of the Venezuelan coast. It became a Dutch colony in the seventeenth century. First a colony of the Netherlands, the Netherlands Antilles of which Aruba was a part, became a constituent country of the Kingdom of the Netherlands in 1954. Since the 1930s there had been a movement to separate Aruba from the Netherlands Antilles. This movement finally resulted in Aruba becoming a country of the Kingdom of the Netherlands in its own right in 1986, separate from the remaining Netherlands Antilles ('*status aparte*'). This '*status aparte*' was expected to be a transition to full independence, but this ambition seems to have been abandoned and after the dissolution of the Netherlands Antilles in 2010, Aruba became one of the four 'countries' of the Kingdom of the Netherlands, together with the Netherlands, Curaçao and Sint Maarten.[2]

Aruba is a parliamentary democracy within the constitutional monarchy of the Kingdom of the Netherlands. Aruba's head of state is the Dutch monarch, who appoints the governor of Aruba as his or her representative. The governor watches over the general interest of the Kingdom in Aruba and ensures that no decisions are taken by legislative and administrative bodies in Aruba that could damage the unity

With special thanks to Ass. Prof. Mr. Dr. Carlos Bollen of the Law Faculty of the University of Aruba for reviewing the report on Aruba; our thanks also go to Mrs. Mr. Glenda Gil and Mrs. Mr. Marisol Tromp for their precious information.

[1]For general data and figures, see: Country Profiles (2020) and World Factbook (2020).

[2]Oostindie and Klinkers (2001), pp. 175 and 223–224.

D. Pieters, *Social Security Law in Small Jurisdictions*, The World of Small States 8,
https://doi.org/10.1007/978-3-030-78247-4_3

of the Kingdom or that are contrary to the provisions of the Statute of the Kingdom[3] or to international law.

Given the mainly symbolical and advisory role of the monarch, the real political and legislative power lies with the parliament and the Council of Ministers, headed by the prime minister. The governor in turn appoints the ministers, who form the government; the Government needs the confidence of, and is politically responsible to, the Parliament.

The parliament of Aruba ('*Staten*') consists of one chamber with 21 directly elected members. Two political parties dominate the political scene and alternate power: the Christian-Democrat Aruban People's party (AKV) and the Social-Democrat People's Electoral Movement (MEP). The latter tends to favour the idea of full independence. In last elections both obtained 9 seats and the MEP, together with smaller parties, constituted a coalition Government.

A plenipotentiary minister represents Aruban interests in the Kingdom of the Netherlands, but is not a member of the Aruban Cabinet.[4] He/she participates in the decision making in the Council of Ministers for the Kingdom, consisting of the members of the Council of Ministers of the Netherlands and the three plenipotentiary ministers from the three Caribbean countries of the Kingdom. The three countries may also delegate a national minister in an advisory capacity, in addition to the authorised minister. There is no Parliament for the Kingdom, but only the Dutch Parliament, that also deals with matters reserved to the Kingdom after consultation with the parliaments of the three other components of the Kingdom.

According to a 2010 estimate, three quarters of the population is Roman Catholic and about one-tenth belongs to one of the Protestant denominations.

Aruba has a rich culture of trade unions.[5] Furthermore, an important role is played by the (Aruban) Social and Economic Council ('*Sociaal Economische Raad*', SER),[6] which is composed of representatives from employers' and workers' organisations and independent experts. The task of the SER is to advise the government on all important subjects of a social and/or economic nature. The SER delivers its opinions at the request of one or more ministers; it can also advise the Government on its own initiative on issues of a socio-economic nature. The opinions shall mention dissenting opinions of the minority.[7]

It is clear that Aruba has strong ties with the Netherlands and the two other countries of the Kingdom of the Netherlands. The Kingdom is *inter alia* also responsible for its foreign relations and defence.

[3]The Statute of the Kingdom of the Netherlands is the constitutional act of 28 October 1954 establishing the Kingdom of the Netherlands as a union of the Netherlands and Aruba, Curaçao and St. Maarten.

[4]See: https://secure.overheid.aw/bestuur-organisatie/samenstelling_3395/.

[5]See: https://www.refworld.org/docid/3ae6ae688.html; and https://www.bearingpointcaribbean.com/en/government-news/arubaanse-vakbonden-trekken-samen-op-tegen-aov-plannen/.

[6]See: https://ser.aw.

[7]See: https://www.overheid.aw/bestuur-organisatie/sociaal-economische-raad_3381/.

The Kingdom of the Netherlands is a member of the European Union, but Aruba has the status of an 'overseas country and territory' (OCT)[8] and is therefore not part of the European Union. However, there is only one type of citizenship within the Kingdom of the Netherlands, and all citizens of the Kingdom of the Netherlands, including those of Aruba, are EU citizens as well.[9] This implies strong bonds with the European Union, which provides funds to Aruba through the European Development Fund.

3.2 Legal Framework of Rights to Social Security

3.2.1 Constitutional Context

Aruba is one of the 'countries' constituting the Kingdom of the Netherlands. The Charter ('*Statuut*') for the Kingdom of the Netherlands regulates the constitutional relationship between the four countries that make up the Kingdom: the Netherlands, Aruba, Curaçao and Sint Maarten. The Charter stipulates that the four countries manage their own affairs autonomously and are jointly responsible for Kingdom affairs. It also lays down rules governing mutual assistance, consultation and cooperation and the constitutional organisation of the countries. The Charter may only be amended with the agreement of all four countries, and it takes precedence over the individual countries' constitutions. Kingdom affairs, over which individual countries have no control, include foreign relations, defense and citizenship of the Netherlands. The Charter also stipulates how the countries should conduct Kingdom affairs in cooperation. All matters that the Charter does not define as Kingdom affairs are country affairs. Each country must promote the realisation of human rights, legal certainty and good governance within its borders. It is the Kingdom's responsibility to safeguard these values.[10]

Each Caribbean country of the Kingdom of the Netherlands has its own Constitution ('*Staatsregeling*'). In the Aruban *Staatsregeling* we read that "The Government shall take measures to promote public health. [...]. Promotion of sufficient housing is a matter of concern for the Government [as well]."[11] Furthermore, the *Staatsregeling* states that "Dutch nationals here in the country who cannot provide for their existence and who meet the requirements to be laid down in the National Ordinance, have a right to government assistance to be regulated by the National Ordinance".[12]

[8]The Netherlands secured a provision in the Treaty of Lisbon that says that any Caribbean part of the Netherlands can opt for a change of status to Outermost Region (OMR) if it so wishes, without having to change the Treaties of the European Union.

[9]See: https://en.wikipedia.org/wiki/Dissolution_of_the_Netherlands_Antilles [and the references made therein].

[10]See: https://www.royal-house.nl/topics/legislation/charter-for-the-kingdom-of-the-netherlands.

[11]Art. V.23 *Staatsregeling*.

[12]Art. V.24 *Staatsregeling*.

Aruban law belongs to the civil law group as it is strongly influenced by Dutch law.

3.2.2 Social Security Legislation and Structure

Aruba has, partly as a result of the pre-existing legislation of the Netherlands Antilles, and partly as new pieces of legislation, regulated all social security schemes through its own Aruban *landsverordeningen* or national ordinances.

The most important are the following ordinances:

- the General Old-Age Insurance (AOV) of 1990;[13]
- the General Widow(ers) and Orphans Insurance (AWW) of 1996;[14]
- the General Illness Costs Insurance (AZV) of 1992;[15]
- the Sickness Insurance (ZV) of 1993;[16]
- the Accident Insurance (OV) of 1996;[17]
- the Severance Pay Insurance (*Cessantia*) of 1998;[18]
- the Reparation Allowance of 2010;[19] and
- the Social Care (*bijstand*) of 1988[20] and 1989

all as amended.

The *landsverordening* establishing the country's own social security administration dates from 1995: the national ordinance *Sociale Verzekeringsbank* (SVB) of 1995.[21]

The so-called general insurances, AOV, AWW, AZV are contributory, universal social insurances that in principle cover the entire population; the Sickness Insurance (ZV), the Accident Insurance (OV) and the *Cessantia* are arrangements on a professional basis. Social Care *'bijstand'* is a social assistance scheme.

The AOV provides a pension upon reaching the pension age (whether one retires or not); the AWW grants survivor benefits to the spouse of a deceased and to his/her children.

The General Illness Costs Insurance AZV makes the listed health care provisions (general practitioner, specialist, basic hospitalisation, physiotherapy, pharmaceuticals) available to the insured through contracts concluded between the AZV and the

[13] AB 1990 no. GT 33.

[14] AB 1996 no. GT 30.

[15] AB 1992 no. 18.

[16] AB 1993 no. GT 24.

[17] AB 1996 no. GT 26.

[18] AB 1998 no. GT 18.

[19] AB 2010 no.99.

[20] *Landsverordening maatschappelijke zorg* of 1989 (AB 1989 no. GT27) and *Landsbesluit* of 1988 (AB 1988 no. GT 88).

[21] AB 1995 no. GT1.

providers; the benefits are thus provided in kind. Exceptionally, costs are reimbursed.

The Accident Insurance (OV) covers victims of a labour accident and provides them with income replacement in case of incapacity to work. It also provides benefits to the surviving spouse and children of the victim of a lethal labour accident.

The Sickness Insurance (ZV) provides an income replacement for incapacitated workers (including cases of pregnancy/maternity) for a maximum period of two calendar years.

The *Cessantia* guarantees a one-off payment upon the involuntary termination of the employment of a worker. The benefit is due by the employer, but in case the employer fails to pay (e.g. due to bankruptcy) the benefit can be claimed from the *Sociale Verzekeringsbank.*

The Reparation Allowance provides private sector employees with low wages (between minimum wage and about 45% above minimum wage) with a wage supplement (amount decreasing the higher the wage bracket) and all Aruban pensioners with a fixed pension supplement.

Social Care provides the needy with a means-tested cash benefit, *bijstand*, consisting of a fixed monthly standard amount, potentially plus allowances (child allowance, handicapped allowance, illness allowance). Temporary assistance, covering the costs of food and shelter, is possible in emergency cases.

By virtue of the General Pension national ordinance,[22] second pillar pension arrangements provide workers with an additional pension in addition to the general insurance benefits. The arrangement can take the form of an enterprise-based pension fund or a life insurance contract; in both cases the employer finances in principle at least half the cost.

We do not further discuss the special social protection arrangements for civil servants.[23] Let us merely mention that civil servants as well as other workers for government, government related institutions and publicly subsidised institutions and foundations enjoy a second pillar pension by the General Pension Fund Aruba (APFA) in addition to the AOV.[24] APFA also grants invalidity pensions.

There is a clear influence of the Dutch social security upon the Aruban social security, be it that Aruba has deployed an important legislative activity since it left the Netherlands Antilles. The AOV, AWW, ZV and OV are basically the continuation of the former Antillean arrangements, themselves to a large extent adaptations of the then existing Dutch social security laws. The *Cessantia* also go back to an Antillean arrangement, which was however inspired by Latin American arrangements. The General Illness Costs Insurance AZV and the Reparation Allowance date from after leaving the Netherlands Antilles and are therefore of Aruban creation.

[22]*Landsverordening algemeen pensioen*, AB 2011 no. 85.

[23]See *inter alia*: the *Landsverordening Materieel Ambtenarenrecht*, AB 1989 no. GT 37, as amended.

[24]See: www.apfaruba.org.

3.2.3 *Enforcement of Constitutional and Statutory Rights*

Decisions of the *Sociale Verzekeringsbank* SVB (i.e. the social security administration, *infra*) relating to the AOV, AWW, ZV, OV and *Cessantia* benefits can in principle be appealed to an Appeal Board (*College van Beroep*), consisting of a lawyer, president, a member appointed on proposal of the trade unions, and a member appointed on proposal of the employers.[25] Decisions of the Appeal Board overturning the decision of the SVB, replace this decision; no new decision needs to be taken. In the event that the Appeal Board decides in cases relating to the ZV, the OV and the *Cessantia,* the law explicitly mentions the Appeal Board to be the 'only and highest' level of decision.[26] In recent years, about 30 cases have been brought before the Appeal Board annually.[27]

Appeals against decisions concerning the AZV, the Reparation Allowance and the Social Care ('*bijstand*') follow the procedure established by *the Landsverordening Administratieve Rechtspraak* (LAR).[28] The decision must first be resubmitted to the administration that took the initial decision; this administration must take its final decision after hearing the advice of a special LAR Commission. This final decision of the administration can be appealed to the General (administrative) Court in the country. The General Court sitting in the country belongs to the ordinary judiciary system common to Aruba, Curaçao, Sint Maarten, Bonaire, Sint Eustatius and Saba. Appeals against decisions of the General Court go to the Joint Court of Justice of Aruba, Curaçao, Sint Maarten, Bonaire, Sint Eustatius and Saba (hereinafter JCJ).[29]

3.3 Population and the Personal Scope of the Social Security Schemes

3.3.1 *General Data on the Population and Its Composition*

Aruba has a population of approximately 119,000 people, according to a 2020 estimate. The largest concentration of people live in or around the capital Oranjestad and in the city of San Nicolaas, with several settlements on the less mountainous

[25]Art. 37 *Landsverordening AOV*; Art. 38 *Landsverordening AWW*; Art. 10 *Landsverordening Ongevallenverzekering;* art. 10 *Landsverordening Ziekteverzekering*; Art. 9 *Cessantiaverordening.*

[26]Art 10 §1 *Landsverordening Ongevallenverzekering;* art. 10§ 1 *Landsverordening Ziekteverzekering*; art.9 §1 *Cessantiaverordening.*

[27]Data provided by Mrs. Mr. Marisol Tromp. Exceptionally in 2016, 134 cases were heard, but this exceptionally high figure was due to 113 *Cessantia* appeals that year.

[28]AB 1993 no. 45, as amended.

[29]See: http://gemhofvanjustitie.org/; See also: *Rijkswet cassatierechtspraak voor Aruba, Curaçao, Sint Maarten en voor Bonaire, Sint Eustatius en Saba.*

western side of the island. Slightly less than half of the population lives in urban areas.

Ethnically, inhabitants of Aruba are very diverse. Based on a 2010 estimate, two thirds of the inhabitants were born in the country. Colombia (9%), the Netherlands (4%) and the Dominican Republic are the most important of the many countries of origin.

The diversity of the population is reflected in a diversity of languages. Papiamento is the official language and mother tongue of about seven-tenths of the population, whereas Dutch, the other official language, accounts for 6% of native speakers. Spanish (14%) and English (7%) are the other major first languages.

The labour force in Aruba was estimated at about 52,000 people in 2007, with two thirds of workers employed in the service sector and about one third active in industry. Roughly one-third of the active population was not born in Aruba. In 2016, the unemployment rate was estimated at approximately 8%.

According to a 2020 estimate, the net migration rate is 8.4 migrants per 1000 persons; this high figure is mainly due to people fleeing from Venezuela.

3.3.2 Personal Scope of the Social Insurance and Social Assistance Schemes

The General Insurances AOV and AWW apply to residents and non-residents who receive a wage from the country for activities performed outside Aruba or in relation to studies or training. Some residents are not covered: residents who by virtue of international agreements do not pay income tax in Aruba, and residents who are mandatorily covered for the relevant risks by a statutory arrangement elsewhere.

At the end of 2019, 21,455 persons received an AOV pension and 1748 people an AWW benefit.[30]

The AZV applies to all persons registered in the basic population administration who are entitled to stay in the country and who have their main residence in Aruba. Persons who are not registered in the basic administration but who are in the service of the country and their family members can also be covered. Persons who fall within this personal scope of application of the AZV can be freed of this insurance if they demonstrate they are covered by a foreign statutory arrangement that provides at least similar benefits. The AZV does not apply to residents who are freed from social insurance in Aruba, by virtue of international arrangements to which Aruba is party. The AZV also does not apply to residents (and their family members) who have an income out of employment elsewhere for an employer established elsewhere in the Kingdom of the Netherlands.

The Reparation Allowance benefits wage earners registered in the population register and earning a monthly salary of at least the minimum wage and not more

[30]See: https://www.svbaruba.org/organsacion/estadistica/.

than a fixed amount (approximately 140% of the minimum wage). Wage earners are defined as persons employed by a private sector employer with neither the spouse nor themselves receiving a pension; persons registered in the population register receiving a pension. If these pensioners have another income than this pension, the total amount of income should not exceed a fixed threshold.

The professional social insurance ZV and OV apply to employees, i.e. to anyone performing work for an employer in an employment contract or in a personal capacity, except in a number of cases. The most important exceptions are: employees designated as employers, parents and children living at home with the employer unless the employment is for a normal wage, domestic staff and homeworkers, captains and seamen on national seagoing vessels, and people in service of a public authority covered for the risk by their legal status. Persons earning a daily wage above an established limit are also excluded from the field of application of the ZV. At the beginning of 2020, about 36,500 people were ZV insured and 41,500 OV insured.[31]

The *Cessantia* arrangement applies to all workers as defined in the Civil Code, with the exception of persons in public service and persons employed by subsidised special schools. At the end of 2018, 45,133 workers participated in the *Cessantia* fund; in the same year 34 workers applied for a *Cessantia* benefit.[32]

The following qualify for Social Care (*bijstand*): persons who are registered in the population registers in Aruba and

- are born in Aruba and possess citizenship of the Kingdom of the Netherlands; or
- have resided in Aruba in the three preceding years.

In case of absence from Aruba for more than 4 consecutive weeks or more than 8 weeks per year, the *bijstand* is suspended; however, stays in an hospital abroad or in a holiday camp abroad are not counted if the stay does not exceed 4 weeks.

There is also a possibility of granting social care to non-citizens who are born in Aruba. Foreigners only qualify for social care in the form of transitory assistance ('*overbruggingshulp*') that covers the period between the application for naturalisation and the decision whether or not to grant the citizenship. Foreigners who are not in that situation may only qualify for emergency assistance in the form of a one-off interest-free loan.

The national ordinance General Pensions obliges all employers residing or established in Aruba to ensure their workers take part in an enterprise-based pension fund or a life insurance. Workers are defined as all persons of at least 18 years of age and who have not reached the AOV pensionable age, who have a labour contract and who are registered in the population registers.

---

[31] See: https://www.svbaruba.org/organsacion/estadistica/.

[32] Sociale Verzekeringsbank Aruba, Sociale zekerheid voor iedereen. Jaarverslag 2018, p.12. Accessed on: https://www.svbaruba.org/wp-content/uploads/jr/2018/SVb%20jaarverslag%202018.pdf.

3.4 Administration of Social Security

According to a national ordinance of 2013,[33] the competences and political responsibilities in the area of social security are distributed across the Ministry of Tourism, Public Health and Sports, competent, among other things, for 'the social and people's insurances' and the Ministry of Social Affairs and Labour, competent, amongst other things, for 'social, labour and family affairs'. The Reparation Allowance falls under the competence of the Ministry of Finance and Economic Affairs, which is also competent for supervising the application of the national ordinance General Pensions.

An administration for all social insurances, except the AZV, has been established by *landsverordening*: the Social Insurance Bank (SVB), an autonomous public agency. The Bank is managed by a Director, nominated by the Government on proposal of the Supervisory and Advisory Board. The Supervisory and Advisory Board provide supervision and advice. The Board consists of seven members nominated by Government, two from the circle of the employers, two from the circle of the employees and three, amongst which the president, from other socio-economic circles.

Within the SVB there are separate funds to finance the different schemes. An additional scheme, the *Schommelfonds* OV and ZV, collects the money not used for the OV or ZV benefits that year, and respectively adjusts the deficits in these funds when the incomes that year do not cover the expenses.

The AZV Fund is administrated by its Executive Organ ('*uitvoeringsorgaan*'), an autonomous public agency. The Minister of Health may give instructions to the Executive Organ, which in principle must be followed by the Executive Organ. A Council of Commissioners is in charge of the general supervision of the activities of the Executive Organ. The Council consists of five members: two independent members, one nominated by the most representative trade unions, one nominated by the most representative organisations of the employers; the fifth member is nominated by the four other members and will be the president. The Executive Organ is managed by a direction, composed of maximum two directors. Health care is in principle provided by autonomous health care providers (medical doctors, hospitals, pharmacies) who have entered into a contract with the Executive Organ.

The collection of the contributions for the general insurances is the competence of the income tax authorities; collection of the employment related contributions is carried out by the SVB. The Reparation Allowance is paid by the SVB to the pensioners, and by the employers to the wage earners entitled to this allowance. Employers can reduce the amount of the income taxes and social contributions they owe by the amount of the reparation allowances paid to their employees.

A division within the Ministry of Social Affairs is competent for social care (*bijstand*).

---

[33] *Landsverordening instelling ministeries* 2018, AB 2013 no. 94, as amended by AB 2018 no. 22.

3.5 Coordination

The Charter for the Kingdom of the Netherlands stipulates that the Kingdom is in charge of international relations and not the country. Article 37 of the Charter stipulates that the Netherlands and the country shall consult as much as possible on the interests of both countries. The charter explicitly states that social relations between the countries are a matter of mutual interest.

As stated above, the country is not a member state of the EU. Therefore, European social security coordination rules do not apply.

Although Aruba is a part of the Kingdom of the Netherlands, coordination treaties concluded by the Netherlands explicitly state, as a general rule, that these treaties only apply to the European part of the Kingdom.[34] A treaty on the coordination of social security schemes between the Netherlands and the country does not exist.[35] Nevertheless, the Netherlands has made arrangements regarding the export of Dutch social security benefits to the country.[36]

Since foreign relations are part of the Kingdom affairs to be regulated by the Netherlands (*supra*), the coordination of social protection schemes with third countries should be discussed and enacted through the Kingdom's relevant bodies. However, no treaties on social coordination can be found for the country.

The Executive Organ of the General Illness Costs Insurance AZV has made agreements with health care providers in the Netherlands, Curaçao, Sint Maarten, the USA, Colombia and Venezuela to provide the needed health care absent on the island.

Elements of what would otherwise be regulated in coordination agreements, can be found spread over the various relevant national ordinances, this however without a clear comprehensive logic behind them.

For instance, in case the AOV or the AWW is paid abroad, the relevant law stipulates that transfer costs are at the expense of the pensioner.[37] In order to preserve his/her rights, an AOV insured person can request, on the basis of article 21 §1 AOV, to receive a declaration of the rights he/she has accrued up to that point upon permanently leaving the island. The same article in its second paragraph adds that the entitlement to and payment of AOV for persons living outside Aruba will be regulated by a *landsbesluit*. However, the latter could not be found.

---

[34] See, for example, the following treaty between the Netherlands and Belgium (art. 4) https://wetten.overheid.nl/BWBV0005135/2015-10-01 or a similar treaty between the Netherlands and Suriname (art. 15): https://wetten.overheid.nl/BWBV0001496/2002-11-01.

[35] See: https://www.uwv.nl/particulieren/overige-onderwerpen/internationaal/overzicht-verdragslanden/detail/met-welke-landen-heeft-nederland-een-verdrag.

[36] See: https://www.uwv.nl/particulieren/overige-onderwerpen/internationaal/handhavingsverdrag-naar-welke-landen-kan-uitkering-mee/detail/overzicht-landen-waar-u-uw-uitkering-mee-naartoe-kunt-nemen.

[37] Art. 13 §3*Landsverordening* AOV; Art. 16 § *3 Landsverordening* AWW.

At the end of 2018, approximately 10% of the AOV beneficiaries lived outside Aruba; 6% lived in the European part of the Kingdom.[38]

The national ordinance OV provides the possibility of transforming the OV recurrent benefit into a capital in favour of a worker who is not a citizen of the Kingdom of the Netherlands, who him/herself or their spouse is established or settling outside of Aruba.[39] The work-incapacitated worker who leaves Aruba without permission of the SVB loses entitlement to the OV benefit.[40]

Article 21 of the national ordinance General Illness Costs Insurance mentions the possibility in favour of insured persons temporarily staying abroad, of compensating the costs of health care abroad when the care cannot be delayed until return to Aruba. Article 25 of the same *Landsverordening* AZV stipulates that when the care to which an insured party is entitled cannot be provided in Aruba, the AZV Fund will refer the patient to the health care institution in the Netherlands, Curaçao, Sint Maarten, the United States of America, Colombia or Venezuela, that provides the needed care at the lowest cost. If the patient accepts this, the organisational and financial aspects of the journey, the stay and the treatment will be taken care of by the ASZ. However, if the patient refuses treatment by the indicated provider, the Executive Organ of AZV will offer the patient a choice between one health care provider in each of the other mentioned countries. In the latter case the patient must take care of all organisational and financial aspects and he/she will only be reimbursed for the costs to the extent of the amount that would have been covered if the first indicated health care provider had been chosen.

The national ordinance General Pension provides for the possibility of paying the value of the general pension arrangement (minus costs and possible open social security debts) to participants who have left the country and who have been unregistered since at least 3 years.[41]

3.6 Additional Relevant Information

Occasionally Aruba is hit by hurricanes, although the island lies outside the Caribbean hurricane belt and is therefore rarely threatened.

The country's economy is highly dependent on tourism and other services, earlier also on petroleum bunkering and refinery. The environmental impact of both tourism and oil refining calls for concern. Aruba deals with difficulties to manage waste; freshwater must be produced through desalination.

---

[38]Sociale Verzekeringsbank Aruba, Sociale zekerheid voor iedereen. Jaarverslag 2018, p.13. Accessed on https://www.svbaruba.org/wp-content/uploads/jr/2018/SVb%20jaarverslag%202018.pdf).

[39]Art.5 §7 b & c *Landsverordening* OV.

[40]Art. 7 §1, g.

[41]Art. 24 *Landsverordening Algemeen Pensioen*, AB 2011 no. 85.

Whereas Aruba fights corruption and is in favour of more integrity in the public administration, bribery and corruption are less present in the social sector than in other sectors of society. Yet according to the *Sociaal Economische Raad*, there is definitely a problem of developing the social security system for 'electoral gain'. Benefits have been increased considerably, in which party political interests have played an important role. In doing so, the cost aspect has been lost sight of and the need for sound economic support was neglected. The bankruptcy of the General Pension Fund could only barely be averted. Moreover, the almost limitless possibilities of the General Illness Costs Insurance AZV also exceeded the country's financial possibilities by far. In recent years, constant corrections had to be made to prevent the bankruptcy of the social schemes and the Country, which is the guarantor.

Websites

http://gemhofvanjustitie.org/
https://secure.overheid.aw/bestuur-organisatie/samenstelling_3395/
https://ser.aw
https://en.wikipedia.org/wiki/Dissolution_of_the_Netherlands_Antilles
www.apfaruba.org
www.refworld.org/docid/3ae6ae688.html
www.royal-house.nl/topics/legislation/charter-for-the-kingdom-of-the-netherlands
www.svbaruba.org/organsacion/estadistica/
www.uwv.nl/particulieren/overige-onderwerpen/internationaal/overzicht-verdragslanden/detail/met-welke-landen-heeft-nederland-een-verdrag
www.uwv.nl/particulieren/overige-onderwerpen/internationaal/handhavingsverdrag-naar-welke-landen-kan-uitkering-mee/detail/overzicht-landen-waar-u-uw-uitkering-mee-naartoe-kunt-nemen

References

Country Profiles (2020) International Social Security Association. https://www.issa.int/en_GB/country-profiles. Accessed 12 Feb 2020
Oostindie G, Klinkers I (2001) Knellende koninkrijksbanden: het Nederlandse dekolonisatiebeleid in de Caraïben, 1940-2000. Amsterdam University Press, Amsterdam
Sociale Verzekeringsbank Aruba, *Sociale zekerheid voor iedereen. Jaarverslag 2018.* https://www.svbaruba.org/wp-content/uploads/jr/2018/SVb%20jaarverslag%202018.pdf
World Factbook (2020) Central Intelligence Agency. https://www.cia.gov/the-world-factbook/countries/aruba. Accessed 12 Feb 2020

Chapter 4
Buthan

4.1 Context

Bhutan[1] is a multi-ethnic, landlocked country in the Himalayas between Tibet and India. In the nineteenth century the country was unified and in 1907 Ugyen Wangchuck was proclaimed King, the first king or *Druk Gyalpo*, of the currently still-reigning dynasty. In 1919, Bhutan and the United Kingdom signed the Treaty of Punakha whereby the British agreed not to interfere in Bhutanese internal affairs, while Britain directed Bhutan's foreign affairs and provided an annual subsidy. In 1949, the Indo-Bhutanese Friendship Treaty made the newly independent India take over the commitments of the United Kingdom. Slavery was only abolished in the early 1950s. Until then, Bhutan had remained a very closed country, but now the country has slowly opened up to the world and to modernity, resulting in the presentation in 2005 by the fourth *Druk Gyalpo* of Bhutan's first written constitution, which was adopted by popular referendum. In 2007, India and Bhutan renegotiated their Friendship Treaty, eliminating the provision that Bhutan would be 'guided by' India in its foreign policy. In 2008, the first parliamentary elections were held, after which parliamentary majorities and governments have alternated every 5 years.

Whereas the country was governed by royal decrees before the constitution of 2005, today the Kingdom of Bhutan can be qualified as a constitutional monarchy.

The legislative power is bestowed upon the King and the two houses of parliament, the *Chi Tshog*. The non-partisan National Council consists of 25 members, 20 of whom are directly elected in single-seat constituencies and 5 of whom are

With special thanks to Prof. Michael Peil and Prof. Mahesh Gajmer, both of Jigme Singye Wangchuck School of Law, for reviewing the report on Bhutan.

[1]General information, data and figures, see: Country Profiles (2020), UNICEF(2009) and World Factbook (2020).

D. Pieters, *Social Security Law in Small Jurisdictions*, The World of Small States 8,
https://doi.org/10.1007/978-3-030-78247-4_4

appointed by the King. The other chamber, the National Assembly, consists of 47 members who are all directly elected in single-seat constituencies. National Assembly elections consist of two phases: a primary phase, in which all registered parties are permitted to contest, and a general phase, which only the top two vote-getting parties are permitted to contest. In the last primary elections (the third in Bhutan's history), three parties each received one third of the votes: the social-democrat United Party of Bhutan DNT, the royalist-conservative Bhutan Peace and Prosperity Party DPT (which controlled the first government from 2008 until 2013) and the royalist-progressivist People's Democratic Party PDP (which controlled the second government from 2013 until 2018). In the general election, DNT took two-thirds of the seats and DPT took the remaining one third.

The head of state is the King and the head of the government is the prime minister. The prime minister is the head of the majority party in Parliament, formally appointed by the King. The cabinet members are nominated by the Prime Minister and formally appointed by the King.

According to article 3, section 1 of the Constitution, Buddhism is the spiritual heritage of Bhutan, which promotes the principles and values of peace, non-violence, compassion and tolerance.

Bhutan has gained worldwide attention for its promotion of the philosophy of Gross National Happiness, based on four pillars: sustainable and equitable socio-economic development, preservation and promotion of culture, conservation and sustainable use and management of the environment, and promotion of good governance. The concept is enshrined in the Bhutanese Constitution, where article 9, section 2 directs the State "to promote those conditions that will enable the pursuit of Gross National Happiness".[2] The emphasis on community strengthening, education and health is consistent with the Gross National Happiness philosophy.

Bhutan maintains many and good links with neighbor India, with which Bhutan is linked with a Friendship Treaty. Bhutan is dependant upon India, monetarily as well as economically.

4.2 Legal Framework of Rights to Social Security

4.2.1 Constitutional Context

The Bhutanese Constitution enumerates in article 7 a list of fundamental rights, but none of them is directly related to social security. Article 7, Section 1, states that "All persons shall have the right to life, liberty, and security of person and shall not be deprived of such rights except in accordance with the due process of law." This provision is based on the Buddhist principle of '*Sok choepa*'. Buddha said, "Every

[2]On the Gross National Happiness idea, see amongst others: K.P. Lama & S.T. Dorji, Gross National Happiness and SCP in Bhutan, in: *Sustainable Asia*, Chapter 6. Available from: www.worldscientific.com.

living being deserves to enjoy a sense of security and well-being. We should protect life and bring happiness to others." *Prima facie* this provision would appear to include rights such as the protection of the physical integrity of the citizens against external threats, such as invasion and terrorism, and against abuse by official authorities and other citizens. However, according to Former Chief Justice, Sonam Tobgay, the provision is beginning to include other social rights, such as the right to the necessities of life, the right to social security, and protection of health and safety.[3]

Article 8 summarises the fundamental duties and here we find in section 6: "A person shall have the responsibility to provide help, to the greatest possible extent, to victims of accidents and in times of natural calamity." More interesting for our purposes is article 9, which enumerates the principles of State Policy, where we read:

> 1.The State shall endeavour to apply the Principles of State Policy set out in this Article to ensure a good quality of life for the people of Bhutan in a progressive and prosperous country that is committed to peace and amity in the world.
>
> 2.The State shall strive to promote those conditions that will enable the pursuit of Gross National Happiness. [...]
>
> 7.The State shall endeavour to develop and execute policies to minimize inequalities of income, concentration of wealth, and promote equitable distribution of public facilities among individuals and people living in different parts of the Kingdom. [...]
>
> 11.The State shall endeavour to promote those circumstances that would enable the citizens to secure an adequate livelihood. [...]
>
> 19.The State shall endeavour to promote those conditions that are conducive to co-operation in community life and the integrity of the extended family structure.
>
> 20.The State shall strive to create conditions that will enable the true and sustainable development of a good and compassionate society rooted in Buddhist ethos and universal human values.
>
> 21.The State shall provide free access to basic public health services in both modern and traditional medicines.
>
> 22.The State shall endeavour to provide security in the event of sickness and disability or lack of adequate means of livelihood for reasons beyond one's control.[...]

Two more provisions of the Constitution are worthy of our attention: article 2, section 16, sub b) where we can read that the King in exercise of His Royal Prerogatives, may: "grant citizenship, land kidu and other kidus"; and section 19 of the same article 2 stating: "The State shall endeavour to promote those conditions that are conducive to co-operation in community life and the integrity of the extended family structure."

Bhutanese law is considered to belong to the civil law group, but its content is based on Buddhist law and morals.

[3]See: http://www.judiciary.gov.bt/education/constitutionphilosophies.pdf.

4.2.2 Social Security Legislation and Structure

Social security, in the usual sense of the concept of a public, statutory system that provides cash benefits in case of certain eventualities, is rather limited in Bhutan, both in terms of the number of social risks and the number of people covered. Many social protection arrangements also operate outside of a formal statutory framework. Social security in Bhutan only started in 1962 with the introduction of a lump sum benefit upon retirement, in line with what existed at that moment in many former British colonies, and especially in India. The actual pension schemes were inspired by studies of the United Nations Development Programme and the Asian Development Bank.

The only statutory social insurances (except the rural life insurance) are governed by the Government Executive Order of 1 July 2002; the National Pension and Provident Fund (Amendments of 2010 and 2013) Rules and Regulations of Bhutan 2002; and the Armed Forces Pension and Provident Fund Scheme (Amendment 2011) Rules and Regulations 2002.

The social protection to be provided by employers to their employees is based on the Labour and Employment Act 2007 and more specifically the Workers' Compensation Regulation, 2009; the Gratuity Regulation 2009; and the Provident fund Regulation 2009.

It is not clear on what legal basis the rural life insurance scheme has been established. This scheme provides a lump sum upon the death of an insured person in order to cover the (traditionally very high costs of the) funeral rites.[4]

The health care system is based on the constitutional obligation of the state to provide free health care.

The social assistance benefits under the *kidu* system are directly based on the King's prerogatives according to the constitution.

The National Pension and Provident Fund Plan[5] consists of two tiers: tier 1, a defined benefit pension plan and tier 2, a defined contribution provident fund.

Under tier 1, the pension plan, monthly pension benefits are provided upon retirement of a member of the plan, or upon his/her permanent disability prior to his/her retirement. Upon the death of a member prior to or after retirement, monthly benefits are given to the surviving spouse and surviving children. Tier 1 is a partially funded, pay-as-you-go plan. The pension amount is in principle based upon the salary upon retirement and the number of years of service. When the member of the plan has less than 10 years membership, no retirement pension will be paid, but a lump sum equivalent to his/her pension contributions will be paid out. In case of a permanent disability pension a minimum of 3 years membership is required.

Under tier 2, the provident fund plan, a lump sum equivalent to all the contributions to a member's tier 2 account, together with the returns on this account, are paid on the date of his/her retirement or death while in service. Tier 2 is a defined

[4]Dorji et al. (2017), p. 32.

[5]See: www.nppf.org.bt.

contribution, fully funded plan. If a member of the plan leaves the service after more than 1 year but before retirement or death, he/she will receive the accumulated contributions credited to his/her tier 2 account, along with the returns credited on the account, minus possible withdrawals. Early withdrawals of tier 2 benefits are not allowed other than during exit from employment, "but the National Pension Board may allow at its sole discretion withdrawals for the construction of a house or the purchase of a flat or financing the education of his/her children."[6]

Members of the National Pension and Provident Fund Plan are also eligible for loans provided by the Fund, such as housing and commercial housing loans, education and student loans or loans to help members settle and establish themselves at the start of their careers.

Under the Provident Fund Regulation 2009, all enterprises that employ five or more employees for a duration of at least 1 year under the Labour and Employment Act 2007, must provide a provident fund for their employees. A provident fund here is a scheme with the purpose of making a lump sum payment and/or a payment in installments to entitled employees at the severance of the employer-employee relation. It must be a defined contribution scheme; the employer and employee each contributing at least 5% of the wage. The employee provident fund account is segregated from the other assets of the enterprise and an assured account is maintained with an authorised financial institution. The latter maintains a provident fund account for each individual employee. When the employment ends due to retirement, termination of the employment (except when the employee is at fault), becoming disabled, or death, the employee (or his/her nominee in case of death) is entitled to receive the full amount of the employee and employer contributions plus interest, credited to his/her account. In case less than 5 years of continuous contributions have been made, the employer contributions are not included. After 5 years of continuous contributions, an employee is entitled to withdraw up to half of the amount in his/her account, but shall not be permitted to make further withdrawals until a further period of 5 years has elapsed.

Under the Workers' Compensation Regulation, all enterprises covered by the Labour and Employment Act 2007, must provide income compensation to their employees and their dependants as a result of injury, diseases or death arising from their work or related to the tasks and duties they are required to perform. The benefits include compensation for the loss of earning capacity, death benefits and the payment of medical and related costs not covered by the public health system. The employer has the duty to insure with an authorised insurer that all types and levels of compensation prescribed by the regulation are covered by an insurance policy; if this is not done, the employer is liable to pay all compensations him/herself.

The Gratuity Regulation 2009, establishes the nature and the arrangements for gratuity payments to employees who retire from employment or otherwise end their employment relation with their employer. Gratuity involves a lump sum payment

[6]Section 70 of the National Pension and Provident Fund Plan Rules and Regulation of the Kingdom of Bhutan. 2002.

made to an employee at the separation from an employee from service. Here, the obligation upon the employers is to operate a defined gratuity system as foreseen by the Regulation, for the benefit of all employees who have completed a minimum of 10 years of continuous employment.

In conformity with the Constitution, health care is provided freely in the public health system. Traditional and modern (allopathic) methods are practiced and implemented on an equal basis. Modern (allopathic) health care first appeared in Bhutan in the middle of the twentieth century. Bhutan now has a public health system with 28 hospitals, 156 basic health units and 654 outreach clinics.[7] Health care is provided in kind and freely, user charges are limited (for dental care for instance). The primary and secondary levels of care are to be situated on district level or below; tertiary care is provided through a network of three regional referral hospitals, including the national referral hospital, which provides specialised medical and surgical care services. Patients are referred outside Bhutan for specialist care not available in the country, with the cost of care funded by the Government (see further). Traditional health care services are integrated into the modern health care systems at all levels of care.[8]

Patients are nevertheless confronted with often high transportation costs that are not covered The expenses incurred for ritual healing prayer practices based on Buddhist culture, such as *rimdo* and *puja*, are not covered by the public health care system either, although they apparently accounted for more than half of the total health expenditure according to the Bhutan Living Standards survey of 2012.[9]

It may be significant that an insurance company, the Royal Insurance Corporation Bhutan, started a private health insurance to cover user charges and for treatment abroad. In 2012, about one quarter of the funds disbursed covered health expenditure abroad, nearly all in India.[10] Also *kidu* coverage of health care abroad is reported (see further on).

4.2.3 Enforcement of Constitutional and Statutory Rights

None of the social programmes seem to contain specific appeal procedures against the decision taken.

The Supreme Court is the highest jurisdiction in the country and acts as constitutional court. There is a High Court and there are subordinate courts on district and sub-district level. According to Article 7(23) of the Constitution, all persons in

[7]See: www.moh.gov.bt/about/overview.

[8]Sharma et al. (2014), pp. 226–237, here pp. 227–228.

[9]World Health Organization (2017), p. 68. Accessed on: https://apps.who.int/iris/bitstream/handle/10665/255701/9789290225843-eng.pdf?sequence=1&isAllowed=y.

[10]World Health Organization (2017), pp. 68–69. Accessed on: https://apps.who.int/iris/bitstream/handle/10665/255701/9789290225843-eng.pdf?sequence=1&isAllowed=y.

Bhutan shall have the right to initiate appropriate proceedings in the Supreme Court or High Court for the enforcement of their constitutional rights. However, in Bhutan there appears to have been no social security litigation to date.[11]

Finally, it is important to note that the development of social security that provides individual entitlements is seen as somehow conflicting with the mandate of article 2, section 19 of the Constitution to uphold the integrity of the extended family system and community life.[12] It must be recognised that to this day, social protection is largely the responsibility of family and community. "Bhutan has had strong informal social security systems built on family and community solidarity".[13]

> The traditional old-age care and support system (based on filial piety) still exists. The informal care and support system rests on the principles of hierarchy, obligation, obedience, and commitment (*tha dhamtshi*). The traditional joint family system ensures the continuity of the family and contributes towards maintenance of family solidarity.[14]

Or, as the Ministry of Labour and Human resources put it in 2013:

> Community-based social support forms the foundation of social protection in Bhutanese society and contributed to social security and cohesion long before any formal institution existed. Even today, it plays an important role in promoting individual and family welfare and should serve as an overall guide for policymakers in that it is a representation of the social and cultural values of the Bhutanese people.[15]

Charity and social welfare programmes of non-governmental organisations play a role in protecting the poorest sections of the population as well.[16]

The influence of Western individualism, the migration of young people away from their parents and village, the decline in the birth rate are all factors that now endanger this informal social protection system.[17]

Somewhere between the formal public social protection and informal support, we can place the '*kidu*' system.[18] The King has the prerogative, but also the fundamental responsibility to provide '*kidu*' or well-being to his people, in the first place the most vulnerable sections of society. Traditionally the '*kidu*' consisted of providing land to poor households, but now it has extended to encompass all that is absent but seen to be needed or desirable for the well-being of the citizens. The '*kidu*' may be provided under certain 'schemes' or outside any such scheme. As such the '*kidu*' may function

[11]RICB senior agent Kyshab reports that he has not heard of any social security litigation, so far.

[12]See e.g. Dorji et al. (2017), p. 7.

[13]Dorji et al. (2017), p. 24.

[14]Dorji et al. (2017), p. 1.

[15]Ministry of Labour and Human resources, Draft National Social Protection Policy for Workers in Bhutan, 2nd July 2013, p. 1. Accessed on: https://www.gnhc.gov.bt/en/wp-content/uploads/2017/05/Draft-Social-Protection-Policy-2-July-2013.pdf.

[16]Dorji et al. (2017), p. 32.

[17]Dorji et al. (2017), pp. 23–24.

[18]See: https://kidufoundation.org/about-us/; Shaw (2015), pp. 1–22. Accessed on: http://www.bhutanstudies.org.bt/publicationFiles/JBS/JBS_Vol33/1.JBS_Vol33%20Notes%20Concerning%20the%20Political%20Role%20of%20Kidu.pdf; and Dorji et al. (2017), pp. 32–33.

as a form of social assistance, but it is important to keep in mind that it operates outside the realm of the bureaucracy of the state and outside the ambit of the political democratic powers; it remains a royal prerogative. This is justified as follows:

> While binding people more closely to the monarch in the Bhutanese 'social contract', the *kidu* authority and practice also has the practical effect of keeping open an avenue of review and possible redress for the people, at a time when the political institutions of the country (notably legal and political) are still in the process of growth and maturation.[19]

Schemes of '*kidu'* exist to provide support for the education of children from humble families and scholarships to study at universities abroad.[20] The '*kidu*' may also consist of financing the medical referral abroad.[21] Elderly people who have no family are also the object of a special scheme.

A Kidu Foundation was established in 2009 after Bhutan was hit by a natural disaster: the victims were assisted by the Foundation, which received many donations to that effect. Now the Foundation has significantly expanded its area of interest beyond disaster relief to include, amongst other things, education and culture.

Another example of '*kidu*' was the King's Relief Kidu, created in 2020 to provide immediate financial support (fixed amounts of cash) for a period of three months to people who have lost their income from work as a consequence of the COVID-19 pandemic and of the measures to contain it. Bhutanese citizens who were working abroad and have returned home and do not have any other source of income may also benefit. Within the first month of operation of the Relief Kidu, over 13,000 recipients were already identified.[22]

The '*kidu'* system also operates by setting up or supporting civil society organisations (NGOs), such as the Tarayana Foundations that support the most vulnerable, amongst other things, by implementing the food-for-education programme in some communities.[23]

---

[19]Shaw (2015), p. 19. Accessed on: http://www.bhutanstudies.org.bt/publicationFiles/JBS/JBS_Vol33/1.JBS_Vol33%20Notes%20Concerning%20the%20Political%20Role%20of%20Kidu.pdf.

[20]In 2014, for instance, 161 students were pursuing higher education abroad with such a scholarship.

[21]In 2014: 95 persons.

[22]Press Release from the Druk Gyalpo's Relief Kidu, https://bhutanfound.org/press-release-from-the-drul-gyalpos-relief-kidu.

[23]Dolkar (2012), p. 19. Accessed on: https://www.adb.org/sites/default/files/project-document/76052/44152-012-reg-tacr-04.pdf.

4.3 Population and the Personal Scope of the Social Security Schemes

4.3.1 General Data on the Population and Its Composition

The population of Bhutan is estimated at about 782,000 (2020), mainly spread over three main ethnic groups: the Tshanglas in the East, the Ngalops in the West, and the Lhotshampas on the Southern foothills of Bhutan. Next to these three groups, there are several smaller ethnic groups. Dzongkha is the official language, but it is the mother tongue of only a quarter of the population.

Three quarters of the population adheres to Vajrayana Buddhism, while a fifth of the population is Hindu. Some animistic traditions and beliefs are also still practiced by the people.[24]

About one quarter of the population lives in the capital city. A large majority of the population lives outside urban areas, but there is an important internal migration trend from the countryside to the cities underway. Migration in and out of Bhutan is in equilibrium, resulting in a zero net migration rate.

The labour force was estimated at about 311,000 in 2018. Unemployment was estimated at 3.4% in that year, whereas youth employment was estimated at more than three times as much.[25] There is a major shortage of skilled labour. In 2012, 12% of the population was estimated to live below the poverty line.

4.3.2 Personal Scope of the Social Insurance and Social Assistance Schemes

The National Pension and Provident Fund Plan (NPPFP) has two types of members:

- those who are covered both in tier 1 and 2 of the Plan, the so-called simultaneous members, and
- those covered only in tier 2, the provident fund.

Bhutanese nationals who are regular employees enjoy simultaneous membership when working in the following sectors:

- armed forces;
- civil service;
- public organisations, projects and institutions of the Government; and
- fully owned government, joint sector, and public companies.

[24]See: https://www.bhutan.travel.page/our-people-society-religion.

[25]Figures taken from: National Statistics Bureau (2019).

Foreign ('expatriate') members of the armed forces and of the above-mentioned agencies, as well as contract employees working in the above agencies only enjoy tier 2 provident fund membership.

A member is not entitled to a pension, or a pension shall cease when a member or pensioner has absconded from the country as declared by an appropriate authority, or when he/she relinquishes Bhutan citizenship.

In 2018, the NPPFP counted some 55,000 members (representing about 8% of the population) and some 6500 pensioners.[26]

The rural life insurance scheme includes all persons aged 8 years old and over in its personal scope. It remains unclear whether all persons are covered, or the insurance is open to all persons who want to affiliate and pay the insurance premium. It is also unclear whether only people living in the rural areas are to affiliate, or all households.[27]

The number of workers of the (formal) private sector who effectively enjoy the protection in case of an industrial risk, a gratuity scheme or a provident fund is very limited.[28]

The public health care system serves all citizens of Bhutan. The voluntary health insurance operated by the Royal Insurance Corporation of Bhutan covers some 1% of the population, mainly through insurance policies contracted by employers for their employees.

4.4 Administration of Social Security

The National Pension and Provident Fund (NPPF) was established as an autonomous public agency to manage and implement the National Pension and Provident Fund Plan (NPPFP).

The powers of the NPPF are vested in a Board of Directors, the National Pension Board, which is responsible for policy decisions and general supervision. The National Pension Board consists of a member of the Council of Ministers as chairperson; the CEO of the NPPF as member secretary; and the Secretary of Finance, the Secretary of the Royal Civil Service Commission, the Director of the Department of Employment and Labour, all ex officio, plus four other Directors appointed for a renewable term of 3 years. These four Directors are nominated by their respective sectors from the CEOs of financial institutions and public

[26]National Pension and Provident Fund, Annual Report 2017–2018, Thimphu, 2019; p. 6. Accessed on: http://www.nppf.org.bt/eng/publication/annual-report/2017-2018-Annual-Report.pdf.

[27]Dolkar (2012), p. 23. Accessed on: https://www.adb.org/sites/default/files/project-document/76052/44152-012-reg-tacr-04.pdf.

[28]In the study *Social Protection in South Asia* (p. 54) it was estimated that the formal private sector in Bhutan stands roughly for one per cent of the total labour force. Accessed on: https://www.unicef.org/socialpolicy/files/social_protection_in_south_asia_-_a_review_-_unicef_rosa_2009.pdf.

corporations, and the representatives from the armed forces and the private sector. The Board is independent and autonomous in the discharge of its functions. The Board appoints a CEO to be in charge of the NPPF and responsible to the Board for the implementation of its policy and the day-to-day administration.

From the contributions paid to the National Pension and Provident Fund Plan (NPPFP), two separate funds are established, the Tier 1 Fund and the Tier 2 Fund.

The funds of the NPPFP shall be invested by the NPPF in accordance with the investment policy prescribed by the National Pension Board. The NPPF is nowadays one of the main sources of funding for most projects in the country (mainly hydropower and hotels) and has in this way contributed to its economic development. NPPF is also one of the biggest real estate developers in the country.[29]

In the Annual Report of the NPPF we read:

> In the absence of a clear legal framework within which NPPF functions, NPPF is regulated like a State Owned Enterprise (SoE) under the Ministry of Finance (MoF). The MoF takes the lead in governance matter such as appointment of Board Directors, Chief Executive Officer (CEO. [. . .] The RMA [Royal Monetary Agency, i.e. the central bank, also plays a quasi-regulatory role since NPPF is categorized as a financial institution. Therefore, all Board and CEO are appointed after issuing of "Fit and Proper" test. For some of the business aspects, such as loans, the operations is regulated by all applicable laws and regulations issued applied by RMA. [. . .]
>
> [T]he lack of a proper supervisory and regulatory authority, especially in the case of pension schemes, have left NPPF vulnerable.[30]

The rural life insurance scheme is under the supervision of the Minister of Home and Cultural Affairs. The Ministry of Labour and Human Resources and the Ministry of Finance supervise, each within their field of competence, the gratuity schemes, workers' compensation arrangements and provident funds.

Companies such as Bhutan Insurance, and the Royal Insurance Corporation of Bhutan manage such insurances, provident funds and gratuity schemes. The Royal Insurance Corporation of Bhutan also administers the rural life insurance scheme.

The Ministry of Health provides general supervision over the delivery of health care. District-level health services' planning and management are decentralised to district health management teams that function within the framework of local government. The regional referral hospitals work under the Ministry of Health. There are no private hospitals in Bhutan.

Let us also observe that according to article 8 of the Executive Order of 1 July 2002, the Board of NPPF may make investments outside Bhutan with the approval of the Government and may for this purpose engage the services of professional investment managers.

[29]National Pension and Provident Fund, Annual Report 2017–2018, Thimphu, 2019, p. 1. Accessed on: http://www.nppf.org.bt/eng/publication/annual-report/2017-2018-Annual-Report.pdf.

[30]National Pension and Provident Fund, Annual Report 2017–2018, Thimphu, 2019, pp. 13–14. Accessed on: http://www.nppf.org.bt/eng/publication/annual-report/2017-2018-Annual-Report.pdf.

4.5 Coordination

Bhutan has no social security coordination agreements with other states. The law seems to also neglect residence conditions for accessing social benefits; it suggests exportability of benefits, which might however be contradicted by reality.

It is not known whether there are special agreements between Bhutan and its health care system and foreign, i.e. Indian, health care providers and hospitals. In principle, if (life-saving) specialist health services are not available in the country, patients will be referred by the three referral hospitals of Bhutan to hospitals outside Bhutan (to India) and the costs of the care will be funded by the Government of Bhutan.[31] Referrals abroad expenditure amounted to 5.35% of the total health expenditure in 2014–2015; 1126 patients benefitted from a referral abroad in the same period. However, data on diseases and costs of treatment abroad for individual cases are unfortunately not available.[32]

4.6 Additional Relevant Information

Bhutan is occasionally hit by violent storms from the Himalayas. Earthquakes occur rather frequently; an earthquake in 2009 was disastrous and destroyed many houses and infrastructure. There are frequent landslides during the rainy season.

Bhutan is confronted with a lack of skilled workers that hinders the development of the private sector. Moreover, the fact that social insurances are in fact restricted to the public sector may push (young) jobseekers to prefer employment in the public sector.[33]

Bhutan's economy is based on hydropower, agriculture and forestry. Imports and exports account for 90% and more to and from India, a country with which Bhutan has a monetary union. Moreover, Bhutan is dependant on India for financial assistance and migrant workers for development projects, especially for road construction. In total, India finances nearly a quarter of Bhutan's budget expenditures. For several years, an effort has been made to promote (sustainable and up-market) tourism. This sector is however very volatile.

Bhutan is also largely dependant on international development aid for most of its educational, social and environment programmes. Since the country reached the status of low middle income country, this development aid is being reduced.

---

[31]World Health Organization (2017), p. 24. Accessed on: https://apps.who.int/iris/bitstream/handle/10665/255701/9789290225843-eng.pdf?sequence=1&isAllowed=y.

[32]World Health Organization (2017), pp. 58–59. Accessed on: ttps://apps.who.int/iris/bitstream/handle/10665/255701/9789290225843-eng.pdf?sequence=1&isAllowed=y.

[33]Ministry of Labour and Human Resources, *Draft National Social Protection Policy for Workers in Bhutan*, July 2nd 2013, p. 10. Accessed on: https://www.gnhc.gov.bt/en/wp-content/uploads/2017/05/Draft-Social-Protection-Policy-2-July-2013.pdf.

It should also be observed that Bhutan only started with democratic government in 2008. Since then, many efforts have been made to develop a more comprehensive social policy. Some legislation has been developed since then, but there seems to be a long road ahead.

Websites

https://bhutanfound.org/press-release-from-the-drul-gyalpos-relief-kidu
https://kidufoundation.org/about-us/
www.bhutan.travel.page/our-people-society-religion
www.judiciary.gov.bt/education/constitutionphilosophies.pdf
www.nppf.org.bt
www.moh.gov.bt/about/overview

References

Country Profiles (2020) International Social Security Association. https://www.issa.int/en_GB/country-profiles. Accessed 12 Feb 2020

Dolkar C (2012) Kingdom of Bhutan: updating and improving the social protection index. Asian Development Bank. Accessed on: https://www.adb.org/sites/default/files/project-document/76052/44152-012-reg-tacr-04.pdf

Dorji L, Jamtsho C, Norbu T, Bhujel GD (2017) Understanding the situation of elderly citizens in Bhutan. National Statistics Bureau, Thimphu

Lama KP, Dorji ST. Gross National Happiness and SCP in Bhutan. In: Sustainable Asia, Chapter 6. Available from: www.worldscientific.com

Ministry of Labour and Human Resources (2013) Draft National Social Protection Policy for Workers in Bhutan. Accessed on: https://www.gnhc.gov.bt/en/wp-content/uploads/2017/05/Draft-Social-Protection-Policy-2-July-2013.pdf

National Pension and Provident Fund (2019) Annual Report 2017–2018. National Pension and Provident Fund, Thimphu. Accessed on: http://www.nppf.org.bt/eng/publication/annual-report/2017-2018-Annual-Report.pdf

National Statistics Bureau (2019) Bhutan at a glance. National Statistics Bureau, Thimphu

Sharma J, Zangpo K, Grundy J (2014) Measuring universal health coverage; a three-dimensional composite approach from Bhutan. WHO South-East Asia J Public Health 3(3–4)

Shaw BC (2015) Bhutan: notes concerning the political role of Kidu. J Bhutan Stud 33 (winter). Accessed on: http://www.bhutanstudies.org.bt/publicationFiles/JBS/JBS_Vol33/1.JBS_Vol33%20Notes%20Concerning%20the%20Political%20Role%20of%20Kidu.pdf

UNICEF (2009) Social protection in South Asia. Accessed on: https://www.unicef.org/socialpolicy/files/social_protection_in_south_asia_-_a_review_-_unicef_rosa_2009.pdf

World Factbook (2020) Central Intelligence Agency. https://www.cia.gov/the-world-factbook/countries/bhutan. Accessed 12 Feb 2020

World Health Organization (2017) Regional Office for South-East Asia, The Kingdom of Bhutan health system review. Health Syst Transit 7(2). Accessed on: https://apps.who.int/iris/bitstream/handle/10665/255701/9789290225843-eng.pdf?sequence=1&isAllowed=y

Chapter 5
Curaçao

5.1 Context

Curaçao[1] is a Lesser Antilles island, located in the South Caribbean Sea, situated about 60 km north of the Venezuelan coast. It became a Dutch colony in the seventeenth century and was an important centre of the Caribbean slave trade until the abolition of slavery in 1863. Curaçao was part of the Netherlands Antilles. The Netherlands Antilles were decolonised in 1954 to become a constituent country of the Kingdom of the Netherlands.

After referendums held in 2005 and 2009, by which the citizens of Curaçao expressed the will to become a self-governing country within the Kingdom of the Netherlands, the Netherlands Antilles were dissolved in 2010. Since then, Curaçao has been a country of the Kingdom of the Netherlands with full sovereignty in internal affairs.[2]

Curaçao is a parliamentary democracy within the constitutional monarchy of the Kingdom of the Netherlands. Curaçao's head of state is the Dutch monarch, who appoints the Governor of Curaçao as his or her representative. The Governor watches over the general interest of the Kingdom in Curaçao and ensures that no decisions are taken by legislative and administrative bodies in Curaçao that could damage the unity of the Kingdom or that are contrary to the provisions of the Statute of the Kingdom or to international law.

Given the mainly symbolical and advisory role of the monarch, the real political and legislative power lies with the parliament and the Council of Ministers, headed by the prime minister. The governor in turn appoints the ministers, who form the

With special thanks to Prof. Dr. Flora Goudappel, dean of the Law Faculty of the University of Curaçao and Mr. Philip Martis, director of SVB for reviewing the report on Curaçao.

[1]For general data and figures, see: Country Profiles (2020) and World Factbook (2020).
[2]Oostindie and Klinkers (2001), pp. 175 & 223–224.

D. Pieters, *Social Security Law in Small Jurisdictions*, The World of Small States 8,
https://doi.org/10.1007/978-3-030-78247-4_5

government; the Government needs the confidence of and is politically responsible to the directly elected Parliament.[3]

The parliament of Curaçao ('*Staten*')[4] consists of one chamber with 21 directly elected members. The political scene is very divided, with only three parties having more than two seats: the liberal Partido Alternativa Real, PAR (6), the social-democratic Movishon Antia Nobo, MAN (5) and the centre-left Movementu Futuro Korsou, MFK (5); four other parties have one or two seats. Governments are coalition governments (in 2020 of PAR and MAN).

A plenipotentiary minister represents Curaçaoan interests in the Kingdom of the Netherlands, but is not a member of the Curaçaoan Cabinet. He/she participates in the decision making in the Council of Ministers for the Kingdom, consisting of the members of the Council of Ministers of the Netherlands and the three plenipotentiary ministers from the three Caribbean countries of the Kingdom. The three countries may also delegate a national minister in an advisory capacity, in addition to the authorised minister. There is no Parliament for the Kingdom, but only the Dutch Parliament, which also deals with matters reserved to the Kingdom, after consultation with the parliaments of the three other countries of the Kingdom.

Based on a 2011 estimate, around three quarters of the population is Roman Catholic and around 15% belongs to various Protestant denominations.

Trade unions are important social actors in the country.[5]

It is clear that Curaçao has strong ties with the Netherlands and the two other countries of the Kingdom of the Netherlands. For example, Curaçao has a monetary union with Sint Maarten. The Kingdom is also responsible for its foreign relations and defence.

The Kingdom of the Netherlands is a member of the European Union, but Curaçao has the status of an 'overseas country and territory' (OCT)[6] and is therefore not part of the European Union. However, only one type of citizenship exists within the Kingdom of the Netherlands, and all citizens of the Kingdom of the Netherlands, also those of Curaçao, are EU citizens as well.[7] This implies strong bonds with the European Union, which provides funds to Curaçao through the European Development Fund.

[3]Art. 28 *Staatsregeling Curaçao*. Accessed on: https://gobiernu.cw/nl/regering/.

[4]Art. 40 and 41 *Staatsregeling Curaçao*. Accessed on: http://www.parlamento.cw/nederlands/zittingsperiode_3125/.

[5]See: https://antilliaansdagblad.com/nieuws-menu/19809-solidaridat-sindikal-roept-bonden-op.

[6]The Netherlands secured a provision in the Treaty of Lisbon that says that any Caribbean part of the Netherlands can opt for a change of status to Outermost Region (OMR) if it so wishes, without having to change the Treaties of the European Union.

[7]See: https://en.wikipedia.org/wiki/Dissolution_of_the_Netherlands_Antilles [and the references made therein].

5.2 Legal Framework of Rights to Social Security

5.2.1 Constitutional Context

Curaçao is one of the 'countries' constituting the Kingdom of the Netherlands. The Charter ('Statuut') for the Kingdom of the Netherlands regulates the constitutional relationship between the four countries that make up the Kingdom: the Netherlands, Aruba, Curaçao and Sint Maarten. The Charter stipulates that the four countries manage their own affairs autonomously and are jointly responsible for Kingdom affairs. It also stipulates rules governing mutual assistance, consultation and cooperation and the constitutional organisation of the countries. The Charter may be amended only with the agreement of all four countries, and it takes precedence over the individual countries' constitutions. Kingdom affairs, over which individual countries have no control, include foreign relations, defence and citizenship of the Netherlands. The Charter also stipulates how the countries should conduct Kingdom affairs in cooperation with each other. All matters that the Charter does not define as Kingdom affairs are country affairs. Each country must promote the realisation of human rights, legal certainty and good governance within its borders. It is the Kingdom's responsibility to safeguard these values.[8]

Each Caribbean country of the Kingdom of the Netherlands has its own Constitution ('Staatsregeling'). The Constitution of Curaçao entered into force on 10 October 2010, on the date of the dissolution of the Netherlands Antilles.[9]

The Constitution clearly stipulates that the livelihood of the population and the distribution and promotion of wealth are the subject of the State's concern and duties.[10] Entitlements to social protection are regulated by national ordinance ('*landsverordening*'), which is a legislative act by the parliament.[11] Social assistance is provided to Dutch citizens with insufficient means to support their livelihood.[12] Finally, according to article 23 of the *Staatsregeling*, the authorities also have the duty to provide sufficient housing.[13]

Curaçaoan law belongs to the civil law group as it is strongly influenced by Dutch law.

[8]See: https://www.royal-house.nl/topics/legislation/charter-for-the-kingdom-of-the-netherlands.

[9]See: https://en.wikipedia.org/wiki/Constitution_of_Cura%C3%A7ao [and the references made therein].

[10]Art. 23, 1) *Staatsregeling Curaçao.*

[11]Art. 23, 2) *Staatsregeling Curaçao.*

[12]Art. 23, 3) *Staatsregeling Curaçao.*

[13]Art. 25, 2) *Staatsregeling Curaçao.*

5.2.2 Social Security Legislation and Structure

Social security is mostly still regulated by national ordinances or '*landsverordeningen*' of the time when the country belonged to the Netherlands Antilles, with some later amendments. These are the national ordinances concerning

- the General Old-Age Insurance (AOV) of 1960;[14]
- the General Widow(ers) and Orphans Insurance (AWW) of 1960;[15]
- the General Insurance Exceptional Medical Expenses (AVBZ) of 1996;[16]
- the Sickness Insurance (ZV) of 1966;[17]
- the Accident Insurance (OV) of 1966;[18]
- the Severance Pay Insurance (*Cessantia*) of 1983;[19] and
- the financial assistance (financiële bijstand) of 1996.

The *landsverordening* establishing the country's own social security administration also dates from before the dissolution in 2010 of the Netherlands Antilles: the national ordinance Sociale Verzekeringsbank (SVB) of 1960.[20]

Since the dissolution of the Netherlands Antilles, Curaçao has only added the following schemes to complete the social security regime:

- a national ordinance Basic Illness Costs Insurance (BVZ) of 2013;[21] and
- a national ordinance holding Additional Provisions for Public Servants and Declared Assimilated Persons of 2014.[22]

The so-called General Insurances, AOV, AWW, AVBZ, as well as the Basic Illness Costs Insurance BVZ are contributory, universal social insurances that cover in principle the entire population; the Sickness Insurance, the Accident Insurance and the *Cessantia* are arrangements on a professional basis. Financial assistance is a social assistance scheme.

The AOV provides a pension upon reaching the pension age (whether one retires or not) while the AWW grants survivor benefits to the spouse of the deceased and to his/her children. The AVBZ covers the (high) costs of treatment and care for the chronically ill and disabled.

[14]See: https://svbcur.org/wetten/aov/.

[15]See: https://svbcur.org/wetten/aww/.

[16]See: https://svbcur.org/wetten/avbz/; this law is commonly known as '*Lei di Labizjan*'.

[17]See: https://svbcur.org/wetten/zv/.

[18]See: https://svbcur.org/wetten/ov/.

[19]See: https://svbcur.org/wetten/cessantia/.

[20]See: https://decentrale.regelgeving.overheid.nl/cvdr/xhtmloutput/Historie/Nederlandse/Antillen/36310/363101.html.

[21]See: https://gobiernu.cw/wp-content/uploads/2019/07/P.B_2013__no._3.pdf.

[22]See: https://svbcur.org/wp-content/uploads/Voorlichting-aanvullende-voorzieningen-ambt-BVZ.pdf.

The Accident Insurance covers victims of a labour accident and provides them with compensation of their medical costs, as well as with income replacement in case of incapacity to work. It also provides benefits for the surviving spouse and children of the victim of a lethal labour accident.

The Sickness Insurance provides an income replacement for incapacitated workers (including cases of pregnancy/maternity). For the small group of persons who are not residents (and thus are not covered by the Basic Illness Costs Insurance) and who are legally employed on Curaçao, the Sickness Insurance also covers the cost of health care services.

The *Cessantia* guarantees a one-off payment upon the involuntary termination of employment.

The Basic Illness Costs Insurance covers the costs of enumerated health care provision (general practitioner, basic hospitalisation costs, etc.) The national ordinance that contains Additional Provisions for Public Servants and Declared Assimilated Persons complements this covered health care package with more health care and related costs being compensated in favour of civil servants as well as assimilated persons and their family members.

Financial assistance or *'onderstand'* is provided to support citizens who lack sufficient means for a decent livelihood.

Let us observe that most of the Curaçaoan social security schemes date back to the time the country was part of the Netherlands Antilles and have largely been based on the Dutch social security law of that time. The main innovation since Curaçao became an autonomous part of the Kingdom of the Netherlands was the introduction in 2013 of a basic illness costs insurance that provides a basic coverage of health care costs for all residents. As a consequence, the ZV has primarily been dealing with income replacement benefits ever since. Minor changes have occurred in the other schemes (e.g. in the AOV, where the pension age was raised).[23]

5.2.3 Enforcement of Constitutional and Statutory Rights

The *Sociale Verzekeringsbank* SVB (i.e. the social security administration, *infra*) is obligated to take decisions on medical issues in conformity with the opinion of the Medical Advisory College, consisting of two medical doctors appointed by the Minister and the medical advisor of SVB.[24]

Decisions taken by the SVB with relation to the above mentioned insurances can be appealed to the competent Minister. Decisions by the Minister can be contested before the General Court.[25] The General Court sitting in the country belongs to the

[23] See: http://svbcur.org/wetten/aov/.

[24] Art. 8 *Landsverordening Basisverzekering ziektekosten*.

[25] Art. 38 *Landsverordening Algemene Ouderdomsverzekering*; art. 39 *Landsverordening Algemene Weduwen en Wezenverzekering*; art. 10 *Landsverordening Ongevallenverzekering*; art.

ordinary judiciary system common to Aruba, Curaçao, Sint Maarten, Bonaire, Sint Eustatius and Saba. Appeals go to the Joint Court of Justice of Aruba, Curaçao, Sint Maarten, Bonaire, Sint Eustatius and Saba (hereinafter: JCJ). Decisions may eventually be appealed to the Supreme Court of the Netherlands (Hoge Raad), which, in the case where it upholds the appeal, will send the case back to the JCJ.[26]

Transparency International finds in its Curaçao National Integrity System Assessment that, although Curaçao's legislative framework is fairly strong, there are some considerable gaps between the law in the books and the law in action in many areas. In numerous cases, it appears that existing legislation is not consistently applied in practice, and those who are responsible for the execution of the laws, or who are required to comply with them, do not always know how to correctly do so. This would be particularly true with regards to transparency, where much of the information that should legally be made public, is not consistently or systematically published.[27]

5.3 Population and the Personal Scope of the Social Security Schemes

5.3.1 General Data on the Population and Its Composition

The population of Curaçao is estimated at some 151,000 inhabitants (2020). The largest concentration of people live in or around the capital Willemstad; about 90% of the population lives in urban areas.

Ethnically, inhabitants of Curaçao are very diverse. Whereas most people belong to an Afro-Caribbean majority, there are many other ethnic groups on the island. Three quarters of the population is born on Curaçao, whereas people of Dutch origin make up more than 6% of the population, and all other countries of origin account for less than 4%.

Of the three official languages, Papiamento is the first language of 81% of people, Dutch of 8% and English of 3%.

In 2018, the labour force in Curaçao consisted of about 70,000 people. More than four fifths of the labour force is active in the services sector, while about 17% is

---

36 *Landsverordening Algemene Verzekering Bijzondere Ziektekosten*; art. 10 *Landsverordening Zieklteverzekering*; art. 9 *Landsverordening Cessantia*.

[26]See: http://gemhofvanjustitie.org/; See also: *Rijkswet cassatierechtspraak voor Aruba, Curaçao, Sint Maarten en voor Bonaire, Sint Eustatius en Saba*.

[27]See: https://www.transparency.org/news/pressrelease/transparency_internationals_Curacao_study_highlights_weaknesses_in_the_publ.

employed in industry. In 2018, the unemployment rate amounted to 13.5%, with youth unemployment just above 29%.[28]

Curaçao shows a negative net migration rate of minus 1.3 migrants per 1000 population (2020 estimates).

5.3.2 Personal Scope of the Social Insurance and Social Assistance Schemes

The General Insurances AOV, AWW and AVBZ apply to:

- residents, i.e. persons who according to real circumstances are registered to live in the country; and
- non-residents who are taxed for income tax purposes as a taxpayer living in the country.

Those who stay in Curaçao temporarily (no longer than 6 months) and either live in the Netherlands or who are considered to live there under locally applicable legislation on income-dependent taxation are considered not to be living in the country. The insurances also do not apply to any foreigner who cannot be considered to permanently live in the country and who enjoys a salary or wages payable by another power for work performed in the country.

The BVZ applies to residents. A resident is a person who is enlisted with the population registers under a valid residence title, and who is effectively established in Curaçao. However, residents who already enjoy the coverage of at least the same health care costs under a private health care policy when the BVZ came into operation are excluded from the BVZ. The same goes for employees who already enjoy coverage by a commitment of their employer at that time. Residents with a labour contract elsewhere in the Kingdom of the Netherlands and who are insured for their health care costs are also excluded.

The professional social insurances ZV and OV apply to employees, i.e. to anyone performing work for an employer in an employment contract or in a personal capacity, except in a number of cases. The most important exceptions are: employees designated as employer, parents and children living at home with the employer unless the employment is for a normal wage, domestic staff and homeworkers, captains and seamen on national seagoing vessels, and people in service of a public authority covered for the risk by their legal status.

Persons earning a daily wage above an established limit are also excluded from the field of application.

[28]See: https://www.cbs.cw/website/press-releases-2018_3499/item/results-labour-force-survey-2018_2584.html.

The *Cessantia* arrangement applies to all workers as defined in the Civil Code, with the exception of persons in public service and persons employed by subsidised special schools.

The complementary health care insurance coverage provided by national ordinance, holding Additional Provisions for Public Servants and Declared Assimilated Persons, benefits civil servants, the personnel of the special education schools, some other assimilated persons and the family members of the aforementioned groups.

The means-tested financial assistance scheme applies to citizens of the Kingdom of the Netherlands who have been resident in the country for at least 3 months before applying for the benefit. A resident is understood to be a person enrolled in the population register and effectively living in the country. The condition of citizenship does not apply to persons who fulfill the following conditions:

- the applicant is temporarily or for an undetermined period allowed to stay in the country;
- he/she has been a resident for at least 5 years immediately preceding the application for benefit; and
- the financial help by the guarantor of the stay of the foreigner, cannot reasonably be expected.

Non-citizens who do not fulfill the condition of residence during the previous 5 years may exceptionally be provided assistance if the assistance is needed to tackle life-threatening circumstances.

5.4 Administration of Social Security

The minister responsible for social security policy in the broadest sense is the Minister for Social Development, Labour and Well-being. The Minister for Health, the Environment and Nature is responsible for the AVBZ and ZV. He/she is also politically responsible for health policy, be it that health care provision is privately organised.

An administration for all social insurances has been established by *landsverordening*: the Social Insurance Bank (SVB), an autonomous public agency. Within the SVB there are separate funds to finance the different schemes. If, at the end of any calendar year, a scheme-related fund exceeds the amount required for the benefits, costs and reserve in that year, the surplus will be put into a separate fund, the '*Schommelfonds*' ('Swing Fund'). This Fund will then be used to supplement the resources of a scheme-related fund if and to the extent that the scheme-related fund should prove insufficient to cover all expenses.

The SVB is monitored by a Supervisory Board and managed by a director, nominated by the Government on proposal of the Surpervisory Board. The Supervisory Board consists of six members, one of whom is appointed as representative of the employees and one as representative of the employers; the other four, including the director, come from other socio-economic circles.

5.5 Coordination

The Charter for the Kingdom of the Netherlands stipulates that the Kingdom is in charge of international relations rather than the individual countries. Article 37 of the Charter stipulates that the Netherlands and the country shall consult each other as much as possible involving the interests of both countries, explicitly stating the social relations between the countries as a matter of mutual interest.

As stated above, the country itself is not a member state of the EU. Therefore, European social security coordination rules do not apply.

Although Curaçao is a part of the Kingdom of the Netherlands, coordination treaties concluded by the Netherlands explicitly state, as a general rule, that these treaties only apply to the European part of the Kingdom.[29] A treaty on the coordination of social security schemes between the Netherlands and the country does not exist.[30] Nevertheless, the Netherlands has made arrangements regarding the export of Dutch social security benefits to the country.[31]

Since foreign relations are part of the Kingdom affairs to be regulated by the Netherlands (*supra*), the coordination of social protection schemes with third countries should be discussed and enacted through the Kingdom's relevant bodies. However, no treaties on social coordination can be found for the country.

The Sociale Verzekeringsbank has made agreements with health care providers outside of Curaçao, mainly in Colombia and the Netherlands, to provide the needed health care absent on the island.

5.6 Additional Relevant Information

Unlike many other Caribbean countries, Curaçao is seldom threatened by hurricanes due to its location south of the Caribbean hurricane belt.

Curaçao's economy is mainly based on tourism, petroleum refining and bunkering as well as offshore finance. The oil was imported from Venezuela, but the refinery has not been active the last few years. The processing of heavy crude oil from Venezuela caused significant environmental damage. Problems in waste management threaten environmental sustainability, including pollution of marine areas from domestic sewage. Industrial effluents and agricultural runoff, the

[29]See, for example, the following treaty between the Netherlands and Belgium (art. 4): https://wetten.overheid.nl/BWBV0005135/2015-10-01 or a similar treaty between the Netherlands and Suriname (art. 15): https://wetten.overheid.nl/BWBV0001496/2002-11-01.

[30]See: https://www.uwv.nl/particulieren/overige-onderwerpen/internationaal/overzicht-verdragslanden/detail/met-welke-landen-heeft-nederland-een-verdrag.

[31]See: https://www.uwv.nl/particulieren/overige-onderwerpen/internationaal/handhavingsverdrag-naar-welke-landen-kan-uitkering-mee/detail/overzicht-landen-waar-u-uw-uitkering-mee-naartoe-kunt-nemen.

mismanagement of toxic substances and ineffective regulations to combat such negative effects are other examples of such threats.[32]

Confidence in Curaçao's key institutions is generally low. A 2019 survey showed that more than three quarters of the Curaçaoan population is not satisfied with the fight against corruption, and more than half of the population believes corruption has increased significantly in recent years.[33] Such corruption problems have also impacted social protection on the island.[34]

The role of political parties was one of the main causes of the lack of trust in the public institutions. A potential risk of dominance of party discipline over governance, both among member of the *Staten* as well as the government, exists, blurring the separation of powers and diminishing the use of oversight instruments at the disposal of the *Staten* to hold the government accountable.[35] Curaçaoan ministers have indeed been under the suspicion of corruption,[36] and some have even been convicted.[37] In 2016, former Prime Minister Schotte was sentenced to 3 years unconditional imprisonment and 5 years disqualification from public office for corruption and forgery.[38]

In contrast to political parties, the judiciary and the supervisory institutions, among others, scored relatively well in the Curaçao National Integrity System assessment. The judiciary and the supervisory institutions were found to be largely independent and considered adequately resourced. They therefore have the potential to create an effective system of checks-and-balances over the social sectors of the country and serve as a key defence against those who repeatedly get away with acts of corruption.[39]

[32]See: https://www.cia.gov/library/publications/the-world-factbook/geos/cc.html.

[33]See: http://www.nostisia.com/Curacao/23-lokal/7766-the-elephant-in-the-room-corruption-in-Curcao-economic-growth-good-governance-corruption-remuneration.html.

[34]See also: https://www.medischcontact.nl/nieuws/laatste-nieuws/artikel/chirurgen-op-Curcao-vervalsten-dossiers.htm.

[35]See: https://www.transparency.org/news/pressrelease/transparency_internationals_Curacao_study_highlights_weaknesses_in_the_publ.

[36]See: https://web.archive.org/web/20190526101936/http://www.dutchcaribbeanlegalportal.com/news/latest-news/9138-om-seponeert-zaak-tegen-steven-martina.

[37]See: https://antilliaansdagblad.com/nieuws-menu/20862-minister-alcala-walle-dient-ontslag-in-bij-gouverneur.

[38]See: https://www.ad.nl/politiek/veroordeling-oud-premier-Curacao-gerrit-schotte-definitief~a915ce16/?referrer=https://www.google.com/.

[39]See: https://www.transparency.org/news/pressrelease/transparency_internationals_Curacao_study_highlights_weaknesses_in_the_publ.

Websites

https://antilliaansdagblad.com/nieuws-menu/19809-solidaridat-sindikal-roept-bonden-op
https://antilliaansdagblad.com/nieuws-menu/20862-minister-alcala-walle-dient-ontslag-in-bij-gouverneur
https://decentrale.regelgeving.overheid.nl/cvdr/xhtmloutput/Historie/Nederlandse/Antillen/36310/363101.html
https://en.wikipedia.org/wiki/Dissolution_of_the_Netherlands_Antilles
https://en.wikipedia.org/wiki/Constitution_of_Cura%C3%A7ao
http://gemhofvanjustitie.org/
https://gobiernu.cw/wp-content/uploads/2019/07/P.B_2013__no._3.pdf
https://svbcur.org/wetten/aov/
https://svbcur.org/wetten/aww/
https://svbcur.org/wetten/avbz/
https://svbcur.org/wetten/zv/
https://svbcur.org/wetten/ov/
https://svbcur.org/wetten/cessantia/
https://svbcur.org/wp-content/uploads/Voorlichting-aanvullende-voorzieningen-ambt-BVZ.pdf
https://www.ad.nl/politiek/veroordeling-oud-premier-Curacao-gerrit-schotte-definitief~a915ce16/?referrer=https://www.google.com/
https://web.archive.org/web/20190526101936/http://www.dutchcaribbeanlegalportal.com/news/latest-news/9138-om-seponeert-zaak-tegen-steven-martina
www.cbs.cw/website/press-releases-2018_3499/item/results-labour-force-survey-2018_2584.html
www.cia.gov/library/publications/the-world-factbook/geos/cc.html
www.medischcontact.nl/nieuws/laatste-nieuws/artikel/chirurgen-op-Curcao-vervalsten-dossiers.htm
www.nostisia.com/Curacao/23-lokal/7766-the-elephant-in-the-room-corruption-in-Curcao-economic-growth-good-governance-corruption-remuneration.html
www.royal-house.nl/topics/legislation/charter-for-the-kingdom-of-the-netherlands
www.transparency.org/news/pressrelease/transparency_internationals_Curacao_study_highlights_weaknesses_in_the_publ
www.uwv.nl/particulieren/overige-onderwerpen/internationaal/overzicht-verdragslanden/detail/met-welke-landen-heeft-nederland-een-verdrag
www.uwv.nl/particulieren/overige-onderwerpen/internationaal/handhavingsverdrag-naar-welke-landen-kan-uitkering-mee/detail/overzicht-landen-waar-u-uw-uitkering-mee-naartoe-kunt-nemen

References

Country Profiles (2020) International Social Security Association. https://www.issa.int/en_GB/country-profiles. Accessed 12 Feb 2020

Oostindie G, Klinkers I (2001) Knellende koninkrijksbanden: het Nederlandse dekolonisatiebeleid in de Caraïben, 1940–2000. Amsterdam University Press, Amsterdam

World Factbook (2020) Central Intelligence Agency. https://www.cia.gov/the-world-factbook/countries/curaçao. Accessed 12 Feb 2020

Chapter 6
Cyprus

6.1 Context

Cyprus, an island in the Mediterranean Sea, was a British colony until 1960, when an independent, bi-communal Republic of Cyprus was established.[1]

In 1974, Turkey occupied more than one third of the island. In 1983 the Turkish-administered area proclaimed itself to be the 'Turkish Republic of Northern Cyprus', which was only internationally recognised by Turkey. The Republic of Cyprus still claims sovereignty over the whole island, but has no control over the territory of Northern Cyprus. In reality, although not constitutionally, this meant the end of the bi-communal character of the Republic of Cyprus.

The Republic of Cyprus joined the European Union in 2004. The application of EU law is suspended in Northern Cyprus; however, individual Turkish Cypriots who are able to document their eligibility for citizenship of the Republic of Cyprus legally enjoy the same rights as EU citizens.

In principle we shall hereafter only deal with the Republic of Cyprus as it functions today.

The Republic of Cyprus is a presidential republic. The president is also head of the Government and appoints the ministers. Parliament consist of the House of Representatives (*Vouli Antiprosopon*). The constitutionally guaranteed representation of the Turkish minority in both government and parliament cannot be realised since the Turkish Cypriots went out.

Apart from the general comparative sources, Country Profiles (2020) and World Factbook (2020), we consulted for Cyprus especially: Amitsis (2020); See also: www.mlsi.gov.cy and www.mof.fov.cy.

---

[1]The United Kingdom retained two Sovereign Base Areas on Cyprus: the base of Akrotiri and the base of Dhekelia.

D. Pieters, *Social Security Law in Small Jurisdictions*, The World of Small States 8,
https://doi.org/10.1007/978-3-030-78247-4_6

The most important political parties are the liberal conservative DISY, the communist AKEL and the smaller centrist DIKO. DISY provides the current president; the current parliamentary majority consists of DISY and a smaller party.

The Greek Orthodox Church plays a powerful role in (Greek-)Cypriot society.

As a former British colony, Cyprus maintains a special relationship with the United Kingdom. Cyprus is member of the Commonwealth. The Republic of Cyprus, being member of the European Union, must comply with EU law.

Traditionally, Greece exercised an important influence upon Cyprus and there was even a movement in favour of unification of Cyprus with Greece. This culminated in the failed coup to overthrow the elected president of Cyprus, which was supported by the Greek military junta in 1974. This coup triggered the Turkish occupation of the northern part of the island.

6.2 Legal Framework of Rights to Social Security

6.2.1 Constitutional Context

The Constitution dates back to 1960 and has already been amended 14 times.[2] In the second part of the Constitution entitled 'Fundamental Rights and Freedoms' we find article 9, "The right to social security and decent living". The article states that "Everyone shall have the right to decent living and social security. Issues related to the protection of labourers, the assistance coverage of poor persons and the development of the social insurance system shall be regulated by law." Here, the term social security is explained as the basic objective of social protection, promoted through the application of two different techniques: social insurance for the working population and social assistance for needy persons or groups ('assistance to the poor').[3]

The Republic of Cyprus inherited a common law tradition from its previous colonial power and can today be characterised by its mixed or hybrid legal system as the law of Cyprus was also influenced by Greek law. Since independence in 1960, the legal system has been based on the Constitution, the (English) pre-independence laws, the post-independence laws enacted by the House of Representatives, and the principles of common law and equity. Since the accession to the European Union, the supremacy of EU law has been constitutionally recognised.

---

[2]In principle, the constitutional provisions establishing a presidential regime (with a Greek-Cypriot president and a Turkish-Cypriot vice-president), as well as all those provisions ensuring the bi-communal character of the state and the separation of powers are not open for revision. The constitution is to be amended by at least 2/3 of the representatives of each community. However, on the basis of the law of necessity, constitutional amendments were adopted by the Greek Cypriot representatives only, as the Turkish-Cypriots withdrew from Parliament (and Government).

[3]Amitsis (2015), p. 55.

6.2.2 *Social Security Legislation and Structure*

Social security in Cyprus is regulated by:

- The Social Insurance Law N° 59/2010 (as amended) and associated regulations dealing with the social insurance schemes. The following benefits are distinguished: old-age pension, old-age settlement, disability pension, orphan's pension, spouse's pension, spouse's settlement, unemployment benefits, missing person's allowance,[4] funeral grant, cash sickness benefit, cash maternity benefit, cash paternity benefit, cash maternity grant, and benefits related to work injury;
- The Social Pension Law N° 25(I)/1995-2005 (as amended) establishing a non-contributory pension for residents of 65 and over who are not entitled to another pension or similar payment from any source;
- The Child Benefit Law N°167(I)/2002 (as amended) that provides means-tested child benefits and means-tested single parent benefits; and
- The General Minimum Income and Other Social Benefits Law N°109/2014 introducing a means-tested benefit to any person whose income and other financial resources are insufficient to satisfy his/her basic and specific needs, as defined by law. Next to the cash benefit services may also be provided according to this law.

We leave the special (pension) schemes for civil servants and other public sector employees aside here.[5]

In 2001, the General Heath Care Scheme Law N° 89/2001[6] established (the principle of) a contributory health insurance system covering the entire population, providing a free choice of doctors and providers from the services of both the public and private sector. Provision and funding of health care would be separated and the health care services would be purchased by the Health Insurance Organisation (HIO) that manages the system. However, this General Health Care Scheme has not yet been fully implemented due to financial and other constraints.

Medical services are currently provided in kind by government hospitals, clinics and health centres. About 15% of the population does however not have access to public health care that is either offered free of charge or provided at a reduced cost and therefore has to rely on the private health sector. In fact, due to inefficiencies and long waiting lists, a majority of the population is forced to use the private health care services and bear the total expense.[7] The current public health care services are governed by the Government Medical Institutions and Services Laws of 1978–2013.

[4]This benefit introduced after the Turkish invasion of 1974, covers the wives and children of men declared missing after the invasion.

[5]See Retirement Benefits of State Employees and of Employees of the Broader Public Sector Law No. 113/2011 and Law N°216/2012.

[6]Information on the General Health System can be found on https://www.gesy.org.cy/launchpad.html.

[7]Amitsis (2015), pp. 103–104.

The first Social Insurance System in Cyprus was established in 1957 by the adoption of the Law N° 31/1956 under the strong influence of the UK Administration. Accordingly, both contributions and benefits were 'flat-rate', irrespective of the insured person's earnings. In 1964, substantial changes were made to the 1957 scheme, in terms of both its personal and material scope. Compulsory insurance was thus extended to every person gainfully occupied in Cyprus, including the self-employed, while the material scope was expanded to include maternity allowance and benefits for industrial accidents and occupational diseases. This process led to the establishment of a hybrid social insurance system that was radically reformed between 1973 and 1980. After the major crisis due to the Turkish occupation of the Northern part of the island, the so-called missing persons' allowance was introduced in 1980. In the same year, a major structural change occurred as the current repartition based earnings-related social insurance scheme was introduced. Since the beginning of the 2010s, the Government has adopted a new set of successive fiscal packages, such as the introduction of a contribution by civil servants to their government pension and the abolishment of the special pension scheme for new entrants into the public service, and targeting criteria for social benefits.[8] The Agreement reached with the Troika in 2013 forced the Government to take even more restrictive measures.[9]

6.2.3 *Enforcement of Constitutional and Statutory Rights*

Any decision of a social security body is subject to appeal to the Administrative Court that was established in 2015.[10] The Supreme Court is competent to hear appeals against the decisions of the Administrative Court.

The Cypriot Supreme Court acts as both a constitutional court and an appellate court. Moreover, the President of the Republic may submit all texts voted by parliament to the Supreme Court as Constitutional Court before signing them: if the text is found to be unconstitutional, the text may not be signed and will thus not become law.

Jurisprudence is a significant source of social security law. Let us observe in passing that, unlike other areas of law, the administrative law of Cyprus is largely based upon and reproduces the principles to be found in the jurisprudence of the Greek Council of State and therefore in other continental European jurisdictions.[11]

[8]Amitsis (2015), p. 36.

[9]See further under 'additional relevant information'.

[10]Previously The Supreme Court was competent in first instance to deal with appeals against administrative decisions, including those concerning social security.

[11]Annaliza Kyprianou in: https://www.kourtelaw.com/uc/wp-content/uploads/2015/08/Cyprus-Establishment-of-new-Administrative-Court.pdf.

6.3 Population and the Personal Scope of the Social Security Schemes

6.3.1 General Data on the Population and Its Composition

By mid-2020, the population of the Republic of Cyprus was estimated at about 1,270,000 persons, of which 855,000 live in the territory controlled by the Republic of Cyprus. The Cypriot citizens living in that territory are nearly all ethnic Greek people (Greek Cypriots), who speak Greek and in their vast majority belong to the Greek Orthodox Church. About one fifth of the population of that territory consists of foreign citizens (some 13% from other EU countries, mainly Greeks, British, Romanian and Bulgarians; and some 7% from outside the EU, mainly from the Philippines). The population is concentrated in the capital Nicosia and the major cities Paphos, Limassol and Larnaca.

The net migration rate in 2020 amounts to 7.6 per thousand persons. There is an important influx of asylum seekers from the Middle East.

The active population, estimated at about 427,000 persons in 2017, works for more than 80% in the services sector; unemployment amounted to 11% in 2017.

6.3.2 Personal Scope of the Social Insurance and Social Assistance Schemes

The Social Insurance System[12] compulsorily covers every person gainfully occupied in Cyprus, either as an employed person or as a self-employed person. Persons working abroad in the service of Cypriot employers and persons who interrupt their compulsory insurance are allowed to be insured voluntarily under certain conditions. The insured persons are classified into three categories: employed persons, self-employed persons and voluntary contributors. Employed persons qualify for all benefits of the Social Insurance System. Self-employed persons are excluded from unemployment benefits. Self-employed persons as well as voluntary contributors working abroad for Cypriot employers are excluded from the benefits relating to occupational accidents and professional diseases. Other voluntary contributors are only entitled to the survivor and old-age benefits.

The number of persons socially insured under the Social Insurance System amounted to 414,000 in 2018, of which 82.5% are employees of the private and semi-public sector, 6.6% are self-employed, 10.8% are employees of the public sector, and 0.1% are voluntarily insured. Cypriots constitute 66.5% of the total number of the socially insured (of which only 0.3% are Turkish-Cypriots); other

[12]Also called General Social Insurance Scheme or GSIS; we prefer to speak of the Social Insurance System, as 'scheme' suggests an arrangement dealing with a single social risk.

EU citizens[13] account for 21.1% and other aliens for 12.4%. The number of pensioners of the social insurance system amounts to 140,000.[14]

The Social pension covers persons aged 65 and older who are habitual residents of Cyprus and have been so for at least 20 years after the age of 40 or 35 years after the age of 18. At the end of 2019, there were 16,356 beneficiaries of a social pension.[15]

The Child benefits and single parent benefits cover all habitual residents of Cyprus. Habitual residents are persons who have the centre of their interests in Cyprus and intend to stay in Cyprus in the near future.

According to Law N° 89/2001, those eligible to be insured by the General Health Care Scheme are: all Cypriots and citizens of the European Union who permanently reside in Cyprus, as well as their dependants. Also qualifying are all persons contributing to the scheme and permanently residing in Cyprus or lawfully working in Cyprus and their dependants. As we have mentioned earlier, the General Health Care Scheme is not fully operational yet and important parts of the population are still formally or *de facto* excluded from free public health care services. According to the still applied Government Medical Institutions and Services Laws of 1978–2013, no health care is granted (in the public health care institutions) unless the patients have contributed to the Social Insurance System for at least three years and has submitted personal income tax declaration at the time he/she applies for health care benefits. Health care services of the public system are free for a range of categories of people, including active and retired civil servants, social assistance beneficiaries and people with a yearly income below the set threshold.

The General Minimum Income only benefits persons who are citizens of the European Union or have long-term resident status in Cyprus as well as political refugees. They must be lawful and habitual residents and they must have been so in the five preceding years, except for the refugees. They must satisfy income and property tests and belong to one of the following categories: persons over 28 years old; married persons; single parents; orphans or disabled persons; or adults who were in the care of the director of social welfare services before reaching the age of 18. Monks in a monastery, students, and intentionally unemployed persons disqualify in principle.

Information on social security is available in the official languages, Greek and Turkish, and mostly also in English. Legislation and other legal documents dating from before independence may only exist in English.

---

[13]Including citizens of the UK and possibly also citizens of the European Economic Area.

[14]See:http://www.mlsi.gov.cy/mlsi/sid/sidv2.nsf/All/CE878DFA37B78D70C22585270033FE68?OpenDocument, pp. 1–3.

[15]See: http://www.mlsi.gov.cy/mlsi/sid/sidv2.nsf/All/CE878DFA37B78D70C22585270033FE68?OpenDocument, p. 5.

6.4 Administration of Social Security

The Ministry of Labour, Welfare and Social Insurance oversees social security. The Ministry includes the departments of:

- Social Insurance Services, which oversees the social insurance schemes, the social pensions law, and advice on social security policy in general; and
- The Social Welfare Services, which oversees the child benefits, the single parent's allowance, and the general minimum income scheme.

The Head Office of the Social Insurance Services is responsible for the application of social policy, decision making and payment of benefits as well as coordinating the district offices, which are mainly responsible for receiving claims, collecting contributions and for inspections. There are district offices in Nicosia, Limassol, Larnaka, Paphos and Ammochostos.

The Social Welfare Services personnel consist of 257 Social Welfare Services Officers and 149 Residential Officers who occupy posts at all levels of the Services hierarchy. The Secretarial personnel consists of 8 Secretarial Officers and 41 Assistant Secretarial Officers. Social Welfare Officers are placed at the Central Office of the Social Welfare Services, the five Social Welfare Services District Offices in Nicosia, Limassol, Larnaca, Pafos and Ammochostos (seat in Paralimni), and the nine local offices in Nicosia, Limassol and Larnaca. The Social Welfare Services also staff a series of welfare institutions across the country.

The Ministry of Health is responsible for the organisation of the health care system and the provision of state-financed health care services. By Law N° 73/2017, the State Health Services Organisation (OKYY) was established to take over the management, control, supervision and development of the public hospitals and primary health care centres from the Ministry of Health. A semi-governmental, public organisation, the Health Insurance Organsiation (HIO) was established by Law N° 89/2001 to manage the funding of the General Health Scheme to be implemented. HIO would contract with the health care providers who will deliver their services in the General Health Scheme.

The Cyprus Academy of Public Administration[16] aims to contribute to the efficiency, effectiveness and continuous improvement of the Public Service for the benefit of the individual citizens and society at large, mainly through the formulation and implementation of a comprehensive learning policy for the Public Service, at individual, group, and organisational levels.

The investment policy of the social insurance system has been the subject of important debates. A reform bill regulating investment policy was already promised in 2009. Also in the subsequent years, there was a call for a more diversified investment portfolio and for allowing more investment in non-government assets. The competence for setting up the investment policy of the social insurance system lies with the Ministry of Finance.

[16]See: www.mof.gov.cy/mof/capa/cyacademy.nsf/index_en/index_en?OpenDocument.

A recent ILO report comments:

In order to enhance the financial governance of the GSIS and thus the security of GSIS members' benefits and inter-generational equity, it is recommended to revise the current investment policy of the GSIS.

A diversification of the investment portfolio of the GSIS into non-government securities should be contemplated in order to increase the rates of return through these diversified investments. In addition, investing, in the near future, part of GSIS reserves in non-government assets would help in the containment of longer term future increases in government debt towards the GSIS and provide more flexibility to the GSIS in periods of significant economic difficulties. The GSIS could then draw on these funds, if necessary, from any of the GSIS borrowers and not necessarily from the Government, which might itself face cash flow problems at the same time.[17]

6.5 Coordination

Cyprus, being a member state of the European Union, has its social security system coordinated with those of the other EU states, Iceland, Liechtenstein, Norway, Switzerland and (until now) the United Kingdom[18] according to the EU Regulations 883/04 and 987/09.

Bilateral social security coordination treaties have been concluded with the following other states: Egypt, Canada and Quebec, Australia, Serbia, and Syria.[19]

The EU coordination mechanism provides:

- the principle of non-discrimination on the basis of nationality;
- rules concerning the determination of the applicable legislation;
- the exportability of acquired social security benefits;
- the aggregation and apportionment of periods of residence, work or insurance; and
- administrative co-operation agreements.

The EU mechanism is applicable to all persons insured under the social security of a member state and to all social insurance schemes.

The bilateral coordination agreements with states which are not members of the EU coordination mechanism have a similar content, except that they mostly only apply to nationals of the two concerned countries and that they do not apply to unemployment benefit schemes nor to child benefits, sickness, and maternity benefits. Sometimes benefits for victims of occupational accidents or professional

[17]International Labour Office, Public Finance, Actuarial and Statistics Services Branch (SOC/PFACTS), Social Protection Department, *Cyprus: report to the Government: actuarial valuation of the General Social Insurance Scheme as of 31*, December 2014, Geneva: ILO, 2017, p. xi.

[18]There is still also a bilateral treaty with the United Kingdom dating back to 1957.

[19]See the official Website of the Republic of Cyprus, Social Insurance Services, Bilateral Agreements: http://www.mlsi.gov.cy/mlsi/sid/sidv2.nsf/page92_en/page92_en?OpenDocument.

diseases are also excluded in these bilateral agreements. The agreement with Serbia however does not include all these exceptions.

There is a sponsorship scheme in place to sponsor patients going abroad for receiving health care, after having obtained an authorisation by the Special Medical Board of the Ministry of Health. The sponsored patients are subject to means testing and must contribute to the expenses of the treatment abroad according to their level of income. In 2012, it was said:

> Despite the improvements in health infrastructure more than 2000 patients every year seek treatment in specialized centres and hospitals abroad [. . .]. More than half of these patients choose the United Kingdom, followed by Israel and Greece. [. . .]. Apart from the severity of illness, current legislation stipulates that financial criteria must be taken into account to determine eligibility to be sent for treatment abroad.[20]

Amitsis reports that the Ministry currently terminated the practice of sending patient abroad for treatment; instead the EU law on cross border heath care will be applied.[21] This would mean that health care provided in Israel, and possibly in the future also health care provided in the United Kingdom, will not be covered anymore.

6.6 Additional Relevant Information

A major shock for all sectors of life and government was the separation of Northern Cyprus in 1974 and the flows of internal displaced persons that resulted from it: Greek Cypriots fled from the Turkish occupied area, whereas Turkish Cypriots fled the Greek Cypriot controlled territory of the Republic. The total number of internally displaced persons was estimated at 228,000 in 2018, many of them already since 1974.

The events of 1974 and the subsequent de facto separation of the Turkish and Greek parts of Cyprus also impacted social security. Restrictive measures to safeguard the social insurance system against the risk of bankruptcy included the reduction of pension rates and the suspension of the rights to unemployment and certain other benefits. A new benefit was introduced, the so-called missing persons' allowance, for the families of persons missing as a result of the Turkish invasion.

Cyprus' economy is mainly based on the services sector, which accounts for more than four fifths of GDP; tourism, finance, shipping and real estate have traditionally been the most important services. Cyprus has belonged to the Eurozone since 2008. In 2009, Cyprus was hit by the global financial crisis and the resulting low demand in the tourism and construction sectors. In 2013, the Cypriot Government reached an agreement with the Troika (European Commission, European Central Bank and IMF) on a 10 billion euro bailout, which was conditional upon passing financial and

[20]Theodorou et al. (2012), pp. 1–128, here p. 33.

[21]Amitsis (2015), p. 104.

structural reforms, which also affected social security. Pension amounts were frozen for the period 2013–2016 and an automatic adjustment of the statutory retirement age every 5 years, in line with changes in life expectancy, was introduced while early retirement was being penalised. The minimum contributory period was gradually extended from 10 to 15 years in the period 2013–2017.

Websites

www.gesy.org.cy/launchpad.html

www.kourtelaw.com/uc/wp-content/uploads/2015/08/Cyprus-Establishment-of-new-Administrative-Court.pdf.

www.mlsi.gov.cy/mlsi/sid/sidv2.nsf/All/CE878DFA37B78D70C22585270033FE68?OpenDocument

www.mlsi.gov.cy/mlsi/sid/sidv2.nsf/page92_en/page92_en?OpenDocument

References

Amitsis G (2015) Cyprus social security. Wolters Kluwer Law

Amitsis G (2020) Cyprus. In: The international Encyclopedia of social security law. Wolters/Kluwer

Country Profiles (2020) International Social Security Association. https://www.issa.int/en_GB/country-profiles. Accessed 12 Feb 2020

International Labour Office, Public Finance, Actuarial and Statistics Services Branch (SOC/PFACTS), Social Protection Department (2014) Cyprus: report to the Government: actuarial valuation of the General Social Insurance Scheme as of 31. ILO, Geneva

Theodorou M, Charalambous C, Petrou C, Cylus J (2012) Cyprus: health system review. Health Syst Transit 14(6)

World Factbook (2020) Central Intelligence Agency. https://www.cia.gov/the-world-factbook/countries/cyprus. Accessed 12 Feb 2020

Chapter 7
Faroe Islands

7.1 Context

The Faroe Islands are an archipelago situated in the Northern Atlantic Ocean, halfway between Norway and Iceland, about 300 kms north of Scotland. They are a self-governing nation with a high degree of autonomy within the Kingdom of Denmark. The political link with Denmark goes back to the fourteenth century.

The autonomy of the Faroe Islands was established by the Home Rule Act of 1948,[1] after a majority of Faroese people had voted for establishing the Faroes as an independent state in 1946.[2] The Home Rule Act was amended and supplemented by the 2005 law on transfer of competence to the Faroese authorities. The Faroese can unilaterally decide that all areas of competence can be transferred to the Faroese authorities, except the Danish State's constitution, citizenship, Supreme Court and foreign, security and defence policy as well as the currency.

The periodically elected legislative assembly of the Faroe Islands, the *Løgting*,[3] is one of the oldest parliaments in the world. The executive government, *Føroya Landsstýri*, is headed by the Prime Minister (the *løgmaður*). Additionally, two Faroese representatives are elected to the Danish Parliament in Copenhagen.

Of the 33 seats of *Løgting* four parties have more than 2 seats: the conservative People's Party *Fólkaflokkurin* (8), the Social Democratic Party *Javnaðarflokkurin*

With special thanks to Ms. Eline Mortensen of the Mission of the Faroe Islands in Brussels and the Ministry of Social Affairs; thanks also to Mr. Jan Sjóstein of Almannaverkið for reviewing the report on the Faroe Islands.

[1]Home Rule Act of the Faroe Islands (No. 137 of March 23rd, 1948). Accessed on: https://www.government.fo/en/foreign-relations/constitutional-status/the-home-rule-act/.

[2]See: https://www.government.fo/en/foreign-relations/the-political-and-legal-status-of-the-faroe-islands/.

[3]See: https://www.logting.fo/files/File/2016/Faldari%202016/Faldari%20Logtingi%20hefti%20UK.pdf.

D. Pieters, *Social Security Law in Small Jurisdictions*, The World of Small States 8,
https://doi.org/10.1007/978-3-030-78247-4_7

(7), the centre-right-wing unionist Union Party *Sambandsflokkurin* (7) and the pro-independence left-wing Republic party Tjóðveldi (6). The current Government is composed of a coalition of the People's Party, the Union Party and a smaller centre party.

The Faroe Islands have the exclusive right to independently legislate and govern in a wide range of areas, including taxation and social security. According to an agreement between the Faroe Islands and Denmark, translated in the Foreign Policy Act 2005, the Faroe Islands can negotiate and conclude agreements under international law on behalf of the Kingdom of Denmark, where such agreements relate solely to matters that have been fully transferred to the Faroese Authorities. This includes labour market issues and social security.

On the official website of the Faroese Government, we read:

> The collaborative effort of trade unions and employers' associations has shaped the Faroese labour market, making it both fair and efficient.
>
> There are more than 50 trade unions in the country. The trade union movement dates back to the turn of the twentieth century and has played a large role in ensuring fair wages, good working conditions and ample employment benefits for the Faroese workforce. Employers' associations exist to promote legislation and industrial policies that are conducive to a prosperous business climate. They work together to accomplish this through an umbrella organisation based in the 'House of Industry'.[4]

The Faroe Islands obviously have very strong ties with Denmark, which is still in control of defence, police and judicial policies. However, for many decades there has been a strong political movement striving for sovereignty and full independence. The Faroese in favour of independence and those in favour of maintaining the union with Denmark more or less balance each other out.

Economic aid from Denmark accounts for 3.5% of the total GDP. The Faroe Islands are in a monetary union with Denmark.

The Faroe Islands are an active member of the Nordic Council and are present in a number of other international organisations.[5]

In 1973, the Faroe Islands did not follow Denmark in joining the European Communities. As a consequence, the European Union Treaty confirms that the Faroe Islands are not part of the Union. A Protocol to the Treaty of Accession of Denmark stipulates that Danish nationals residing in the Faroe Islands are not considered Danish nationals within the meaning of the EU Treaty. Formal relations between the EU and the Faroe Islands are currently based on three separate bilateral agreements dealing with fisheries, trade in goods and scientific and technological cooperation.

---

[4]See: https://www.faroeislands.fo/people-society/work-live/.

[5]See: https://www.government.fo/en/foreign-relations/the-faroe-islands-in-the-international-community/.

7.2 Legal Framework of Rights to Social Security

7.2.1 Constitutional Context

From the perspective of Denmark, the constitutional setting of the Faroe Islands is determined by the Danish Constitution, as well as the Danish statutes granting home rule to the Faroe Islands of 23 March 1948 and of 24 June 2005.[6] According to these laws, the Faroe institutions may legislate and administer in all matters except the Constitution, nationality, the Supreme Court (*Højesteret*) and foreign, security and defence policy, as well as the monetary policy.

The Faroese *Styrisskipanarlóg* (law on the government) of 26 July 26 1994[7] acts as a constitution for the Faroe Islands, regulating the legislative, executive, and (partially) the judicial powers and containing some other provisions on the functioning of the administration. It does not contain references to social security. Attempts by the Faroese to draft their own constitution have until now not gained unified support among the political parties and are at a standstill, as the Danish government requires the Danish constitution to be supreme and not equal to a potential Faroese constitution in terms of hierarchy of laws.

By Law no. 315 of 1995, concerning social benefits on the Faroe Islands, as amended by Law no. 130 of 2001, the Faroese parliament took over competence from Denmark in the following areas: people's pensions (i.e. the universal state pensions) and early pensions, special provisions for persons with a handicap, child allowance for single parents, and benefits in case of sickness, pregnancy or birth.[8]

7.2.2 Social Security Legislation and Structure

Social security is now completely regulated by Faroese laws.[9] The Faroese social security system includes state pensions, supplemental pensions, and compulsory savings in a pension scheme.

The universal state pension scheme includes a flat-rate old age pension for people reaching the age of 67, and a state disability pension for total or partial loss of capacity to work. The supplemental pension is compulsory for all workers. The

[6]Law nr. 578 of 24th of June 2005, concerning the take-over of matters and areas by the Faroes. Accessed on: http://stm.dk/_p_5618.html.

[7]See: https://logting.elektron.fo/logkjak/logir/Styrisklog/styrlog.htm.

[8]Lov no. 315 af 17. maj 1995 om sociale ydelser på Færøerne, sum broytt við løgtingslóg nr. 130 frá 8. oktober 2001. Accessed on: https://logir.fo/Lov/315-fra-17-05-1995-om-sociale-ydelser-pa-Faeroerne-sum-broytt-vid-logtingslog-nr-130.

[9]For a good summary see: Útlendingastovan, *New to the Faroe Islands. Practical Information from public agencies*, Føroyaprent, Torshavn, 2016. Accessed on: http://d1d6zxt0xmx99c.cloudfront.net/media/1861/national-handbook-online-version.pdf; See also: https://www.norden.org/en/info-norden/old-age-pension-faroe-islands.

pension insurance is taken out with the Labour Market Supplemental Pension Fund (*Samhaldsfasti*).

In case of temporary incapacity to work, workers may qualify for an earnings-related sickness benefit from *Almannaverkið* (when the employer has no obligation to continue payment of salary). For the self-employed, this insurance is optional. Benefits that compensate for the loss of income of the career in case of pregnancy, birth or adoption are paid by the Parental Leave Fund. For employed persons the insurance is compulsory, for self-employed persons this insurance is optional. Persons who do not qualify for a benefit of the Parental Leave Fund may apply for a parental allowance from *Almannaverkið*.

Sailors and fishermen are governed by special social insurance arrangements, granting them, amongst other benefits, a sickness benefit even if they become sick whilst being ashore or an unemployment benefit if the ship has to go into reparation.

Employees are insured for work-related injuries. The employment service ALS provides unemployment benefits and labour mediation to wage earners and, optionally, to self-employed.

Child allowance takes the form of a deduction from the tax returns of the parents of children under the age of 18. The deduction is given per child and is independent of the income of the parents.[10]

The National Health Insurance covers general and specialist medical treatment and subsidises a proportion of medication, dental treatment and other specialist treatments. The National Health Insurance oversees travel expenses related to treatment and expenses related to burial.[11]

There is also temporary public assistance that can be applied for at *Almannaverkið*.

7.2.3 Enforcement of Constitutional and Statutory Rights

Faroese law belongs to the civil law group, as it has strong ties with Danish law. The Faroese court system is part of the Danish judiciary system, with the Supreme Court, Højesteret, at the top. The court of the Faroe Islands (Tórshavn) hears the same cases as the district courts in other regions of Denmark. Appeal goes to the High Court of Eastern Denmark. According to Danish tradition, there is no separate administrative court.

[10]See: https://www.norden.org/en/info-norden/child-benefit-faroe-islands.

[11]See: http://www.heilsutrygd.fo.

7.3 Population and the Personal Scope of the Social Security Schemes

7.3.1 General Data on the Population and Its Composition

In 2020, the population of the Faroe Islands was estimated at about 53,000 and the labour force at 27,300. The unemployment rate was less than 1% at the beginning of that year.

The Faroese population is spread across 17 of the 18 islands of the archipelago. The island of Streymoy, with the capital Torshavn, hosts more than 40% of the population, the second island, less than half that number and seven of the inhabited islands have fewer than one hundred inhabitants. Most people live on the small coastal lowlands. Nearly the entire Faroese population is native, of Scandinavian and Gaelic descent. Persons of Danish origin accounted for about 7% of the population and other backgrounds accounted for about 3% in 2018.

As the Faroe Islands faced a deep economic crisis in the '90s of the last century, many Faroese (youth) emigrated. Today, however, there is a net immigration, amongst other factors, due to the immigration of Asian women (in 2011, there were 2155 more men than women between the age of 0 to 59). In 2020, immigration and emigration kept in balance (net migration rate equal to 0). In 2017, the Faroese population passed 50,000 for the first time. The growth is primarily caused by the economic prosperity in the Faroe Islands, which has contributed to more expats returning to the Faroe Islands, fewer young people emigrating (or staying abroad after studies), and the growing number of children being born.[12]

Faroese is the mother tongue of nearly all Faroese and is also the official language. In 2011, a little less than 90% of the population said to be Christian (with large predominance of the Evangelical Lutheran church).

The Faroese society is founded on the Scandinavian welfare model. The standard of living in the Faroe Islands is comparable to the other Nordic countries. Citizens and residents are entitled to a range of publicly financed services such as social security, healthcare and education.[13] In 2015, it was estimated that about one tenth of the population lived below the poverty line.

7.3.2 Personal Scope of the Social Insurance and Social Assistance Schemes

The general requirements for obtaining pension rights in the Faroe Islands are either Danish citizenship or marriage to a person with Danish citizenship, living in the

[12]See: https://www.faroeislands.fo/people-society/people-of-the-faroe-islands/population/.

[13]See: https://www.faroeislands.fo/people-society/society/.

Faroe Islands or having worked on a ship registered in the Faroe Islands, and having lived in the Danish Kingdom (i.e. the Faroe Islands, Greenland or Denmark) for at least 3 years between the ages of 15 and 67.

By agreement with the Nordic countries, the Danish citizenship expands to include Scandinavian citizenships, and furthermore, the right to receive earned pension rights in EEA-countries is based on this agreement.[14]

To benefit from a supplemental pension, the worker must have lived in the Faroe Islands at least 3 years between the age of 15 and the state pension age. Unlike the state pension, the supplemental pension is also paid out to people who have left the Faroe Islands.

People employed in the Faroe Islands may qualify for an earnings-related sickness benefit from *Almannaverkið*; for the self-employed, this insurance is optional. Workers who live and are liable to pay full taxes in the Faroes, and who have had an income from work in the previous year, qualify for the benefits of the Parental Leave Fund. For self-employed persons, this insurance is optional. All workers contribute to the employment service ALS, which provides unemployment benefits and labour mediation. To qualify for the benefits, one must live in the Faroe Islands or be resident there. The self-employed may join on a voluntary basis.

Child allowance is paid for all children below the age of 18 living in the Faroe Islands.

The National Health Insurance covers all residents in the Faroe Islands who have a Faroese ID number.[15]

7.4 Administration of Social Security

The Department of Social Services, *Almannaverkið*,[16] administers a range of social welfare schemes. As a cornerstone of the Faroese welfare community, *Almannaverkið* is staffed by around 1000 people, of whom 140 are social workers, occupational therapists and administrative personnel, and 860 provide services for people with special needs (nurses, physiotherapists, health visitors etc.). *Almannaverkið* provides, amongst other services, old-age pensions to approximately 8.600 individuals, disability pensions for 2050 persons, services for people with special needs to approximately 640 people, and sickness benefits to approximately 3045 individuals.[17]

---

[14]Útlendingastovan, *New to the Faroe Islands. Practical Information from public agencies*, Føroyaprent, Torshavn, 2016, p. 35. Accessed on: http://d1d6zxt0xmx99c.cloudfront.net/media/1861/national-handbook-online-version.pdf.

[15]See: https://www.heilsutrygd.fo.

[16]See: www.av.fo.

[17]Útlendingastovan, *New to the Faroe Islands. Practical Information from public agencies*, Føroyaprent, Torshavn, 2016, p. 26. Accessed on: http://d1d6zxt0xmx99c.cloudfront.net/media/

The Faroese Labour Market Supplemental Pension Fund (*Samhaldsfasti*),[18] the Parental Fund (*Barsilsskipanin*),[19] and the Unemployment Fund (*Arbeiðsloysisskipanin*)[20] manage the corresponding social insurance schemes. They are managed by a Board in which the trade unions and employers' organisations are represented.

The *Føroya Vanlukkutryggingarráð* is the part of the Faroese judiciary that assesses insurance claims regarding work-related accidents and work-related illnesses and disabilities.

The Faroese National Health Insurance, *Heilsutrygd*,[21] oversees the implementation of public health insurance legislation. The agency administers allowances and benefits covering the cost of most primary health services available on the islands.[22]

TAKS[23] is the Faroese Tax Administration, a public agency under the Ministry of Finance. The staff numbers around 120 and TAKS has departments in five locations. TAKS administers laws regarding taxes, customs and other levies. TAKS also manages the Parental Leave Fund.[24] In addition to taxes, it also collects the contributions for the Faroese Labour Market Supplemental Pension Fund, the Parental Fund, the Unemployment fund and the National Health Insurance.

7.5 Coordination

The Faroe Islands have joined[25] the revised Convention on Social Security between the Nordic countries (2012, into force 2014), which replaced the previous Nordic Convention on Social Assistance and Social Service, which itself replaced the previously existing bilateral treaties between the concerned Nordic states. The Nordic Convention facilitates mobility between Finland, the Åland Islands, Sweden, Norway, Denmark, Faroe Islands, Greenland and Iceland and ensures that people travelling between the countries have a right to social security benefits. The convention simplifies work between social security administrations of the Nordic countries. The agreement supplements (and in principle does not alter) the social

1861/national-handbook-online-version.pdf; See also: https://www.fmr.fo/fo/logir-og-reglur/figgjarlog/figgjarlog-2004-2020/.

[18]See: http://www.samhaldsfasti.fo/.

[19]See: http://www.barsil.fo.

[20]See: http://www.als.fo.

[21]See: http://www.heilsutrygd.fo.

[22]See: http://www.heilsutrygd.fo.

[23]See: http://www.taks.fo.

[24]Útlendingastovan, *New to the Faroe Islands. Practical Information from public agencies*, Føroyaprent, Torshavn, 2016, p. 90. Accessed on: http://d1d6zxt0xmx99c.cloudfront.net/media/1861/national-handbook-online-version.pdf.

[25]See: Bekendtgørelse no. 15 af 23. august 2019 om udvidelse til Færøerne og Grønland af nordisk konvention af 12. juni 2012 om social sikring med tilhørende administrativ aftal.

security coordination mechanism agreed between the countries of the European Economic Area. The agreement expands the application of the EU's social security regulations to include the Faroe Islands and Greenland, as well as citizens of non-union countries who reside in the Nordic countries. It may furthermore extend the social security rights to the benefit of the migrant workers according the EU mechanism. The EU coordination mechanism provides:

- the principle of non-discrimination on the basis of nationality;
- rules concerning the determination of the applicable legislation;
- the exportability of acquired social security benefits;
- the aggregation and apportionment of periods of residence, work or insurance; and
- administrative co-operation agreements.

The EU mechanism applies to all persons insured under the social security of a member state and to all social insurance schemes.

The Faroe Islands have concluded no bilateral coordination agreements. Danish bilateral agreements exclude their application upon the Faroe Islands' social security since the law of 24 June 2005.[26] It is unclear whether earlier Danish bilateral treaties apply to Faroe social security schemes, as they do not mention any exclusion of the Faroe Islands but neither sum up Faroese schemes in their scope of application.[27]

The law on the Faroese Hospital Service states that superintendents in the Faroese health service have the possibility to send patients abroad when there is a need for a treatment that is not offered in the Faroe Islands. The majority of Faroese patients who go abroad are sent to *Rigshospitalet* in Copenhagen. In this regard, a new agreement is made between the Faroese hospital service and *Rigshospitalet* every year, which allows Faroese patients to be treated in the facilities at *Rigshospitalet.*[28]

A considerable proportion of the Faroese workforce has been employed abroad. In 2014, their wages accounted for about 7% of GNP, a record in a European context. This group has typically been employed as skilled workforce, e.g. carpenters or electricians in Norway, as sailors in the Danish merchant fleet or on foreign fishing vessels.[29]

---

[26]So e.g. the bilateral treaty with Australia: Bekendtgørelse no. 6 af 22. februar 2001 om overenskomst af 1. juli 1999 med Australien om social sikring med tilhørende administrativ aftale.

Law nr. 578 of 24th of June 2005, concerning the take-over of matters and areas by the Faroes, http://stm.dk/_p_5618.html.

[27]Take for instance the bilateral agreement with New-Zealand, of 6 May 1997 or the Agreement with Québec of 23 November 1987.

[28]See: https://www.hmr.fo/en/what-we-do/health-and-prevention/hospitals/special-treatment-abroad/.

[29]Útlendingastovan, *New to the Faroe Islands. Practical Information from public agencies*, Føroyaprent, Torshavn, 2016, p. 26. Accessed on: http://d1d6zxt0xmx99c.cloudfront.net/media/1861/national-handbook-online-version.pdf.

7.6 Additional Relevant Information

The economy of the Faroe Islands was and still is largely based on fishing and fish farming. These sectors account for nearly all exports and half of the GDP. The collapse of the Faroese fishing industry in the early 1990s brought the Faroe Islands into economic problems, leading to unemployment rates of 10 to 15% by the mid-1990s. Since 2000, efforts have been made to diversify the economy. Favourable prices and growing stock quotas on fisheries as well as the rise of the salmon farming industry and growing tourism have diversified the economy somewhat. The economy has been recovering and unemployment dropped at the beginning 2020 below 1%.

Websites

https://logting.elektron.fo/logkjak/logir/Styrisklog/styrlog.htm
www.av.fo
www.barsil.fo
www.faroeislands.fo/people-society/people-of-the-faroe-islands/population/
www.faroeislands.fo/people-society/society/
www.faroeislands.fo/people-society/work-live/
www.fmr.fo/fo/logir-og-reglur/figgjarlog/figgjarlog-2004-2020/
www.government.fo/en/foreign-relations/the-faroe-islands-in-the-international-community/
www.government.fo/en/foreign-relations/the-political-and-legal-status-of-the-faroe-islands/
www.heilsutrygd.fo
www.hmr.fo/en/what-we-do/health-and-prevention/hospitals/special-treatment-abroad/
www.logting.fo/files/File/2016/Faldari%202016/Faldari%20Logtingi%20hefti%20UK.pdf
www.norden.org/en/info-norden/child-benefit-faroe-islands
www.norden.org/en/info-norden/old-age-pension-faroe-islands
www.samhaldsfasti.fo/
www.taks.fo

References

Country Profiles (2020) International Social Security Association. https://www.issa.int/en_GB/country-profiles. Accessed 12 Feb 2020

Útlendingastovan (2016) New to the Faroe Islands. Practical Information from public agencies. Føroyaprent, Torshavn. Accessed http://d1d6zxt0xmx99c.cloudfront.net/media/1861/national-handbook-online-version.pdf

World Factbook (2020) Central Intelligence Agency. https://www.cia.gov/the-world-factbook/countries/faroeislands. Accessed 12 Feb 2020

Chapter 8
Fiji

8.1 Context

The Republic of Fiji groups over 330 islands and over 500 islets, scattered over about 190,000 km^2 in the South Pacific Ocean, of which less than 10% is land. About 100 islands are inhabited and two major islands, Viti Levu (with the capital city Suva) and Vanua Levu, account for about three-quarters of the land area and a little less than 90% of the population.

Fiji, a former British colony, gained independence in 1970. It became a republic in 1987. Periods of democratic rule were interrupted several times by coups d'état. Political turmoil due to the often tense relations between the two major ethnic communities, disturbed the orderly functioning of democratic institutions. The current prime minister, after successfully leading the most recent military coup in December 2006, was elected in 2014 and re-elected in 2018 in parliamentary elections deemed fair and free. The current constitution dates to 2013.

Fiji has a parliamentary republican form of Government, according to the Westminster model. The president, elected by Parliament, has a mainly representative function. Head of Government is the prime minister. The cabinet is responsible to Parliament.

The unicameral Parliament is elected according to proportional representation in a nationwide constituency. Of its 51 seats, Fiji-First obtained 27 seats and the Social Democratic Liberal Party (SODELPA) 21 seats in the last elections (2018). Fiji-First is a centre-left party, SODELPA a Christian, conservative center party. Whereas political parties claim to be multiracial, the Indo-Fijian community mainly supports

Apart from the general comparative sources, Country Profiles (2020) and World Factbook (2020), we consulted the following source for Fiji: https://www.ssa.gov/policy/docs/progdesc/ssptw/2016-2017/asia/fiji.html.

D. Pieters, *Social Security Law in Small Jurisdictions*, The World of Small States 8,
https://doi.org/10.1007/978-3-030-78247-4_8

FijiFirst, whereas SODELPA has been characterised as an ethno-nationalist party of the iTaukei.[1]

The level of political tension between the major ethnic groups varies among the different islands.

The ethnic divide between the iTaukei and the Indo-Fijians is also a land tenure divide: most sugar cane farmers are Indo-Fijians, whereas over 80% of the land is held by iTaukei under the collective ownership of the traditional iTaukei clans. The former lease the land from the latter.

Protestants of various denominations represent 45% of the population, Roman Catholics 9%, and other Christian faiths 10%. Hinduism is the religion of 28% of the population and Islam of 6% (2007 estimates). It may be observed that the Methodist (protestant) Church comprises over two-thirds of the iTaukei, Fiji being the country with the highest percentage of Methodists in the world.

The concept of family, kinship (clans) and community are of great importance to the iTaukei. Kinship is determined through a child's lineage to a particular spiritual leader. Descent is patrilineal and all titles and statuses are derived from the father's side. The traditional chiefs, who, for instance, previously elected the president, have lost much power with the democratic institutions under the current Constitution.

Fiji is member of the Commonwealth of Nations and as such maintains important ties with the United Kingdom, Australia and New Zealand. Fiji is a leading member of the Pacific community and hosts many international organisations' regional offices.

8.2 Legal Framework of Rights to Social Security

8.2.1 Constitutional Context

The Constitution of Fiji declares in its first article that the Republic is founded, amongst others, on the value of 'equality for all and care for the less fortunate'. The Constitution furthermore recognises the right to reasonable access to transportation (sect. 34), to housing and sanitation (sect. 35), to adequate food and water (sect. 36) and to a clean and healthy environment (sect. 40). Section 41 declares that every child has the right to basic nutrition, clothing, shelter, sanitation and health care. Most important to us are the sections 37 and 38 on the right to social security schemes and the right to health, respectively. These state as follows:

Section 37:

(1) The State must take reasonable measures within its available resources to achieve the progressive realisation of the right of every person to social security schemes, whether private or public, for their support in times of need, including

[1]iTaukei are the ethnic group native to Fiji. The iTaukei are predominantly of Melanesian extraction, with some Polynesian influence.

the right to such support from public resources if they are unable to support themselves and their dependents.

(2) In applying any right under this section, if the State claims that it does not have the resources to implement the right, it is the responsibility of the State to show that the resources are not available.

Section 38:

(1) The State must take reasonable measures within its available resources to achieve the progressive realisation of the right of every person to health, and to the conditions and facilities necessary to good health, and to health care services, including reproductive health care.
(2) A person must not be denied emergency medical treatment.
(3) In applying any right under this section, if the State claims that it does not have the resources to implement the right, it is the responsibility of the State to show that the resources are not available.

Fiji has a common law system based on the English model. It has a written constitution and courts can test the constitutionality of Acts of Parliament and other acts of Government.

8.2.2 Social Security Legislation and Structure

Social security is regulated in the following Acts:

- The Fiji National Provident Fund Act N°19 of 1966, as amended and provided of further regulations;[2] and
- The Public Health Act 1935 N°29 of 1935, and the Public Hospitals and Dispensarics Act N° 13 of 1955, both as amended.[3] Hereafter, we shall not discuss the older special pension schemes for civil servants, the military and the police, which still cover some of these groups.[4]

The social welfare (assistance) schemes are not founded on a statutory basis.

The Fiji National Provident Fund[5] is a defined contribution fund that provides superannuation services to its members. It is entirely financed by its members and their employers. There are two types of individual accounts for each member: a Preserved Account primarily meant for retirement (although first-time homebuyers may withdraw a portion of the balance prior to retirement) and a General Account,

---

[2]The Fiji National Provident Fund Act, cap. 219 Laws of Fiji.

[3]The Public Health Act, cap. 111 and the Public Hospitals and Dispensaries Act, cap. 110 Laws of Fiji.

[4]Cfr. the Pensions (1979) Act, the Pensions and Retirement Allowances Act 2010.

[5]https://myfnpf.com.fj;Seealso: http://www.parliament.gov.fj/wp-content/uploads/2019/11/Fiji-National-Provident-Fund-2019-Annual-Report.pdf.

which may be accessed prior to retirement to cover the costs of education, medical care, unemployment, housing or other approved expenses. The amount of the preserved account balance may be taken at reaching the retirement age in the form of a lump sum, a single-life or joint-life annuity or a term annuity (for terms of 5, 10 or 15 years) or a combination of those options. The total account balance may be taken at any age if the member is emigrating permanently. The total account balance may also be taken at any age when permanent disability occurs (to be withdrawn in same manner as retirement benefit). The total account balance is paid at the death of the member as a survivor benefit, again to be withdrawn in the various forms possible for the retirement benefit. Upon the death of the member, an additional amount is credited to the deceased's balance, the so-called 'special death benefit', part of which can be used for the deceased's funeral expenses.

In the event of a natural disaster, such as cyclone Winston in 2016, members are also allowed to withdraw a certain amount from their accounts.[6]

Due to the many possibilities of early withdrawals from the accounts and the widely used options for receiving a lump sum payment at retirement, monthly payments by the Fund provide income security for only a minority of older persons.[7]

Free health care, including preventive, generalist and specialist services as well as hospitalisation is provided by the public health system. There are three specialised or national referral hospitals and three divisional hospitals. Furthermore, there are sub-divisional hospitals, health centres and nursing stations across the country. These services are complemented by specialised clinical services from abroad that visit according to a set programme. If the required diagnostics or treatment cannot be delivered in Fiji, referral to foreign health care institutions is possible (see later).[8]

Social welfare or assistance[9] benefits are provided by the Ministry of Women, Children and Poverty alleviation, under the following schemes:

- The Poverty Benefit Scheme (PBS), providing a flat rate assistance benefit for a maximum duration of 3 years to needy households. The need is assessed according to a proxy means test, which looks at the properties, land ownership and household items owned by the applicants. The PBS replaced a former scheme, the family assistance programme, after it was evaluated by the World Bank as not reaching even one-tenth of the poor. The PBS is provided for up to four persons per household;
- The flat rate means-tested Care & Protection Allowance, paid to the benefit of children below 18, to needy single mothers, abandoned spouses, widows, prisoners' dependents, and foster parents or guardians without any source of income.

[6]Naidu et al. (2016), p. 22.

[7]Naidu et al. (2016), pp. 22–24.

[8]See: http://www.health.gov.fj/wp-content/uploads/2014/09/Fiji-Specialised-Clinical-Services-Visiting-Team-Manual-20131.pdf.

[9]Annual report of the Ministry of Women, Children & Poverty Alleviation, 2016–2017, pp. 26–28. Accessed on: http://www.mwcpa.gov.fj/images/stories/Files/2018/MOWCPA_AR2016-2017_final%20approved_web.pdf.

The conditions that the child must attend school and that the benefit may not be paid more than 5 years would not be enforced;[10]

- The Social Pension Scheme, paid to persons aged 66 and older who do not have any income nor benefit from any other social assistance scheme, pension or provident fund benefit. As such, the social pension scheme is primarily aimed at people having worked in the informal sector;
- The Food Voucher Program, which is available to recipients of PBS and Care & Protection Allowance; and
- The non-means-tested Food Voucher Programme for Rural Pregnant Mothers, which creates an incentive for these (future) mothers to register early in their health facilities to avoid complications during later stages of pregnancy or during child birth. Civil servants are not eligible nor recipients of other social assistance benefits.

It may be observed that traditionally the informal social protection systems, such as those provided by family kinship networks and through faith-based organisations, have been important. However, at the beginning of the twenty-first century, these seemed less robust than they once were and seemed increasingly unable to meet existing needs.[11]

8.2.3 Enforcement of Constitutional and Statutory Rights

If one is not satisfied with a decision of the Fiji National Provident Fund, the decision can be re-examined by the Fund's Complaints Management Officer or the Contribution, Compliance and Collections team. If, after re-examination, one is still not satisfied, the decision will be reviewed by the Review of Decisions Committee of the Fund, consisting of staff members who were not involved in the initial decision making. If the complaint was declared ineligible by the Fund's Review of Decisions Committee or one is not satisfied with the latter's decision, the case can be submitted to the Chief Manager of the Financial Systems Development & Compliance group, of the Reserve Bank of Fiji.

There is a Grievance and Complaints Mechanism for the social welfare benefit within the Ministry of Women, Children and Poverty Alleviation. Complaints about the functioning of the public health system are also dealt with internally by the Ministry of Health. Persons aggrieved by the decisions of the Overseas Medical Treatment Committee may appeal to the Permanent Secretary for Health.[12]

[10]Child-sensitive social protection in Fiji. Assessment of the Care and Protection Allowance, UNICEF, Pacific & Fiji Ministry of Women, Children and Poverty Alleviation, 2015. Accessed on: https://www.unicef.org/Child-Sensitive_Social_Protection_in_Fiji.pdf, p. 8.

[11]Naidu et al. (2016), p. 15.

[12]See: http://www.health.gov.fj/wp-content/uploads/2014/09/Fiji-Specialised-Clinical-Services-Visiting-Team-Manual-20131.pdf, section 3.

It is not clear whether the aforementioned administrative complaint decisions can also be challenged before the Courts of Fiji. At the top of the judiciary hierarchy in Fiji we find the Supreme Court; under it the Court of Appeal. Below the latter, the High Court has both original competence and hears appeals against decisions of subordinate courts, such as the Magistrate's Courts. The Supreme Court, Court of Appeal and High Court are competent to review violations of individual rights provided by the Constitution. The decisions of the Supreme Court are final.

8.3 Population and the Personal Scope of the Social Protection Schemes

8.3.1 General Data on the Population and Its Composition

The population of about 936,000 persons (2020) mainly consists of indigenous Fijians, called iTaukei, and descendants of the indentured labourers imported from British India under colonial rule, the Indo-Fijian.[13] The iTaukei represent about 57% of the population, the Indo-Fijian 37% (2007 estimates).

The labour force was estimated at about 353,000 in 2017; unemployment at 4.5% in the same year. Most people work in agriculture or in the services sector. Many people are employed in civil service, although the role of the private sector has developed since independence. In 2002, the military employed about 6% of the total labour force, with more than a quarter of the military deployed on missions abroad.[14]

Although Fiji is considered as an upper middle-income country, the population living below the poverty line was estimated at 28% in 2017.[15]

Fiji has a negative net migration rate of minus 6.2 per thousand (2020). Many of Fiji's skilled workers emigrated to Australia, New Zealand and the United States.[16] In the '90s, many Indo-Fijians left the country as they felt discriminated against by the indigenous Fijians in power. This led to economic difficulties, but also caused the indigenous Fijians to become the majority in the Republic.

[13]The notion 'Fijian' covers according to section 5 of the Constitution all citizens of Fiji. This was contested as the iTaukei considered themselves as indigenous people, the only ones entitled to be called 'Fijians'.

[14]Narayan (2011), section 4.6.

[15]See: https://fijivillage.com/news/22826-families-being-assisted-under-Poverty-Benefit-Scheme-r529ks/.

[16]Narayan (2011), section 6.

8.3.2 Personal Scope of the Social Insurance and Social Assistance Schemes

The following persons between 15 and 55 years of age are compulsorily registered as members of the Fiji National Provident Fund:[17]

(a) Persons employed in Fiji under a contract of service or apprenticeship or learnership, whether written or oral, or whether expressed or implied;
(b) Persons in Fiji under a contract for the performance of manual labour entered into either as an individual person or as one of a group of persons;
(c) Fijian citizens employed as meant sub (a) and (b) outside Fiji by an employer with a place of business in Fiji;
(d) Fijian citizens employed under a contract of service entered into in Fiji as member of the crew of a vessel or an aircraft, the owners of which have a place of business in Fiji;
(e) Designated employees of the Government; and
(f) Members of co-operative societies employed by the society of which they are a member.

On application of an employee and his/her employer, employees who are not Fijian citizens may be exempted if the employee is employed by an employer whose principal registered office is outside Fiji, under an employment contract entered into outside Fiji, while the employee is entitled under a scheme established outside Fiji to benefits on retirement that are adequate in the circumstances. Also exempted are:

- non-citizen Government employees recruited by the UK, Australian or New Zealand Government under staffing assistance schemes enjoying adequate provision of a kind similar to that of the Fiji National Provident Fund Act; as well as
- non-citizen expatriates applying for exemption within 3 months of employment in Fiji, on condition that they are part of a scheme established outside Fiji that provides adequate benefits on retirement.

According to the Fiji National Provident Fund (Exemptions) Order, a person is exempted from all the provisions of the Fiji National Provident Fund Act if the employee or employer applies for exemption within 3 months after commencement of the employment and the Board is satisfied that the employee is a contributing member of a scheme that provides benefits at retirement and that the applying employee or employer would suffer hardship if the Act applied to the employee.

Fijian citizens from the age of 6 who have not reached the age of 55 may voluntarily become member if they are not eligible for the compulsory scheme. The following may become voluntary members in this way: students, self-employed persons, unemployed persons or persons working in the informal sector. Fijian

[17]See: https://myfnpf.com.fj/.

workers who are excluded from compulsory membership, such as domestic servants working for a private employer in a domestic house, may also become members on a voluntary basis. Voluntary members constitute only 1% of total membership of the Fund.[18]

Employees whose employer's principal place of business is outside Fiji, as well as military and police personnel, are excluded from membership of the Fiji National Provident Fund. Additionally, persons who were civil servants before November 1971 and have opted to remain under the Civil Service Pension Scheme are excluded as well. The Fiji National Provident Fund had 442,000 members in 2019.[19]

The public health care and the social assistance schemes are open to all citizens of Fiji.

8.4 Administration of Social Security

The Fiji National Provident Fund[20] is governed by the Fiji National Provident Board, the members of which are appointed by the Minister of Finance. The Board consists of two civil servants, two representatives of the employers and two representatives of the employees. The Board is the Trustee of the Fund, managing its money, subject to general directions of the Minister of Finance.

The Fiji National Provident Fund is a major investor in Fiji and one of the country's largest property owners.

The Division of Public Health and Hospital Services of the Ministry of Health and Medical Services oversees the provision of public health care. The Deputy Secretary of Public Health coordinates primary and preventive care services through a network of local health facilities and hospitals. The Deputy Secretary of Hospital Services coordinates secondary and tertiary care through a network of national hospitals.

The Social Welfare Division of the Ministry of Women, Children & Poverty Alleviation[21] is in charge of the several social assistance programmes. There are 15 social welfare offices across the country where people can apply for assistance benefits.

8.5 Coordination

No bilateral or multilateral social security agreement with Fiji could be identified.

[18]Naidu et al. (2016), p. 19.

[19]See: http://www.parliament.gov.fj/wp-content/uploads/2019/11/Fiji-National-Provident-Fund-2019-Annual-Report.pdf, p. 2.

[20]See: https://www.myfnpf.com.fj/.

[21]See: http://www.mwcpa.gov.fj.

The Fiji National Pension Fund Act explicitly provides in section 44 that the Fund may make payments to a member in any country in which the member is resident.

Section 65 of the same Act deals with reciprocal agreements, stating:

(1) The Minister, after consulting the Board, may enter into a reciprocal agreement with the government of any other country or territory in which a fund similar to the Fund has been established and such agreement may provide, amongst other matters that:

   (a) any period of work for an employer in that country or territory shall be treated as a period of work in Fiji for that employer for the purpose of the definition of "employee" [. . .]; and
   (b) subject to such conditions as may be laid down in the reciprocal agreement, any amount standing to the credit of any member of the Fund who works for any employer in that country or territory may be transferred to his credit in such fund, and any amount standing to the credit in such fund of any person who becomes a member of the Fund may be transferred to his credit in the Fund, [. . .].

(2) Any reciprocal agreement made under the provisions of subsection (1) shall be published in the Gazette and shall come into force on the date of such publication or on such later date as may be provided in the agreement.

But as was mentioned, no such agreements could be found.

An arrangement is established within the Ministry of Health an Overseas Medical Treatment[22] that provides funds for patients where the diagnostic and/or treatment intervention is not available in Fiji, nor can be delivered by a visiting team or specialist, and where there is a good prognosis for the patient having a healthy life for at least 3 to 5 years after treatment.

The funds can cover the cost of return airfares and/or treatment and/or accommodation. The airfares of a parent accompanying a child under the age of 15 or of an accompanying doctor where appropriate, may also be covered by the Fund. Funding should, as far as possible, be on a shared costs basis with the patients. The shared funding arrangement is determined on the basis of financial status of the patient and his/her family. No funds will be provided to persons covered by a health insurance company or who have access to personal funds or a funding agency.

Decisions are taken by the Overseas Medical Treatment Committee (OMTC) chaired by the Director of Curative Health Services. Upon approval, the overseas service provider in countries such as Australia, New Zealand and India is contacted for a cost estimation and appointment date for acceptance of the patient.

[22] See: http://www.health.gov.fj/wp-content/uploads/2014/09/Fiji-Specialised-Clinical-Services-Visiting-Team-Manual-20131.pdf, section 3.

8.6 Additional Relevant Information

Fiji is currently one of the most developed and connected of the Pacific islands' economies. Tourism, the sugar industry, fishery and the export of bottled water are the most important economic sectors. Remittances from Fijians working abroad are an important source of foreign exchange.

Tourism, fishery and the sugar industry are all sensitive to natural disasters, such as cyclones, floods, hurricanes and earthquakes. The tropical Cyclone Winston in 2016, for instance, destroyed thousands of homes as well as sugar crops and a sugar mill. In general, cyclones occur about 10 to 12 times per decade.

Fiji is well aware of the dangers climate change may pose to its islands and their population.

The unstable political situation that continued from independence until the first years of the twenty-first century deterred foreign investment. Social crises followed the several military coups with an increase in unemployment and poverty as a consequence.[23]

It may be significant that a page on the website of the Fiji National Provident Fund is especially dedicated to becoming a whistleblower.[24] We read there that

> with Accountability and Integrity being part of our corporate values, the Fund has in place a Whistle Blower Policy. [...]
>
> These concerns include (but are not limited to):
>
> 1. Fraud, theft or misappropriation
> 2. Use of inside information by an employee for private gain
> 3. Giving or receiving of bribe, gifts, benefits or anything of value which would impair objectivity in the performance of an employee's responsibilities
> 4. Inappropriate disclosure of FNPF's confidential information (including intellectual property)
> 5. Engaging in activities that compromise or are potentially in conflict with the interests of the Fund
> 6. Breach of FNPF policies
> 7. Any illegal act
>
> The proxy means test operated by the department of Social Welfare for the allocation of PBS and other social assistance benefits may raise some concern about the way it is operated.

Websites

https://fijivillage.com/news/22826-families-being-assisted-under-Poverty-Benefit-Scheme-r529ks/
https://myfnpf.com.fj
https://myfnpf.com.fj/index.php/about-fnpf/become-a-whistleblower

---

[23]Naidu et al. (2016), sections 5 and 6.4.

[24]See: https://myfnpf.com.fj/index.php/about-fnpf/become-a-whistleblower.

www.health.gov.fj/wp-content/uploads/2014/09/Fiji-Specialised-Clinical-Services-Visiting-Team-Manual-20131.pdf
www.mwcpa.gov.fj
www.parliament.gov.fj/wp-content/uploads/2019/11/Fiji-National-Provident-Fund-2019-Annual-Report.pdf
www.ssa.gov/policy/docs/progdesc/ssptw/2016-2017/asia/fiji.html

References

Country Profiles (2020) International Social Security Association. https://www.issa.int/en_GB/country-profiles. Accessed 12 Feb 2020

Ministry of Women, Children & Poverty Alleviation (2016–2017) Annual report of the Ministry of Women, Children & Poverty Alleviation, 2016-2017. Accessed on: http://www.mwcpa.gov.fj/images/stories/Files/2018/MOWCPA_AR2016-2017_final%20approved_web.pdf

Naidu V, Plange NK, Achary P (2016) Income security for older persons in Fiji. ESCAP/SSD, Bangkok. (DD-SPPS Project Working Paper Series. Income Security for Older persons in Asia and the Pacific)

Narayan PK (2011) Draft paper prepared for the joint Commonwealth Secretariat/UNRISD project on social policies in small states. UNRISD, Geneva

UNICEF, Pacific & Fiji Ministry of Women, Children and Poverty Alleviation (2015) Child-sensitive social protection in Fiji. Assessment of the Care and Protection Allowance. Accessed on: https://www.unicef.org/Child-Sensitive_Social_Protection_in_Fiji.pdf

World Factbook (2020) Central Intelligence Agency. https://www.cia.gov/the-world-factbook/countries/fuji. Accessed 12 Feb 2020

Chapter 9
Gibraltar

9.1 Context

Gibraltar[1] is a territory of 6.5 km^2 south of Spain, bordering the Strait of Gibraltar, which links the Mediterranean Sea and the North Atlantic Ocean.

In the Treaty of Utrecht of 1713, Spain ceded Gibraltar to Great Britain. In 1830, Gibraltar became a colony of the United Kingdom. Both in 1969 and 2002, the population of Gibraltar voted for maintaining British sovereignty, rejecting joint sovereignty with Spain. In 1969 Gibraltar was granted autonomy and in 2007 the current non-colonial constitution was adopted. Gibraltar has the status of a British Overseas Territory; its citizens are British citizens, but Gibraltar is not part of the United Kingdom. Gibraltar is self-governing, but the United Kingdom remains responsible for its external relations (defence and foreign affairs).

The British monarch is the head of state and is represented by a Governor. Gibraltar has the Westminster type of parliamentary democracy. There is a unicameral Parliament,[2] consisting of 17 directly elected members in a single Gibraltar-wide constituency, and a speaker of Parliament appointed by the 17 elected members. An alliance of the Liberal Party of Gibraltar and the Gibraltar Socialist Labour Party obtained 10 seats in Parliament, whereas the centre-right Gibraltar Social Democrats obtained 6 seats.

The Chief Minister, head of the Executive, is in principle the leader of the majority party (or coalition). A particularity of Gibraltar is that the Chief Minister

[1] For data and figures, see: Country Profiles (2020) and World Factbook (2020).

[2] See H.K. Budhrani, The Gibraltar Parliament, in: N.D.J. Baldwin, *Legislatures of Small States: A comparative study*, Library of Legislative Studies, Routledge, pp. 102–106. Accessed on: https://books.google.nl/books?id=VNd8hxn3Vh0C&pg=PA105&lpg=PA105&dq=gibraltar+parliamentary+workings&source=bl&ots=8BJlFnxaHD&sig=ACfU3U0Uep2PwreC9WUj-soNJvXYFj_V q w & h l =e l & s a =X & ved=2ahUKEwjktJnf1uXoAhXNKewKHaDKAw8Q6AEwAnoECAkQLg#v=onepage&q=gibraltar%20parliamentary%20workings&f=false.

D. Pieters, *Social Security Law in Small Jurisdictions*, The World of Small States 8,
https://doi.org/10.1007/978-3-030-78247-4_9

and the other cabinet members must be chosen from amongst the elected members of Parliament, and that therefore no or few members of Parliament belong to the majority who are not a Minister.

All political forces are against a change in the self-government status under British sovereignty; in the Brexit-referendum, all were in favour of remaining in the European Union. Upon consultation, the population of Gibraltar followed these positions of the political parties with majorities of over 90%.

Roman Catholics constitute a little less than three quarters of the population, the Church of England represents about 8%. Other faiths represent less than 4% (2012).

The constitutional status of Gibraltar means that it has very strong ties with the United Kingdom. Relations with its big neighbor Spain are difficult, as the country continues to oppose self-government under British sovereignty, advocating shared sovereignty if not a return of Gibraltar to Spain. The preamble to the Gibraltar Constitution Order contains the commitment that the UK Government will never transfer sovereignty over Gibraltar against the freely and democratically expressed wishes of the people of Gibraltar.

The relations with Spain were eased by the United Kingdom and Spain both being members of the European Union. Although Gibraltar is not part of the United Kingdom, it was part of the European Union as a British Overseas Territory. It did however not participate in the EU customs union or the EU agricultural policy, nor did it participate in the Schengen Area.

The United Kingdom left the European Union on 31 January 2020 and thus Gibraltar is no longer part of it either, although the Brexit referendum saw more than 95% of the participating Gibraltarians voting against leaving the European Union. It remains to be seen how the interests of Gibraltar will be taken into account in the follow-up Brexit negotiations between the United Kingdom and the European Union. Spain, also as a member state of the European Union, takes a special interest in the matter. Since the foreign affairs of Gibraltar are handled by the United Kingdom, Gibraltar has no direct say in the negotiations.

9.2 Legal Framework of Rights to Social Security

9.2.1 Constitutional Context

There is no constitutional provision regarding (a right to) social security or the like.

Common law and rules of equity apply to Gibraltar. However, the Gibraltarian Parliament has complete legislative powers except for foreign affairs and defence. Gibraltar can override English law with its own statutes. Most Gibraltarian enactments are modelled on UK equivalents.[3]

[3]Ch. Gomez & others, https://www.lawequitygibraltar.com/gibraltars-legal-system.

9.2.2 Social Security Legislation and Structure

Social security in Gibraltar is completely regulated by Acts of the Gibraltarian Parliament and Regulations of the Gibraltarian Government. The most important acts are:

- The Social Security (Employment Injuries Insurance) Act;[4]
- The Social Security (Insurance) Act;[5]
- The Social Security (Non-Contributory Benefits and Unemployment Insurance) Act;[6]
- The Medical (Group Practice Scheme) Act;[7]
- The Medical (Gibraltar Health Authority) Act;[8]
- The Social Security (Closed Long-Term Benefits and Scheme) Act;[9] and
- The Social Security (Open Long-Term Benefits Scheme) Act 1997;[10]

all as amended later and provided of regulations.
There are three contributory schemes of Social Insurance:

- The Employment Injuries Insurance Scheme provides cash benefits to those who are unable to work or are disabled due to an accident at work or certain industrial diseases and for widows and widowers and certain other dependents of industrial casualties. It also provides free medical treatment for the victims of the employment injury or occupational disease;
- The Social Security Short-Term Benefits Scheme provides maternity grants, maternity allowances, death grants and unemployment benefits; and
- The Social Security Open Long-Term Benefits Scheme provides cash benefits for widowhood, old-age pensions and benefits for guardians of orphans.

All these benefits are provided in return of contributions, which are earnings related, subject to a pre-determined minimum and maximum rate. The benefits are flat rate.[11]

Health care is delivered by the Gibraltar Health Authority using a healthcare model closely linked to the UK National Health Service. However, the coverage of

---

[4]The Social Security (Employment Injuries Insurance) Act, Act N°1952-10.

[5]The Social Security (Insurance) Act, Act N° 1955-14.

[6]The Social Security (Non-Contributory Benefits and Unemployment Insurance) Act, Act N° 1955-15. It may be observed that no non-contributory benefits are still in place in Gibraltar's social security system.

[7]The Medical (Group Practice Scheme) Act, Act N° 1973-14.

[8]The Medical (Gibraltar Health Authority) Act, Act N°1987-34.

[9]The Social Security (Closed Long-Term Benefits and Scheme) Act, Act N° 1996-06. This Act will not be discussed here as it exclusively deals with periods of insurance before 1994.

[10]The Social Security (open long-term benefits scheme) Act 1997; Act N° 1997-16.

[11]For a summary description, see: HM Government of Gibraltar, Department of Social Security. *Guide to Social Security Benefits*, 2018.

the health care costs is based on a contributory system, called the Group Practice Medical Scheme (GPMS). It provides the registered persons (and dependants) access to (in principle) free health care.

There is social assistance, including a minimum guaranteed income scheme, but it functions on a rather narrow legislative basis. In a regulation on the social assistance fund, we read that it is the purpose of the Social Assistance Fund "to provide assistance to meet identified social needs of individuals" according to criteria determined by the Government, by means of direct payments or interest-free loans or contributions to charitable institutions and the like.[12]

9.2.3 *Enforcement of Constitutional and Statutory Rights*

The judicial system of Gibraltar[13] echoes the English judicial system.

Appeals against decisions of the Director of Social Security concerning employment injuries insurance, short term benefit insurance schemes, and long-term benefits schemes, will be decided by the Employment Injuries Appeals Board, the Social Insurance Appeals Board and the Closed Long-Term Benefits Appeals Board respectively. Each of these consists of a chairperson and a representative of the insured persons and a person representing the employers. Appeals against the decisions of the Medical Board established by the Social Security (Employment injuries Insurance) Act lie with the Medical Appeals Tribunal.

There is a Supreme Court of Gibraltar, which has both an original and appellate jurisdiction. It hears appeals from the magistrates' courts and tribunals, such as the Employment Injuries Appeals Board, the Social Insurance Appeals Board, the Closed Long-Term Benefits Appeals Board and the Medical Appeals Tribunal. The Supreme Court only hears cases when it concerns a question of law or a question of mixed fact and law.

There is a Court of Appeal for Gibraltar that hears appeals from the Supreme Court. It is a non-resident court that holds two sessions a year in Gibraltar. The Justices of Appeal are mainly drawn from active or retired English Court of Appeal judges.

Appeals beyond the Court of Appeal are heard by the Judicial Committee of the Privy Council in London.

[12]Public Finance (control and audit) Act, Social Assistance Fund (amendment) regulations. 1992, amending the Social Assistance Fund Regulations 1988, section 3 (legal notice n° 33 of 1992).

[13]English Law (Application) Act; See also: Gibraltar Courts Service, Overview of the Justice System. Accessed on: http://www.gcs.gov.gi/index.php/justice-system/overview.

9.3 Population and the Personal Scope of the Social Protection Schemes

9.3.1 General Data on the Population and Its Composition

The population of Gibraltar is estimated at about 29,600 people in 2020. About four fifths of them are native Gibraltarians, whereas the British make up about 13% according to 2012 estimates. Gibraltar shows a negative net migration rate of minus 3.3 per thousand (2020).

The labour force is estimated at 24,500 (2014) and the unemployment rate at 1% (2016). These figures must be taken with the knowledge that about 2000 British and 9000 Spanish workers cross the border with Spain every day in order to work in Gibraltar.

9.3.2 Personal Scope of the Social Insurance and Social Assistance Schemes

Employment Injuries Insurance is mandatory for employed persons, i.e. persons occupied in employment under a contract of service, whether written or oral and whether expressed or implied, or in employment with the Government. Apprentices and learners under agreement are also included. Some categories are however excluded, such as employment in the service of one's own partner or employment for a relative with whom the employed person cohabits. Under certain conditions, mariners on board of a ship registered in Gibraltar or contracted in Gibraltar are also included.

The short term-insurance and long-term insurance schemes are mandatory for all persons below the pensionable age who are either self-employed or in insurable employment under the Social Security (Employment Injuries Insurance) Act. A self-employed person is defined as a person who is occupied in gainful employment in Gibraltar and who is not an employed person, or a person exercising functions in Gibraltar as an ordained minister of religion or as a member of a religious order who is not an employed person. The following will be disregarded as employment or self-employment:

- casual employment;
- employment or self-employment of less than 15 h a week; and
- employment as a student during a period of vacation.

A person who ceases to be a self-employed or employed person may elect to pay contributions on a voluntary basis. Members of the Gibraltar Regiment may under special conditions also qualify as insured person.

Unemployment insurance covers all persons insured under the Social Security (Insurance) Act, who are not self-employed.

In principle,[14] in order to qualify for the above-mentioned short-term benefits, the beneficiary is required to be in Gibraltar or the Campo district.[15]

A person will however not be disqualified from a maternity grant or maternity allowance because the birth occurred outside Gibraltar or the Campo district, nor due to absence from Gibraltar or the Campo district. A person is not disqualified from receiving a death grant when the death occurs outside Gibraltar or the Campo district nor due to absence from Gibraltar or the Campo district.

Persons insured under the Social Security (Employment Injuries Insurance) Act or under the Social Security (Insurance) Act should be registered under the Medical Group Practice Scheme. Persons who are ordinarily resident in Gibraltar can also register. The dependants of the registered persons will be covered as well.[16]

Social assistance has benefited over 450 persons per month in 2018.[17]

9.4 Administration of Social Security

The Department of Social Security is responsible for the administration of the three contributive social insurances and social assistance. It functions under the political responsibility of the Chief Minister. The Minister of Health, Care and Justice is politically responsible for healthcare. The medical and health services have been transferred from the Government to the Gibraltar Health Authority. The Income Tax Office is in charge of collecting social security contributions.

An appropriate Fund has been established for each of the three social insurance schemes—employment injury insurance, short-term benefits, and long-term benefits.[18] At the head of these Funds is a director appointed by the Government.

All decisions and claims are settled by the Director. The Director is assisted by the Employment Insurance Advisory Committee and the Social Insurance Advisory Committee, respectively. Both consist of a chairperson and two members appointed after consultation with the representative employers' organisations, two members appointed after consultation with the representative workers organisations, one representative of the Director and one independent member.

Decisions of a medical nature with relation to the Employment Injury Insurance are determined by the Medical Board established for that purpose.

The Gibraltar Health Authority (GHA) consists of the Minister of Health, the Chief Secretary of Government, the medical Director of the Authority, five medical practitioners, one representative of the Gibraltar Trades Council, three other

[14] Social Security (Insurance) Act, section 23 of the Social Security (insurance) Act.

[15] The Campo (de Gibraltar) district is the district of Spain next to Gibraltar.

[16] See: https://www.gha.gi/healthcare&registration/.

[17] Department of Social Security, Statistics, Table SS7, updated 10 December 2018.

[18] In fact, there are two distinct long-term benefit Funds, one covering the rights built up before 1994, the 'closed Fund' and those relating to contributions as of 1994, the 'open' Fund.

members, one of whom shall be a barrister or solicitor of the Supreme Court, and the Financial Secretary. The Health Authority must arrange services to provide a comprehensive, preventive, diagnostic and treatment service in respect of physical and mental health.[19]

The GHA has a primary care centre, a hospital and a mental health facility. It employs about 1.000 persons. A visitation programme by UK medical consultants covers certain specialities not provided in Gibraltar. Moreover, tertiary referrals are also delivered by the UK National Health Service or nearby Spanish hospitals.

As mentioned already, the GHA operates the contributory Group Practice Medical Scheme.

9.5 Coordination

Since the external relations of Gibraltar are handled by the United Kingdom, we need to examine on a case-by-case basis whether the bilateral and multilateral social security coordination instruments ratified by the United Kingdom also apply to Gibraltar in its relations with other states.

Gibraltar as an Overseas British Territory was part of the European Union and thus participated in the EU mechanism of social security coordination, which also applies to the EEA countries and Switzerland.

The EU coordination mechanism provides:

- the principle of non-discrimination on the basis of nationality;
- rules concerning the determination of the applicable legislation;
- the exportability of acquired social security benefits;
- the aggregation and apportionment of periods of residence, work or insurance; and
- administrative co-operation agreements.

The EU mechanism applies to all persons insured under the social security of a member state, and to all social insurance schemes.

In the context of the European coordination mechanism, Gibraltar is treated by the United Kingdom as another EEA country; other EEA countries treat Gibraltar as part of the United Kingdom.[20] This follows from the Interim Agreement on Social Security arising from the UK accession to the European Economic Community.[21] According to this agreement, any social security law reference to a territory shall be

[19]Medical (Gibraltar Health Authority) Act, 1987, Act N° 1987-34. Accessed on: https://www.gha.gi/.

[20]Avato (2008). Accessed on: http://siteresources.worldbank.org/INTLM/Resources/390041-1244141510600/Avato-UK.pdf.

[21]Social Security (reciprocity) order (LN 1974/059) giving full force and effect to the provision set out in the letters exchanged between the Secretary of State for Foreign and Commonwealth Affairs and the Governor of Gibraltar of 12 December 1973 and 30 January 1974.

construed as a reference to the territory of the UK or Gibraltar or both, as the case may be. Any period during which a person was present or ordinarily resident in the other territory shall be treated as a period during which he/she was present or ordinarily resident in the territory of the competent country.

Gibraltar has now left the European Union, but the specifics of the practical arrangements of the Brexit have not been established, it remains unclear what the coordination situation will be. In the worst case scenario that no agreement (on this matter) would be reached between the United Kingdom and the European Union, the Government of Gibraltar has already reflected on the matter. In a technical notice[22] we can read:

> It is [. . .] the intention, [. . .], to initially maintain status quo, on a unilateral basis, ensuring that citizens' acquired rights are protected in relation to social security matters even in the context of a No-Deal Brexit. However, in circumstances where the EU system of social security coordination relies on cooperation and reciprocity from other EU Member States, it should not be assumed that this will continue in a No-Deal scenario in relation to other EU Member States. Gibraltar cannot, as a matter of domestic legislation, require EU Member States to cooperate with Gibraltar authorities, provide information, or apply the rules contained in EU law to individuals moving to/from Gibraltar. Notwithstanding the above, it should be noted that the EU have recently adopted an EU Regulation which is intended to safeguard, in case of a No-Deal Brexit, the social security rights of (1) citizens of EU Member States in the UK and Gibraltar; and (2) UK nationals (including Gibraltarians) in the EU who have benefitted from the right of free movement prior to the UK and Gibraltar's exit from the EU. Moreover, with regard to the position in Spain specifically, it should be noted that the Government of Spain has enacted national legislation outlining contingency measures applicable in the case of a No-Deal Brexit. The legislation, which has been extended to cover Gibraltar, and which will apply for a period of 21 months following a No-Deal exit, complements legislation adopted at EU level on matters concerning the coordination of social security systems. In the medium to long term, and in the absence of a future agreement covering social security matters, [the Government of Gibraltar] will develop policy in this area, amending legislation where necessary, to take into account the level of reciprocity guaranteed by individual EU Member States. Lastly, it is also important to underline that a No-Deal exit from the EU would be of no practical effect on the coordination of social security as between Gibraltar and the UK. Longstanding bilateral arrangements, already in place as between the UK and Gibraltar, will be maintained.

In the meantime, Spain and the United Kingdom have signed a bilateral memorandum relating to citizens' rights, which is referred to in the Protocol on Gibraltar annexed to the Agreement on the Withdrawal of the United Kingdom from the European Union. The Protocol is part of an EU-UK agreement, while the memorandum focuses on the same issues from a United Kingdom-Spain bilateral perspective. The agreement on citizens provides the specific modalities of the rights and guarantees for cross-border workers in Gibraltar that the Withdrawal Agreement confers to citizens and workers in general. The rights of workers are therefore guaranteed, including their social benefits, which shall be enjoyed on equal terms with the locals according to the principle of non-discrimination. In addition,

[22]Technical Notice, No deal Brexit, Social Security Coordination, March 2019. Accessed on: https://www.gibraltar.gov.gi/uploads/Brexit%20Page/216-2019.pdf.

mechanisms for coordination and the exchange of information between authorities are provided to ensure effective compliance. Likewise, the British authorities have undertaken to reimburse Spain for the difference in unemployment benefits advanced by Spain to cross-border workers.[23]

According to Act n° 10 of 2019, the Minister of Social Affairs is given the power to issue regulations to modify EU legislation dealing with retained social security coordination (such as regulation EC N°883/2004 and N°987/2009).[24]

According to the Social Security (Insurance) Insurability and Special Classes Regulation, the Director of Social Security may exempt a person employed or self-employed both in Gibraltar and in another country (other than UK or a EU country) from social insurance in Gibraltar if the concerned person is covered by the insurance of the other country, entitling him/her to benefits no less favourable than those provided in Gibraltar.[25]

The Minister of Health is competent to make payments and to arrange for payments to be made with regards to the cost of health care provided outside Gibraltar.[26] In fact, tertiary referrals by the Gibraltar Health Authority are often delivered in the UK National Health System as well as in nearby Spanish hospitals.[27]

The Sponsored Patient Department of the Medical Directorate of the Gibraltar Health Authority is in charge of facilitating health care abroad, which has been approved by a Gibraltar medical consultant. Travel costs, a maintenance allowance and in-patient pocket money are provided to persons obtaining health care in Spain and, most often, the United Kingdom.

9.6 Additional Relevant Information

Gibraltar faces occasional droughts; the drinking water is provided by desalination and stored rainwater.

Gibraltar is self-sufficient and does not receive funds from the United Kingdom. Its economy is mainly based on the financial sector (offshore banking, duty-free shopping), tourism, the shipping sector, (online) gaming and e-commerce.

Gibraltar has a land border with Spain, which has been closed for some periods in the past due to Spain's claims on Gibraltar. This could be repeated, especially now

[23]Signing of the Memoranda on Gibraltar between Spain and the UK, http://www.exteriores.gob.es/Portal/en/SalaDePrensa/Comunicados/Paginas/2018_COMUNICADOS/20181129_COMU172.aspx.

[24]Healthcare (international agreements) and social security coordination Act, Act N° 2019-10, Part 3.

[25]Social Security (Insurance) Insurability and Special Classes Regulation, (Subsidiary 1955.08;04-7), Section 4.

[26]Healthcare (international agreements) and social security coordination Act, Act.N° 2019-10, sections 4 and 5.

[27]See: https://www.gha.gi/about-us/.

that the United Kingdom and Gibraltar have left the European Union. This would endanger the economy of Gibraltar, the tourism industry in the first place, and reduce the attractiveness for frontier workers to come and work in Gibraltar.

Websites

www.exteriores.gob.es/Portal/en/SalaDePrensa/Comunicados/Paginas/2018_COMUNICADOS/20181129_COMU172.aspx
www.gha.gi/about-us/
www.gha.gi/healthcare&registration/
www.gcs.gov.gi/index.php/justice-system/overview
www.gibraltar.gov.gi/uploads/Brexit%20Page/216-2019.pdf

References

Avato J (2008) Portability of social security and health care benefits in the United Kingdom. The World Bank, Background Study. Accessed on: http://siteresources.worldbank.org/INTLM/Resources/390041-1244141510600/Avato-UK.pdf

Budhrani HK. The Gibraltar Parliament. In: Baldwin NDJ (ed) Legislatures of small states: a comparative study. Library of legislative studies. Routledge, pp 102–106. Accessed on: https://books.google.nl/books?id=VNd8hxn3Vh0C&pg=PA105&lpg=PA105&dq=gibraltar+parliamentary+workings&source=bl&ots=8BJlFnxaHD&sig=ACfU3U0Uep2PwreC9WUj-s o N J v X Y F j _ V q w & h l =e l & s a =X & ved=2ahUKEwjktJnf1uXoAhXNKewKHaDKAw8Q6AEwAnoECAkQLg#v=onepage&q=gibraltar%20parliamentary%20workings&f=false

Country Profiles (2020) International Social Security Association, https://www.issa.int/en_GB/country-profiles. Accessed 12 Feb 2020

HM Government of Gibraltar, Department of Social Security (2018) Guide to Social Security Benefits

World Factbook (2020) Central Intelligence Agency. https://www.cia.gov/the-world-factbook/countries/gibraltar. Accessed 12 Feb 2020

Chapter 10
Greenland

10.1 Context

Greenland[1] may be called a small state because of its small population, but it is also the largest island in the world. The island spans four time zones and is situated in the North Atlantic Ocean between Europe and America.

Greenland was a colony of Denmark from the eighteenth century until 1953, when Denmark made an amendment of the Danish Constitution in which Greenland had its status renewed and became a constituency in the Danish Kingdom. In January 1979, a referendum on greater autonomy was held in which 63% of the voters voted in favor of a Home Rule, and on 1 May 1979 Greenland Home Rule was established. Home Rule became self-government in 2009, following a referendum the year before where three quarters of the voters expressed their desire for more autonomy.[2] The Act on Greenland Self-Government of 2009[3] was an extension of the powers enacted in the Home Rule act of 1979.[4]

The Greenlandic parliament (*Inatsisartut*) is elected proportionally by the population. It approves the executive government '*Naalakkersuisut*', which is responsible for the central administration headed by a Premier with a cabinet. In addition, two Greenlandic representatives are elected to the Danish Parliament in Copenhagen. Currently, three parties hold more than five of the 31 seats of *Inatsisartut*: the social-democratic Forwards (9), the centre-right Democrats (6), and the left-wing

With special thanks to Mrs. Kirsten Olesen and Mrs. Signe Haugaard Christensen for reviewing the report on Greenland.

[1]For data and figures, see: Country Profiles (2020) and World Factbook (2020).

[2]See: https://naalakkersuisut.gl/en/About-government-of-greenland/About-Greenland/Politics-in-Greenland.

[3]Danish Act nr. 473 of 12 June 2009.

[4]Danish Act. nr. 577 of 29 November 1978.

D. Pieters, *Social Security Law in Small Jurisdictions*, The World of Small States 8,
https://doi.org/10.1007/978-3-030-78247-4_10

independentist Inuit Community (8). Greenland has a coalition government lead by Forwards.

Under the Self-Government Act, there is the possibility that Greenland will take over jurisdiction in many areas, except nationality, the Supreme Court, foreign affairs, defence and security policy as well as exchange rate and monetary policy. All these matters remain the competence of the Parliament and Government in Copenhagen. The Danish parliament's adoption of an agreement with the Greenland Government[5] provided full powers to the Government of Greenland to conclude certain international agreements on behalf of the Kingdom of Denmark on matters of exclusive material competence of Greenland.

The Greenlandic Inuit culture differs fundamentally from the European Nordic culture.

Greenlandic people belong in their vast majority to the Danish Evangelical Lutheran Church, while some Greenlandic people also follow traditional Inuit spiritual beliefs.

Social issues are gaining a lot of public interest in the press and other media.

The country is a constituent part of the Kingdom of Denmark and highly depends on the Danish block grant it receives annually from Copenhagen. The latter amounted to more than half of the Greenlandic revenues and a quarter of Greenlandic GDP in 2017.Imports and exports are also more than 70% to Denmark. Still, there is an important movement for independence in Greenland. Greenland joined the European Communities in 1973 as a part of Denmark. However, Greenland withdrew from the European Communities as early as 1985 due to a dispute over fishing quota. Greenland remained a member of the Overseas Countries and Territories Association (OCTA) of the European Union. Greenland actively participates in Nordic and Arctic co-operation.

10.2 Legal Framework of Rights to Social Security

10.2.1 Constitutional Context

The Danish Act on Greenland Self-Government[6] states in article 1:

> The Greenland Self-Government authorities shall exercise legislative and executive power in the fields of responsibility taken over. Courts of law that are established by the Self-Government authorities shall exercise judicial power in Greenland in all fields of responsibility. Accordingly, the legislative power shall lie with *Inatsisartut*, the executive power with *Naalakkersuisut*, and the judicial power with the courts of law.

[5]Danish Act nr. 577 of June 24, 2005 "Concerning the conclusion of agreements under international law by the Government of Greenland".

[6]Danish statute no. 473 of 12 June 2009.

Pursuant to the Greenland statute on *Inatsisartut* and *Naalakkersuisut* (Parliament and Government),[7] Greenland has already assumed legislative and administrative responsibility in a substantial number of areas that affect the daily lives of Greenlandic citizens, including social security and health.

Danish law applies to areas that are not covered by Greenlandic law. The legal system of Greenland is highly influenced by Danish law and belongs with it to the civil law group.

10.2.2 Social Security Legislation and Structure

Social security in Greenland is governed by a number of (recent) statutes of the Greenlandic parliament on old-age pensions,[8] early retirement,[9] labour market benefits,[10] child benefits,[11] and social assistance.[12] Health care is regulated by Greenlandic law as well.[13] It is noteworthy that although some inspiration was drawn from Danish legislation, all social matters have been regulated by Greenlandic statutes.

Some of the above-mentioned statutes allow the municipalities some freedom with regard to the level or the conditions for the benefits they administer in their municipality.

Old-age pensions and their supplements are flat rate. The early retirement pensions provide a flat rate income replacement in case of long-term work incapacity. The labour market insurance covers both the risk of unemployment and loss of income due to sickness. Again, the benefits are not wage related. Child benefits are also flat rate benefits. The social assistance provides both occasional and recurrent financial aid to those in need.

10.2.3 Enforcement of Constitutional and Statutory Rights

Decisions of the municipalities in social affairs can be appealed against with the Social Appeals Commission (*Det Sociale Ankenaevn*) of Greenland.[14] The members

---

[7]Inatsisartutlov n° 26 of 18 November 2010.

[8]Inatsisartutlov nr. 20 af 23. november 2015 om alderspension.

[9]Inatsisartutlov nr. 40 af 9. december 2015 om førtidspension.

[10]Inatsisartutlov nr. 2 af 15. maj 2014 om arbejdsmarkedsydelse.

[11]Inatsisartutlov nr. 9 af 7. december 2009 om børnetilskud.

[12]Landstingsforordning nr. 15 af 20. november 2006 om offentlig hjælp.

[13]Landstingsforordning nr. 15 af 6. november 1997 om sundhedsvæsenets ydelser m.v.

[14]Landstingsforordning nr. 11 af 12. November 2001 om socialvaesenets styrelse og orgnaisation, §§ 8 ff.

of Det Sociale Ankenaevn are appointed by the Government. The decisions of *Det Sociale Ankenaevn* are not open for further administrative appeal.

Questions relating to the evaluation of a person's work capacity are dealt with by the Early Pension Complaints Commission (*Førtidspensionsklagenævnet*), an independent commission whose members are nominated by the Government. Decisions of the *Førtidspensionsklagenævnet* cannot be appealed to any other administrative authority. Decisions regarding the health system (unrelated to health professionals' activities) can be appealed with the directorate of health, with no further administrative appeal possible.

There is a Court and a High Court of Greenland. Appeals beyond the High Court of Greenland are heard by the Supreme Court in Copenhagen.

10.3 Population and the Personal Scope of the Social Security Schemes

10.3.1 General Data on the Population and Its Composition

The population of this vast island is estimated at about 57,500 people (2020), of which about 90% are native Greenlandic (Inuit) and about 8% Danish. (West-) Greenlandic (*Kalaallisut*) is the official language; Danish may also be used for official purposes. The population is concentrated on the Southwest shore; there are limited settlements scattered along the remaining parts of the coast. The cities and settlements on the shore are not interconnected by roads. The interior of Greenland is uninhabited. About one quarter of the population lives in the capital Nuuk.

Greenland has a negative net migration rate of minus 6 migrants per thousand. A declining population due to emigration and a lack of qualified labourers hinder economic development. Unemployment amounted to 9% in 2015. The population that is estimated to live below the poverty line amounted to 16% in 2015.

10.3.2 Personal Scope of the Social Insurance and Social Assistance Schemes

The right to an old-age pension[15] and the right to early pension[16] are conditional on the applicant being a Danish citizen. However, this condition does not apply to persons who are covered by the Nordic Convention on Social Security, or persons who have been permanent residents in Greenland for at least 3 years immediately prior to the date of application. The two rights are also conditional upon the applicant

[15]Inatsisartutlov nr. 20 af 23. november 2015 om alderspension, §§ 1-4 and 7.

[16]Inatsisartutlov nr. 40 af 9. december 2015 om førtidspension, §§1-4 and 7.

having permanent residence in Greenland or in one of the other Nordic countries, or in a country that is a party to the EEA Agreement.

Furthermore, to qualify for a Greenlandic old-age pension or early pension in Greenland, the applicant must have had at least 3 years of permanent residence in Greenland, Denmark or the Faroe Islands between the age of 15 and the age of pensioning. To qualify for a full old-age pension, one must show 40 years of residence; for a full early pension, one must have had permanent residence during at least four fifths of the period between the age of 15 and the beginning of the early pension. In 2019, 3820 persons received an old-age pension and 2391 an early pension.[17]

To qualify for the labour market insurance benefit,[18] one must be registered in the people's register in Greenland and have worked as a wage earner for at least 13 weeks. All persons employed by an employer according to a contract or agreement, and who are subject to the instructions of the employer, are regarded as wage earners. In 2018, 2518 persons received the unemployment benefit; 1014 women received maternity benefit.[19]

To be entitled to child allowance,[20] the following conditions must be met:

- The child must have his/her home in a Greenlandic municipality, and the person to whom the allowance will be paid has to have their permanent residence in Greenland and has to be in the people's register in Greenland; and
- The child or the one who will get the benefit paid, must be a Danish citizen or have had his/her residence in Greenland during the last year.

The condition that the child needs to have his/her home municipality in Greenland is not valid for people entitled to receive social security benefits by virtue of the Nordic Social Security Convention or other international agreements. In 2019, 3679 persons received child allowances.[21]

Persons who are registered in the people's register in Greenland and have their permanent residence in Greenland, qualify for health care regardless of their nationality. Persons staying in Greenland temporarily may also qualify according to the conditions set by the law.[22]

The purpose of public help or social assistance[23] is to create an economic safety net for all persons staying in Greenland who cannot cope in another way.

---

[17]Information on the website of the Statistical Office. Accessed on: http://bank.stat.gl/pxweb/en/Greenland/.

[18]Inatsisartutlov nr. 2 af 15. maj 2014 om arbejdsmarkedsydelse,§§ 2 and 6.

[19]Information on the website of the Statistical Office. Accessed on: http://bank.stat.gl/pxweb/en/Greenland/.

[20]Inatsisartutlov nr. 9 af 7. december 2009 om børnetilskud, §1.

[21]Information on the website of the Statistical Office. Accessed on: http://bank.stat.gl/pxweb/en/Greenland/.

[22]Landstingsforordning nr. 15 af 6. november 1997 om sundhedsvæsenets ydelser m.v., §2.

[23]Landstingsforordning nr. 15 af 20. november 2006 om offentlig hjælp, §§ 3-4.

All people staying in Greenland are entitled to social assistance in case of urgent necessity. However, to qualify for recurrent help, the coverage of fixed expenses or for occasional help, one must have permanent residence in Greenland and be registered in the people's register. Moreover, one must be a Danish citizen or have been married to a Danish citizen for at least one year. The latter condition does not apply to people covered by agreements with other countries or by international organisations that give them a right to continued social assistance and a right to fixed expenses when staying in Greenland. In 2019, 4760 persons received public help.[24]

10.4 Administration of Social Security

The Government of Greenland, through its departments of Health and of Social Affairs and Justice, is responsible for social security lawmaking and policy in Greenland. The department of Social Affairs and Justice includes a Control Unit in charge of controlling the municipalities in the way they administer social affairs.

The administration of the social security benefits is the competence of the municipalities where the beneficiary lives. The country consists of 5 municipalities. If the beneficiary does not live in any of these, the tasks of the municipalities are carried out by the Department of Social Affairs and Justice. Municipal administrations are governed by an elected municipal council.

It is noteworthy to observe that Greenlandic law[25] explicitly contains an obligation for the Government to organise courses for the members of the municipal administrations (council members) dealing with social affairs, and this within one year after elections for these municipal administrations. The same law requires the president of *Det Sociale Ankenaevn* to have a degree in law or otherwise provide proof of deep knowledge of social law in Greenland. Two members of *Det Sociale Ankenaevn* should have social legal insight, whereas the two remaining members should have social policy insight.

[24]Information on the website of the Statistical Office. Accessed on: http://bank.stat.gl/pxweb/en/Greenland/.

[25]Landstingsforordning nr. 11 af 12. November 2001 om socialvaesenets styrelse og orgnaisation, §§ 5 and 9.

10.5 Coordination

In article 12. (1) of the Danish Act on Greenland Self-Government,[26] it is established that "Naalakkersuisut may, on behalf of the Realm, negotiate and conclude agreements under international law with foreign states and international organisations, including administrative agreements which exclusively concern Greenland and entirely relate to fields of responsibility taken over."

Greenland has joined[27] the revised Convention on Social Security between the Nordic countries (2012, into force 2014), replacing the previous Nordic Convention on Social Security from 2003, which itself had replaced the previously existing bilateral treaties between the concerned Nordic states. The Nordic Convention facilitates mobility between Finland, Sweden, Norway, Denmark and Iceland and gives people travelling between the countries a right to social security benefits. The convention simplifies work between social security administrations of the Nordic countries. The agreement supplements (and in principle does not alter) the social security coordination mechanism agreed between the countries of the European Economic Area. The agreement expands the application of the EU's social security regulations to include the Faroe Islands and Greenland, as well as citizens of non-union countries who reside in the Nordic countries. It may furthermore extend the rights of the migrant workers according to the EU mechanism. The EU coordination mechanism provides:

- the principle of non-discrimination on the basis of nationality;
- rules concerning the determination of the applicable legislation;
- the exportability of acquired social security benefits;
- the aggregation and apportionment of periods of residence, work or insurance; and
- administrative co-operation agreements.

The EU mechanism applies to all persons insured under the social security of a member state and all social insurance schemes.

Greenland has not concluded bilateral coordination agreements. Danish bilateral agreements are excluded from application upon Greenlandic social security.[28] It is unclear whether earlier Danish bilateral treaties apply to Greenlandic social security schemes, as they do not mention any exclusion of Greenland but neither sum up Greenlandic schemes in their scope of application.[29]

---

[26] Danish statute no. 473 of 12 June 2009.

[27] See Bekendtgørelse no. 15 af 23. august 2019 om udvidelse til Færøerne og Grønland af nordisk konvention af 12. juni 2012 om social sikring med tilhørende administrativ aftal.

[28] So e.g. the bilateral treaty with Australia: Bekendtgørelse no. 6 af 22. februar 2001 om overenskomst af 1. juli 1999 med Australien om social sikring med tilhørende administrativ aftale.

[29] Take for instance the bilateral agreement with New-Zealand, of May 6th, 1997 or the Agreement with Québec of 23 November 1987.

Let us observe here that in article 12. (2) of the Danish Act on Greenland Self-Government,[30] we find the possibility of co-operation between two small jurisdictions:

> Agreements under international law which exclusively concern Greenland and the Faroe Islands and entirely relate to fields of responsibility taken over may, subject to decision by Naalakkersuisut as well as the Faroe Islands Landsstyre [Government of the Faroes], be negotiated and concluded jointly on behalf of the Realm by Naalakkersuisut and the Faroe Islands Landsstyre.

Given the extent of the country and the limited health care institutions in Greenland, it is important to note that people registered with the people's register in Greenland and have their permanent residence in the country, as well as other persons being treated for epidemic or venereal diseases, are entitled to medically prescribed free transportation to the appropriate district hospital, central hospital (Dronning Ingrids Hospitalet) or hospital abroad. A Visit Commission (*Visitationsnaevn*) decides upon the examination and treatment of a person outside the district where he/she stays. The decision of the *Visitationsnaevn* cannot be appealed before any other administrative authority. Referral to examination or treatment outside of Greenland is only possible to treatment institutions with which the Greenlandic Government has made an agreement to receive patients from Greenland.[31]

10.6 Additional Relevant Information

Greenland's economy is highly dependant upon fishing. Fish and shellfish accounted for more than 90% of export. This makes the country very much dependant upon fluctuations in the fish and shellfish market. Necessary diversification is only starting, with tourism and the exploitation of mineral resources in the forefront.[32]

Until the beginning of the twentieth century, hunting for seals and whales was the most important source for the survival of the Greenlandic people; to this day about a tenth of the workforce is indirectly involved in the hunting industry.[33] One has to observe that both hunting seals and whales are critically viewed by many in the world, which may constitute a risk for the sector.

Greenland is very vulnerable to climate change and the consequent disruption of the Arctic environment.

---

[30] Danish statute no. 473 of 12 June 2009.

[31] Landstingsforordning nr. 15 af 6. november 1997 om sundhedsvæsenets ydelser m.v., §§19-23.

[32] See: https://naalakkersuisut.gl/en/About-government-of-greenland/About-Greenland/Economy-and-Industry-in-Greenland.

[33] See: https://naalakkersuisut.gl/en/About-government-of-greenland/About-Greenland/Economy-and-Industry-in-Greenland.

Greenland's high dependency on Danish subventions is another risk factor, especially in the perspective of political pressure for independence. This pressure is partly based on high hopes for the exploitation of Greenland's natural resources. A lacking infrastructure has thus far hindered the exploitation of uranium, iron and other mineral products.

The public sector, including publicly owned enterprises (also in the fish industry) and the municipalities, plays an important role in the economy.

Websites

http://bank.stat.gl/pxweb/en/Greenland/

https://naalakkersuisut.gl/en/About-government-of-greenland/About-Greenland/Economy-and-Industry-in-Greenland

https://naalakkersuisut.gl/en/About-government-of-greenland/About-Greenland/Politics-in-Greenland

References

Country Profiles (2020) International Social Security Association. https://www.issa.int/en_GB/country-profiles. Accessed 12 Feb 2020

World Factbook (2020) Central Intelligence Agency. https://www.cia.gov/the-world-factbook/countries/Greenland. Accessed 12 Feb 2020

Chapter 11
Grenada

11.1 Context

The state of Grenada[1] is composed of three main islands—Grenada, Carriacou and Petite Martinique—and a number of very small, largely uninhabited islands. They are situated between the Caribbean Sea and the North Atlantic Ocean and constitute the most southern of the Windward islands.

After its discovery by Columbus, Grenada was first colonised by the French and from 1762 by the British. It gained full independence in 1974 but maintained the Queen of England as its monarch and head of state. A leftist revolution movement seized power in 1979. This revolutionary period ended with internal struggle between factions and the US invasion in 1983. The constitutional order of a Westminster type parliamentary democracy has been restored and since then two moderate main parties alternate power in a stable political context. The monarch is represented in Grenada by a Governor General. Executive power is exercised by the Government headed by the Prime Minister, who is usually the leader or the majority party. The Government itself is answerable to the House of Representatives. The 15 members of the House of Representatives are elected in single-seat constituencies. The members of the other house of the legislature, the Senate, are appointed by the Governor General, 10 on advice of the prime minister (of whom 3 represent the Labour Movement, the Private Sector and Agriculture, respectively) and 3 on advice of the leader of the opposition. Currently, the conservative New National Party occupies 14 seats of the House; the other political party, the social-democratic National Democratic Congress none, although it obtained 40% of the votes in the latest elections.

It may be important to mention that the labour movement is historically related to the emergence of the national political consciousness, which led the country to independence.

[1]For data and figures, see: Country Profiles (2020) and World Factbook (2020).

D. Pieters, *Social Security Law in Small Jurisdictions*, The World of Small States 8,
https://doi.org/10.1007/978-3-030-78247-4_11

Nearly half of the population are members of the various protestant denominations, while just over one third of the inhabitants are Roman Catholic.

Grenada is member of both the Organisation of the Eastern Caribbean States and the Caribbean Community, CARICOM. The Organisation of Eastern Caribbean States (OECS) groups together 7 small jurisdictions (Grenada, Antigua & Barbuda, Dominica, St Kitts and Nevis, St. Lucia, St. Vincent and Grenadines and Montserrat). They strive for a close (economic and monetary) union and share the Eastern Caribbean dollar as currency. They were formerly united in the British West Indies. The Caribbean Community (CARICOM) groups the OECS jurisdictions plus Barbados, the Bahamas, Belize, Guyana, Jamaica, Haiti, Suriname and Trinidad and Tobago. Cooperation within OECS and CARICOM is very important to Grenada.

Grenada as a Commonwealth realm has maintained strong ties with its former colonial ruler, the United Kingdom.

11.2 Legal Framework of Rights to Social Security

11.2.1 Constitutional Context

The Constitution does not contain any right to social security, but limits itself in articles 92 and 93 to provide special protection for the pensions of judges and public officers as well as their survivors.

Grenada's legal system, strongly influenced by English law, belongs to the common law group. However, the High Court, the Court of Appeal and the Privy Council may test the constitutionality of Acts of Parliament.

11.2.2 Social Security Legislation and Structure

Social insurance is mainly regulated by the National Insurance Act, N°14/1983 (as amended) and related regulations.[2] We shall not deal here with the special pensions and other benefits for judges, public officers and their survivors, as provided in articles 92 and 93 of the constitution.[3] We shall also not comment on the private schemes established by employers for their employees.

The National Insurance Scheme (NIS) provides seven benefits, grouped in three branches:

- Long-term benefits, including age benefits (both pensions and grants), survivors' benefits (both pensions and grants) and invalidity benefits (both pensions and grants);

---

[2]National Insurance Act, Chapter 205 of the Laws of Grenada.

[3]Main legal acts in relation with the special public service pensions are to be found in Chapters 233–236 of the Laws of Grenada.

- Short-term benefits, including sickness benefits, maternity benefits and funeral grants; and
- Employment injury benefits, including injury benefits, disability benefits, medical expenses, death benefits, and funeral grants.

Each of the branches is financially autonomous from the other two.

Self-employed persons qualify just like employees for all benefits offered by NIS.[4] Voluntarily insured persons qualify for age, invalidity, survivors' and funeral benefits.

The public health care system[5] provides care of various levels against modest user charges; drugs at public pharmacies are sold at subsidised prices. Children under the age of 17 and adults over 60 are exempted from all user fees, as well as individuals considered as 'indigent'. Plans to introduce a national health insurance have not yet materialised.

Social assistance is not adequately regulated by law. It consists of a number of means-tested benefits in kind and in cash, most of which are provided by the Division of Social Services of the Ministry of Social Development, Housing & Community Empowerment, and some also by the Prime Minister's Office.[6] Some of the programmes are of a temporary nature or pilots. Moreover, some of the benefits are very much linked to foreign support grants. According to the information provided by the Ministry of Social Development, Housing & Community Empowerment, the Safety Net programme in 2020 consists of:[7]

- Public assistance to vulnerable families who fall below the poverty line. Cash transfers are made to the elderly, mentally ill, and persons who are physically and mentally challenged;
- Necessitous Fund: financial support to children to ensure that they remain in school by means of allowances made to the school or to the family;
- Burial Assistance granted to families whose relatives need assistance to ensure a proper burial of their loved ones; and
- Disaster Fund: financial support provided to families who have suffered a personal disaster (such as fire, floods. . .).

The conditions for these benefits, the operated (proxy) means tests and the amounts of the benefits granted are determined by the respective programmes;

---

[4]This information was provided by the official website of the NIS. Accessed on: http://www.nisgrenada.org/contributors/details/self-employed as last consulted on 9 April 2020. It is in contradiction with many other sources denying the self-employed the NIS sickness benefits (see e.g.: https://www.issa.int/en/country-details?countryId=GD&regionId=AME&filtered=false) and in contradiction with Article 3 section 2 of the National Insurance (Self-Employed Persons) Regulations, stating: "For the avoidance of doubt regulations relating to Sickness Benefit contained in the National Insurance (Benefit) Regulations do not apply to self-employed persons."

[5]See: http://www.health.gov.gd/.

[6]See: https://www.mgovernance.net/needy-assistance#.

[7]Information provided on the official website of the Ministry. Accessed on: https://www.gov.gd/ministries//social_development.html.

they often lack transparency. There is an enormous fragmentation of various types of assistance benefits.

Currently, all social assistance, including the Social Safety Net, is undergoing a reform process known as "Support for Education, Employment and Development" or SEED, funded by the World Bank.

The Needy Assistance programme run by the Prime Minister's Office for needs-based assistance on a case-by-case evaluation, which was due to be stopped in 2018,[8] is apparently still available.[9]

11.2.3 Enforcement of Constitutional and Statutory Rights

Questions concerning the liability of a person to pay contributions or concerning a person's right to benefits are decided by the NIS Director, subject to a right of appeal to the Board. Questions concerning the status of the insured person or the status of the employer, or questions concerning which person(s) should be granted survivors' benefits, are reserved for decision by the Board.

Appeals against decisions of the Board will be decided by an Appeal Tribunal, whose decisions are final, except for questions of law. The Appeal Tribunal consists of an independent chair and one member who represents the employers and one who represents the insured persons. Questions of law arising from decisions of the Appeal Tribunal may be referred to the High Court.

Grenada's judicial power is exercised by the Eastern Caribbean Supreme Court (ECSC), which consists of a Court of Appeal and a High Court. The Court of Appeal is itinerant, travelling to the member states of the Organisation of Eastern Caribbean States to hear appeals from the High Court and subordinate courts. Two High Court judges reside in Grenada. Appeals beyond the ECSC must be dealt with by Judicial Committee of the Privy Council in London.

11.3 Population and the Personal Scope of the Social Security Schemes

11.3.1 General Data on the Population and Its Composition

The population is estimated at 113,000 (2020). Most people live along the coast lines; one third lives in the capital city of St. George's. More than four fifths of the

---

[8]See: https://www.nowgrenada.com/2018/04/seed-not-suspended-only-safety-net-programmes-under-the-opm/.

[9]See: https://www.mgovernance.net/needy-assistance.

population are of African descent, while more than one tenth are considered of mixed origin.

The labour force was estimated at about 55,000 in 2017, unemployment at 24% in the same year. 38% of the population was reported to live below the poverty line in 2008.

Grenada has a negative net migration rate of minus 2.6 migrants per thousand. Remittances from the many Grenadians working abroad are an important source of income. However, this does not compensate for the loss of human capital: more than four fifths of the educated workforce left the country, as have two thirds of the tertiary educated and nearly all physicians.[10]

11.3.2 Personal Scope of the Social Insurance and Social Assistance Schemes

All persons in employment are covered by the National Insurance Scheme (NIS).[11] The category of 'employed persons' includes both the employees and the self-employed persons. Employees are persons who perform services under a contract of service or apprenticeship with a public or private employer. Self-employed persons are defined as persons who are not in the employment of a registered employer, but otherwise gainfully occupied in employment. Also temporary and part-time workers and students with summer or part-time jobs must also register. Persons previously insured in the NIS may, when they are between age 16 and 60 and not in the employment of another person, register as voluntarily insured persons. Employees of diplomatic or consular missions or international organisations are exempted from national insurance according to international law.

To be insured, one must in principle be ordinarily resident in Grenada and the insurable employment must be performed in Grenada. However, people who were employed in Grenada and continue to work for the same or another employer abroad, remain under the national insurance for up to 1 year.

In principle, a person is disqualified for a national insurance benefit when staying abroad. There are, however, important exceptions to this rule. A person will not be disqualified from receiving sickness or maternity benefits when they have temporarily left the country for the specific purpose of being treated abroad. A person will also not be disqualified from receiving invalidity benefits when they are absent from Grenada for such period as the NIS Director may allow, provided that the entitlement

[10]Rata and Xu as referred to in: P. Lewis, Social Policies in Grenada, *Social Policies in Small States Series*, N°.2, Commonwealth Secretariat/UNRISD, p. 35. Accessed on: http://www.unrisd.org/80256B3C005BCCF9/httpNetITFramePDF?ReadForm&parentunid=50F82735B441C66DC12577EB004CDC41&parentdoctype=book&netitpath=80256B3C005BCCF9/(httpAuxPages)/50F82735B441C66DC12577EB004CDC41/$file/Grenada%20(small).pdf.

[11]See: http://www.nisgrenada.org/contributors.

to the invalidity was established before leaving. A person will not be disqualified from receiving age benefits or survivors' benefits or employment injury benefits because they are absent from Grenada.

As the NIS covers workers of the formal sector, it leaves many workers of the informal sector uninsured. This would leave a majority of the workforce without coverage.[12]

Public health care institutions are open to all citizens.[13] Social assistance is available for all needy vulnerable citizens and families.

11.4 Administration of Social Security

The Ministry of Health and Social Security is politically responsible for social security and gives directions to the National Insurance Board, which must carry them out.

The National Insurance Fund, which operates the National Insurance Scheme, is for the rest an autonomous body administered by the National Insurance Board. The Board consists of 7 members: the Director and three times two members, representing respectively the Government, employers and employees. The Board appoints the Director of the Fund who manages the staff and is responsible for the administration of the National Insurance Scheme.

The Board is assisted by a number of Committees, such as the Investment Committee, which consists of five members appointed by the Minister. These members include an officer of the Ministry of Finance who acts as chairperson, the Director and another member of the Board, as well as two members representing employers and employees respectively. The Investment Committee gives directions on the investment of the assets of the Fund that are in surplus of the current needs.

The Ministry of Health and Social Security is the sole public institution responsible for the provision of health care. It is responsible for policy development, planning, implementation, monitoring and evaluation of the services provided by the public health care system. There are four hospitals, six district health centres and thirty medical stations throughout the country that provide health care.[14]

The Ministry of Social Development, Housing & Community Empowerment is responsible for the social assistance programmes. A specific SEED unit within the

---

[12] P. Lewis, Social Policies in Grenada, *Social Policies in Small States Series*, N°.2, Commonwealth Secretariat/UNRISD, p. 31 referring also to Barrientos. Accessed on: http://www.unrisd.org/80256B3C005BCCF9/httpNetITFramePDF?ReadForm&parentunid=50F82735B441C66DC12577EB004CDC41&parentdoctype=book&netitpath=80256B3C005BCCF9/(httpAuxPages)/50F82735B441C66DC12577EB004CDC41/$file/Grenada%20(small).pdf.

[13] See: http://www.health.gov.gd/.

[14] See: http://www.health.gov.gd/.

Ministry provides the Safety Net benefits. Some social assistance interventions may be claimed with the Prime Minister's Office.[15]

11.5 Coordination

Two social security coordination instruments deserve some special attention, since Grenada is party to both: the CARICOM Agreement on Social Security (CASS) of 1996 and the OECS Convention on Social Security of 1991.

CASS has been concluded between all CARICOM states except Haiti and Suriname, the latter country having an insufficiently similar social security system. It came into effect on 1 April 1997. CASS protects nationals of the member states who belong to the following groups of workers: workers in transnational enterprises, workers in international transport and on ships, workers in diplomatic missions, consulates and international organisations, self-employed workers and itinerant workers (i.e. working in more than one member state) as well as eventually their dependant family members. To be covered by CASS, the worker must move to work or must have worked in two or more member states. CASS only includes in its material scope (contributory) pensions in case of invalidity, disablement, old-age and retirement, survivors' benefits and death benefits. CASS contains a non-discrimination on the basis of nationality clause. CASS ensures that workers who have not made enough contributions to receive an independent pension from their state's social security system enjoy a totalisation with contributions in other member states. The worker then also enjoys an apportioned pension in the first state. CASS leaves untouched pensions that have been acquired solely on the basis of one member state's social security. Furthermore, CASS contains rules on posting of workers of international enterprises (in principle up to 2 years) and contains rules on assigning the competent country (or countries) for the other groups of workers.

The OECS Convention has a broader scope than CASS as it also covers short-term benefits such as maternity and illness-related benefits. Yet it only covers 7 small jurisdictions. Grenada has signed the Convention but has not yet ratified it.

Although many people from Grenada emigrate for work outside the Caribbean, Grenada has concluded only one bilateral social security coordination agreement, i.e. with Canada.[16] The agreement with Canada is applicable to contributory national insurance age, invalidity, and survivors' benefits and to the funeral grant. The agreement applies to persons, regardless of their nationality, who are socially insured in Canada or Grenada. The agreement contains provisions on the equal treatment of each other's citizens, the export of benefits, the designation of the applicable

[15]See: https://www.gov.gd/ministries/social_development.html and https://www.mgovernance.net/needy-assitance.

[16]Agreement on Social Security between the Government of Canada and the Government of Grenada. Accessed on: https://www.treaty-accord.gc.ca/print-imprimer.aspx.

legislation, the aggregation of periods of social insurance and administrative co-operation between the two countries. Interestingly, if a person is not entitled to the payment of a benefit based on the creditable periods under the legislation of both countries, totalised as stipulated in the agreement, that person's entitlement to the payment of that benefit will be determined by totalising these periods and creditable periods under the legislation of a third state to which Grenada and Canada are bound by separate social security instruments, which provide for totalising periods.

The public health care system does not provide any coverage of health care abroad.

11.6 Additional Relevant Information

The islands of Grenada lie on the edge of a hurricane belt. In 2004 and 2005 Grenada was struck by hurricanes Ivan and Emily, devastating Grenada's economy by damaging 70% of the touristic infrastructure, 85% of the nutmeg crop and 60% of the cocoa tree stock. More than 80% of the public and commercial buildings were damaged.[17] Two active volcanos are situated in or near the island of Grenada. Both hurricanes and volcanos constitute a permanent threat to the islands.

Today, Grenada mainly relies on tourism and remittances for its foreign exchange. Traditionally very important agricultural exports such as cocoa, nutmeg and bananas are of decreasing importance, whereas the services sector is growing. Dependency upon agricultural exports makes the country sensitive to price fluctuations on the international markets, but also to destruction of crops by natural disasters.

Dependency upon tourism, remittances and financial services, left the economy severely affected by the 2008/2009 financial crisis.[18] Grenada has also engaged in a policy of citizenship in exchange for investment; such a passport-selling practice does not go uncriticized.

Social assistance programmes rely heavily on external (foreign) funding, which makes them very vulnerable as these funds could be terminated overnight.[19]

---

[17] Charles (2014), p. 27.

[18] P. Lewis, Social Policies in Grenada, *Social Policies in Small States Series*, N°.2, Commonwealth Secretariat/UNRISD, p. 47. Accessed on: http://www.unrisd.org/80256B3C005BCCF9/httpNetITFramePDF?ReadForm&parentunid=50F82735B441C66DC12577EB004CDC41&parentdoctype=book&netitpath=80256B3C005BCCF9/(httpAuxPages)/50F82735B441C66DC12577EB004CDC41/$file/Grenada%20(small).pdf.

[19] P. Lewis, Social Policies in Grenada, *Social Policies in Small States Series*, N°.2, Commonwealth Secretariat/UNRISD, p. 35. Accessed on: http://www.unrisd.org/80256B3C005BCCF9/httpNetITFramePDF?ReadForm&parentunid=50F82735B441C66DC12577EB004CDC41&parentdoctype=book&netitpath=80256B3C005BCCF9/(httpAuxPages)/50F82735B441C66DC12577EB004CDC41/$file/Grenada%20(small).pdf.

The lack of clear eligibility criteria and targeting procedures is considered by some to lead to abuse of social assistance benefits, as well as to non-take-up by others. Subjectivity in Safety Net implementation and processes open to interference fraud and corruption are the consequence.[20] It was even reported that the eligibility for social assistance depended, amongst other factors, upon subjective criteria and pressures by the local sections of the ruling party.[21] The reform process that the Social Safety Net is currently undergoing, under the name SEED, and which is funded by the World Bank, tries to provide answers to these flaws of social assistance in Grenada. But in the Throne Speech at the opening of the 10th Parliament (2018), the Governor General mentioned enduring weaknesses in the administration of some safety net programmes. Speaking on behalf of the Government, she said:

> My government has been apprised that some who do not merit certain benefits, have been able to access them because of weaknesses in the administration of those programmes, or because they provide false information that the checks and balances have not been able to flag.

She added that the government recognised and accepted responsibility for the weaknesses and abuses and would make every effort to ensure that all social programmes service the needs of those they are intended to serve.[22]

Also with respect to the public health care system, voices are heard complaining about favouritism and partisanship.[23]

Websites

www.health.gov.gd/
www.gov.gd/ministries//social_development.html
www.issa.int/en/country-details?countryId=GD&regionId=AME&filtered=false
www.mgovernance.net/needy-assistance#
www.nisgrenada.org/contributors
www.nisgrenada.org/contributors/details/self-employed
www.nowgrenada.com/2017/07/will-better-healthcare-made-available-grenadians/

[20]Ministry of Social development and Housing, Social Safety Net Policy framework. Final, December 2012. Accessed on: https://www.mgovernance.net/sites/mocr/files/docs/Documents/grn149451.pdf.

[21]P. Lewis, Social Policies in Grenada, *Social Policies in Small States Series*, N°.2, Commonwealth Secretariat/UNRISD, p. 32. Accessed on: http://www.unrisd.org/80256B3C005BCCF9/httpNetITFramePDF?ReadForm&parentunid=50F82735B441C66DC12577EB004CDC41&parentdoctype=book&netitpath=80256B3C005BCCF9/(httpAuxPages)/50F82735B441C66DC12577EB004CDC41/$file/Grenada%20(small).pdf.

[22]See: https://www.nowgrenada.com/2018/04/seed-not-suspended-only-safety-net-programmes-under-the-opm/.

[23]See: https://www.nowgrenada.com/2017/07/will-better-healthcare-made-available-grenadians/.

www.nowgrenada.com/2018/04/seed-not-suspended-only-safety-net-programmes-under-the-opm/

References

Charles L (2014) Country document on disaster risk reduction for Grenada. ECHO/UNISDR, Santo Domingo/Ciudad del Saber (Clayton)

Country Profiles (2020) International Social Security Association. https://www.issa.int/en_GB/country-profiles. Accessed 12 Feb 2020

Lewis P. Social Policies in Grenada. Social Policies in Small States Series, N°.2, Commonwealth Secretariat/UNRISD. Accessed on: http://www.unrisd.org/80256B3C005BCCF9/httpNetITFramePDF?ReadForm&parentunid=50F82735B441C66DC12577EB004CDC41&parentdoctype=book&netitpath=80256B3C005BCCF9/(httpAuxPages)/50F82735B441C66DC12577EB004CDC41/$file/Grenada%20(small).pdf

World Factbook (2020) Central Intelligence Agency. https://www.cia.gov/the-world-factbook/countries/grenada. Accessed 12 Feb 2020

Chapter 12
Guyana

12.1 Context

Guyana[1], originally under Dutch colonial rule, became a British possession in 1815. It declared independence in 1966. It is situated in the north-eastern part of South America, bordering the Northern Atlantic Ocean.

Today, the Co-operative Republic of Guyana has a presidential regime, where the pre-designated leader of the party winning the parliamentary elections becomes Head of State and Head of Government. The Prime Minister and other cabinet members are appointed by the President and need the confidence of the directly elected one-chamber Parliament, the National Assembly.

Guyana basically operates a two-party system. Both parties are socialist, but fiercely oppose each other as they are organised along ethno-cultural lines: the People's Progressive Party represent the Indo-Guyanese and the People's National Congress Reform Party act for the Afro-Guyanese, the latter being in power until the end of 2019. Both parties occupy about half of the seats in Parliament. The divide between the two major ethnic-cultural groups has resulted in political troubles, ethnic tensions, and incidents since independence.

Christians of many denominations account for about 60% of the population, Hindus account for about one fifth of the population and Muslims for about 7% (2012).

As a former colony of the British, Guyana remained a member of the Commonwealth after independence, which means that ties with the United Kingdom remain important.

As the only English-speaking country of South America, Guyana has close bonds with the English-speaking Caribbean countries, with which it is bound by the Caribbean Community (CARICOM) in a single market union.

[1]For data and figures, see: Country Profiles (2020) and World Factbook (2020).

D. Pieters, *Social Security Law in Small Jurisdictions*, The World of Small States 8,
https://doi.org/10.1007/978-3-030-78247-4_12

12.2 Legal Framework of Rights to Social Security

12.2.1 Constitutional Context

The Constitution of Guyana does not contain a right to social security as such.

That said, article 149B, introduced in 2013, reads as follows: "Every public sector worker shall enjoy an absolute and enforceable right to any pension or gratuity granted to him or her under the provision of any law or collective agreement of any kind whatsoever". The civil servants and other persons in public service enjoy specific pension arrangements, which we shall not discuss hereafter.[2]

Notwithstanding minor remnants of Roman-Dutch civil law, Guyana clearly belongs to the group of common law legal systems.

12.2.2 Social Security Legislation and Structure

National Insurance is regulated by the National Insurance and Social Security Act, N°15/1969 (as amended).[3] The National Insurance Scheme provides for the payment of all social insurance benefits, which are grouped under three branches:

- The long-term benefits, including old-age benefits, funeral benefits, invalidity pensions, survivors' benefits and constant attendance benefits;
- The short-term benefits, including sickness benefits, maternity benefits and sickness benefits/medical care; and
- The industrial benefits, including injury benefits, injury benefits/medical care, industrial death benefits and disablement benefits.

Old-age benefit is payable to insured persons who have reached the age of 60, and it can take the form of a Periodical Payment (Old-Age Pension) or a lump-sum (Old-Age Grant). Invalidity pension is paid to an insured person who is incapable of working if this is not the result of employment injury, the person has been incapable for a period of no less than 26 weeks, and is likely to be permanently incapable. Survivors' benefits are payable to or for the benefit of the dependants of a deceased insured person; it may take the form of a pension or a grant. The constant attendance benefit is a recurrent fixed amount payable to an invalidity or a disablement pensioner who is dependent on custodial care for performing the activities of daily living.

Sickness benefits are payable to an insured person who is temporarily incapable of working, if this is not the result of an employment injury. Maternity benefits (Allowance and Grant) are payable in the case of pregnancy and labour of a woman who is an insured person, or whose spouse is an insured person. Sickness benefit

---

[2]See Cap. 27 of the Laws of Guyana.

[3]Cap. 36.01 of the Laws of Guyana.

medical care involves the limited reimbursement of medical expenses incurred by an insured person who is in principle temporarily incapable of working. This benefit is available for medical care expenses incurred both locally and overseas.

Injury benefits, injury benefit medical care, industrial death benefits and disablement benefits all fall under the industrial benefit branch. These benefits are payable as a result of an injury or prescribed disease that arises during or directly as a result of employment.

In Guyana, health care is provided by both public and private suppliers. There are five levels of public sector health care in Guyana, starting from local health huts, posts and centres over district, community and regional hospitals, to the national hospital providing tertiary care. The public health care system provides health care services and goods. Essential health care is free; for other health care, an income test may be applied or a copayment required.

There is also a private health sector operating on a fee-for-service basis. Sickness benefit medical care and injury benefit medical care cover (part of) the costs of medical care that would normally have to be borne by the patient.

The Poor Relief Act of 1903[4] (with only minor amendments after independence) still governs social assistance. According to section 24 of the Act, every aged or infirm person and every child under the age of fourteen who is destitute and unable to earn sufficiently for their maintenance, shall be entitled to poor relief. The benefit is made conditional on children's regular attendance at school and at medical appointments. Poor people aged 65 and older may also qualify for a means-tested old-age pension according to the Old Age Pensions Act of 1944 (as amended).[5]

12.2.3 Enforcement of Constitutional and Statutory Rights

Claims and questions concerning the right to benefits of the NIS (and some other issues) are decided by the General Manager of NIS, with the possibility of appeal to an Appeals tribunal, composed of three members, one chosen by the Board to represent employers, another to represent insured persons and an independent chairman. Appeals against decisions of the tribunal must be decided by the independent National Insurance Commissioner, appointed by the president.

Questions concerning the status of insured persons or about the contribution states (and some other issues) are directly decided by the Board. Appeals (on questions of law) against the decisions of the Board must be heard by the High Court, with the possibility of higher appeal with the Supreme Court.

Decisions concerning (means-tested) old-age pensions may be appealed to the Old Age Appeal Boards that have been created for this purpose.

---

[4]Cap.36:02 Laws of Guyana.

[5]Cap.36:03 Laws of Guyana.

The Supreme Court of Judicature is the highest court on the Guyanese Judiciary. The High Court functions below it. In 2009, Guyana acceded to the Caribbean Court of Justice as final court of appeal, replacing the Judicial Committee of the Privy Council in London.

12.3 Population and the Personal Scope of the Social Security Schemes

12.3.1 General Data on the Population and Its Composition

The population, estimated at about 750,000 (2020), consists mainly of descendants from slaves coming from Africa and descendants of contract workers imported from India (after the abolition of slavery, in order to work on the sugar plantations). In 2012, the Afro-Guyanese accounted for about 29% and the Indo-Guyanese for about 40% of the population. People of mixed background made up 20% and the original Amerindian population about 10% of the population. The official language for all is English. Creole, Hindi, Urdu and indigenous languages are also spoken. The population is concentrated in the northeast in and around the capital Georgetown. Part of the population also lives along the Berbice River. The rest of the country is sparsely populated.

The labour force[6] was estimated at about 490,000 in 2017; in the same year the unemployment amounted to about 12%. About half of the employed labour force was holding informal jobs. About one-third of the Guyanese population is considered to live below the poverty line; indigenous people (Amerindians) are disproportionately affected.

Guyana's emigration rate is amongst the highest in the world, with about half of its citizens living abroad. Guyana is one of the largest recipients of remittances relative to GDP amongst Latin American and Caribbean counties. More than 80% of Guyanese nationals with tertiary level educations have emigrated. Yet due to important immigration from Venezuela, the number of immigrants and emigrants is in balance (net migration rate 0.0% in 2020).

[6]Bureau of Statistics Guyana, *Guyana Labour Force Survey*, July 2018. Accessed on: https://statisticsguyana.gov.gy/wp-content/uploads/2019/10/GLFS_2017_Quarter4_Final-PDF-1.4MB.pdf.

12.3.2 *Personal Scope of the Social Insurance and Social Assistance Schemes*

The National Insurance Scheme extends social insurance coverage on a compulsory basis to all persons between the ages of 16 and 60 years who are engaged in insurable employment. The following is considered to be insurable employment according to article 1 of schedule 2 of the National Insurance and Social Security Act: "employment in Guyana under any contract of service or apprenticeship, written or oral, and whether expressed or implied". According to article 2, such employment outside Guyana may also be taken into consideration to the benefit of some people employed on vessels or aircraft under Guyanese flag, members of the army or diplomatic personnel. Some types of employment may be excluded, such as casual work or work for a relative.

Coverage is also extended on a voluntary basis to persons who cease the indicated employment before reaching the age of 60, until the attainment thereof. Employed persons outside this age range who are in insurable employment are also covered, but for industrial benefits only.

Self-employed persons in the same age brackets are also covered, but not for benefits under the Industrial branch. A self-employed person is a person gainfully occupied in employment in Guyana who is not an employed person.

Unless exceptions are made, the National Insurance and Social Security Act also applies to persons employed by or under the State.[7]

Public health care is in principle available to all.

Whereas the Poor Relief Act does not mention specific residence or nationality requirements to be met, it is different as far as the (means-tested) old-age pension is concerned. Apart from an age requirement (65 or older) and the passing of a means and income test, the law on old-age pensions requires that the beneficiary must have been a citizen of Guyana for at least 10 years immediately preceding his/her claim and that he/she must have been ordinarily resident in Guyana during the 20 years immediately preceding the claim. Temporary absences from Guyana for an aggregate period of no more than 2 years during these 20 years are not taken into account.[8] The latter condition has not always been verified in the past.[9] The old-age pension will not be paid if the beneficiary is out of the country.[10]

[7]Art. 47 National Insurance and Social Security Act, Cap. 36:01 Laws of Guyana; see also Cap. 27 of the Laws of Guyana.

[8]Cap. 36:03 Laws of Guyana, art. 4.

[9]See: https://dpi.gov.gy/statement-on-old-age-pension-eligibility/ of 2016.

[10]Cap. 36:03 Laws of Guyana, art. 9.

12.4 Administration of Social Security

The National Insurance Scheme (NIS)[11] is governed by a Board and the Chief Executive Officer of the organisation is the General Manager who plans, organises and controls the internal administrative policies of NIS. The National Insurance Board, the members of which are appointed by the Minister of Finance, is accountable to the same Minister and is responsible for:

- The monitoring of the performance of the National Insurance Scheme; and
- The revision and approval of the organisation's procedures.

The mission of NIS is:

- To establish and maintain a system of Social Security through which enough income is secured to take the place of earnings when such are interrupted by sickness or accident.
- To provide for retirement through age, sudden death of a breadwinner and to meet exceptional expenses as those concerned with birth and death.
- To ensure that monies collected which have to be used for future payments are invested in such a manner that the economy of the country would reap maximum benefit.

Within NIS, a National Insurance Fund has been created to administer the financial means of NIS. Any assets forming part of the Fund may from time to time be invested by the Board in such securities as may be approved by the Administration of Finance.[12] Within the NIS, a National Insurance Medical Board for medical evaluations is established as well.

Public health care is coordinated by the Ministry of Health to ensure a uniform health care system across the country. However, the delivery of public health care is decentralised throughout the country and is administered by the Regional Democratic Councils with ministerial oversight vested in the Ministry of Communities.

Poor relief is administered by a board, called the Poor Relief Commission, appointed by the Minister of Social Protection. The Poor Relief Commission operates in Georgetown, and in the rest of the country through local boards at district level.[13]

The means tested old-age pension is administered by the Poor Relief Commissioners and local boards too, under supervision of the Minister of Social Protection.

It may be observed that the Minister of Social Protection has no competence in social insurance matters.

[11]See: http://nis.org.gy.

[12]Article 33 National Insurance and Social Security Act, Cap. 36:01 Laws of Guyana.

[13]Cap. 36:02 Laws of Guyana.

12.5 Coordination

First of all, let us recall that Guyana is party to the CARICOM Agreement on Social Security (CASS) of 1996. CASS protects nationals of the member states who belong to the following groups of workers: workers in transnational enterprises, workers in international transport and on ships, workers in diplomatic missions, consulates and international organisations, self-employed workers and itinerant workers (i.e. working in more than one member state) as well as eventually their dependant family members. To be covered by CASS, the worker must move to work or have worked in two or more member states. CASS includes in its material scope only (contributory) pensions in case of invalidity, disablement, old-age and retirement, survivor's benefits and death benefits. CASS contains a non-discrimination on the basis of nationality clause. CASS ensures that workers who have not made enough contributions to get an independent pension from their state's social security system enjoy a totalisation with contributions in other member states. The worker then also enjoys an apportioned pension in the first state. CASS leaves untouched pensions that have acquired solely on the basis of one member state's social security. Furthermore, CASS contains rules on posting of workers of international enterprises (in principle up to 2 years) and contains rules on assigning the competent country (or countries) for the other groups of workers.

Although many Guyanese emigrate for work outside the Caribbean, no bilateral social security coordination agreements between Guyana and another country could be found. There is only an arrangement with the United Kingdom concerning British officers designated for service in Guyana.[14]

However, the National Insurance and Social Security (persons abroad and voluntary contributors) regulations[15] determine that when a person in insurable employment ceases to be so employed in Guyana, but is employed (whether by the same or by a different employer) outside Guyana in continuation of such employment, that employment outside Guyana shall be treated as insurable employment for the period of 1 year or until the employment outside Guyana ceases. All this on condition that the employer has a place of business in Guyana and that the concerned person is ordinarily resident in Guyana.

Old-age and survivors' benefits of NIS are payable abroad, disability benefits of NIS are not, nor are (means-tested) old-age pensions.

No agreements between the Guyanese public health system and foreign health care authorities or providers could be found. However, let us recall that the sickness and injury benefit medical care involves limited reimbursement of medical expenses incurred both locally and overseas. Many Guyanese go to Northern America, Trinidad and Tobago or Cuba for their health care.

---

[14]Exchange of notes constituting an agreement concerning officers designated by the Government of the United Kingdom in the service of the Government of Guyana. Georgetown, 29 March 1971.

[15]Cap. 36:01 Laws of Guyana, pp. 64–68.

12.6 Additional Relevant Information

In the two rainy seasons, the country is prone to flash floods.

The Guyanese economy depends heavily upon the export of sugar, gold, bauxite, shrimp, timber and rice, which represents nearly 60% of the country's GDP and is highly susceptible to adverse weather conditions and fluctuations in commodity prices. Guyana recently drastically reduced the sugar production, but increased gold production. Guyana is hoping to become a petroleum producer.

Furthermore, the country constantly struggles with a shortage of skilled labour and a deficient infrastructure. Although remittances are a vital source of income for most citizens, the pervasive emigration of skilled workers is depriving Guyana of professionals in health care and other key sectors. Brain drain and the concentration of limited medical resources in Georgetown are hampering Guyana's ability to meet the health needs of its predominantly rural population.

The country also has issues as a source of and destination for human trafficking.

Websites

https://dpi.gov.gy/statement-on-old-age-pension-eligibility/ of 2016
http://nis.org.gy

References

Bureau of Statistics Guyana (2018) Guyana Labour Force Survey. Accessed on: https://statisticsguyana.gov.gy/wp-content/uploads/2019/10/GLFS_2017_Quarter4_Final-PDF-1.4MB.pdf

Country Profiles (2020) International Social Security Association. https://www.issa.int/en_GB/country-profiles. Accessed 12 Feb 2020

World Factbook (2020) Central Intelligence Agency. https://www.cia.gov/the-world-factbook/countries/guyana. Accessed 12 Feb 2020

Chapter 13
Iceland

13.1 Context

Iceland,[1] an island of 103,000 km^2 in the North Atlantic Ocean, is proud to have the oldest legislative assembly in the world, the *Althingi*,[2] established in 930. It has been independent for over 300 years, after which Iceland was ruled by Norway and later Denmark. Denmark granted limited home rule in 1874, the status of sovereign state under the Danish crown in 1918 and complete independence in 1944.

Iceland is a republic with a parliamentary government. The directly elected president is head of state and has a rather representative function. The government is headed by the prime minister and needs the confidence of the proportionally elected *Althingi*.[3]

Iceland has had a rather turbulent political life following the financial collapse in 2008/2009. One of the political challenges Iceland faces, concerns the loss of trust in politics, political parties and the parliament, especially after the collapse. Polarisation has since been part of the developments in party politics. The political scene is rather fragmented with 8 parties represented in the *Althingi*. Only the (liberal-conservative, Eurosceptic) Independence Party received a quarter of the votes, while all other parties received between 17% and 7% (i.e. the (Eurosceptic) Left-Green Movement, the Social-Democratic Alliance, the (Eurosceptic, centre-right) Centrist Party, the (centre-right, Eurosceptic) Progressive Party, the Pirate Party (in favour of direct democracy), the (centre-left) People's Party and the (centre-right) Reform Party). Governments are coalition Governments; since 2017, the

With special thanks to Mrs. Hildur Sverrisdóttir Röed for reviewing the report on Iceland.

[1]For data and figures, see: Country Profiles (2020) and World Factbook (2020).

[2]For more information about Althingi, see: https://www.althingi.is/english.

[3]Government of Iceland, *How is Iceland governed*? Accessed on: https://www.government.is/topics/governance-and-national-symbols/how-is-iceland-governed/.

D. Pieters, *Social Security Law in Small Jurisdictions*, The World of Small States 8,
https://doi.org/10.1007/978-3-030-78247-4_13

coalition has been formed by the Independence Party, the Progressive Party and the Left-Green Movement.

The Icelandic labour union movement has had one of the highest membership levels in the world in recent years. The Icelandic labour movement has a high level of organisation and also a high level of centralisation in confederations. This strength of the Icelandic labour union movement has been influential in shaping the society in Iceland.[4] In general we can say that Iceland has very strong and influential labour market partners, as the employers' organisations are also strong. Together they form a power block that can influence governmental decisions and policies, both through external pressures and through cooperative undertakings, within a corporatist framework.[5]

In a small-scale, mutually supportive society that is transparent and where the social fabric is strong, the role of self-help organisations of people suffering from a certain disease, charities or rescue and emergency services tends to be important. The sector of voluntary non-governmental organisations can count on broad participation.[6]

Iceland has historically had strong bonds with the other Nordic countries, especially Denmark and Norway. Icelandic policy makers have looked to these countries for models in economic and social matters, as witnessed by the influence of the latter systems on Icelandic politics and laws. This resulted in similar timing of many of the landmarks in the development of the welfare system. The principle of universalism of social security benefits, tax-financed benefits and services, public healthcare and education, even the entitlements of different welfare programmes, are all features that Iceland shares with the Nordic countries. However, considering the (lower) levels of the Icelandic benefits, Iceland is more comparable to Beveridgean countries like Australia, Ireland, Britain and New Zealand.[7] Icelandic benefits are indeed mostly flat-rate and to a high degree means or income tested.

Iceland plays an active role in the Nordic Council and in the Nordic Council of Ministers. In the welfare sphere, this resulted in the participation in the Icelandic leadership programme in the Nordic Council of Ministers, *the Nordic Welfare Watch* (2014), which examined the welfare consequences of financial crises.[8] Since then, a Nordic Welfare Forum is held biannually to deal with future challenges for the welfare systems.

---

[4]Olafsdottir and Olafsson (2014), p. 13.

[5]Olafsson (2011), p. 11, referring to Edvaldsson and Ólafsdóttir.

[6]Olafsson (2011), p. 21.

[7]S. Olafsson as referred to in Hauser Global Law School Programme, Researching Icelandic Law. Accessed on: https://www.nyulawglobal.org/globalex/Iceland.html.

[8]See: http://norden.diva-portal.org/smash/record.jsf?pid=diva2%3A1155301&dswid=-3517.

13.2 Legal Framework of Rights to Social Security

13.2.1 Constitutional Context

The Constitution of Iceland dates back to 1944 and has been amended various times since then. Article 76 of the Icelandic Constitution states:

> The law shall guarantee for everyone the necessary assistance in case of sickness, invalidity, infirmity by reason of old-age, unemployment and similar circumstances.
>
> The law shall guarantee for everyone suitable general education and tuition.
>
> For children, the law shall guarantee the protection and care which is necessary for their well-being.[9]

Iceland has a civil law legal system influenced by Danish law. Major sources of law in Iceland include the Constitution, statutes and regulations. Other legal resources are precedents and customary law.[10]

13.2.2 Social Security Legislation and Structure

Social security is mainly governed by statutes. The most important are:

- the Social Security Act, N° 100/2007;
- the Act on Health Insurance, N° 112/2008;
- the Act on Social Security Occupational Injury Insurance, N°45/2015;
- the Unemployment Insurance Act, N° 54/2006;
- the Social Assistance Act, N° 99/2007;
- the Municipalities Social Services Act, N° 40/1991;
- the Act on Mandatory Pension Insurance and on the Activities of Pension Funds, N°129/1997; and
- the Welfare Appeals Committee Act, N°85/2015 (all as amended).[11]

The social security pension insurance includes old-age pensions, invalidity pensions, age-related invalidity supplements, pension supplements, invalidity allowances and child pensions.

Health insurance covers both health care services and cash benefits. The cash benefits include the coverage of travel costs to obtain medical care, subsistence

[9]For the English translation, see: https://www.government.is/Publications/Legislation/Lex/?newsid=89fc6038-fd28-11e7-9423-005056bc4d74.

[10]Icelandic Financial Services Association, *The Icelandic Legal System*. Accessed on: https://www.sff.is/en/legislation/legal-system-iceland.

[11]Most laws to be found in English translation on: https://www.government.is/publications/legislation/.

expenses for the parent upon hospitalisation of a child in a distant hospital, as well as per diem sickness benefits.

Unemployment insurance provides unemployment benefits.

The Social Security Occupational Injury Insurance comprises medical assistance, per diem cash benefits, invalidity benefits and death grants.

General child benefits are paid with every child under the age of 18 years and are based on both parents/supporters' total income for the previous year.

The occupational pension funds provide life-long old-age pensions, disability pensions and death benefits. Currently, the occupational pension funds have slightly higher expenditures on pensions than the social security system (for state pensions) and the share of that system is set to increase slightly each year, as rights mature with time and new pensioners thus have higher occupational pensions than those already within the system. There is a system of income testing in the social insurance system that reduces the public pension as the occupational pension (and other earnings) increases.

State social assistance benefits consist of: single parent's allowance, child pension in connection with school studies or vocational training of young people aged 18–20, home-care allowance, spouse's benefit, homecare benefit, death grant, rehabilitation pension, household supplement, additional supplements, automobile purchase grant, automobile purchase supplements, automobile operation supplements and reimbursements of substantial expenses in connection with medical assistance and medications.

The basic social protection is at local level. General social assistance, handled at the municipality level, provides financial assistance to individuals and families who have an income and assets below the set amounts. The assistance may take the form of a loan or a grant.

13.2.3 Enforcement of Constitutional and Statutory Rights

Administrative appeals against administrative decisions concerning all social insurance and social assistance schemes are handled by the Welfare Appeals Committee.[12] The Welfare Appeals Committee consists of twelve members appointed as follows. The Minister appoints the chairman and three members on a fulltime basis. They shall meet the conditions of eligibility for appointment as District Court judges. The Minister shall also appoint eight other members of the committee and the same number of alternates. Three of them shall have law degrees; one shall be a physician and one shall have specialised knowledge in the field of child welfare. Care shall be taken to ensure that the necessary specialised knowledge within the fields covered by the committee exists at all times.

[12]See: https://www.urvel.is.

The Welfare Appeals Committee is independent and autonomous in its work. Its decisions are final at the administrative level and cannot be referred to a higher authority. Now all decided cases are published. In 2019, the appeals committee published 245 decisions on social security cases that had been appealed. In more than four fifths of those cases, the administrative decision was confirmed.

Decisions of the Welfare Appeals Committee can be appealed (both by the concerned persons and the administration) to the Court of Appeal, provided that specific conditions for appeal are met. Persons can also sue directly without first referring the decision of the social administration to the Welfare Appeals Committee.

Cases before the courts are few, but those cases usually attract attention. The main issues have been the entitlement ratio and the income-testing of the social security benefits against other income, especially pension payments from the mandatory employment pension scheme.

In special cases, and with the permission of the Supreme Court, it will be possible to refer the decision of the Court of Appeal to the Supreme Court.

13.3 Population and the Personal Scope of the Social Security Schemes

13.3.1 General Data on the Population and Its Composition

The population of Iceland was estimated at about 360,000 persons in 2020.[13] Nearly all of them live in settlements along the coast; about half of the population lives in the area of the capital Reykjavik. The population with a foreign background was estimated at 19% in 2018. The rest of the population is homogeneously Icelandic. More than two thirds of the population belong to the state church, the Evangelical Lutheran Church of Iceland.

The labour force was estimated at about 210,000 persons for 2020, about three quarters worked in the services sector. The unemployment rate was estimated at about 3% in 2020.[14]

The net migration rate for 2020 was estimated at 3.3 migrants per thousand.

[13]Information on the population, see: https://px.hagstofa.is/pxen/pxweb/en/Ibuar/Ibuar__mannfjoldi__1_yfirlit__yfirlit_mannfjolda/MAN00000.px; and https://statice.is/statistics/population/inhabitants/overview/.

[14]See: https://px.hagstofa.is/pxen/pxweb/en/Samfelag/Samfelag__vinnumarkadur__vinnumarkadsrannsokn__1_manadartolur/VIN00001.px.

13.3.2 *Personal Scope of the Social Insurance and Social Assistance Schemes*

Any person (legally) resident in Iceland is social security insured. However, certain conditions must be met to become entitled to benefits, for example regarding age, disability and periods of legal residence. Income and family circumstances can also influence entitlement.[15]

Insurance cover ceases to apply when the individual moves his/her residence from Iceland. Although no longer residing in Iceland, the following categories of people may upon application continue to be social security insured:

- for an additional period of up to 1 year, the person who was permanently domiciled in Iceland for a period of not less than five continuous years prior to departure when the purpose of the journey is not to seek medical treatment;
- for an additional period of up to 5 years, the person studying abroad; and
- for an additional period for up to 5 years, the person in question working abroad for a party that is established in Iceland and conducts operations in Iceland on condition that social security tax is paid in Iceland on his/her wages.

In the two last hypotheses, the accompanying spouse and children also continue their insurance.

At the end of 2019, about 35,500 people received and old-age social security pension and about 18,500 an invalidity pension from SIA.[16]

A health insured person is a person who is resident in Iceland and has been resident in Iceland for a minimum of six months. Children under the age of 18 who are resident in Iceland are covered by health insurance with their parents. A regulation may provide for exemptions from the requirement of 6 months' residence. The health insurance coverage will also be continued, even though the persons concerned no longer reside in Iceland for the same categories as mentioned above regarding the social security insurance, be it that there is no maximum period of 5 years established for the last two categories. Persons who have been granted refugee status or have obtained a residence permit on humanitarian grounds will also be covered by the health insurance when staying in Iceland.

'Residence' is defined in both the Social Security Act and the Health Insurance Act, as the 'domicile' according to the Domicile and Residence Act. This defines domicile as the place where you are registered as having your permanent residence, i.e. the place where you spend your free time, keep your belongings and where you sleep.[17]

---

[15] For detailed information see: Social Insurance in Iceland. Accessed on: https://www.asa.is/social-insurance-in-iceland.

[16] See: https://www.tr.is/tryggingastofnun/frettir/nanar/699/70-000-vidskiptavinir-fengu-greitt-i-desember.

[17] See: https://www.sjukra.is/english/; see also: EC, *Your Social Security rights in Iceland.* Accessed on: https://ec.europa.eu/social/main.jsp?catId=1114&langId=en.

Unemployment insurance covers wage-earners and self-employed individuals on the Icelandic labour market if they become unemployed. Wage-earners are understood to be persons who engage in paid employment in the service of others in at least 25% of full job capacity (full-time employment) each month, and for whom social security tax is paid according to the Social Security Tax Act. Self-employed individuals are persons who work at their own business or independent activity to the extent that they themselves are obliged to pay tax deductions at source regarding calculated wages and social insurance tax in respect of their work, either monthly or in another regular manner.

General child benefits are paid with respect to every child under the age of 18 years, provided that the child is domiciled in Iceland and dependant on a person or persons who have an unlimited tax liability in Iceland.

All employees and employers or self-employed persons are obliged to insure their (occupational) pension rights through membership in a pension fund from the age of 16 until the age of 70. There is generally no free choice of pension fund.

Social assistance benefits are only paid to persons who are legally domiciled in Iceland, in accordance with the Domicile and Residence Act.

13.4 Administration of Social Security

The Minister of Social Affairs exercises overall supervision of the Social Insurance Administration (SIA) as well as over the implementation of the Unemployment Insurance.

The Social Insurance Administration handles the implementation of the social security pension insurance. It is also responsible for paying the state social assistance. The general social assistance is administered by the municipalities.

The Minister of Health is responsible for the central administration of health insurance and contracting for health services and other assistance under the Health Insurance Act. He/she is also in charge of the Health Insurance Administration. The Health Insurance Administration is also responsible for the implementation of the social security occupational injury insurance.

The Board of SIA and the Board of governors of the Health Insurance Administration are appointed by the Minister of Social Affairs and the Minister of Health respectively; the director of SIA and the director general of the Health Insurance Administration are also appointed by the respective Ministers. The law stipulates that the director and the director general shall have completed studies at university level and shall have experience in management that is of practical use for their work. They must monitor the activities of the SIA and the Health Insurance Administration respectively and ensure that their operations are in accordance with their policy and remain within the framework of the national budget at any given time.

The unemployment insurance is paid from the Unemployment Insurance Fund, or for farmers, small fishing-vessel owners and lorry-drivers, from the Self-Employed Individuals' Insurance Fund. The Directorate of Labour manages the assets of the

Funds. The board of the Directorate of Labour appoints an allocation committee to ensure consistency in decisions concerning entitlements and penalties and to attend to the processing of cases. The allocation committee consists of one member nominated by the Icelandic Confederation of Labour; one nominated jointly by the Federation of State and Municipal Employees and the Alliance of University Graduates; one nominated by the Minister of Social Affairs; one nominated jointly by the minister of Social Affairs and the Union of Local Authorities in Iceland; and one shall be nominated by the Confederation of Icelandic Employers.

The Minister of Social affairs also appoints a nine-member board of the Unemployment Insurance Fund to ensure the fund has sufficient resources to meet its obligations. The Board must also draw up budgets covering the operation and payments made. Two of the directors (members of the board) shall be nominated by the Icelandic Confederation of Labour; one shall be nominated by the Federation of State and Municipal Employees; one shall be nominated by the Alliance of University Graduates; one shall be nominated by the Minister of Social Affairs; one shall be nominated by the Union of Local Authorities in Iceland and two shall be nominated by the Confederation of Icelandic Employers.

The Minster of Social Affairs likewise appoint a Board of the Self-Employed Individuals' Insurance Fund. One director (member of the board) shall be nominated by the Icelandic Farmers' Association; one by the Union of Small Fishing Vessel Owners and one by the National Federation of Lorry-Drivers. The Minister shall appoint one director, without nomination, who shall be the chairman of the board of the fund.

The Directorate of Labour, operating under the Ministry of Social Affairs, is also responsible for the Maternity and Paternity Leave Fund.[18]

The Directorate is established in the capital and has 8 regional offices around the country.[19] In recent years, both social partners have asked to transfer the custodianship of the Unemployment Insurance fund from the public Directorate of Labour to labour market partners.[20]

Child benefits are administered by the Directorate of Internal Revenue[21] operating under the Minister of Finance and Economic Affairs.

Social assistance in Iceland is twofold and comprises both state social assistance and local general social assistance.[22] The state social assistance is the responsibility of the Social Insurance Administration. General social assistance is administered by the local authorities. Social assistance at state and local level is supervised by the Ministry of Social Affairs. Local authorities are also responsible for social services, such as home help, institutions and the care of children and young people, as well as

---

[18]See Act on Maternity/paternity and Parental Leave, N°95/2000.

[19]See: https://vinnumalastofnun.is/en/about-us.

[20]Olafsdottir and Olafsson (2014), p. 50.

[21]See: https://www.rsk.is/english/individuals/child-benefits.

[22]Nordic Social Statistical Committee, 'Social Protection in the Nordic Countries; Scope, Expenditure and Financing', no. 63, 2015/2016, p. 19.

disabled people. Local councils, in cooperation with the national government, are also responsible for services to elderly people.[23]

The mandatory occupational pension scheme is administered by individual occupational pension funds, regulated by the Ministry of Finance and Economic Affairs and under the supervision of the Financial Supervisory Authority. The Directorate of Internal Revenue of the Ministry of Finance and Economic Affairs is responsible for ensuring that the pension contributions are paid for each individual subject to mandatory (occupational) pension insurance.

The occupational pension funds, the sickness funds, the occupational, educational and retraining system, the life-long learning system and rehabilitation and activation funds are operated mainly by the unions or the social partners. The occupational pension funds are operated from separate institutions that are co-governed by representatives of the unions' and employers' federations.[24] Unions also have sickness funds (paid out of bargaining agreements) that provide supplementary grants to pay for costs of minor operations, physiotherapy, glasses etc.

13.5 Coordination

By virtue of the European Economic Area Agreement, the EU coordination mechanism also applies to Iceland. The EU coordination mechanism provides:

- the principle of non-discrimination on the basis of nationality;
- rules concerning the determination of the applicable legislation;
- the exportability of acquired social security benefits;
- the aggregation and apportionment of periods of residence, work or insurance; and
- administrative co-operation agreements.

The EU mechanism applies to all EEA citizens and their family members insured under the social security of a member state and to all social insurance schemes.

The revised Convention on Social Security between the Nordic countries (2012, into force 2014) replaces the previous Nordic Convention on Social Assistance and Social Service, which itself had replaced the previously existing bilateral treaties between the concerned Nordic states. The Nordic convention facilitates mobility between Finland, Sweden, Norway, Denmark and Iceland and gives people travelling between the countries the right to social security benefits. The convention simplifies work between social security administrations of the Nordic countries.

[23]See The Municipalities' Social Services Act, N°40/1991 and the Act on the Affairs of the Elderly, N°125/1999; as well as the Act on the Affairs of Disabled Persons, N°59/1992; see also Nordic Social Statistical Committee, 'Social Protection in the Nordic Countries; Scope, Expenditure and Financing', no. 63, 2015/2016.

[24]Olafsdottir and Olafsson (2014), p. 52.

The agreement supplements (and in principle does not alter) the social security coordination mechanism agreed between the countries of the European Economic Area. The agreement expands the application of the EU's social security regulations to include the Faroe Islands and Greenland, as well as citizens of non-union countries who reside in and move between the Nordic countries. It furthermore may extend to the rights of the migrant workers according the EU mechanism.

Iceland has concluded bilateral coordination agreements with the United States of America (2016, into force 2019)[25] and Canada (1988, into force 1989);[26] these agreements are restricted to enumerated pension benefits.

The US Agreement with Iceland, which was signed on 27 September 2016, is similar to US social security agreements already in force with many other countries.[27] The Agreement eliminates dual social security coverage. The Agreement also helps eliminate situations where workers suffer a loss of benefit rights because they have divided their careers between the two countries. Under the Agreement, workers may qualify for partial US benefits or partial Icelandic benefits based on combined (totalised) work credits from both countries.[28]

The Agreement with Canada also contains provisions on equality of treatment of each other's nationals, exportability of the pensions, designation of the competent country, rules concerning the satisfaction of required periods of insurance (aggregation and apportionment) and administrative co-operation arrangements.

Persons receiving social security pension insurance benefits living abroad will only receive their benefits when international agreements have been concluded to that effect.

Apart from the provisions of the EU/EEA arrangements within the framework of the EU coordination regulations or the directive on the mobility of patients, and what has been agreed within the context of the Nordic Council, predetermined health care abroad is also possible by virtue of domestic Icelandic law.[29] The Icelandic Health Insurance will cover predetermined medical treatment abroad in the following cases:

- If medical treatment cannot be provided in Iceland and the treatment is not experimental or long-time care; or
- If the necessary medical treatment is not provided in Iceland within a time limit that can be justified by medical examination, based on the current health status of the patient and the likely progression of the disease.

[25]See: https://www.ssa.gov/international/Agreement_Texts/iceland.html.

[26]See: https://www.canada.ca/en/services/benefits/publicpensions/cpp/cpp-international/iceland.html.

[27]PWC, United States; More social security agreements—consider both new and existing mobile populations, 2019, see: https://www.pwc.com/gx/en/services/people-organisation/publications/assets/pwc-us-social-security-agreements-with-slovenia-and-iceland.pdf.

[28]See: https://www.federalregister.gov/documents/2019/02/26/2019-03271/agreement-on-social-security-between-the-united-states-and-iceland-entry-into-force.

[29]See: https://www.sjukra.is/english/health-insurance-abroad/medical-treatment-abroad/.

In both cases, the patient's doctor sends an application for treatment abroad. A special committee/advisory board evaluates the application. If the application is approved, the Icelandic Health Insurance Administration will pay for the medical care, travel expenses and living expenses (fixed amount). If a patient needs an escort, professional or other, the patient's doctor must apply for the escort and confirm that it is necessary for the patient. The Health Insurance Administration will determine where the health insured person should undergo treatment abroad. If a health insured person opts for treatment in another and more expensive location abroad than decided by the Administration, health insurance will only pay the cost that would have been paid at the location decided by the Administration.

Iceland, as a member of the European Economic Area, has adhered to the EU coordination mechanism. Moreover, the cross-border health care directive 2011/24/ESB gives patients the right to receive medical care in another EEA country and be reimbursed for the same amount it would have cost in Iceland.

13.6 Additional Relevant Information

It is important to remember that Iceland is a volcanic island with regular earthquakes and volcanic activity. In 1875, the eruption of the Askja volcano devastated Iceland, causing famine and massive emigration. This environmental situation did however not lead to specific social security measures.

Since independence, the economy has developed substantially, mainly based on the fishing industry. The economy diversified after the country joined the European Economic Area in 1994. The Icelandic labour market is characterised by a high level of union density, high labour force participation rate, long working hours and low incidence of part-time employment, as well as late retirement.

In the early years of this century Icelandic banks expanded aggressively in foreign markets; consumers and businesses borrowed heavily in foreign currencies. In 2008/2009, Iceland was especially hard hit by the global financial crisis. The international financial crisis caused the bubble built in the previous years to burst. The (previously overvalued) national currency, the *Krona*, lost much of its value in relation to other currencies and the three major Icelandic banks collapsed. Households, firms and eventually also the government were confronted with serious debt problems. The real disposable earnings of households fell by almost 20%. Lower wages, along with shorter working hours and increased unemployment, as well as the higher debt burden, were the main aspects of the cuts in living standards that the crisis inflicted on households.[30]

Before the financial crisis, the Icelandic welfare was characterised by ample social services and rather modest social security cash benefits. This changed since the crisis years:

[30]Olafsdottir and Olafsson (2014), p. 10.

> Public expenditures on education and health care were significantly cut, (...), at the same time as transfers to households were increased. The policy of the left-wing government that came to power in early 2009 was to soften the crisis consequences for the lower income groups and balance the budget by a mixture of tax increases and expenditure cuts. Public welfare expenditures were targeted towards the lower and middle-income groups. Hence, expenditures on transfers to households have in fact been raised, mostly on unemployment benefits and household debt relief, but also on minimum pension guarantees and social assistance.[31]

The economy has since recovered, fueled primarily by a tourism and construction boom. In 2016, inflation had already dropped below 2% and unemployment below 3%; at the beginning of 2020 unemployment was around 3.5%.[32]

In their 2014 report, Katrin Olafsdottir and Stefan Olafsson wrote:

> Another element of difference that should be taken into account is the exceptionally small size of the population in Iceland (about 325.000). The small scale does not free Iceland from having the main institutional architecture that a modern affluent society requires. Hence, resources for common tasks may be small in absolute numbers, even though relative proportions may be similar. The small scale of the society makes for more transparency and better connections between grassroots and top levels of the governance system. This may provide good conditions for voices from below to be heard in higher places, while at the same time increasing the danger of cronyism.[33]

Websites

https://hagstofa.is/media/51192/iceland_in_figures_2018.pdf
http://norden.diva-portal.org/smash/record.jsf?pid=diva2%3A1155301&dswid=-3517
https://px.hagstofa.is/pxen/pxweb/en/Ibuar/Ibuar__mannfjoldi__1_yfirlit__yfirlit_mannfjolda/MAN00000.px
https://px.hagstofa.is/pxen/pxweb/en/Samfelag/Samfelag__vinnumarkadur__vinnumarkadsrannsokn__1_manadartolur/VIN00001.px
https://statice.is/statistics/population/inhabitants/overview/
https://vinnumalastofnun.is/en/about-us
www.althingi.is/english
www.asa.is/social-insurance-in-iceland
www.canada.ca/en/services/benefits/publicpensions/cpp/cpp-international/iceland.html
www.federalregister.gov/documents/2019/02/26/2019-03271/agreement-on-social-security-between-the-united-states-and-iceland-entry-into-force
www.government.is/publications/legislation/

---

[31] Olafsdottir and Olafsson (2014), p. 9.

[32] https://hagstofa.is/media/51192/iceland_in_figures_2018.pdf.

[33] Olafsdottir and Olafsson (2014), pp. 13–14.

www.government.is/Publications/Legislation/Lex/?newsid=89fc6038-fd28-11e7-9423-005056bc4d74
www.pwc.com/gx/en/services/people-organisation/publications/assets/pwc-us-social-security-agreements-with-slovenia-and-iceland.pdf
www.rsk.is/english/individuals/child-benefits
www.ssa.gov/international/Agreement_Texts/iceland.html
www.sjukra.is/english/
www.sjukra.is/english/health-insurance-abroad/medical-treatment-abroad/
www.tr.is/tryggingastofnun/frettir/nanar/699/70-000-vidskiptavinir-fengu-greitt-i-desember
www.urvel.is

References

Country Profiles (2020) International Social Security Association. https://www.issa.int/en_GB/country-profiles. Accessed 12 Feb 2020
EC. Your Social Security rights in Iceland. Accessed on: https://ec.europa.eu/social/main.jsp?catId=1114&langId=en
Government of Iceland. How is Iceland governed? Accessed on: https://www.government.is/topics/governance-and-national-symbols/how-is-iceland-governed/
Icelandic Financial Services Association. The Icelandic Legal System. Accessed on: https://www.sff.is/en/legislation/legal-system-iceland
Nordic Social Statistical Committee. 'Social Protection in the Nordic Countries; Scope, Expenditure and Financing', no. 63, 2015/2016
Olafsdottir K, Olafsson S (2014) Economy, Politics and Welfare in Iceland; Booms, busts and challenges. NorMod 2030, Fafo, Sub-report 4
Olafsson S (2011) Iceland's Social Inclusion Environment. Social Research Centre University of Iceland, Working Paper no. 2
World Factbook (2020) Central Intelligence Agency. https://www.cia.gov/the-world-factbook/countries/iceland. Accessed 12 Feb 2020

Chapter 14
Liechtenstein

14.1 Context

Liechtenstein is a double landlocked country situated between Austria and Switzerland. First established in the eighteenth century as a principality within the Holy Roman Empire of the German Nation, it became fully independent in 1806.

The Principality of Liechtenstein is a constitutional monarchy with the Reigning Prince as head of state; currently the Reigning Prince is permanently replaced by the regent in his official duties. The Head of Government is the prime minister; he/she and the other members of the Government are answerable to both the monarch and the Parliament. The monarch appoints the ministers nominated by the Parliament.

The Parliament, the *Landtag*, consists of one chamber of 25 members that is directly elected according to the system of proportional representation in two constituencies, Upper Country and Lower Country. Traditionally there are two main political parties, both of Christian-Democrat conservative tendency: The Fatherland Union (VU) and the Progressive Citizens' Party (FBP), which obtained 8 and 9 seats respectively at the last election. A newer party, the right-wing

With special thanks to Prof. Dr. iur. Patricia Schiess, Head of Research Law, Liechtenstein Institute in Bendern, Principality of Liechtenstein, for her critical reading and additional comments. Thanks also to Mag. Patricia Hornich, LL.M., Research Associate, Liechtenstein Institute in Bendern, Principality of Liechtenstein.

Apart from the general comparative sources, Country Profiles (2020) and World Factbook (2020), we also consulted:

– Office of Statistics of the Principality of Liechtenstein, Liechtenstein in Figures 2020, Vaduz 2020. Accessed on: https://www.llv.li/files/as/liechtenstein_in_figures_2020.pdf;

– Liechtensteinische AHV-IV-FAK-Anstalten, Geschäftsbericht 2019, Vaduz 2020. Accessed on https://www.ahv.li/fileadmin/user_upload/Dokumente/Ueber/Jahresberichte/AHV-IV-FAK-Jahresbericht%2D%2D2019.pdf; and

– AXA Winterthur, All you need to know about social security. Pension system in the Principality of Liechtenstein, 2013. Accessed on: https://www.igpinfo.com/igpinfo/public_documents/ss_summaries/Liechtenstein.pdf.

D. Pieters, *Social Security Law in Small Jurisdictions*, The World of Small States 8,
https://doi.org/10.1007/978-3-030-78247-4_14

conservative-nationalist Independents (DU) obtained 5 seats. The Free List (FL), founded in 1985 as a democratic and ecological alternative, obtained 3 seats. The Government is mostly made up of a coalition of the VU and FBP, the larger one providing the Prime Minister and two Ministers, and the smaller coalition partner the other two Ministers. Both Upper Country and Lower Country are guaranteed two Ministers.[1]

The Liechtenstein population is about three-quarters Roman-Catholic, whereas various Protestant denominations, with the Protestant Reformed ahead, account for about 17% of the population. About 6% of the inhabitants are Muslim.

The employers' associations[2] and the medical association (*Ärztekammer*)[3] are powerful and well organised to defend the interests of their members.

There is an important public interest (as indicated in the press, media and politics) in social security matters, especially for items such as the financial sustainability of the AHV pensions and the health care system, the medical overconsumption and the export of benefits abroad.

Liechtenstein, as a small country, has always entertained strong ties with its two neighbouring states, Austria and Switzerland. Until the end of World War I, Liechtenstein was most closely tied to Austria. Afterwards, the ties with Switzerland became stronger. Liechtenstein has a customs and monetary union with Switzerland. United with Switzerland in the European Free Trade Association (EFTA), it also strengthened its ties with Austria and the rest of the European Union, when EFTA and the European Union set up the European Economic Area (EEA) in 1995. Liechtenstein is also member of the Schengen Area.

14.2 Legal Framework of Rights to Social Security

14.2.1 Constitutional Context

The current constitution of Liechtenstein dates back to 1921, but has been revised several times. The most important constitutional reform dates from 2003.

The following articles of the Liechtenstein Constitution (LV) are relevant to social security:[4]

Article 18: "The State shall be responsible for the public health system, shall support measures for the care of the sick, and shall seek by way of law to combat alcoholism and work-shy persons."

[1] See: https://www.regierung.li/regierung.

[2] Liechtensteinische Industrie- und Handelskammer: https://www.lihk.li/en/ and Wirtschaftskammer für Gewerbe, Handel und Dienstleistung: https://wirtschaftskammer.li/.

[3] Liechtensteinische Ärztekammer: https://www.aerztekammer.li.

[4] See: https://socialprotection-humanrights.org/instru/social-security-provisions-in-the-constitution-of-liechtenstein/; For an extensive commentary article by article, see: Liechtenstein-Institut (ed.), Kommentar zur liechtensteinischen Verfassung. Online-Kommentar, Bendern 2016. Accessed on: https://verfassung.li/.

Article 20 § 1:

To improve the ability to work and to advance its economic interests, the State shall promote and support agriculture, the cultivation of alps, trades and industry; in particular, it shall promote insurance against damage that endangers work and goods and shall take measures to combat such damage.

Article 25:

Public services for the poor shall be administered by the municipalities under the conditions set forth in specific laws. The State shall, however, exercise overall supervision of such services. It may grant appropriate subsidies to the municipalities, especially for the proper care of orphans, the mentally ill, the terminally ill, and the infirm.

Article 26: "The State shall support and promote insurance schemes for health, old age, disability, and fire."

These articles belong to the chapter of the Constitution on the tasks of the state and not to the chapter on fundamental rights and duties of the citizens. They are therefore not qualified as "the rights guaranteed by the Constitution" ("*verfassungsmässig gewährleistete Rechte*") mentioned in Article 104 LV. According to jurisprudence, the Constitutional Court cannot be used by individuals (in an "*Individualbeschwerde*") to have court decisions tested on their conformity with these articles. But in principle, all legislation can be tested on conformity with these articles in the context of a direct challenging of the constitutionality when the Government, one of the municipalities or a court asks for such a control (*Normkontrollverfahren*).[5]

Liechtenstein is a civil law country, with a strong influence of Austrian law, and since the end of World War I of Swiss law.[6] The latter is especially the case in administrative law, labour law and also social security law. German law has also influenced the law of Liechtenstein. Of course, the directives and regulations incorporated into the EEA Agreement are also of great importance for Liechtenstein.

[5]Schiess Rütimann (2016a). Accessed on: https://verfassung.li/Einführende_Bemerkungen_zum_III._Hauptstück.

[6]S. Wolf et al. (2018), p. 186. Accessed on: https://www.um.edu.mt/sst/sst12nov2018.

14.2.2 Social Security Legislation and Structure

Social security consists of a number of social insurances[7] and social assistance, all of them regulated by a statute and application ordinances.[8]

The statutes that govern the social insurances are the statutes concerning:

- the Old-Age and Survivors' Insurance (*Alters- und Hinterlassenenversicherung*, hereafter AHV) of 1952;[9]
- the Invalids' Insurance (*Invalidenversicherung*, hereafter IV) of 1959;[10]
- the Complementary Benefits of the Old Age, Survivors' and Invalids' Insurance (*Ergänzungsleistungen zur Alters-, Hinterlassenen- und Invalidenversicherung*, hereafter EL) of 1965;[11]
- the Family Allowances (*Familienzulage*, hereafter FAK) of 1985;[12]
- the Unemployment and Insolvency Compensation (*Arbeitslosenversicherung*, hereafter ALV) of 2010;[13]
- the mandatory Accident Insurance (*Unfallversicherung*, hereafter UVers) of 1989;[14]
- the Occupational Pension Plans (*betriebliche Personalvorsorge*, hereafter BPV) of 1987;[15]
- the Sickness Insurance (*Krankenversicherung*, hereafter KV) of 1971;[16] and
- the Blind People Allowance (*Blindenbeihilfe*) of 1970;[17]

all as later amended.

Social assistance (*Sozialhilfe*, hereafter SH) is governed by a statute of 1984, later amended.[18]

---

[7]We use the notion social insurance in its internationally accepted meaning; in Liechtenstein it may be that the notion is reserved for these arrangements which are contribution based, excluding thus schemes wholly financed by the state. See in this respect: Schiess Rütimann (2016c), nrs. 40–42. Accessed on https://verfassung.li/Art._26.

[8]All laws of Liechtenstein are officially coordinated and can be found on https://www.gesetze.li/konso/suche under the appropriate reference number. The statutes themselves are usually indicated by the abbreviation of the subject, see hereafter e.g. AHV, followed by a G for Gesetz or statute.

[9]Coordinated laws of Liechtenstein, LR 831.10.

[10]Coordinated laws of Liechtenstein, LR 831.20.

[11]Coordinated laws of Liechtenstein, LR 831.30.

[12]Coordinated laws of Liechtenstein, LR 836.0.

[13]Coordinated laws of Liechtenstein, LR 837.0.

[14]Coordinated laws of Liechtenstein, LR 832.20.

[15]Coordinated laws of Liechtenstein, LR 831.40.

[16]Coordinated laws of Liechtenstein, LR 832.10.

[17]Coordinated laws of Liechtenstein, LR 854.0.

[18]Coordinated laws of Liechtenstein, LR 851.0.

AHV, IV, FAK and ALV are labelled as first pillar insurances whereas the BPV and the UVers are seen as second pillar insurances.[19]

The AHV provides wage-related old-age pensions (plus eventually also a child pension), widow(er)s' pensions, orphan pensions and some assisting tools for the handicapped. To benefit from AHV benefits, the insured person must have been contributing to the AHV for at least 1 year. The IV provides reintegration measures, and in case the worker is unable to recover earnings capacity, wage-related invalidity pensions. The family benefits from FAK include child allowances, birth allowances and lone parent allowances.

There are also two sorts of benefits for people who need the care and assistance of another person, called *Hilflosenentschädigung* and *Betreuungs- und Pflegegeld*, as well as allowances of a fixed amount for the sight-impaired, called *Blindenbeihilfe*. They are administered by the administration of the AHV, IV and FAK.

The complementary benefits EL complement the income of AHV and IV pensioners up to a minimum income. The monthly cash benefits are means tested. EL also includes a compensation of the health care or handicap costs. *Hilflosenentschädigung* and *Betreuungs- und Pflegegeld* are stipulated in the statue of the Complementary Benefits of the Old Age, Survivors' and Invalids' Insurance, so that—as for the services of EL—only persons living in Liechtenstein may receive benefits.

The ALV provides wage-related unemployment benefits, partial unemployment benefits and compensation of wages in case of insolvency of the employer. The ALV also pays contributions to the Occupational Pension Plan BPV of the worker.

The UVersG makes accident insurance mandatory; it covers the risk of an occupational accident or a non-occupational accident. The accident insurance covers daily benefits in case of temporary incapacity, disability pensions and survivors' pensions, indemnities for physical and mental impairment, coverage of medical treatment and transportation costs, and a care allowance.

The BPVG makes it mandatory to insure workers with an Occupational Pension Plan BPV. The BPV should include retirement, disability and child pensions, as well as widow(er)'s pensions and orphan's pensions. Exceptionally, the pension plan may accept withdrawal of a lump sum instead of a recurrent pension.

The KVG makes sickness insurance compulsory; it covers the risk of becoming ill and being pregnant/giving birth (maternity leave). The insurance must cover defined health care services and goods, and wage-related income replacement sickness benefits for temporary work incapacity of the worker.

In addition to social services, social assistance (*Sozialhilfe*) also includes means-tested cash benefits that enable families and persons to live a dignified existence and overcome extraordinary problems that they cannot overcome themselves or with the

[19]See: https://www.li-makler.li/downloads/files/Uebersicht%20Sozialver.%202020.pdf.

The third pillar stands for the individual private arrangements. On the three pillar concept, followed, but not legally enshrined, in Liechtenstein, see: Schiess Rütimann (2016c), nrs. 28–32. Accessed on: https://verfassung.li/Art._26.

help of others. Social assistance is subsidiary to social insurance benefits. It is paid to persons resident in Liechtenstein who are not entitled to social security benefits or—if they are—if their pensions of social insurance are too low.

In general, it can be said that most social security legislation in Liechtenstein is strongly inspired by the Swiss social security legislation. This is especially the case for the AHVG, the IVG, the ELG, the ALVG, the UVersG, the BPVG, the KVG, the *Hilflosenentschädigung*, but not for the *Betreuungs- und Pflegegeld* (inspired by Austria) and not so much for the family allowance. However, the Liechtenstein arrangements are no copy of the Swiss ones and even if a law was at first more or less a copy of its Swiss model,[20] some important differences may exist, mainly as far as the level of benefits (higher in Liechtenstein) and the administrative organisation of social security is concerned. Liechtenstein also lacks a general law on social security that unifies concepts and procedures for the various schemes (as Switzerland has).[21]

14.2.3 Enforcement of Constitutional and Statutory Rights

The procedures to challenge the decisions of the various social security administrations[22] differ and are not systematically designed.[23]

Appeals concerning AHV-IV-FAK are first dealt with internally with possibility of appeal with the Court of Appeal *(Obergericht)*, and further by way of revision with the Supreme Court *(Oberster Gerichtshof OGH)*. Appeals against decisions concerning the EL taken by AHV-IV-FAK go to the Government and appeals against decisions of the Health Office concerning the maternity benefits also go to the Government.

Appeals against decisions of the accident insurers (under UVersG) and appeals against decisions of private sickness funds (under KVG) are first dealt with internally with possibility of appeal with the Court of Justice *(Landgericht)*. According to the BPVG, appeals against decisions of the Financial Market Authority FMA or of the Security Fund can be lodged with the Complaints Commission of the Financial Market Authority; appeals against their decision are possible with the Administrative Court.[24]

Decisions of the National Economy Office regarding unemployment insurance and decisions of the Social Services Office can be appealed to the Government and

[20]When Liechtenstein copies foreign norms, they are copied literally so that the Liechtenstein administration and courts can copy the foreign jurisprudence too.

[21]P.M. Schiess Rütimann, *Kommentar zur liechtensteinischen Verfassung. Online Kommentar*, Bendern 2016, Art. 26, nrs. 13–14 and 17–21. Accessed on: https://verfassung.li/Art._26; Weiss (2019), pp. 66–68.

[22]For this chapter see: Weiss (2019), pp. 58–68, and Weiss, Nachtrag (2019), p. 102.

[23]Weiss (2019), p. 65.

[24]Art. 23b BPVG.

the governmental decision can be appealed to the Administrative Court.[25] Experts from abroad, generally from Switzerland, are called in for the evaluation of long term work incapacity.

The Liechtenstein judiciary is composed of a Court of Justice *(Landgericht)*, the Court of Appeal (*Obergericht*), and, at the top, the Supreme Court (*Oberster Gerichtshof OGH*). There is also an Administrative Court (*Verwaltungsgerichtshof*) that hears appeals from government actions. To preserve impartiality in a small country, the Administrative Court and the Constitutional Court have a mixed composition: for many years, three of their five judges are Liechtensteiner, one Swiss and one Austrian. In the ordinary courts, many judges are also judges with Austrian nationality who have previously worked in Austrian courts; a few come from Switzerland. The president of the Supreme Court is traditionally a well-respected judge of a higher court in Tyrol in Austria.

There is also a Constitutional Court (*Staatsgerichtshof StGH*) that tests the constitutionality of laws. The Constitutional Court may be addressed by individuals to preserve their fundamental rights (given by the Constitution or international Conventions as the EHCR), but not for testing the conformity with the provisions of the tasks of the state. When a law or regulation in a case is found to be contrary to the Constitution, the Constitutional Court squashes the decision and sends it back for decision to the previous court (*Kassation*). In addition, the Constitutional Court cancels the concerned article(s) of the law or regulation.

In matters dealing with the European Economic Area (EEA) and its law, such as the social security coordination regulations, Liechtenstein recognises the competence of the EFTA Court.[26]

14.3 Population and the Personal Scope of the Social Security Schemes

14.3.1 General Data on the Population and Its Composition[27]

The population was estimated at approximately 39,000 (2020), of which two thirds are of Liechtensteiner nationality. About 10% are Swiss and about 6% of Austrian citizenship; other nationalities account for less than 5%.

[25]P.M. Schiess Rütimann, in: Liechtestein-Institut (ed.), *Kommentar zur liechtensteinischen Verfassung. Online-Kommentar*, Bendern 2016, Article 25 nr. 80 and Art. 26, nrs. 49-53. Accessed on: https://verfassung.li/Art._25 and https://verfassung.li/Art._26.

[26]See EFTA Court Case E-13/15 Abuelo Insua Juan Bautista v Liechtensteinische Invalidenversicherung concerning the Coordination of social security systems: https://eftacourt.int/cases/e-13-15/.

For a survey of sentences concerning social security from about 2008 util 2014 see: Augustin (2015), pp. 1–12.

[27]See also, Brunhart (2019).

Liechtenstein has a net migration rate of 4.9 per thousand.

The labour force was estimated at 39,500 in 2018; more than half of them are commuters who come from Austria, Switzerland or Germany daily. About two-thirds of the active population works in the services sector. About half of the residents are in gainful employment. The unemployment rate is estimated at less than 1.7% (2018).

14.3.2 Personal Scope of the Social Insurance and Social Assistance Schemes[28]

The AHV[29] defines its personal scope as follows:

the following are mandatorily insured:

- persons who have their civil law domicile (*Wohnsitz*) in Liechtenstein;
- persons who exercise a professional activity in Liechtenstein;
- persons posted by an employer with establishment in Liechtenstein on condition that the employee is paid by the Liechtenstein employer and that an insurance relation pre-existed to the posting; and
- persons who work abroad in the Liechtenstein public service;

always on the condition that this situation is not for too brief a period.

Persons who belong to a foreign pension insurance are excluded from the obligatory insurance, in so far their insurance in Liechtenstein too would constitute an unreasonable double levy.

The following can join the AHV on a voluntary basis:

- Liechtenstein citizens living abroad aged less than 50 years old; and
- Liechtenstein citizens leaving the mandatory insurance;

---

[28]The statistical data were provided by P. Schiess of the Liechtenstein Institute and are based on:

- for persons working in Liechtenstein: https://www.llv.li/files/as/ibeschaeftigung_ve_2019.pdf;
- for AHV, IV and FAK: Liechtensteinische AHV-IV-FAK-Anstalten, Geschäftsbericht 2019, Vaduz 2020: https://www.ahv.li/fileadmin/user_upload/Dokumente/Ueber/Jahresberichte/AHV-IV-FAK-Jahresbericht%2D%2D2019.pdf;
- for BPV: FNA, Betriebliche Personalvorsorge in Liechtenstein, Vaduz 2020: https://www.fma-li.li/de/fma/publikationen/betriebliche-personalvorsorge-in-liechtenstein.html;
- for ALV: Amt für Statistik, Arbeitslosenstatistik 2019, Vaduz 2020: https://www.llv.li/files/as/arbeitslosenstatistik-2019.pdf;
- for KVG: Amt für Statistik, Krankenkassenstatistik 2018, Vaduz 2019: https://www.llv.li/files/as/ikk_2018.pdf;
- for UVers: Amt für Statistik, Unfallversicherungsstatistik 2018, Vaduz 2019: https://www.llv.li/files/as/iunfallversicherungs_2018.pdf;
- for Social assistance: Amt für Soziale Dienste, Jahresbericht 2019, Schaan 2020: https://www.llv.li/files/asd/asd-jahresbericht-2019.pdf.

[29]Art. 34-35 AHVG.

always on the condition that Liechtenstein has no social security agreement with the country they live in.

In total 24,621 persons received an AHV benefit in 2019, about 65% of them living abroad. It is noteworthy that as far as the total amounts of AHV money transferred abroad, these represent only 36% of the total AHV payments.

The personal scope of the IV is the same as that of the AHV.[30] In 2019, 1976 persons received an IV benefit, 51% of them living abroad.

The following are in principle entitled to family allowances:

- persons who have their civil law domicile (*Wohnsitz*) in Liechtenstein;
- persons who have lived or worked in Liechtenstein and who are posted by an employer with establishment in Liechtenstein on condition that the employee is paid by the Liechtensteiner employer and that an insurance relation pre-existed to the posting; and
- frontier workers who are employed by a Liechtenstein employer or who are self-employed and mandatorily insured for the AHV.

Children who are entitled to the various benefits of the FAK (family allowances) should, in principle,[31] have their domicile in Liechtenstein.[32] A total of 6085 persons received a family allowance in 2019.

The means-tested EL complements the benefits of the AHV, IV, the *Blindenbeihilfe*, are granted on condition that the recipients of these benefits:

- are Liechtenstein citizens with civil law domicile in Liechtenstein; and
- are non-Liechtenstein citizens with civil law domicile in Liechtenstein and have resided in Liechtenstein in the immediately previous uninterrupted period of 10 years.

As far as the *Blindenbeihilfe* is concerned, there is an exception in favour of non-citizens who have not reached the age of 20: they qualify from the age of six if their father and mother meet the 10 years condition. As far as the EL is concerned, an exception to the 10 years condition is made in favour of refugees and stateless persons, where the period is reduced to 5 years.[33] 875 persons received EL benefits in 2019; only 50 *Blindenbeihilfe*.

Persons who heavily depend on the help and care of another for their daily activities qualify for *Hilflosenenstchädigung* and *Betreuungs- und Pflegegeld* on condition that they have their civil law domicile in Liechtenstein, irrespective of their financial circumstances.[34] In 2019, 466 persons received *Hilflosenenstchädigung* and 485 persons *Betreuungs- und Pflegegeld.*

---

[30] Art. 26 IVG.

[31] This is the national law; on the basis of bilateral and multilateral coordination rules, this condition is however waived in most cases.

[32] See: https://www.ahv.li/leistungen/fak/allgemeines/.

[33] Art. 1 ELG; Art. 3 Blindenbeihilfe Gesetz.

[34] Art. 3bis and Art. 3octies ELG.

The unemployment insurance ALV covers persons employed in Liechtenstein for an employer with its head or branch office in Liechtenstein, as well as persons employed abroad who are within the personal scope of the AHV. The personal scope of the ALV furthermore requires the unemployed persons to have their domicile in Liechtenstein. Foreigners are considered to have their domicile in Liechtenstein, as long as they effectively reside in Liechtenstein with a permit to stay for professional activity, with a permanent stay permit or with permission to establish in Liechtenstein.[35] In 2019, only 291 persons received ALV benefit.

The following must be insured under the mandatory accident insurance scheme UVers: all wage earners employed in Liechtenstein, including home workers, apprentices and voluntary workers. If the employee of an employer in Liechtenstein is temporarily employed abroad, this does not interrupt insurance; conversely, employees temporarily posted by a foreign employer in Liechtenstein are not covered by UVers. The family members of an employer when they receive cash wages and pay AHV contributions, as well as persons who have a secondary source of income or hold an office and whose salary is subject to AHV contributions, are also compulsorily insured. Part-time employees who work less than 8 hours a week are only insured against occupational accidents, including accidents on the way to work, but not for other accidents.

Self-employed persons with domicile in Liechtenstein and their not-mandatorily-insured collaborating family members can join the accident insurance on a voluntary basis. Non-active employers with only domestic servants are not admissible to the voluntary accident insurance.[36]

The BPVG obliges employers to cover the same employees with an occupational pension plan as those covered by the AHV and earning a salary of at least three-quarters of the maximum retirement pension. Unemployed persons who receive a daily unemployment benefit should also be compulsorily covered. Employees of legal persons in which they take part and exercise employer's functions, employees who are more than two-thirds invalided, and employees who are not permanently active in Liechtenstein and who have adequate insurance coverage abroad, are freed from the compulsory insurance, but may join voluntarily. Employees posted abroad and the self-employed can also join on a voluntarily.[37] In 2018, 5300 persons received a BPV benefit, 42% of them living abroad.

The Sickness Insurance (KV) distinguishes for its personal scope between the health care costs compensation and the income replacement benefit. The insurance in its health care branch is mandatory for persons with their civil law domicile in Liechtenstein as well as for people working in Liechtenstein. The income replacement scheme in case of illness is mandatory for wage earners over the age of 15 who work in Liechtenstein for an employer with its seat or an establishment in Liechtenstein. Mandatorily insured persons can insure themselves on a voluntary basis for

[35] Art. 8 and 14 ALVG.

[36] Art. 1, 2 and 4 UVersG.

[37] Art. 2, 4c and 5 BPVG.

benefits that go beyond those of compulsory insurance. Persons older than 15 years who are not mandatorily insured can insure themselves for income replacement benefits on a voluntary basis.

Due to international arrangements, Swiss cross-border commuters are not insured by the Liechtenstein insurance concerning health care costs compensation (*Krankenpflegeversicherung*), as everybody living in Switzerland is obliged to be insured in Switzerland, whereas Austrian frontier workers have the choice of being insured in Austria or Liechtenstein. With regard to the income replacement benefit (*Krankengeldversicherung*), everybody must be insured by his/her employer in Liechtenstein.

The *Sozialhilfe* defines its personal scope as follows:

- needy citizens of Liechtenstein; and
- needy non-citizens, if they are in one of the following situations:
  - such as established by treaty;
  - the country of origin of the foreigner treats the Liechtensteiners as if they were its own nationals (reciprocity condition);[38] or
  - it is in the general interest or imperative in the interest of the needy person to preserve him/her of neglect.[39]

In 2019, 923 persons received financial social assistance.

14.4 Administration of Social Security

The Minister for Society is competent for social policy and handles, amongst other things, social insurance and social assistance issues. The Minister supervises the AHV-IV-FAK.

The AHVG, IVG and FZG establish the *Liechtensteinische AHV* respectively *IV* and the *Liechtensteinische Familienausgleichkasse* (FAK) as public law agencies. The Administration Board of AHV is the authority responsible for the Agency and consists of five to seven members appointed by Government and should include, as far as possible, people with enterprise management, financial and property management expertise. The Direction of AHV is responsible for the daily management of the Agency and is appointed by the Board.

The Administration Board and the Direction of AHV also operate as Administration Board and Direction of the IV of the FAK respectively. As a consequence, the administration is often referred to as AHV-IV-FAK.[40] The AHV-IV-FAK is competent for AHV, IV, family allowance from FAK, EL, *Blindenbeihilfe*, *Betreuungs- und Pflegegeld* and *Hilflosenentschädigung*.

---

[38] In reality this reciprocity condition would not be checked.

[39] Art. 3 Sozialhilfegesetz.

[40] See: http://www.ahv.li.

AHV-IV-FAK also collects the contributions for the ALV, but the benefits are paid by the National Economy Office (*Amt für Volkswirtschaft*), a public service of the Ministry of Infrastructure, Economy and Sports.

The UVers is administered by private insurance companies registered with the Health Office of the Ministry for Society. The employer has a choice of insurer; if no choice is made, the Office may appoint one.[41]

Occupational pension plans according to the BPVG are operated by private foundations registered in Liechtenstein. The employer chooses the occupational pension plan. The staff of the state, communes and other public entities are insured in the *betriebliche Personalvorsorge des Staates*, which was established as a foundation.[42] The decision making bodies of a foundation operating a mandatory occupational pension plan must, in principle, have an equal (paritarian) representation of the workers and the employers. Important decisions, such as the choice of the risk carrier, cannot be taken against the will of all employers or the will of all employee representatives. Foundations that operate non-compulsory occupational pension plans must have decision making bodies in which employee representatives participate, at least in accordance with their part in the financing of the pension plan.[43] The benefits of all occupational pension plans are guaranteed (in case of their insolvency) by a Security Fund, *Sicherheitsfonds*, in which all occupational pension plans participate. The Security Fund's Council is composed by as many representatives of the employers as representatives of the employees.

Occupational pension plans and the Security Fund of the BPV are supervised and monitored by the Financial Market Authority (*Finanzmarktaufsicht FMA*), an important independent public institution.[44]

The KV has been administered for many years by three accredited, private sickness funds (*Krankenkassen*), one of which was originally founded in Liechtenstein and the other two are part of Swiss sickness funds. Foreign sickness funds may also be accredited if they have an establishment in Liechtenstein.[45]

The *Sozialhilfe* is administered by the Social Services Office (*Amt für Soziale Dienste*) of the Ministry for Society, assisted in its tasks by the municipalities. The latter, however, has no decision power. Municipalities bear half the costs of all social assistance on the basis of their number of inhabitants.[46]

---

[41] Art. 57-62 UVersG.

[42] See: Gesetz vom 6. September 2013 über die betriebliche Personalvorsorge des Staates (SBPVG), LR 174.40.

[43] Art.13-15 BPVG.

[44] Art. 22 e, 22 f and 23 BPVG.

[45] Art. 1b-4a KVG; see also Schiess Rütimann (2016c), nr. 37 and 44. Accessed on https://verfassung.li/Art._26.

[46] Art. 19 ff SHG; see also Schiess Rütimann (2016b), nrs. 23–24. Accessed on https://verfassung.li/Art._25.

14.5 Coordination

Considering the high number of foreign workers in Liechtenstein and the significant number of frontier workers coming to work in the Principality every day, the coordination of Liechtenstein's social security schemes with those of the neighbouring countries is of paramount relevance. This is illustrated by the fact that today half of the AHV pensions are being exported.[47]

By virtue of the European Economic Area Agreement (EEA) and the Agreement between the European Union and Switzerland, the EU social security mechanism applies to Liechtenstein and its relations with the countries of the European Union and the other EFTA countries. The EU coordination mechanism provides:

- the principle of non-discrimination based on nationality;
- rules concerning the determination of the applicable legislation;
- the exportability of acquired social security benefits;
- the aggregation and apportionment of periods of residence, work or insurance; and
- administrative co-operation agreements.

The EU mechanism applies to all citizens insured under the social security of a member state and to all social insurance schemes.

Bilateral social security coordination agreements have been signed with Switzerland, Austria, Germany and Italy.[48] There is also a 1977 quadrilateral agreement between Liechtenstein, Germany, Switzerland and Austria.[49] It is clear that the agreements with Switzerland are most important.[50]

In principle, the country that is competent for the AHV (old-age and survivors' pensions) will also be competent for all other social insurances. Only in the case of the KV (regarding compensation of health care costs) is a split possible: a person can be sickness insured in Switzerland and for all other schemes covered by Liechtenstein.

Liechtenstein also has a very partial agreement on social security with the Netherlands (which deals with mutual cost compensation within the framework of the EU social security coordination mechanism)[51] and one with the United States of

[47]J.Seeliger, AHV-IV-FAK-Beiträge (Skriptum), 2020, p. 7. Accessed on: https://www.ahv.li/fileadmin/user_upload/Dokumente/Online-Schalter/Beitrags-Skriptum/Beitragsskriptum-2020.pdf.

[48]These agreements can be found in the Coordinated Laws of Liechtenstein under the numbers: LR 0.831.109.101 and LR 0.837.910.11 for Switzerland; LR 0.831.109.102 for Austria, LR 0.831.109.103 for Germany; and LR 0.831.109.104 for Italy.

[49]Coordinated laws of Liechtenstein, LR 0.831.109.101.21.

[50]J. Seeliger, AHV-IV-FAK-Beiträge (Skriptum), 2020, p. 5. Accessed on: https://www.ahv.li/fileadmin/user_upload/Dokumente/Online-Schalter/Beitrags-Skriptum/Beitragsskriptum-2020.pdf.

[51]Coordinated laws of Liechtenstein, LR 0.831.109.114.1.

America (concerning reciprocity in the payment of certain social insurance pensions).[52]

Of a special nature is the agreement between Liechtenstein and the Swiss Confederation whereby Liechtenstein mandates the Swiss Security Fund, *Stiftung Sicherheitsfonds BVG*, to take over the tasks of the Security Fund of Liechtenstein. The Security Fund guarantees the payment of benefits if the occupational pension plans BPV would fail to pay these (in case of bankruptcy and alike). The Liechtenstein occupational pension plans will affiliate under the same conditions as the Swiss pension funds.[53]

Since the hospital in the capital Vaduz *(Landesspital)* offers only a limited number of treatments, the Government of Liechtenstein made an agreement with the Swiss Canton of Sankt Gallen regarding the admission of patients from Liechtenstein to hospitals in this neighbouring Swiss canton.[54] Patients who have their tax residence in Liechtenstein are to be treated equally to patients who have their tax residence in the Canton Sankt Gallen. Liechtenstein commits itself to pay for the care provided to Liechtensteiner patients and to share in the operational costs of the Cantonal Hospitals.

Other agreements with hospitals and other health facilities in Switzerland and Austria exist, but are not enshrined in an international treaty.

14.6 Additional Relevant Information

Liechtenstein is in many ways linked to its two neighbours, Switzerland and, to a lesser extent, Austria. Its fate is therefore very much linked to that of these countries. Though double landlocked, Liechtenstein benefits from access to the main European markets through its simultaneous membership in the European Economic Area (EEA) and its customs union with Switzerland. Liechtenstein remains one of the wealthiest countries in the world on a per-capita basis due to its strong manufacturing sector, with several industrial niche players, and numerous financial service providers.

Although Liechtenstein's economy is widely diversified, with many small and medium-sized enterprises, the country derives approximately one third of its revenue from attracting companies with low business taxes and easy incorporation rules, causing companies to establish their nominal offices in Liechtenstein.

[52]This is not a treaty, but an agreement based on an exchange of letters between ambassadors, Coordinated laws of Liechtenstein, LR 0.831.109.131.1.

[53]Vereinbarung vom 19. Dezember 2006, Coordinated Laws of Liechtenstein, LR 0.831.409.101.1.

[54]Vereinbarung vom 28. September 1977, Coordinated laws of Liechtenstein, LR 0.813.410.11.

Websites

https://socialprotection-humanrights.org/instru/social-security-provisions-in-the-constitution-of-liechtenstein/
https://wirtschaftskammer.li/
www.ahv.li
www.ahv.li/fileadmin/user_upload/Dokumente/Ueber/Jahresberichte/AHV-IV-FAK-Jahresbericht%2D%2D2019.pdf
www.ahv.li/leistungen/fak/allgemeines/
www.aerztekammer.li
www.fma-li.li/de/fma/publikationen/betriebliche-personalvorsorge-in-liechtenstein.html
www.gesetze.li/konso/suche
www.lihk.li/en/
www.li-makler.li/downloads/files/Uebersicht%20Sozialver.%202020.pdf
www.llv.li/files/as/ikk_2018.pdf
www.llv.li/files/as/iunfallversicherungs_2018.pdf
www.llv.li/files/as/arbeitslosenstatistik-2019.pdf
www.llv.li/files/as/ibeschaeftigung_ve_2019.pdf
www.llv.li/files/asd/asd-jahresbericht-2019.pdf
www.regierung.li/regierung

References

Augustin V (2015) Neuere sozialversicherungsrechtliche Rechtsprechung der liechtensteinischen Höchstgerichte. Liechtensteinische Juristen-Zeitung LJZ 36

AXA Winterthur (2013) All you need to know about social security. Pension system in the Principality of Liechtenstein. Accessed on: https://www.igpinfo.com/igpinfo/public_documents/ss_summaries/Liechtenstein.pdf

Brunhart A (2019) Economic and financial data on Liechtenstein: data as of 30th May 2019. Government of the Principality of Liechtenstein, Vaduz. https://www.liechtenstein-institut.li/application/files/8215/7435/8095/Datenbroschuere-2019-EN.pdf

Country Profiles (2020) International Social Security Association. https://www.issa.int/en_GB/country-profiles. Accessed 12 Feb 2020

Liechtenstein-Institut (ed) (2016) Kommentar zur liechtensteinischen Verfassung. Online-Kommentar. Bendern. Accessed on: https://verfassung.li/

Liechtensteinische AHV-IV-FAK-Anstalten (2020) Geschäftsbericht 2019. Vaduz. Accessed on https://www.ahv.li/fileadmin/user_upload/Dokumente/Ueber/Jahresberichte/AHV-IV-FAK-Jahresbericht%2D%2D2019.pdf

Office of Statistics of the Principality of Liechtenstein (2020) Liechtenstein in Figures 2020. Vaduz. Accessed on: https://www.llv.li/files/as/liechtenstein_in_figures_2020.pdf

Schiess Rütimann PM (2016a) Einführende Bemerkungen zum III. Hauptstück. In: Kommentar zur liechtensteinischen Verfassung. Online-Kommentar (ed) Liechtenstein-Institut. Bendern. Accessed on: https://verfassung.li/Einführende_Bemerkungen_zum_III._Hauptstück

Schiess Rütimann PM (2016b) Article 25. In: Kommentar zur liechtensteinischen Verfassung. Online-Kommentar, (ed) Liechtenstein-Institut. Bendern. Accessed on https://verfassung.li/Art._25

Schiess Rütimann PM (2016c) Article 26. In: Kommentar zur liechtensteinischen Verfassung. Online-Kommentar (ed) Liechtenstein-Institut. Bendern. Accessed on https://verfassung.li/Art._26

Seeliger, J. 2020. *AHV-IV-FAK-Beiträge (Skriptum)*. Accessed on: https://www.ahv.li/fileadmin/user_upload/Dokumente/Online-Schalter/Beitrags-Skriptum/Beitragsskriptum-2020.pdf

Weiss M (2019) Grundriss über das liechtensteinische Sozialversicherungsverfahren. Liechtensteinische Juristen-Zeitung (LJZ) 40

Wolf S, Bussjäger P, Schiess Rütimann PM (2018) Law, small state theory and the case of Liechtenstein. Small States Territories 1(2):183–196. Accessed on: https://www.um.edu.mt/sst/sst12nov2018

World Factbook (2020) Central Intelligence Agency. https://www.cia.gov/the-world-factbook/countries/liechtenstein. Accessed 12 Feb 2020

Chapter 15
Maldives

15.1 Context

The Maldives,[1] a chain of about 1190 coral islands grouped into 26 natural atolls in the Indian Ocean, had—but for 15 years—always been an autonomous sultanate since the twelfth century. The sultanate was a British protectorate from 1887 until 1965. In 1968, the Maldives became a republic under a one-party regime. Multipartism was introduced in 2005, and in 2008 the actual democratic constitution was adopted. However, political life continued to be troubled by real or purported coups d'état and a period of restrained political freedom. Stability seems to have returned after the presidential and parliamentary elections in 2018/2019.

The Maldives is a presidential republic, with the directly elected President as both head of state and of Government. He appoints the cabinet members who need approval of the unicameral Parliament, the People's Majlis. The 87 members of the People's Majlis are elected in single-seat constituencies. The centre-right Maldivian Democratic Party (of the president) occupies 65 seats. The next political party, the Islamic right-wing, Progressive Party of Maldives, occupies only 5.

(Sunni) Islam is the state religion and, in principle, the religion of all citizens.

The Maldives is a member of the Commonwealth of Nations.

With special thanks to the National Social Protection Agency's Policy and Planning Section for reviewing the report on Maldives.

[1]For data and figures, see: Country Profiles (2020) and World Factbook (2020).

D. Pieters, *Social Security Law in Small Jurisdictions*, The World of Small States 8,
https://doi.org/10.1007/978-3-030-78247-4_15

15.2 Legal Framework of Rights to Social Security

15.2.1 Constitutional Context

The Constitution of the Republic of Maldives declares the state to be an Islamic state and guarantees fundamental rights and freedoms "in a manner not contrary to any tenet of Islam" (section 16). Section 23 of the Constitution states that every citizen has a number of economic and social rights, such as the right to good standards of health care, both physical and mental care, and that the state undertakes to achieve the progressive realisation of these rights by reasonable measures within its ability and resources. Furthermore, the Constitution contains a number of fundamental rights, including a right to protection and special assistance by the family, the community and the state, for children and young people, as well as for the elderly and disadvantaged persons (section 35), and a right to pension for everyone engaged in employment by the state (section 38).

The legal system of Maldives can be categorised as hybrid: it is an Islamic, sharia-based system with strong English common law influence and a written Constitution.

15.2.2 Social Security Legislation and Structure

Social insurance and health care are governed by statutes, the most important being:

- the Pension Act of 2009;
- the National Social Health Insurance Act of 2008; and
- the Disability Act of 2010;

all as amended.

The Social Protection Act of 2014 (as amended) covers the social assistance programs of the government. It should be noted that since 2008, important legislative work has been done in the social security area.

The Pension Act provides three pension schemes:[2] the Maldives Retirement Pension Scheme (MRPS), the Old-Age Basic Pension Scheme, and the collateralisation of MRPS Funds for Housing Finance Scheme. We will not deal with the defined benefit State Other Pensions here, which benefits civil servants of nine government institutions who did not join the MRPS. In 2018, there were about 7200 State Other Pension recipients. A Disability Insurance Scheme that provides compensation for loss of income and ensures continued benefits in case of total and permanent disability is being developed.

[2]Pension Office. Annual Report 2018, https://storage.googleapis.com/staging.mpao-1327.appspot.com/website/7FKsci1xVuNUE8aGIGEVc067BRabuqpy6QF2H83O.pdf.

The Maldives Retirement Pension Scheme is a defined contribution scheme, which benefits members who have reached the retirement age of 65.[3] The benefit consists of a monthly payment based on the accumulated amount and life expectancy. It is not (yet) possible to have the pension paid in the form of an annuity. It is also not possible to withdraw funds before retirement age, except for the funds that may be disbursed from the retirement savings account of MRPS to cover 80% of the official cost for that year of (a first) obligatory Hajj. The Pension Board Office sets a maximum number of people eligible for the disbursement annually.

MRPS is a scheme operated by investing pension contributions. Investments are determined by the Investment Committee of the Board of Directors of the Pension Office; they have up till 2019 only been made in locally available securities.

In 2018, MRPS had about 95,000 members, about 40,000 from the public and about 55,000 from the private sector. Since MRPS was established only a few years ago, the number of recipients of a MRPS pension was 1240 people.

The Old-Age Basic Pension Scheme is a universal non-contributory scheme that provides citizens aged 65 and above who reside in the country with a flat rate basic pension on condition that they do not receive another pension income more than twice the amount of the Old-Age Benefit Pension. If citizens have another pension income, the basic pension is reduced by 50% of the other pension's value. In 2018, about 16,800 beneficiaries received basic pension monthly.

MRPS members have the opportunity to collateralise their account balance towards the down payment of housing purchases. In 2018, 159 applications for collateralisations were accepted.

The Senior Citizen Allowance is a state-funded benefit provided to Maldivians above the age of 65 years who do not receive monthly pension benefits above a certain amount. This benefit was created by the president in 2014, in addition to the Old-Age Basic Pension. In 2018, approximately 17,300 persons on average received the benefit.

The National Social Protection Agency[4] is in charge of a number of non-contributory and social assistance schemes.

The Disability Allowance programme provides a fixed monthly allowance to all persons registered as 'persons with disabilities'. There were about 6700 beneficiaries in 2016.

The Medical Welfare programme provides financial assistance to those in need to cover costs of traveling abroad for medical care, or for medical care (for instance, in private hospitals), medicines or equipment not covered by *Husnuvaa Aasandha*. The Medical Welfare also provides financial assistance for assistive devices and psychological assessment to 'persons with disabilities'. In 2016, 6777 citizens benefited from the Medical Welfare program.

---

[3]A person can opt to retire earlier from the age of 55 onwards on condition that he accumulated an amount which can provide a monthly benefit equivalent to double the amount of the basic pension until the life expectancy as determined by the Pension Office's Board.

[4]See: http://www.nspa.gov.mv/v2/; see also: IOC-IG and UNICEF (2019).

Furthermore, the National Social Protection Agency is mandated to conduct the following financial social assistance programmes:[5]

- the Single Parent Allowance programme, which provides a monthly cash benefit to single parents who look after an unmarried child below 18 years and receive an income lower than the established income poverty line. Further conditions are that the child attended school at least 80% of the time and that the child, if below 6 years of age, underwent the compulsory vaccinations. In 2016, almost 3000 parents and more than 5000 children benefited from this programme;
- the Foster Parent Allowance programme, which provides similar assistance under similar conditions to foster parents. In 2016, 107 parents and 147 children benefited from the programme; and
- the Food Subsidy programme, which provides financial assistance to people living below the established poverty line in order to purchase staple food (rice, flour and sugar).[6] For children, vaccination and school attendance requirements are set. In 2016, 395 people benefited from this programme.[7]

Public health care facilities in the Maldives function according to a multiple tier referral system for health services. Community and family health workers provide basic curative and preventive health services at the island level. Patients in need of secondary care are referred to a health centre at the sub-atoll level. Hospitals at the atoll level perform surgery and handle obstetric emergencies. Regional hospitals provide secondary curative services and play an important role in health administration by supervising health services at the lower levels and implementing preventive health programmes. At the central level, the Indira Gandhi Memorial Hospital in Malé provides tertiary curative care and acts as the country's central referral hospital.[8] However, it has to be noted that "for many people, foreign medical care remains the preferred option in view of the perceived low quality of domestic medical services." In 2010, nearly one third of all households in the Maldives had a member who had traveled abroad for medical care in the last twelve months.[9]

---

[5]According to clause 3 of the Social Protection Act, 11 areas are identified for social assistance (single parent allowance, destitute allowance, allowance for mental health patients, foster parent allowance, assistance towards electricity bill, assistance for food, assistance for water bill, housing assistance, assistance for victims of disasters and emergencies, assistance for students and assistance for small and medium businesses). However, only the three above mentioned have been implemented, leaving vulnerable and poor people not eligible under these categorical social assistance schemes without public support. The Government is currently planning a harmonisation of the social protection programme, developing a national social protection framework for the country with the aid from the World Bank.

[6]Information on the vaccination and school attendance of the children is collected, but vaccination and school attendance are no requirement for qualifying for this programme.

[7]The Fishermen's Income Assurance scheme, which safeguards a secure income for Maldivian fishermen whose income is affected due to weather conditions and other nature-related causes, was discontinued since 2019.

[8]Asian Development Bank Maldives (2015), p. 73.

[9]Asian Development Bank Maldives (2015), p. 74.

Husnuvaa Aasandha[10] is the universal health care financing scheme aimed at providing affordable and accessible health care for all Maldivians. It covers both inpatient and outpatient treatments and medication, diagnostics and surgical interventions, and transportation fees in case of emergency.

Treatments in Maldives are covered by the universal insurance if provided by public health care providers or private hospitals and clinics empaneled under the insurance scheme (in case of private care, patients may have to pay extra). All prescribed medication is also free of charge. Emergency evacuation involves the transfer of patients who require urgent medical services to the closest health centre where treatment is available. Transport may also include a person accompanying and also a medical escort. *Husnuvaa Aasandha* also provides coverage of overseas treatments and travel (see further).

It must be observed that the Maldives has been modernising their (still very patchy) social protection schemes for about 10 years and are expected to continue doing so. Since the World Bank has been the only (major) contributor in developing the social protection system in Maldives, the Bank has played, and plays, an important role in the reform of social protection in the Republic.

Alternative social protection is still important. The Islamic charity system, *Zakath*, promotes inter-household income redistribution based on religious duty. The collected *Zakath* contributions are distributed to those in need according to the Quranic precepts. However, the average benefit distributed by *Zakath* is low (less than one tenth of the basic pension). In 2005, about 58,000 Muslims have benefited from the *Zakath*.[11]

Remittances from extended family members abroad also play a role in supporting the needs of the population.

15.2.3 Enforcement of Constitutional and Statutory Rights

All administrative decisions regarding Maldivian social insurance and social assistance schemes can be appealed to the Minister of Gender, Family and Social Services, and thereafter to the courts.

The Supreme Court is the highest judiciary institution of the country. Under it function a High Court, superior trial Courts, and at the lowest level, a Magistrate Court on each inhabited island. Moreover, there are many tribunals or quasi-judicial bodies such as the Employment Tribunal or the Tax Appeal Tribunal.[12]

[10]See: https://aasandha.mv/en.

[11]Asian Development Bank Maldives (2015), pp. 78–79.

[12]Hauser Global Law school program, *Research guide on legal system and research on Maldives*, https://www.nyulawglobal.org/globalex/Maldives.html.

15.3 Population and the Personal Scope of the Social Security Schemes

15.3.1 General Data on the Population and Its Composition

Of the approximately 392,000 inhabitants (2020), about one third lives in the capital city-island of Malé and one tenth in the city-island of Addu. The remaining population is scattered over about 200 other islands of less than 10,000 inhabitants; there are 155 island tourist resorts.

The population of the islands of the Maldives is ethnically, culturally, linguistically (Dhivehi) and religiously (Islamic) homogeneous.

The labour force was estimated at approximately 222,000 in 2017, with more than two-thirds of workers active in the services sector, many of whom are in public service. Unemployment in the same year was estimated at less than 3%; youth unemployment was, however, much higher and was estimated around 16% (2016). In 2016, about 8% of the population was considered to live below the poverty line.[13]

The Maldives has a negative net migration rate of minus 12.7 persons per thousand (2020). Yet the labour force and migration figures must be handled with caution as important quantities of mainly Bangladeshi and Indian migrant workers work legally, but also often illegally and under bad circumstances in the construction and tourism sectors of the Maldives. Foreign workers have taken up many manual, semi-skilled or unskilled jobs Maldivians tend to avoid doing, but also a number of highly qualified jobs are performed by foreigners, as there is an important skills mismatch disadvantaging local youth. In 2010, for instance, 42.9% of the employed would have been foreign, with peaks of 69.4% in the manufacturing sector and 56.1% in tourism.[14] In 2010, 82% of the medical doctors and 55% of the nurses active in the Maldives were foreigners.[15]

15.3.2 Personal Scope of the Social Insurance and Social Assistance Schemes

Membership of the Retirement Pension Scheme is compulsory for all employers and their employees, both in the private and the public sector (except for the latter enjoying a State Other Pension). Self-employed persons can join voluntarily. Self-employed persons are defined as those

[13]See: http://statisticsmaldives.gov.mv/nbs/wp-content/uploads/2018/10/HIES2016-PovertyInequality_Report-ENG.pdf.

[14]Asian Development Bank Maldives (2015), pp. 60–65.

[15]Asian Development Bank Maldives (2015), p. 74.

earning a living from selling goods, providing a service, or performing work, in a manner that does not constitute being an employee in accordance with the Employment Act, and is not under control of an employer or working under the supervision of an employer.

In order to receive the Old-Age Benefit, residency in the Maldives is required.

In 2018, the Maldives Pension Administration Office issued a Regulation on Enrollment and Disbursement of Benefits to Foreign Employees under the Maldives Retirement Pension Scheme.[16] The Regulation seems to contradict the mandatory character of membership of foreign employees. A foreign employee may apply to join and can become a member unless the employer objects; an employer can enroll the foreign workers, on condition that the employee consents. If the enrolled foreign employee requests the employer to deregister him/her from the MRPS, then the employer shall facilitate the request. If the employer desires to deregister a foreign employee, the employee shall be notified and s/he may be deregistered by submitting the required document to the Pension Office.

The requirement to be a citizen and reside in the Maldives in order to qualify for the Old-Age Basic Pension can be read in section 33 of the Pension Act.

The social programmes of the National Social Protection Agency[17] benefit only (needy) Maldivian citizens. In 2019,[18] 8 476 'persons with disability' were registered and qualified for the Disability Allowance; 2501 parents and 4233 children received a Single Parent Allowance; 105 parents and 142 children benefitted a Foster Parent Allowance, and 119 households and 495 persons received Food Subsidy.

The *Husnuvaa Aasandha* covers all citizens.

15.4 Administration of Social Security

The Maldives Pension Administration Office or 'Pension Office'[19] is mandated to administer and manage the pension schemes established under the Pension Act, i.e. the retirement pension and the old-age basic pension. It also administers the housing finance collateralisation scheme. Additionally, the Pension Office disburses State Other Pensions under an agency arrangement. It also pays out the Senior Citizen Allowance.

The Pension Office operates autonomously under the management of a Board of Directors and a CEO, all of whom are appointed by the President. The Board consists of Chairman, a (non-voting) senior employee of the Securities Market Regulator, a senior civil servant of the Ministry of Finance, one member of the Ministry

[16]Regulation N° 2018/R-25.

[17]See: http://www.nspa.gov.mv/v2/; See also: IOC-IG and UNICEF (2019).

[18]See: http://statisticsmaldives.gov.mv/yearbook/2019/.

[19]See: http://www.pension.gov.mv; Pension Office. Annual Report 2018, https://storage.googleapis.com/staging.mpao-1327.appspot.com/website/7FKsci1xVuNUE8aGIGEVc067BRabuqpy6QF2H83O.pdf.

responsible for social security and four members from the private sector. An Investment Committee is established consisting of two Board members of the private sector and the Board member from the Ministry of Finance; the Committee formulates the principles of the investment policy.

The Securities Management Regulator has established a Pension Supervision Department in order to supervise the investment of pension assets and their investment performance.

The National Social Protection Agency (NSPA) is charged with overseeing and regulating the social protection programmes of the Government of the Maldives. It is managed by a Chief Executive Officer and a Deputy CEO. NSPA is a State Agency currently under the umbrella of Ministry of Gender, Family and Social Services, managed by a Chief Executive Officer and Deputy Chief Executive Officer, both appointed by the President.

NSPA also oversees the implementation and regulation of the National Social Health Insurance scheme, *Aasandha*. According to the relevant law, this scheme is managed by a seven-member Scheme Management Board, consisting of a representative each from Ministry of Health, Ministry of Finance, from the Insurance sector, from the Government's social security arm, from the finance and investment sector, from an NGO involved in the health sector and NSPA's CEO. The day to day administration of the Scheme is managed by the state owned company, Aasandha Company Limited,[20] led by a Managing Director and Company Board appointed by the Privatization and Corporatization Board (PCB) of the Government. NSPA employed 67 persons in 2020, 24 of them with an academic degree.[21]

15.5 Coordination

No international social security agreement has been concluded by the Republic of Maldives. Some medical hospitals in Sri Lanka and India have made agreements with *Aasandha* for the provision of medical care under its social health insurance (see further).

It is not clear whether beneficiaries of a Maldives Retirement Pension can receive the benefit when they have left the country. For the Old-Age Basic Pension and the social assistance schemes, residence of the citizens in the Maldives is required.

According to the 2018 Regulation on Enrollment and Disbursement of Benefits to Foreign Employees under the Maldives Retirement Pension Scheme,[22] the foreign employee enrolled in the Retirement Pension Scheme who leaves the Maldives permanently prior to attaining the pensionable age will get the entire balance of his retirement savings account (except the accrued pension rights) paid out when

---

[20]See: https://aasandha.mv/en.

[21]Information provided to us by NSPA's Policy and Planning Section.

[22]Regulation N° 2018/R-25.

leaving. The accrued pension rights shall be disbursed as a lump sum when he attains the age of 65.

Aasandha provides coverage for overseas treatment if the required medical treatment is not available in Maldives. Referrals for treatment abroad are made by specialist doctors who treat patients.[23]

Aasandha will review and approve or reject overseas referral applications. Pre-approved treatment costs of the patient at the overseas health facility are covered by the scheme. Airfare expenses of the referred patient are also covered up to four times annually, and once for the person accompanying the patient (in certain cases the scheme covers airfare for the person accompanying the patient up to four times a year). In 2020, overseas treatment under the *Husnuvaa Aasandha* scheme is available from 41 empaneled health facilities in India and Sri Lanka.

Maldivians living and visiting abroad are also covered if the treatment is not available in Maldives, or in case of emergencies, traumas and accidents where the delay in treatment could cause loss of life or permanent disabilities. Again, only care by empaneled hospitals is covered.

15.6 Additional Relevant Information

The islands are all situated at an altitude between 0 and 2 m (80% on 1 m or less), which makes them very sensitive to climate change and the related sea level rise. Tsunamis are a threat to the islands of Maldives. A tsunami in 2004 caused very severe damage.

Fishery (mainly tuna) and tourism are the main economic areas of the country. Tourism in particular experienced serious problems as a consequence of the tsunami of 2004, the global financial crisis of 2008/2009 and the political turmoil in the two first decades of the twenty-first century.

The dispersion of a limited population over a geographical area of 800 kms length by 130 kms width, with limited (public) transportation facilities between the islands, presents an important challenge to an equal distribution of social protection, especially health care.

Corruption and cronyism are generally considered a serious challenge to the country.

Websites

https://aasandha.mv/en
https://aasandha.mv/en/overseas-treatment/

[23]See: https://aasandha.mv/en/overseas-treatment/.

http://statisticsmaldives.gov.mv/nbs/wp-content/uploads/2018/10/HIES2016-PovertyInequality_Report-ENG.pdf
www.nspa.gov.mv/v2/
www.pension.gov.mv

References

Asian Development Bank Maldives (2015) Overcoming the challenges of a Small Island State Mandaluyong City. Asian Development Bank, Philippines. Accessed on: https://www.adb.org/sites/default/files/publication/172704/maldives-overcoming-challenges-small-island-state.pdf

Country Profiles (2020) International Social Security Association. https://www.issa.int/en_GB/country-profiles. Accessed 12 Feb 2020

Hauser Global Law School Program. Research guide on legal system and research on Maldives. https://www.nyulawglobal.org/globalex/Maldives.html

IOC-IG and UNICEF (2019) Social protection in Asia and the Pacific: inventory of non-contributory programmes. International Policy Center for Inclusive Growth, Brasilia. Accessed on: https://ipcig.org/pub/eng/RR28_Social_Protection_in_Asia_and_the_Pacific_Inventory_of_non_contrib.pdf

Pension Office. Annual Report 2018. https://storage.googleapis.com/staging.mpao-1327.appspot.com/website/7FKsci1xVuNUE8aGIGEVc067BRabuqpy6QF2H83O.pdf

World Factbook (2020) Central Intelligence Agency. https://www.cia.gov/the-world-factbook/countries/maldives. Accessed 12 Feb 2020

Chapter 16
Malta

16.1 Context

The Republic of Malta is composed of three inhabited islands of the Mediterranean Sea: Gozo, Comino and Malta, the latter being by far the largest and most populated.

After undergoing various influences, Malta became a British colony in 1814 and gained some form of self-rule in 1921. Malta became independent in 1964 and has been a republic since 1974. Malta joined the European Union in 2004 and the Eurozone in 2008.

Malta is a parliamentary republic. The President, elected by the Parliament, has a mainly ceremonial function. Malta follows the Westminster model of government with a Prime Minister as the leader of the parliamentary majority. The Government is answerable to the Parliament, which is the House of Representatives (*Il-Kamra Tad-Deputati*) and is composed according to proportional representation. There is fierce competition between the two major political parties, the Labour Party and the Nationalist Party, which together occupy more than nine tenths of the seats in the House.

Article 2 of the Constitution of Malta states:

> (1) The religion of Malta is the Roman Catholic Apostolic Religion.
>
> (2) The authorities of the Roman Catholic Apostolic Church have the duty and the right to teach which principles are right and which are wrong.
>
> (. . .)

With special thanks to Mrs. Joyce Grech, Assistant Director at the Ministry for the Family, Children's Rights and Social Solidarity of Malta for reviewing the Malta report.

Apart from the general comparative sources, Country Profiles (2020) and World Factbook (2020), we consulted for Malta also: https://socialsecurity.gov.mt and European Commission, 'Your Social Security Rights in Malta', Report, 2019.

D. Pieters, *Social Security Law in Small Jurisdictions*, The World of Small States 8,
https://doi.org/10.1007/978-3-030-78247-4_16

Malta is a member of the Commonwealth and of the European Union. As a member of the latter, Malta must comply with EU law.

16.2 Legal Framework of Rights to Social Security

16.2.1 Constitutional Context

The Constitution opens by stating in article 1 (1) that "Malta is a democratic republic founded on work and on respect for the fundamental rights and freedoms of the individual."

Article 17 deals with social security and reads as follows:

(1) Every citizen incapable of work and unprovided with the resources necessary for subsistence is entitled to maintenance and social assistance.
(2) Workers are entitled to reasonable insurance on a contributory basis for their requirements in case of accident, illness, disability, old-age and involuntary unemployment.
(3) Disabled persons and persons incapable of work are entitled to education and vocational training.

However, article 21 of the Constitution stipulates that article 17 shall not be enforceable in any court: "the principles therein contained are nevertheless fundamental to the governance of the country and it shall be the aim of the State to apply these principles in making laws."

Let us also note in passing that articles 113 and 114 of the Constitution provide special protection to any benefits payable under any law that provides for the grant of pensions, gratuities or compensation to persons who are, or have been, public officers in respect of their service in the public service, or the widows, children and dependants of these public officers.

Malta is characterised by a hybrid legal system with both common law elements inherited from the former colonial power, and civil law elements based on Roman law and the Napoleonic civil codes.

16.2.2 Social Security Legislation and Structure

Social security is codified in one piece of legislation, the Social Security Act (Cap. 318 of the Laws of Malta).[1] This law provides a plethora of schemes, which can be grouped together in two categories: contributory schemes, which basically require the satisfaction of the specific contribution conditions for entitlement to benefits, and

[1] See: http://justiceservices.gov.mt/DownloadDocument.aspx?app=lom&itemid=8794.

non-contributory schemes, where entitlement depends upon passing a means test and satisfying nationality and residence conditions.

The contributory schemes are repartition-based and provide the following benefits:

- Sickness Benefits;
- Invalidity Pensions and Increased Invalidity Pensions;
- National Minimum Pensions;
- The Guaranteed National Minimum Pensions;
- Widow(er)'s Pensions and Increased Widow(er)s' Pensions;
- Survivor's Pensions;
- Retirement Pensions and Increased Retirement Pensions;
- National Minimum Pensions and Increased National Minimum Pensions;
- Guaranteed National Minimum Pensions;
- Injury Benefits;
- Injury Grants;
- Injury Pensions;
- Unemployment Benefits and Special Unemployment Benefits;
- Parent's Pensions;
- Orphan's Allowances and Orphan's Supplementary Allowances;
- Marriage Grants;
- Maternity Benefits; and
- Maternity Leave Benefits.

The non-contributory schemes include:

- Social Assistance;
- Sickness Assistance;
- Leprosy Assistance;
- Tuberculosis Assistance;
- Free Medical Aid;
- Milk Grants;
- Age Pensions;
- Disability Pensions;
- Pensions for the Visually Impaired;
- Carer's Pensions;
- Children's Allowances;
- Supplementary Allowances; and
- Disabled Child Allowances.

The history of social security in Malta[2] dates back to 1885 with a pension scheme for police officers that was introduced, but really started off in the late '20s of last century.

[2]For historical development of Maltese Social Security and its origins see: Official Report by Maltese Government, 'The History of Social Security in Malta', updated May 2019, available at https://socialsecurity.gov.mt/en/Documents/The%20History%20of%20Social%20Security%20in%20MaltaEN.pdf; see also Malta Department of Social Security, 'How much do you know about

The year 1956 was the most important in the history of social security in Malta, with the introduction of the National Insurance Act and the National Assistance Act and the creation of the Department of Social Security. Legislation on social insurance and social assistance was consolidated in 1987 (and afterwards amended several times).

16.2.3 Enforcement of Constitutional and Statutory Rights

An internal appeal against social security decisions is dealt with by the Director General of the Department of Social Security. These decisions may be appealed before the Social Security Umpire when a question of law or a principle of importance emerging from the decision of the Director General is at stake. Decisions of the Umpire may be appealed with the Court of Appeal on questions of law. On average, there are about 800 appeal cases per year.

16.3 Population and the Personal Scope of the Social Security Schemes

16.3.1 General Data on the Population and Its Composition

By mid-2020, the population of Malta was estimated at about 457,000 persons. According to estimates for 2005–2006, more than 90% of the Maltese population speak Maltese and more than 90% are Roman Catholic.

The net migration rate in 2020 amounts to 6.6 per thousand. As the economy is doing well and the labour market is rather small, there is an increasing labour immigration to be observed.

The active population, estimated at about 206,000 in 2017, works for more than three quarters in the services sector. Unemployment amounted to 4.6% in 2017. More than four fifths of the gainfully employed are employees, less than one fifth are self-employed.[3]

16.3.2 Personal Scope of the Social Insurance and Social Assistance Schemes

The contributory schemes apply, in principle, to all persons between the age of 16 and retirement age (from age 61 for men, and 60 for women to age 65); in this

the history of Social Security in Malta?'. Accessed on: https://socialsecurity.gov.mt/en/Legislation-Publications/Documents/History%20of%20Social%20Security%20SystemEN.pdf.

[3]See: https://nso.gov.mt/en/publicatons/Publications_by_Unit/Documents/A2_Public_Finance/Social_Protection_2010.pdf.

way, the contributory schemes can be labelled as 'universal'. A distinction is made between three groups of insured persons: employed persons, self-employed persons and self-occupied persons.

The following are considered 'employed persons': persons employed in Malta under any contract of service or apprenticeship, written or orally, and whether expressed or implied, including employment by or under the Government of Malta. Employment outside Malta is treated as employment in Malta if the employee concerned is ordinarily resident in Malta and the employer is the Government of Malta or has a business in Malta. Moreover, a person who is employed under a contract of service outside Malta in such a manner that he/she is not in insurable employment and who retains his/her ordinary residence in Malta, may opt for being insured as an employed person.

A 'self-employed person' is a person younger than 65, ordinarily resident in Malta, who is not an employed person nor a self-occupied person. A 'self-occupied person' is a self-employed person who is engaged in any activity from which earnings of more than €910 per annum are derived.[4]

Persons in full time education or training and married persons who are not gainfully employed, as well as persons who receive social assistance and some persons who receive a pension are excluded from social insurance in the contributory schemes.

In 2019, 232,422 people received a contributory benefit.

The non-contributory schemes require Maltese nationality (with exceptions)[5] and habitual residence in Malta (during the period before applying for the benefit and during the receipt of the benefit). The conditions to be met in order to be considered habitually resident in Malta are determined by the laws of Malta and relate, amongst other things, to the family situation (family status and family connections); and the place where the applicant has his/her permanent residence with the intention to live there permanently.[6] Two classes of contributions are distinguished: one to be paid by employed persons (and their employers) and another to be paid by 'self-occupied' and 'self-employed' persons (unless exempted). The total number of non-contributory benefit recipients in 2019 amounted to 30,810 persons.

16.4 Administration of Social Security

The Ministry for the Family, Children's Rights, and Social Solidarity provides, amongst other things, general supervision of the social security.[7]

---

[4]Article 2 Social Security Act (Cap. 318 Laws of Malta).

[5]Most importantly, EU nationals or persons covered by EU Regulation (EC) 883/2004 are put on an equal footing with Maltese citizens.

[6]European Commission, 'Your Social Security Rights in Malta', Report, 2019.

[7]See: https://family.gov.mt.

For the administration of social security, the Department of Social Security is the most important instrument.[8] The Department of Social Security[9] consists of two directorates: the Department of Social Security and the Income Support and Compliance Division. The Director General (Social Security) is responsible for all social security activities including (but not limited to) the implementation and execution of the provisions of the Social Security Act. The strategic development of local policy and standards in the field of social security and the change management function for the implementation of reforms in the social security system also fall under the competence of the Director General (Social Security). The Income Support and Compliance Division is responsible for the initiation, coordination and monitoring of activities related to compliance and investigation matters. This Division is responsible for the execution of ministerial policies in the area of means-tested benefits and assistance. In general, the Director General (Income Support and Compliance) is also competent to oversee the assessment and payment of non-contributory benefits, pensions and assistance in accordance with the provisions of the Social Security Act.

The Department of Social Security operates an online services page called *MyServices*, which gives individuals access to a variety of personalised social security online services. Certain personalised services require a valid e-ID authentication.

The Commissioner of Inland Revenue[10] collects the social security contributions.

The Office of the Deputy Prime Minister and Ministry for Health[11] supervises the health care benefits, whereas the Health Division administers them.

16.5 Coordination

Malta's social security system, as a member state of the European Union, is coordinated with the systems of the other EU states as well as Iceland, Liechtenstein, Norway, Switzerland and the United Kingdom, according to EU Regulations 883/04 and 987/09.

Bilateral social security coordination treaties have been concluded with the following states: Australia, New Zealand, Canada and Libya.[12]

The EU coordination mechanism provides:

---

[8]See: https://socialsecurity.gov.mt/en.

[9]See: https://socialsecurity.gov.mt/en.

[10]See: https://cfr.gov.mt/.

[11]See: https://deputyprimeminister.gov.mt/en/Pages/health.aspx/.

[12]See the Official Website Malta, Social Security Reciprocal Agreements: https://socialsecurity.gov.mt/en/about-us/Pages/Social-Security-Reciprocal-Agreements-.aspx; See also the Official Website Malta, Social Security Reciprocal Agreements: https://socialsecurity.gov.mt/en/Benefits-and%20Assistance/Pages/Bilateral-Agreements.aspx; Camilleri (2014), pp. 10–11.

- the principle of non-discrimination based on nationality;
- rules concerning the determination of the applicable legislation;
- the exportability of acquired social security benefits;
- the aggregation and apportionment of periods of residence, work or insurance; and
- administrative co-operation agreements.

The EU mechanism applies to all persons insured under the social security of a member state and to all social insurance schemes.

The following applies to the coordination with Australia:

> The agreement with Australia has been active since 1 July 1991 and recognizes the need to coordinate further the operation of the respective social security systems so far as to ensure access by people who move between Australia and Malta. Covered in the agreement are: contributory retirement, widowhood, and invalidity. In addition, in Malta, non-contributory pensions and social assistance are also covered.

No nationality requirement is set.[13]

The coordination agreement with Canada entered into force in 1992. It enshrines the principles of non-discrimination and exportability of benefits, determines the competent legislation and renders residence in one country applicable as required contributions in the other. Residence periods completed in Canada until 1965 are considered as paid contributions. Residence periods completed in Canada as from 1966 are not considered, unless the relative contributions were paid. Furthermore, it provides for regulations in order to make social security contribution payments for persons working in one country and residing in the other. It also establishes administrative co-operation procedures. Apart from pensions, it also applies to orphans' and death benefits.

The Social Security Agreement with New Zealand of 2013 provides for equality of treatment with regard to rights and obligations under the laws of Malta and New Zealand and follows a pattern similar to the agreement with Australia, although its material scope is restricted to pensions. However, invalidity pensions are not covered by the Malta-New Zealand Agreement.

The Libya agreement is rather atypical because it mainly provides for the maintenance of the affiliation to the social security of the country of the employer when workers are sent to the other country for work.

Health care abroad is mainly regulated by the patients' rights legislation under EU law and under the EU social security coordination regulations, which apply in relations with the EU, the EFTA- countries and Switzerland. These arrangements are also valid in relation to the United Kingdom until the end of the transitional period. There are no other agreements related to the provision of health care abroad.

[13] Camilleri (2014), pp. 10–11.

16.6 Additional Relevant Information

Malta's economy relies heavily on trade in both goods (export of goods manufactured on the island) and services (tourism, financial services and online gaming), mainly with Europe. Malta sustained the 2009 crisis well and has the most important growth figures in the Eurozone since. The development of the financial sector may be endangered by EU initiatives against tax avoidance constructions. The relatively small labour market is also seen as a potential critical factor.

As we can read in the *History of Social Security* published by the Department of Social Security:[14] "Since the turn of the century, social protection has been invigorated by the activation of social reforms and benefit enhancements aimed at keeping the social security system abreast of changing social needs and challenges."[15]

With regard to pensions, priority was given to measures designed to strengthen the sustainability and adequacy of pensions.

> The reform got underway in 2006 with the raise of retirement age from 61 years for men and 60 years for women to 65 years for both genders. Concurrently, the contributory period has also been increased to 40 years while 10 years later it went up by another year for persons born after 1968. In terms of sustainability, since 2016, adopted measures have been primarily designed to incentivize pensioners to remain active in the labour market beyond statutory retirement age and to ensure that, over time, a fair balance would be kept between contributions and benefits across generations. (. . .) In terms of adequacy, manifold measures have been implemented since 2016 to increase pensionsto improve the living standards of elderly persons, and to make them resilient towards the risk of poverty.[16]

A dozen of such measures are enumerated.

Another reform package contained active labour market initiatives and was rolled out in 2015 to incentivise social beneficiaries and women to enter the labour market. The package comprises the In-Work Benefit scheme and the Tapering of Benefits (allowing to retain part of the social benefits when starting a job).

> Both schemes have been a notable success in encouraging persons on social and unemployment assistance, mostly single parents, to find employment. Coupled with the free Child Care programme, they have contributed to push up the participation of women in the labour market.[17]

The social security of persons was improved and over 20 other new measures were mentioned for the two first decades of the twenty-first century.[18]

---

[14]See: https://socialsecurity.gov.mt/en/Documents/The%20History%20of%20Social%20Security%20in%20MaltaEN.pdf.

[15]*Ibidem*, p. 3.

[16]*Ibidem*, p. 4.

[17]*Ibidem*, p. 5.

[18]*Ibidem*, pp. 6–8.

Websites

https://cfr.gov.mt/
https://deputyprimeminister.gov.mt/en/Pages/health.aspx/
https://family.gov.mt
http://justiceservices.gov.mt/DownloadDocument.aspx?app=lom&itemid=8794
https://nso.gov.mt/en/publicatons/Publications_by_Unit/Documents/A2_Public_Finance/Social_Protection_2010.pdf
https://socialsecurity.gov.mt
https://socialsecurity.gov.mt/en
https://socialsecurity.gov.mt/en/about-us/Pages/Social-Security-Reciprocal-Agreements-.aspx
https://socialsecurity.gov.mt/en/Benefits-and%20Assistance/Pages/Bilateral-Agreements.aspx
https://socialsecurity.gov.mt/en/Documents/The%20History%20of%20Social%20Security%20in%20MaltaEN.pdf

References

Camilleri C (2014) A Report on National Integration Policies in Malta. INTERACT RR 2014/04. Robert Schuman Centre for Advanced Studies. European University Institute, San Domenico di Fiesole (FI)
Country Profiles (2020) International Social Security Association. https://www.issa.int/en_GB/country-profiles. Accessed 12 Feb 2020
European Commission (2019) Your Social Security Rights in Malta. https://socialsecurity.gov.mt
Malta Department of Social Security. How much do you know about the history of Social Security in Malta?. Accessed on: https://socialsecurity.gov.mt/en/Legislation-Publications/Documents/History%20of%20Social%20Security%20SystemEN.pdf
Maltese Government (2019) The History of Social Security in Malta. Available at https://socialsecurity.gov.mt/en/Documents/The%20History%20of%20Social%20Security%20in%20MaltaEN.pdf
World Factbook (2020) Central Intelligence Agency. https://www.cia.gov/the-world-factbook/countries/malta. Accessed 12 Feb 2020

Chapter 17
San Marino

17.1 Context

San Marino is a landlocked small sovereign state on the Italian peninsula. It is the smallest state in Europe after the Holy See and Monaco. It claims to be the oldest republic in the world, with its roots dating back to at least the Middle Ages, if not the late Roman empire. Its institutions partly reflect these ancient roots. The Head of State role is occupied by two Captains Regent, elected by Parliament for a not immediately renewable period of 6 months. The executive power is vested in the Government, called the Congress of State. Its members, the Ministers, who are called Secretaries of State, need the confidence of (a majority) in the Parliament, and are answerable to it. The Secretary of State, to whom is also assigned the competence for political affairs, acts as Prime Minister. The Parliament, called the Great and General Council, is elected every 5 years and is the seat of the legislative power. The Captains Regent preside over the meetings of the Parliament and coordinate the meetings of the Government.

In Parliament, three parties obtained 10 or more seats out of the 60 legislative seats: the Christian Democratic Party (21), the coalition Domani in Movimento[1] (15), and the left wing Libera San Marino (10). The present coalition consists of the first two mentioned parties together with the left wing Noi per la Repubblica (8 seats).

San Marino, being completely surrounded by Italy and distant from any other country, is greatly influenced by Italy. Its population is ethnically similar to the

With special thanks to the authorities of San Marino, and especially ambassador Antonella Benedettini, for reviewing the report on San Marino.
Apart from the general comparative sources, Country Profiles (2020) and World Factbook (2020) we also consulted: http://www.sanmarino.sm/on-line/en/home/institutions/.

[1]This coalition can be compared to the 5 Stelle movement in Italy.

D. Pieters, *Social Security Law in Small Jurisdictions*, The World of Small States 8,
https://doi.org/10.1007/978-3-030-78247-4_17

Italians in the neighbouring regions of Italy. San Marino and the Sanmarinese are culturally, socially and politically aligned with Italy, and, as such, with the European Union, of which they are not a member. De facto they belong to the Schengen Area.

It comes as no surprise that the social security system has been highly influenced by the Italian system, so much so that a bilateral social security agreement between Switzerland and Italy could be declared applicable in the relation between Switzerland and San Marino (see further on).

17.2 Legal Framework of Rights to Social Security

17.2.1 Constitutional Context

The sources of Sanmarinese law reflect the many centuries of existence of the republic and include, in addition to the statutes adopted by the Great and General Council, also old customs and old statutes (dating back to the seventeenth century), as well as *ius commune*. The Great and General Council may adopt both ordinary laws and laws to be passed by qualified majority (constitutional laws). The most important constitutional law is the Declaration of the Rights of Citizens and Fundamental Principles of the San Marino Legal Order of 1974 (and later amended).[2]

In the Declaration, article 9 reads as follows:

> Each citizen shall have both the right and duty to work. Fair remuneration, annual holidays, weekly rest and the right to strike shall be secured by law.
>
> All citizens shall be entitled to social security.

Article 12 enshrines the protection of the family and in the second paragraph states: "Mothers shall be entitled to assistance and protection by the community".

Sanmarinese law belongs to the civil law group, as it is very much influenced by Italian law.

17.2.2 Social Security Legislation and Structure

Social security is governed by a number of laws[3] that can be grouped together under the following headings:

---

[2]Dichiarazione dei Diritti dei Cittadini e dei Principi Fondamentali dell'Ordinamento Sammarinese), approved by law N°59 8 July 1974; Declaration last amended in 2019.

[3]For the texts of the laws, see: https://www.consigliograndeegenerale.sm/on-line/home/archivio-leggi-decreti-e-regolamenti.html.

- The laws on the establishment of the Institute for the Social Security;[4]
- The laws on pensions;[5]
- The laws on complementary social insurance;[6]
- The laws on unemployment benefits and other social shock absorbers;[7]
- The laws on family allowances;[8] and
- The laws on the beneficiaries of health care.[9]

Social security in San Marino is of the Bismarckian type with professional social insurances covering the dependant workers and the self-employed; health care insurance is universal. The health and social security system of San Marino originated with the creation of the Institute for the Social Security (I.S.S.) in 1955. The system drew inspiration from the Italian social security, however Sanmarinese social security is less complex as it has only one pension system that covers all workers (both salaried workers and self-employed), and the entire system is public and managed by a single public institution (I.S.S.).

The social security law establishes the following social insurance schemes:

- Ordinary retirement pensions (i.e. length of service pensions); ordinary old-age pensions; ordinary invalidity pensions; and survivors' pensions;
- Privileged pensions for work incapacity and survivors of victims of labour accidents and professional diseases;
- Means-tested social pensions (old-age and invalidity);
- Temporary cash benefits in case of sickness and unemployment;
- All kinds of special unemployment benefits, such as the benefits in case of temporary unemployment of the Cassa Integrazione Guadagni;
- Cash benefits for absence from work for reason of maternity and *postpartum*;
- Family allowances; and
- Health care.

In 2011, a complementary insurance was introduced.[10] The complementary pensions supplement the ordinary retirement, old-age, survivors' and invalidity pensions. It is a defined contribution arrangement based on capitalisation. Under certain conditions, part of the capital may be withdrawn before or at the moment of obtaining the complementary pension.

[4]Legge n. 42 del 22 dicembre 1955; Legge n. 37 del 30 giugno 1964; Legge n. 13 del 07 marzo 1969; Legge n. 28 del 10 marzo 2015.

[5]Concerning the 'presatazioni virtalizie': see Legge n. 27 del 05 luglio 1968; Legge n. 82 del 11 dicembre 1979; Legge n. 15 del 11 febbraio 1983; Legge n. 156 del 20 dicembre 1990; Legge n. 157 del 8 novembre 2005; Legge n. 47 del 18 marzo 2008; and Legge n. 158 del 5 ottobre 2011.

[6]Legge n. 191/2011 and- Legge n. 118/2013.

[7]Concerning the 'ammortizzatori sociali' and the 'indennità economiche' see Legge n. 73 del 31 marzo 2010; Legge n. 137 del 29 ottobre 2003 and Legge n. 3/2014.

[8]Legge n. 15/1976 and Legge n. 64/2009.

[9]Concerning the 'assitenza sanitaria' see Legge n. 114 del 22 luglio 2014.

[10]Legge n. 191 del 6 dicembre 2011.

17.2.3 Enforcement of Constitutional and Statutory Rights

Decisions by the Institute for Social Security I.S.S. can be appealed internally. The Council for Social Security (see further) is the authority in charge of the assessment and judgement of the appeals against I.S.S. decisions. The Council for Social Security manages the social security, the social security funds, including the assessment of appeals. Appeals against the decisions of the Council for social security can be made to the administrative section of the court system.

The judicial system is organised as a Single Court[11] consisting of two sections: the ordinary and the administrative. In the first instance, administrative cases are heard by the Judge of Appeal in Administrative Matters, and on appeal to the Highest Judge of Appeal in Civil and Administrative matters.

The Guarantors' Panel on the Constitutionality of Rules,[12] established in 2002, has functions similar to those of a Constitutional Court. It consists of three effective members and three substitute members. All members are elected by a two-thirds majority of the Great and General Council's members from university professors of legal subjects, magistrates and law graduates with at least twenty years' experience in the field of law. Sanmarinese citizenship is not required. The main task of the Guarantors' Panel is to verify the conformity of laws, of regulations with force of law and of customary rules with force of law, with the fundamental principles of the Declaration on the Citizens' Rights.

It must be observed that there are only very few cases of social security litigation.

17.3 Population and the Personal Scope of the Social Security Schemes

17.3.1 General Data on the Population and Its Composition[13]

The population is estimated at 34,735 persons (beginning of 2020). They are not ethnically different from the surrounding Italians; they also belong in their vast majority to the Roman Catholic Church. Of the population of San Marino, about 84% are of Sanmarinese nationality and 14% are Italian nationals. About 13,700 citizens of San Marino live abroad, mainly in Italy (43%), USA (24%), France (19%) and Argentina (14%). San Marino has a net migration rate of about 5 per thousand.

[11]Constitutional Law no. 144/2003 and Qualified Law no 145/2003.

[12]Constitutional Revising Law no. 36 of 26 February 2002—with particular reference to Article 7 of this Law, which has amended Article 16 of the "Declaration on the Citizens' Rights and Fundamental Principles of San Marino Constitutional Order".

[13]Information drawn from the national statistics (May 2020), see: https://www.statistica.sm/on-line/home.html.

The work force amounted to 21,634 persons in 2019. Of these, 87% are active as (private or public) employees, 7.5% are self-employed and 5.5% are unemployed. About a third of the population is active in the manufacturing industry.

17.3.2 *Personal Scope of the Social Insurance and Social Assistance Schemes*

All employees, whether of Sanmarinese citizenship or not, who work for the state or private employers within the territory of San Marino are entitled to the temporary cash benefits of I.S.S. Under the existing social security laws, an employee ("*lavoratore dipendente*") is someone who performs manual or intellectual work for a wage and is under the direction of an employer. Domestic workers and members of the clergy are excluded from compulsory social insurance.[14]

Pension insurance also applies to the same categories. The compulsory pension, including the privileged pensions in case of professional risk, and temporary cash benefit schemes in case of sickness and maternity, is extended to self-employed workers who are mainly active in the artisanship and agriculture sectors.[15] Insurance was also extended to the self-employed workers of commerce sector and of the liberal professions registered in San Marino,[16] as well as to other employers established in San Marino.[17]

About 10,000 persons currently receive a social insurance pension.

Sanmarinese citizens who do not belong to the scope of the obligatory pension insurance, as well as some foreigners resident in San Marino, may join the optional insurance scheme.[18]

Social pensions are provided to all elderly persons residing officially ('*anagraficamente*') and effectively on the national territory for at least ten years, who enjoy no other pension and satisfy a means test.[19]

Complementary insurance[20] is obligatory for all persons obligatorily insured in the ordinary pension insurance, such as workers (wage earners and self-employed). Others, such as students and other persons not covered by the social insurances, may join voluntarily.

---

[14]Legge n. 42 del 22 dicembre 1955, art. 19.

[15]Legge n. 37 del 30 giugno 1964, art. 13 and 17.

[16]Legge n. 27 del 5 luglio 1968, art. 1.

[17]Legge n. 82 del 11 dicembre 1979, art. 1.

In the Legge n. 15 del 11 febbraio 1983 the categories are presented together in art.1in a somewhat adapted way.

[18]Legge n. 15 del 11 febbraio 1983, art. 25.

[19]Legge n. 15 del 11 febbraio 1983, art. 23.

[20]Legge n. 191 del 6 dicembre 2011.

The unemployment benefits scheme and the special schemes of income support, such as the *Cassa Integrazione Guadagni*, cover only certain categories of wage earners.[21]

The child allowance scheme only covers wage earners, agricultural workers, artisans and pensioners. In principle, persons caring for children are required to reside within the national territory, except for frontier workers employed in San Marino.[22] For the supplementary (means-tested) family allowance, both the worker and his/her family must officially and effectively reside in San Marino.[23]

All resident citizens of San Marino benefit from free health care insurance provided by I.S.S., as well as foreigners who are officially registered as residents (*residenza anagrafica*) or have a residence permit for work reasons.[24] The requirement to have an effective residence in San Marino was lifted for Sanmarinese citizens working and socially insured in San Marino, as long as they are officially registered as residents ('*anagraficamente residenti*'). The effective residence requirement was also abolished in case of work accidents.[25]

The following also benefit from the health care insurance by I.S.S. subject to the payment of a monthly contribution: foreigners who reside in San Marino or have a residence permit and do not fall under the free coverage, as well as Sanmarinese citizens who do not reside on the national territory, nor work there, nor receive a Sanmarinese pension, nor are covered by a foreign health care insurance.[26]

17.4 Administration of Social Security

Within the Government of the Republic of San Marino, the State Secretary (Minister) for health, social security, equal opportunities, welfare and social affairs, political affairs and technological innovation is in charge of social policy.

The Social Security Institute (*Istituto per la Sicurezza Sociale*)[27] is responsible for the administration of the vast number of social security benefits, including pensions, cash benefits in case of sickness and unemployment, family allowances, health care and the complementary social insurance.

The Council for Social Security, *Consiglio per la Previdenza*, consists of 12 members nominated by the Parliament for 5 years. It is made up of equal numbers of representatives of the political parties and social partners. Three members are nominated by the trade unions of wage earners and three are nominated by the

[21]Legge n. 73 del 31 marzo 2010.

[22]Decreto n. 15 del 26 aprile 1976, art. 2 and 28.

[23]Legge n. .64 del 8 maggio 2009, art. 2 and 3.

[24]Legge n. 42 del 22 dicembre 1955, art. 2.

[25]Legge n. 13 del 18 marzo 1969, art. 1–3.

[26]Legge n.114 del 22 luglio 2014, art. 2 and 3.

[27]Legge n. 165 del 30 novembre 2004, as amended; see https://www.iss.sm/home/chi-siamo/.

organisations of employers and self-employed. The Council for Social Security manages the social insurances and related funds and handles the internal appeals against decisions of the I.S.S. Moreover, the Council advises the Government in social security planning (including the health and socio-sanitary planning) matters and fundamental acts of the I.S.S.

The I.S.S. is managed by the Executive Committee that consists of the Director General, the Administrative Director and the Director for health and public health activities. I.S.S. provides various services. The '*Medicina Legale e Fiscale'* service and the Medical Commission for individual health evaluations ('*Commissione medica, Accertamenti sanitari individuali'*) are in charge of medical evaluation relevant to social security. The Office for health services abroad is in charge of deciding and facilitating the provision of heath care outside San Marino, under the authorisation competence of the Directorate for "Medicina legale e fiscale".

Complementary insurance is administered by Fondiss, a distinct fund within I.S.S. but separate from other assets of I.S.S. Fondiss is managed by an Administration Committee composed of two members appointed by the Parliamentary majority, one member appointed by the opposition, three members (comprising one vote) appointed by the trade unions and three members (comprising one vote) appointed by the associations of employers and self-employed.

The *Cassa Intergazione Guadagni* is administratively managed by I.S.S. and is supervised by a Commission created for that purpose, composed of one of each of the recognised trade unions, one representative of the recognised employers' associations, and one representative of the liberal professions.

A College of Auditors of I.S.S., *Collegio dei Sindaci Revisori*, of three auditors, is in charge of the control of the regularity and legality of the actions and accounts of I. S.S.

The law on complementary pensions specifies that Fondiss may administer its own funds, always to the benefit of the participants. In such a case it will rely on the support of the Central Bank of San Marino, which will provide advice and evaluate each investment choice. In case the Administration Committee of Fondiss should decide to deviate from the advice of the Central Bank, it will have to explain why. The law adds that Fondiss may also use the services of third partics to manage the investments. These third parties must be allowed to engage in investment activities under Sanmarinese law. As the Central Bank is the depository bank of the complementary pension fund, it may not manage the investments itself.

17.5 Coordination

The Agreement of 16 December 1991 on a Cooperation and Customs Union between the European communities and San Marino[28] contains two apparently very relevant articles relating to social security coordination. As such, a non-discrimination clause regarding social security benefits is exceptional for association or cooperation agreements between the European Union and third countries.

Article 21 provides:

1. Subject to the provisions of the following paragraphs, workers of San Marino nationality and any members of their families living with them shall enjoy, in the field of social security, treatment free from discrimination based on nationality in relation to nationals of Member States in which they are employed.
2. All periods of insurance, employment or residence completed by such workers in the various Member States shall be added together for the purpose of pensions and annuities in respect of old age, death and invalidity, and also for the purpose of medical care for the workers and for members of their families resident in the Community.
3. The workers in question shall receive family allowances for members of their families who are resident in the Community.
4. The workers in question shall be able to transfer freely to San Marino, at the rates applied by virtue of the law of the debtor Member State or States, any pensions or annuities in respect of disability, old age, death, industrial accident or occupational disease.
5. The Republic of San Marino shall accord to workers who are nationals of a Member State and employed in its territory, and to members of their families, treatment similar to that specified in paragraphs 1, 3 and 4.

Article 22 states:

1. Before the end of the first year following the entry into force of this Agreement, the Cooperation Committee shall adopt provisions to implement the principles set out in Article 21.
2. The Cooperation Committee shall adopt detailed rules for administrative cooperation providing the necessary management and control guarantees for the application of the provisions referred to in paragraph 1.
3. The provisions adopted by the Cooperation Committee shall not affect the rights or obligations arising from bilateral agreements between San Marino and Member States of the Community where those agreements provide for more favourable treatment of nationals of San Marino or the Member States.

However, we could not find any decision of the Cooperation Committee as referred to in article 22.

[28] *OJ* 2002 L 84/43.

Furthermore, San Marino has concluded bilateral social security coordination treaties with Italy, Belgium, France and Switzerland. The opportunity to conclude a convention with Argentina is under evaluation.

The bilateral social security agreement with Italy[29] is the most important and in line with the EU coordination principles (non-discrimination on the basis of nationality, export of benefits, aggregation and apportionment, administrative cooperation, designation of competent country). It applies to all social insurance branches of both countries. However, it also contains the interesting disposition that if the totalisation of periods under both legislations does not provide a right to a pension, periods of social insurance realised in third countries with which Italy or San Marino have bilateral treaties may also be taken into consideration.

The bilateral agreement with Belgium[30] similarly contains the same principles of coordination, prevailing in the EU mechanism.

The Agreement with the Helvetic Confederation[31] is based on an exchange of letters in which the countries agree that the stipulations of the bilateral agreements between Switzerland and Italy will also be considered to have been concluded between Switzerland and San Marino, be it with some enumerated exceptions and additions.

As mentioned previously, the Office for Health Services Abroad oversees decision-making and facilitation of the provision of heath care outside San Marino, under the authorisation competence of the Directorate for "Medicina legale e fiscale". In order to provide the necessary health assistance to everyone, many agreements have been signed with the health authorities and health institutions of the Italian neighbouring regions.

17.6 Additional Relevant Information

San Marino occasionally experiences earthquakes. Although the Republic of San Marino is geographically included in a seismic area considered to be medium/high risk, studies dating back to the nineties show that its territory should be considered "low seismicity area".

The economy of San Marino is highly dependant on tourism, banking and manufacturing. It was severely hit by the 2008 financial crisis, which created problems for the banks and a drop in demand for manufactured products.

Moreover, San Marino could attract foreign investment in the past through its friendly tax policies. Since some years now, San Marino has been aligning with the

[29]Convention concerning social security between Italy and the Republic of San Marino of 10 July 1974 as amended and complemented by administrative agreement and exchange of letters.

[30]See: https://www.socialsecurity.ne/CMS/en/coming_to_belgium/convention/FODSZ_Convention_-SaintMarin.

[31]See: https://www.admin.ch/opc/it/print.html.

fiscal legislation of the European Union countries and has therefore gradually lost much of its fiscal attractiveness.

Websites

www.admin.ch/opc/it/print.html
www.consigliograndeegenerale.sm/on-line/home/archivio-leggi-decreti-e-regolamenti.html
https://www.iss.sm/home/chi-siamo/
www.sanmarino.sm/on-line/en/home/institutions/
www.socialsecurity.ne/CMS/en/coming_to_belgium/convention/FODSZ_Convention_-SaintMarin
www.statistica.sm/on-line/home.html

References

Country Profiles (2020) International Social Security Association. https://www.issa.int/en_GB/country-profiles. Accessed 12 Feb 2020

World Factbook (2020) Central Intelligence Agency. https://www.cia.gov/the-world-factbook/countries/sanmarino. Accessed 12 Feb 2020

Chapter 18
Seychelles

18.1 Context

The Republic of Seychelles[1] groups 115 islands in the Indian Ocean, northeast of Madagascar. This smallest sovereign country of Africa is more than 1500 km away from any neighbouring state. Seychelles became independent in 1976 after having been under French and, from 1814, British colonial rule. In 1977, a coup d'état put an end to the multiparty democracy established with independence and replaced it with a socialist one-party regime. External pressure from the countries and international organisations that provided foreign and international aid put the country under pressure to transition to democracy during the 1980s and in 1993, a new constitution was adopted by referendum and multiparty elections took place.

Today, Seychelles is a republic with a presidential form of government. The directly elected President is Head of State and of government. He appoints the Government, which requires the approval of a parliamentary majority.

The parliament consists of one chamber, the National Assembly, of which 25 members are directly elected in single seat constituencies and up to 10 members (today) according to proportional representation. Two main parties split the popular vote: the socialist United Seychelles (the successor of the former sole party) and the social-liberal Linyon Demokratik Seselwa (LDS) (Seychellois Democratic Alliance). Together they receive nearly 99% of the votes.

The candidates of the United Seychelles (or its predecessor parties) have won all presidential elections since 1977, the last elections however with a small difference of 0.3% or 193 votes. They also maintained the majority of the members of Parliament until 2016; in that year the LDS took 19 seats and the United Seychelles 14 seats of the National Assembly.

With special thanks to Mrs. Joelle Barnes for reviewing the report on Seychelles.

[1]For data and figures, see: Country Profiles (2020) and World Factbook (2020).

D. Pieters, *Social Security Law in Small Jurisdictions*, The World of Small States 8,
https://doi.org/10.1007/978-3-030-78247-4_18

More than three quarters of the Seychellois adhere to the Roman Catholic Church and about 10% are of the Protestant faith, while other faith groups represent less than 3% of the population.

Seychelles is a member of the Commonwealth.

18.2 Legal Framework of Rights to Social Security

18.2.1 Constitutional Context

The Constitution of the Republic of Seychelles contains a number of provisions related to social protection. In section 29, it says that

> the State recognises the right of every citizen to protection of health and to the enjoyment of the attainable standard of physical and mental health and with a view to ensuring the effective exercise of this right the State undertakes [among other things] to take steps to provide for free primary health care in State institutions for all its citizens.

The rights to special protection of working mothers, of minors, of families, and of the aged and disabled are recognised in respectively sections 30, 31, 32, and 36. The right to social security is formulated as follows in section 37:

> The State recognises the right of every citizen to a decent and dignified existence and with a view to ensuring that its citizens are not left unprovided for by reason of incapacity to work or involuntary unemployment undertakes to maintain a system of social security.

Seychelles has a hybrid legal system, with elements of English common law, French civil law, customary law and modern constitutionalism.

18.2.2 Social Security Legislation and Structure

Universal social security cash benefits are regulated by the Social Security Act.[2]

The earnings (and contribution) related contributory social security benefits are regulated by the Seychelles Pension Fund Act.[3] Let us observe a terminological particularity: according to the Agency for Social Protection Act,[4] section 2, 'social assistance' means all welfare assistance and all social security benefits of the Social Security Act.

The universal social security benefits mentioned by the Social Security Act include sickness benefits, maternity benefits, injury benefits, invalidity benefits, disablement benefits, survivor benefits, funeral benefits, retirement pensions,

[2]Act 11 of 2010 Social Security Act (as amended), cap. 225 Laws of Seychelles.

[3]Seychelles Pension Fund Act, Cap. 220 Laws of Seychelles.

[4]Act 25 of 2011 Agency for Social Protection Act (as amended).

dependant benefits, orphan benefits, abandoned child benefits, and a level of subsistence (supplementary benefit). Universal benefits are flat rate benefits with potential means-tested supplements.

Contributory social security benefits of the Pension Fund include defined-benefit pensions on a pay-as-you-go basis as well as certain other benefits. The Pension Fund Act distinguishes between a life-long monthly retirement pension, a pre-retirement death gratuity, a post-retirement gratuity, a migration allowance, a permanent incapacity pension, a surviving spouse's pension, a children's pension, and the withdrawal of voluntary contributions on retirement. The migration allowance deserves some special attention: when a member of the Fund has migrated, or is about to migrate, from Seychelles to another country as a permanent resident of that country before retirement, he/she shall be entitled to a migration allowance equal to the total amount of his/her credit in the Fund. In the event that the recipient of the migration allowance later returns to Seychelles permanently, the person may rejoin the Fund.

Under the Unemployment Relief Scheme Act,[5] the Agency for Social Protection provides subsistence income for unemployed persons who are assigned to employment projects; the benefit is paid for up to 6 months.

The National Health Plan, i.e. the public health care system, provides free health care through 13 health centres and 6 hospitals, all situated on the three main islands. The Seychelles Hospital offers several specialised services.[6] The Overseas Treatment Act of 2018[7] provides a framework for the highly specialised overseas diagnosis and treatment programme for the citizens of Seychelles. Its contents are described further on.

Social welfare allowances provided by the Agency for Social Protection supplement the income of needy families in order to cover basic household needs according to an established standard measure.

18.2.3 Enforcement of Constitutional and Statutory Rights

Decisions of the Agency for Social Protection may be appealed against to the Review Panel, the five members of which are appointed by the President of the Republic: a chairperson, one representative from the Non-Governmental Organisations, one from the business community, one from religious organisations, and one from the public sector.[8] The decisions of the Review Panel are final.

---

[5]Unemployment Relief Scheme Act, cap. 244A Laws of Seychelles.

[6]See: http://www.health.gov.sc/index.php/hospitals-and-health-centers/.

[7]Overseas Treatment Act, Act 5 of 2018.

[8]See: http://www.asp.gov.sc/index.php/review-panel?tmpl=component&print=1&page=.

The Supreme Court of Seychelles is the highest trial court and the court of appeal for all lower courts and tribunals. It also functions as constitutional court. Decisions of the Supreme Court can be appealed to the Court of Appeal.

18.3 Population and the Personal Scope of the Social Security Schemes

18.3.1 General Data on the Population and Its Composition

The population is estimated at about 96,000 persons, of whom 86% live on the main island Mahé; two other islands, Praslin and La Digue, together account for 11%. The capital city Victoria is situated on Mahé.

With no indigenous population at the time of colonisation, the current citizens of Seychelles are the descendants of white colonisers, African slaves, Indian contract workers, and Chinese and Middle Eastern traders. The Seychellois people today can predominantly be labelled as creole. The Seychellois creole is the mother tongue of 90% of the population, while the other official languages, English and French, account for respectively 5% and 1% (exclusively) native speakers among the population.

The labour force was estimated at about 47,000 in 2017; unemployment amounted to 3% in the same year.[9] The public sector remains a very important employer.

Seychelles show a net migration rate of 1 per thousand (2020). Recently, Seychelles has seen the immigration of mainly young men to be employed in the tuna processing, construction and tourism industries. As of 2011, these migrant workers accounted for nearly a quarter of the workforce. More than half of them come from India, with the Malagasy as the second most numerous group.

Although Seychelles is considered to belong to the group of the high income economies (since 2015), with sustained investment in free health care and free education and a human development index score comparable to Western countries, the number of people that live below the national poverty line remains high (39% of the population in 2013) and income inequality in the country is very significant.[10] It is however interesting to note that according to a Commonwealth/UNRISD study "[p]overty in Seychelles has always been a controversial issue. Even in the early

[9]The low unemployment rate has to be relativized somewhat as there is considerable government employment in the large home-care program (6% of domestic labour force) and a high number of people staying in prison (2% of the domestic labour force); see: http://documents.worldbank.org/curated/en/191181499447495374/pdf/Seychelles-SCD-FINAL-23Jun17-06282017.pdf, p. xx.

[10]In 2013 with a Gini coefficient of 0.47; http://documents.worldbank.org/curated/en/191181499447495374/pdf/Seychelles-SCD-FINAL-23Jun17-06282017.pdf, pp. xiv and 47–48.

twenty-first century it is an almost taboo subject in society, as well as in the political scene".[11]

18.3.2 *Personal Scope of the Social Insurance and Social Assistance Schemes*

A person who is a citizen of Seychelles and is resident in Seychelles is entitled to apply for universal benefits under the Social Security Act. Only the injury benefit and the disablement benefit (benefits in case of a labour accident or professional disease) are reserved to employed persons. According to the Social Security Act, an 'employed person' is a person gainfully employed in Seychelles, whether under a contract of service, as a director or a member of the board of a body corporate, or as the holder of an office, and includes (a) a person, though not bound by a formal contract of service, who is subject to the control of another person as to the manner and method in which the first-mentioned person carries out their duties; and (b) a person working on an approved government employment project or scheme under the Unemployment Relief Scheme Act 1995. It does not include a self-employed person, unless that person is so registered with the Revenue Commissioner.

To qualify for an invalidity benefit, disablement benefits or the retirement benefit, the beneficiary must have been a resident in Seychelles for an aggregate period of at least 12 years from the date of reaching the age of majority until the date of lodging the application for the benefit.[12]

For the disablement benefit and the retirement benefit, the law offers the Minister the opportunity to waive the requirement of the period of residence. In the case of the retirement benefit, it is specified that the waiver can only be made on grounds of undue hardship.

Sickness benefit, maternity benefit, injury benefit, invalidity benefit, disablement benefit, industrial death pension, and dependant benefit are not paid for days when the beneficiary is absent from Seychelles, unless that person is absent for the purposes of receiving medical treatment, which is not available in Seychelles and that person's absence from Seychelles is approved by the Minister. Paternity benefit is not paid for days when the beneficiary is absent from Seychelles unless that person's absence from Seychelles is approved by the Minister. A person is not entitled to receive a retirement pension at any time when the person ceases to be permanently resident in Seychelles. When a beneficiary is absent from Seychelles for a period during which six or more consecutive payments of the monthly retirement

---

[11]Campling et al. (2011), p. 67. Accessed on: http://www.unrisd.org/80256B3C005BCCF9/httpNetITFramePDF?ReadForm&parentunid=3A9A74B074A08D26C12579580049787F&parentdoctype=book&netitpath=80256B3C005BCCF9/(httpAuxPages)/3A9A74B074A08D26C12579580049787F/$file/Seychelles.pdf.

[12]S.I. 53 of 2019, amending the Social Security (Benefits) Regulations 2019.

pension are due, the person is not entitled to the pension during that period, except for the month prior to returning to Seychelles. Again, the Minister may in any particular case authorise payment of the retirement pension on the basis of undue hardship to a beneficiary for any period during which the beneficiary would have been entitled to receive the pension.

Every worker who is a citizen of Seychelles is required to be a member of the Seychelles Pension Fund. Both workers employed by private and public (Government) employers are included. A self-employed person or other person who is a citizen of Seychelles can also become member of the Seychelles Pension Fund. A 'self-employed person' is an individual who runs his/her own business, or who is a partner in a partnership that runs a business and is liable to pay business tax. A worker or self-employed person may also pay voluntary contributions into the Fund.

When a member of the Fund who has paid contributions for at least 5 years ceases to reside in Seychelles, the member may continue to pay the mandatory contribution and the voluntary contribution or either of them. When a member who is not pensioned ceases to be employed, the member may continue to pay the mandatory contribution and the voluntary contribution or either for a period of up to 5 years before resuming employment.

To qualify for a retirement, incapacity or surviving spouse's pension of the Seychelles Pension Fund, one must show at least 10 years of continuous contributions immediately prior to the application or an aggregate of 20 years' contributions. The benefits of the Pension Fund are also paid to beneficiaries living abroad. To qualify for the Unemployment Relief Scheme, the unemployed person must be a citizen of Seychelles.

The health care system is open to all citizens. Medical treatment at the government clinics and hospitals is free for Seychellois and exempted Gainful Occupation Holders. Other foreign workers and their family members pay for the services they receive. The Overseas Treatment programme benefits the citizens of Seychelles domiciled in Seychelles. Exceptionally, the Minister of Health may waive the domicile condition.[13]

The social welfare assistance allowances are provided to any Seychellois citizen above the age of 18 resident in the country for at least 11 months in a year and whose means are insufficient to meet his/her basic household needs.

[13]Overseas Treatment Act, Act 5 of 2018, section 1.

18.4 Administration of Social Security

The Ministry of Family Affairs[14] supervises the universal programme. The Agency for Social Protection[15] is in charge of the management, administration and payment of social assistance, i.e. of the benefits of the universal programme and of other welfare benefits, including those of the Unemployment Relief Scheme.

The Agency is supervised by a Board appointed by the President, consisting of:

- representatives of the ministries of Family Affairs, Finance and Employment (one representative for each ministry);
- a representative of the Chamber of Commerce and Industry;
- a representative of civil society, nominated by the Non-Governmental Organisations' Liaison Unit; and
- two other members of good standing and repute.

A Chief Executive Officer oversees the direction and the day to day management of the Agency.

In 2020, the Agency consists of 75 occupied positions, of which 29 are based in the districts. They provide the first point of contact for persons seeking benefits and social welfare assistance.[16]

All social 'assistance' benefits must be applied for to the Agency. The benefits of the Social Security Act and those under the Unemployment Relief Scheme are paid out of the Social Security Fund. Due to the creation of the Agency for Social Protection, the Social Security Fund has a merely financial function; its Board—consisting of a chairperson, a representative of the Minister of Finance, a representative of the financial sector and three representatives of the employers in the private sector—is responsible for the proper administration of the assets and investments of the Fund.

The Employment Department supervises the Unemployment Relief Scheme.

The Seychelles Pension Fund[17] administers the contributory social insurance schemes and functions under the supervision of the Ministry of Finance. It collects the contributions through the Revenue Commissioner and delivers the benefits. It invests the funds that are currently not required for benefits, according to the investment principles and procedures established by law.

The Fund is administered by a Board of Trustees, which consists of a chairperson, a representative of the Ministry of Finance and no more than 10 other members of whom at least two represent the public sector, two the private sector and two the workers. The Board may set up committees, amongst other things, to assist the Board in investment or audit matters. A Chief Executive Officer is responsible for the day to day management of the Fund.

[14]See: https://www.family.gov.sc/.

[15]See: http://www.asp.gov.sc/.

[16]See: http://www.asp.gov.sc/index.php/about-us.

[17]See: http://www.pensionfund.sc/.

Decisions on medical issues are taken by the Medical Board established within the Fund; a member who is aggrieved by a decision of the Medical Board may appeal to the Appeals Committee of the Medical Board.

The Ministry of Health, and more specifically its Health Care Agency, is responsible for public health care in Seychelles.[18] An Overseas Diagnosis and Treatment Unit is established within the Health Care Agency. The Overseas Treatment Act[19] established an Overseas Diagnosis and Treatment Board, which consists of four specialists working in the public hospitals in Seychelles and one other member with a medical background. This Board proposes the policies and criteria to be followed and evaluates the requests for overseas diagnosis and treatment on a case-by-case basis. The decisions are to be justified with reasons and may be appealed with an Appeals Committee established for that purpose. The Appeals Committee consists of a chairperson and two other members, who are specialists working in Government hospitals in Seychelles.

The Seychelles Pension Fund's investments are subject to the review process performed by an auditor and actuarial consultant. The latter is currently an internationally renowned firm based in Australia.

18.5 Coordination

The Republic of Seychelles apparently has not entered into bilateral social security arrangements with any other state. As far as could be established above, the benefits of the Pension Fund are paid out when beneficiaries are abroad, whereas staying abroad does not always exclude beneficiaries from the receipt of benefits according the Social Security Act.

No special agreements with foreign countries regarding health care abroad are known to exist. However, the Overseas Treatment Act[20] provides ample coverage of foreign diagnosis and treatment under certain conditions.

In principle, in order to be entitled to free diagnosis, treatment and transport abroad, the patient's own specialist of the public health care system must refer him/her to care abroad. He/she should have received all possible treatment, undergone all possible investigations locally and exhausted all options except when it is not medically judicious to do so. The decision to allow travel and care abroad is taken prior to the travel by the Overseas Diagnosis and Treatment Board. If a person chooses to undergo overseas diagnosis or treatment on his/her own initiative without prior approval, he/she is not eligible for reimbursement of the expenses incurred overseas, unless the Board subsequently decides to do so or if one of the following conditions applies:

[18] See: http://www.health.gov.sc/index.php/about-us/.

[19] Overseas Treatment Act, Act 5 of 2018.

[20] Overseas Treatment Act, Act 5 of 2018.

- the person has fallen ill overseas necessitating urgent treatment;
- the person has travelled overseas for a second opinion and was diagnosed with a disease that was not diagnosed in Seychelles but needs urgent treatment; or
- the person chose to undergo a routine medical check-up overseas and was diagnosed with a disease that needed urgent treatment.

Expenses may also be reimbursed if it is proved that the Board committed an error of judgement in determining not to send the person for overseas diagnosis of treatment.

If the approved overseas specialised treatment concerns adults, this is funded by the Ministry of Health; if it concerns children, it is funded by the Agency for Social Protection. The latter also funds the return ticket (not means-tested) for the person accompanying a patient overseas.

18.6 Additional Relevant Information

Since independence, Seychelles has experienced impressive economic growth, mainly due to the development of tourism. Tuna fishing is also very important.

Seychelles were severely hit by the financial crisis of 2008/2009. A reduction in the number of tourists, remittances and foreign investment has led to a depletion of the foreign exchange reserves and a consequent default on interest payments. Although the country was able to overcome the crisis through adapted measures, it showed the vulnerability of the country: Seychelles still very much depend upon tourism and are thus sensitive to declines in tourist supplies, natural disasters and changes in climatic conditions. In particular, long-term resilience to climate change without weakening economic growth is seen as a challenge for a country where nearly all people live on the narrow coastlines. The environmental footprint of the tourism industry is a point of concern, as is the overfishing to the fishing sector.[21] The piracy in the Indian Ocean that was a threat to the fishing and tourism industries has apparently ended.

Although Seychelles lie outside the cyclone belt, it is occasionally severely hit. In 2004, for instance, some islands were hit by a tsunami, which damaged the environment and the economy. In 2013, the tropical cyclone Felleng caused flooding and landslides, destroying hundreds of houses.

As water supplies depend on catchment areas to collect rainwater, some islands occasionally suffer from droughts.

According to the World Bank Group's Systematic Country Diagnostic of Seychelles,[22]

[21] See: http://documents.worldbank.org/curated/en/191181499447495374/pdf/Seychelles-SCD-FINAL-23Jun17-06282017.pdf, p. xv.

[22] See: http://documents.worldbank.org/curated/en/191181499447495374/pdf/Seychelles-SCD-FINAL-23Jun17-06282017.pdf, p.69.

there are also significant risks to governance for SIDS like Seychelles:

- Given the small population size, and close community and extended family ties, strengthening public sector accountability in a SIDS is a greater challenge than in other countries; and Seychelles is no exception.
- Challenges in ensuring broad access to public office and the public service, creating risks of elite capture.
- Risks of conflicts of interest between public and individual interests, due to the reduced transparency and limited access to information.
- Collusion between the public and private sectors, limiting competition (for example, causing procurement problems) and opening opportunities for corruption.

Websites

http://documents.worldbank.org/curated/en/191181499447495374/pdf/Seychelles-SCD-FINAL-23Jun17-06282017.pdf
www.asp.gov.sc/
www.asp.gov.sc/index.php/review-panel?tmpl=component&print=1&page=
www.family.gov.sc/
www.health.gov.sc/index.php/about-us/
www.health.gov.sc/index.php/hospitals-and-health-centers/
www.pensionfund.sc/

References

Campling L, Confiance H, Purvis M-T (2011) Social policies in Seychelles. Commonwealth Secretariat/UNRISD, London. Accessed on: http://www.unrisd.org/80256B3C005BCCF9/httpNetITFramePDF?ReadForm&parentunid=3A9A74B074A08D26C12579580049787F&parentdoctype=book&netitpath=80256B3C005BCCF9/(httpAuxPages)/3A9A74B074A08D26C12579580049787F/$file/Seychelles.pdf

Country Profiles (2020) International Social Security Association. https://www.issa.int/en_GB/country-profiles. Accessed 12 Feb 2020

World Factbook (2020) Central Intelligence Agency. https://www.cia.gov/the-world-factbook/countries/seychelles. Accessed 12 Feb 2020

Chapter 19
Sint Maarten

19.1 Context

Sint Maarten[1] occupies the southern 40% of the divided island of Saint Martin, while the northern 60% of the island constitutes the French overseas collectivity of Saint-Martin.

The island of Saint Martin, situated in the Caribbean Sea (as one of the Leeward Islands), was sighted by Christopher Columbus in 1493 and hence claimed for Spain. However, it was the Dutch who occupied the island in 1631. The Spanish retook the island 2 years later, but the Dutch continued to assert their claims. The Spanish finally relinquished the island of Saint Martin to the French and the Dutch, who divided the island between themselves in 1648.

African slaves were imported in the subsequent centuries to work on the plantations. Slavery was maintained until 1863.

Sint Maarten lost its colonial status in 1954 when it became one of the six island territories that constituted the Netherlands Antilles under the name of the Island Territory of Sint Maarten ('*Eilandgebied Sint Maarten*'). The Netherlands Antilles was one of the constituent countries of the Kingdom of the Netherlands.

After a referendum in 2000, in which the citizens of Sint Maarten expressed the will to become a self-governing country within the Kingdom of the Netherlands, the Netherlands Antilles was dissolved in 2010. Since then, Sint Maarten has been a country of the Kingdom of the Netherlands with full sovereignty in internal affairs.[2]

Sint Maarten is a parliamentary democracy within the constitutional monarchy of the Kingdom of the Netherlands. Sint Maarten's head of state is the Dutch monarch, who appoints the Governor of Sint Maarten as his or her representative. The Governor watches over the general interest of the Kingdom in Sint Maarten and ensures that no decisions are taken by legislative and administrative bodies in Sint

[1]For data and figures, see: Country Profiles (2020) and World Factbook (2020).

[2]Oostindie and Klinkers (2001), pp.175 & 223–224.

D. Pieters, *Social Security Law in Small Jurisdictions*, The World of Small States 8,
https://doi.org/10.1007/978-3-030-78247-4_19

Maarten that could damage the unity of the Kingdom or that are contrary to the provisions of the Statute of the Kingdom or to international law.

Given the mainly symbolic and advisory role of the monarch, the real political and legislative power lies with the Parliament and the Council of Ministers, headed by the Prime Minister. The Governor in turn appoints the ministers who form the Government. The Government needs the confidence of, and is politically responsible to, the directly elected Parliament.

The country is a parliamentary representative democracy with a multi-party system. The Estates of Sint Maarten ('*Staten van Sint Maarten*') consists of 15 elected members. Since the 2020 elections, the Estates have been composed of six different parties, but only two of them have more than two seats: the social-democratic National Alliance (6) and the centre-right United People's Party (4). The Government is a coalition government of the National Alliance with a smaller party.

A plenipotentiary minister represents Sint Maarten's interests in the Kingdom of the Netherlands, but is not a member of the Sint Maarten Cabinet. He/she participates in the decision making in the Council of Ministers for the Kingdom, consisting of the members of the Council of Ministers of the Netherlands and the three plenipotentiary ministers from the three Caribbean countries of the Kingdom. The three countries may also delegate a national minister in an advisory capacity in addition to the authorised minister. There is no Parliament for the Kingdom, but only the Dutch Parliament, which also deals with matters reserved to the Kingdom, after consultation with the parliaments of the three other countries of the Kingdom.[3]

Based on a 2011 estimate, 45% of the population belongs to a Protestant denomination, whereas 42% of the population belongs to the Roman Catholic Church. Hindus account for about 5% of the population, while all other beliefs represent less than 2% of the population.

The Windward Islands Federation of Labour (WIFOL) is the most important trade federation on the island of Sint Maarten. It represents the majority of workers on the island.[4]

Sint Maarten obviously has strong ties with the Netherlands and the two other countries of the Kingdom of the Netherlands. For instance, Sint Maarten has a monetary union with Curaçao. The Kingdom is also responsible for its foreign relations and defence.

The Kingdom of the Netherlands is a member of the European Union, but Sint Maarten has the status of an 'overseas country and territory' (OCT)[5] and is therefore not part of the European Union. However, there is only one type of citizenship within the Kingdom of the Netherlands, and all citizens of the Kingdom of the Netherlands, also those of Sint Maarten, are EU citizens as well. This implies strong

[3]See: https://ecpr.eu/Filestore/PaperProposal/05b0373e-8099-4fdd-b568-87eeef37df87.pdf.

[4]See: http://www.stmaartenlibrary.org/wifol-windward-islands-federation-labour.

[5]The Netherlands secured a provision in the Treaty of Lisbon that says that any Caribbean part of the Netherlands can opt for a change of status to Outermost Region (OMR) if it so wishes, without having to change the Treaties of the European Union.

bonds with the European Union, which provides funds to Sint Maarten through the European Development Fund.

Sint Maarten has also received Dutch and international assistance after the devastating hurricane Irma; a World Bank programme funded by the Netherlands was agreed upon for the reconstruction.

19.2 Legal Framework of Rights to Social Security

19.2.1 Constitutional Context

Sint Maarten is one of the 'countries' constituting the Kingdom of the Netherlands. The Charter ('Statuut') for the Kingdom of the Netherlands regulates the constitutional relationship between the four countries that make up the Kingdom: the Netherlands, Aruba, Curaçao and Sint Maarten. The Charter stipulates that the four countries manage their own affairs autonomously and are jointly responsible for Kingdom affairs. It also stipulates rules governing mutual assistance, consultation and cooperation and the constitutional organisation of the countries. The Charter may be amended only with the agreement of all four countries, and it takes precedence over the individual countries' constitutions. Kingdom affairs, over which individual countries have no control, include foreign relations, defense and citizenship of the Netherlands. The Charter also stipulates how the countries should conduct Kingdom affairs in cooperation. All matters that the Charter does not define as Kingdom affairs are country affairs. Each country must promote the realisation of human rights, legal certainty and good governance within its borders. It is the Kingdom's responsibility to safeguard these values.[6]

Each Caribbean country of the Kingdom of the Netherlands has its own Constitution ('Staatsregeling'). The Constitution of Sint Maarten entered into force on 10 October 2010, on the date of the dissolution of the Netherlands Antilles. The constitution of Sint Maarten ('*Staatsregeling*') determines the social goals and social duties of the state. In the *Staatsregeling*, we read the following:

> Article 18 1. The continuing concern of public authorities shall be to protect children and young people and to promote their right to education, welfare, cultural development and leisure. 2. Continuous care by public authorities shall be aimed at protecting older people and people with disabilities and promoting their health and well-being.

> Article 19 1. The security of the population's livelihood and the distribution of wealth shall be the subject of sustained public concern. 2. Rules on entitlements to social security are laid down by or pursuant to national ordinance. 3. Dutch nationals residing in Sint Maarten who cannot provide for their existence are entitled to assistance from the government, subject to conditions and restrictions to be set by national ordinance.

[6] See: https://www.royal-house.nl/topics/legislation/charter-for-the-kingdom-of-the-netherlands.

Sint Maarten law belongs to the civil law group, as it is strongly influenced by Dutch law.

19.2.2 Social Security Legislation and Structure

Social security is mostly still regulated by national ordinances of the time the country belonged to the Netherlands Antilles, with only minor later amendments. These are the national ordinances[7] concerning

- the General Old-Age Insurance (AOV) of 1960;
- the General Widow(ers) and Orphans Insurance (AWW) of 1960;
- the General Insurance Exceptional Medical Expenses (AVBZ) of 1996;
- the Sickness Insurance (ZV) of 1966;
- the Accident Insurance (OV) of 1966;
- the Severance Pay Insurance (*Cessantia*) of 1983;
- the Medical Assistance of 1996;
- the Medical Expenses of Former Civil Servants Regulation of 1986;[8] and
- the Financial Assistance (*financiële bijstand*) of 1996.

These schemes were largely based on the Dutch social security law of that time. It should be noted that Sint Maarten has not introduced new schemes since the dissolution of the Netherlands Antilles. Since 2010, only minor changes have been introduced, such as raising the pension age and increasing the pension amount.[9]

The *landsverordening,* establishing the country's own social security administration, dates from the dissolution of the Netherlands Antilles in 2010: the national ordinance *Uitvoeringsorgaan Sociale en Ziektekosten Verzekeringen* (USZV) of Sint Maarten.[10]

The so-called General insurances—AOV, AWW, AVBZ—are contributory, universal social insurances that in principle cover the whole population; Sickness Insurance, Accident Insurance and *Cessantia* are arrangements on a professional basis. Medical assistance and financial assistance are social assistance schemes.

The AOV provides a pension upon reaching pensionable age (whether one retires or not); the AWW grants survivor benefits to the spouse of a deceased person and to his/her children. The AVBZ covers the (high) costs of treatment and care for the chronically ill and disabled.

---

[7]Up-to-date versions of all these laws are to be found for Sint Maarten on https://decentrale.regelgeving.overheid.nl/cvdr/xhtmloutput/historie/Sint%20Maarten/.

[8]According to our general approach, we shall not discuss further this arrangement.

[9]See: https://www.bearingpointcaribbean.com/en/government-news/pensioenleeftijd-st-maarten-omhoog/.

[10]See: https://decentrale.regelgeving.overheid.nl/cvdr/XHTMLoutput/Actueel/Sint%20Maarten/207971.html.

Accident Insurance covers victims of a labour accident and provides them with compensation of their medical costs, as well as with income replacement in case of incapacity to work. It also provides benefits for the surviving spouse and children of the victim of a lethal labour accident.

Sickness Insurance covers the health care (costs) on the island of employees and their family members, as well as income replacement benefits for the work incapacitated worker (including in cases of pregnancy/maternity).

Cessantia guarantees a one-off payment upon the involuntary termination of employment.

Financial assistance can be occasional or recurrent. Occasional assistance can, for instance, cover travel between the former Netherlands Antilles islands or cover temporary shelter after calamities. The recurrent financial assistance aims to cover the necessary costs of livelihood. Financial assistance depends on a means test and unemployed people in the active age must also register as job seekers.

Medical assistance covers the costs of a health care insurance to the benefit of needy people. The arrangement is means-tested.

19.2.3 Enforcement of Constitutional and Statutory Rights

Decisions related to financial and medical assistance can be appealed to the competent Minister.

Decisions taken by the *Sociale en Ziektekosten Verzekeringen* (i.e. the social security administration) regarding the above-mentioned insurance schemes can be appealed to the General Court.[11] The General Court in the country belongs to the ordinary judiciary system common to Aruba, Curaçao, Sint Maarten, Bonaire, Sint Eustatius and Saba. Appeals go to the Joint Court of Justice of Aruba, Curaçao, Sint Maarten, Bonaire, Sint Eustatius and Saba (hereinafter: JCJ). Decisions may eventually be appealed to the Supreme Court of the Netherlands (Hoge Raad), which, if it upholds the appeal, will send the case back to the JCJ.[12]

Sint Maarten has a Constitutional Court.[13] The Court assesses laws that have been ratified, but have not yet entered into force upon their compatibility with the Constitution in its entirety.[14] A request for review can only be made by the Ombudsman of Sint Maarten. Referral to the Court suspends the entry into force of the Act in question. "It is reasonable", according to the preparatory works of

[11] Art. 38 *Landsverordening Algemene Ouderdomsverzekering*; art. 39 *Landsverordening Algemene Weduwen en Wezenverzekering*; art. 10 *Landsverordening Ongevallenverzekering*; art. 36 *Landsverordening Algemene Verzekering Bijzondere Ziektekosten*; art. 10 *Landsverordening Ziekteverzekering*; art. 9 *Landsverordening Cessantia*.

[12] http://gemhofvanjustitie.org/ See also *Rijkswet cassatierechtspraak voor Aruba, Curaçao, Sint Maarten en voor Bonaire, Sint Eustatius en Saba*.

[13] See: https://constitutioneelhof.wordpress.com/.

[14] Art. 119 *Staatsregeling*.

article 127 of the Constitution, "for the legislator to draw up a new draft, taking into account the ruling of the Constitutional Court." If desired, the amended law can be referred back to the Constitutional Court, creating a constitutional dialogue.

Only the Constitutional Court may review laws against the entire Constitution, although exceptions apply. For example, there may be no review if there is a lack of sufficient interest, or if the content of the constitutional provision does not lend itself to review. The legislator has left it up to the courts to determine whether a provision is sufficiently concrete and sufficiently clear to be tested. The wording, context and purpose of the provision and its connection to other provisions play a role in this regard.

There are also some important differences between the review by the General Court and the Constitutional Court. The most important difference for citizens is that they can only address the General Court. If this Court finds that a statutory provision is not compatible with the Constitution, it can declare the provision wholly or partially inapplicable in the case at hand, and decide whether or not the effects of the provision declared inapplicable are maintained in whole or in part. Consequently, citizens and interest groups cannot use their claim to nullify a law. If the Constitutional Court considers a law to be contrary to the Constitution, it may annul (part of) the regulation so that it does not enter into force.

19.3 Population and the Personal Scope of the Social Security Schemes

19.3.1 General Data on the Population and Its Composition

The population of Sint Maarten is estimated at 44,000 people (2020). All people live in urban areas.

Ethnically, the inhabitants of Sint Maarten are very diverse. Based on a 2011 estimate, only 30% of the inhabitants were born in Sint Maarten and about 6% in Saint Martin. Approximately 42% were born on other islands of the Caribbean; only 2% originate from the Netherlands.

Based on a 2001 census, English is the first language of about more than two-thirds of the population, whereas the other official language, Dutch, is the first language of only approximately 4%. Spanish is the mother tongue of 13% of the population, Creole of about 8% of the inhabitants and the other languages are all below 5%.

The labour force in Sint Maarten consists of 23,200 people according to a 2008 estimate. About 84% of the labor force is active in a (tourism) service-related occupation, while about 15% is active in industry. In 2012, there was a 12% unemployment rate.

Sint Maarten shows a net migration rate of 6 migrants per 1000 population (2020). The high influx of migrants today is to be explained by the fact that the

'European' standard of living on the island attracts inhabitants of the less-wealthy islands of the Caribbean. The island of Sint Maarten is even more attractive due to the existence of the border with Saint-Martin, which, on the one hand, promotes a special economic dynamism and, on the other hand, complicates the control of migration flows.[15]

19.3.2 Personal Scope of the Social Insurance and Social Assistance Schemes

The General Insurances AOV, AWW and AVBZ apply to:

- residents, i.e. persons who according to real circumstances are registered to be living in the country; and
- non-residents who for purposes of income tax, are taxed as taxpayers living in the country.

Those who stay temporarily (no longer than 6 months) and either live in the Netherlands, or are considered to live there under locally applicable legislation on income-dependent taxation, are considered not to be living in the country. Any foreigner who cannot be considered to permanently live in the country and enjoys a salary or wages payable by another state for work performed in the country is not insured either.

The professional social insurances ZV and OV apply to employees, i.e. to anyone performing work for an employer in an employment contract or in a personal capacity, except in a number of cases. The most important exceptions are persons who are designated as employer, parents and children living at home with the employer unless the employment is for a normal wage, domestic staff and homeworkers, the captains and seamen on national seagoing vessels, and people in service of a public authority covered for the concerned social risks by their legal status. Persons who earn a daily wage above an established limit are also excluded from the field of application of the ZV.

The *Cessantia* arrangement applies to all workers as defined in the Civil Code, with the exception of persons in public service and persons employed by subsidised special schools.

The means-tested financial assistance scheme applies to citizens of the Kingdom of the Netherlands who have been resident in the country for at least 3 months before applying for the benefit. A resident is understood to be enrolled in the population register and to effectively live in the country. The condition of citizenship does not apply to persons who fulfill the following conditions:

[15]See: https://journals.openedition.org/etudescaribeennes/962.

- the applicant is temporarily or for an undetermined period allowed to stay in the country;
- he/she has been a resident for at least 5 years immediately preceding the application for benefit; and
- the financial help by the guarantor of the stay of the foreigner cannot reasonably be expected.

Non-citizens who do not fulfill the condition of residence during the previous 5 years may exceptionally receive assistance if the assistance is needed to address life-threatening circumstances.

Means-tested medical assistance scheme applies to citizens of the Kingdom of the Netherlands who have been residents for at least 3 months before the application, as well as to foreigners who have a permission to stay in the country for an undetermined period and have been residents for at least 5 years preceding the application.

19.4 Administration of Social Security

The minister responsible for social security policy in the broadest sense is the Minister of Public Health, Social Development and Labour. He/she is also politically responsible for health policy. Health care provision is privately organised.

An administration for all social insurances has been established by *landsverordening*: the Administration for Social and Health Costs Insurances (USZV), which is an autonomous public agency.

The USZV is monitored by a Supervisory Board and managed by a director, nominated by the Government on proposal of the Supervisory Board. The Supervisory Board consists of seven members, two of whom are appointed as representatives of the employees and two as representatives of the employers; the other three, including the director, come from other socio-economic circles.

The Department of Social Services, a government executing agency under the Ministry of Public Health, Social Development and Labour, is charged with providing financial and medical assistance.

19.5 Coordination

The Charter for the Kingdom of the Netherlands stipulates that the Kingdom is in charge of international relations and not the country. Article 37 of the Charter stipulates that the Netherlands and the country shall consult as much as possible involving the interests of both countries, explicitly stating the social relations between the countries as such a matter of mutual interest.

As stated above, the country is not a member state of the EU. Therefore, European social security coordination rules do not apply.

Though Sint Maarten is a part of the Kingdom of the Netherlands, coordination treaties concluded by the Netherlands explicitly state, as a general rule, that these treaties only apply to the European part of the Kingdom.[16] A treaty on the coordination of social security schemes between the Netherlands and Sint Maarten does not exist.[17] Nevertheless, the Netherlands has made arrangements concerning the export of Dutch social security benefits to Sint Maarten.[18]

Given that foreign relations are part of the Kingdom Affairs to be regulated by the Netherlands (*supra*), the coordination of social protection schemes with third countries should be discussed and enacted through the Kingdom's relevant bodies. However, no treaties on social coordination can be found for Sint Maarten.

Some international agreements on social security exist, without formally being coordination agreements. Complex care services are accessed outside of Sint Maarten, guaranteed through arrangements between the insurer, mainly the *Sociale en Ziektekostenverzekering* (SZV), and facilities in Aruba, Colombia, Cuba, Curaçao, the Dominican Republic, the United States of America and Venezuela.[19]

19.6 Additional Relevant Information

Sint Maarten is occasionally hit by hurricanes. The impact of the hurricanes Irma and Maria in 2017 was enormous, destroying houses and infrastructure.[20] Sint Maarten's economy depends highly upon tourism. The effects of climate change, and thus also the occurrence of natural disasters such as hurricanes, have a significant impact on Sint Maarten's tourism-based economy.

In August 1990, the public prosecutor of the Netherlands Antilles launched an investigation into the alleged ties between the Sint Maarten Government and the Sicilian Mafia, and in 1991, the Court of Audit of the Netherlands Antilles issued a report concluding that such allegations were not far-fetched.[21] A similar report concluded that Sint Maarten was in a severe financial crisis, that rules of democratic

---

[16]See, for example, the following treaty between the Netherlands and Belgium (art. 4): https://wetten.overheid.nl/BWBV0005135/2015-10-01 or a similar treaty between the Netherlands and Suriname (art. 15): https://wetten.overheid.nl/BWBV0001496/2002-11-01.

[17]See: https://www.uwv.nl/particulieren/overige-onderwerpen/internationaal/overzicht-verdragslanden/detail/met-welke-landen-heeft-nederland-een-verdrag.

[18]See: https://www.uwv.nl/particulieren/overige-onderwerpen/internationaal/handhavingsverdrag-naar-welke-landen-kan-uitkering-mee/detail/overzicht-landen-waar-u-uw-uitkering-mee-naartoe-kunt-nemen.

[19]See: https://www.paho.org/salud-en-las-americas-2017/?p=4304.

[20]See: https://www.Curaçaochronicle.com/post/main/Curaçao-st-maarten-economies-contracted/.

[21]Oostindie and Klinkers (2001), pp. 188–189.

decision making were often broken, and that the Government constituted an oligarchy, rather than a representative democracy.[22]

Allegations of criminal activities in Sint Maarten continue in this century as well. In 2004, a report of the Dutch Ministry of Justice concluded that money laundering and cocaine trade are widespread in Sint Maarten, and that money was used to finance terrorist organisations such as Hamas and the Taliban.[23] After considerable pressure from the Netherlands, the National Ordinance of 28 December 2017 for the establishment of the Integrity Chamber was adopted. The Chamber had to investigate and act upon possible violations of public integrity.

In relation to social security, the *Sociale en Ziektekostenverzekering* (SVZ) has noted an escalation in fraud with the issuing of false employer statements in the past 5 years. At the beginning of the century, one or two companies were involved in issuing such false declarations, whereas the SVZ has declared that in 2011 an estimated 15 companies were involved.[24]

Websites

https://constitutioneelhof.wordpress.com/

https://decentrale.regelgeving.overheid.nl/cvdr/xhtmloutput/historie/Sint%20Maarten/

https://decentrale.regelgeving.overheid.nl/cvdr/XHTMLoutput/Actueel/Sint%20Maarten/207971.html

https://ecpr.eu/Filestore/PaperProposal/05b0373e-8099-4fdd-b568-87eeef37df87.pdf

http://gemhofvanjustitie.org/

https://journals.openedition.org/etudescaribeennes/962

https://wetten.overheid.nl/BWBV0005135/2015-10-01

https://wetten.overheid.nl/BWBV0001496/2002-11-01

www.bearingpointcaribbean.com/en/government-news/pensioenleeftijd-st-maarten-omhoog/

www.Curaçaochronicle.com/post/main/Curaçao-st-maarten-economies-contracted/

www.nrc.nl/nieuws/2007/10/08/sint-maarten-vrijhaven-voor-criminele-gelden-11406650-a905108

www.nrc.nl/nieuws/2007/10/29/sint-maarten-bloeit-politici-leven-in-luxe-11419313-a1366310

www.paho.org/salud-en-las-americas-2017/?p=4304

[22]Oostindie and Klinkers (2001), pp. 188–189 & 191.

[23]See:https://www.nrc.nl/nieuws/2007/10/08/sint-maarten-vrijhaven-voor-criminele-gelden-11406650-a905108; https://www.nrc.nl/nieuws/2007/10/29/sint-maarten-bloeit-politici-leven-in-luxe-11419313-a1366310.

[24]Criminaliteitsbeeldanalyse Sint Maarten, 192. Accessed on: www.sintmaartengov.org.

www.royal-house.nl/topics/legislation/charter-for-the-kingdom-of-the-netherlands
www.sintmaartengov.org
www.stmaartenlibrary.org/wifol-windward-islands-federation-labour
www.uwv.nl/particulieren/overige-onderwerpen/internationaal/overzicht-verdragslanden/detail/met-welke-landen-heeft-nederland-een-verdrag
www.uwv.nl/particulieren/overige-onderwerpen/internationaal/handhavingsverdrag-naar-welke-landen-kan-uitkering-mee/detail/overzicht-landen-waar-u-uw-uitkering-mee-naartoe-kunt-nemen

References

Country Profiles (2020) International Social Security Association. https://www.issa.int/en_GB/country-profiles. Accessed 12 Feb 2020

Oostindie G, Klinkers I (2001) Knellende koninkrijksbanden: het Nederlandse dekolonisatiebeleid in de Caraïben, 1940-2000. Amsterdam University Press, Amsterdam

World Factbook (2020) Central Intelligence Agency. https://www.cia.gov/the-world-factbook/countries/sintmaarten. Accessed 12 Feb 2020

Chapter 20
Suriname

20.1 Context

The Republic of Suriname is the smallest sovereign state of South America, situated on the northeastern Atlantic coast of the continent. From the sixteenth century, European powers have invaded and contested the country. It eventually came under Dutch rule in the late seventeenth century. In 1954, Suriname became one of the constituent countries of the Kingdom of the Netherlands. In 1975, Suriname left the Kingdom to become an independent state.

Suriname is a presidential republic. The President is elected by a two-thirds majority of the National Assembly.[1] He is both Head of State and head of a government that is answerable to him.[2] Parliament consists of one chamber, the National Assembly, elected according to the proportional vote system. In theory, the president is answerable to the National Assembly.[3]

Since independence, democracy in Suriname has been confronted with major challenges. The first constitution of independent Suriname (1975) established a parliamentary republic of the Westminster type. Political life was very divided. A

With special thanks to Ms. Drs. Rachel Perri, director of the Uitvoeringsorgaan Basiszorg, for reviewing the report on Suriname as well as to ambassador Mrs. Sieglien Burleson for her appreciated comments.

Apart from the general comparative sources, Country Profiles (2020) and World Factbook (2020), we also consulted: http://president.gov.sr/ and http://www.gov.sr/ and http://www.dna.sr/; as well as: https://www.wdl.org/en/search/?countries=SR and https://www.ucos.be/landenfiche-suriname/.

[1] Art. 74 a. Constitution. If at least two-thirds of the National Assembly cannot agree to vote for one presidential candidate, a People's Assembly is formed from all National Assembly delegates and regional and municipal representatives who were elected by popular vote in the most recent national election.

[2] Art. 123 Constitution.

[3] Art. 90, 2° Constitution.

D. Pieters, *Social Security Law in Small Jurisdictions*, The World of Small States 8,
https://doi.org/10.1007/978-3-030-78247-4_20

military coup led by Dési(ré) Bouterse de facto suspended this constitution in 1980. The military took over power, but soon they were also confronted with resistance. In 1986, the so-called Jungle Commando started an internal armed rebellion against government, which would last six years. Negotiations from 1985 led to the drafting of a new constitution in 1987, which was adopted through popular referendum. The 1987 Constitution established a presidential regime. In 2010, the leader of the military coup, Bouterse, was elected president; in 2015 he was re-elected. In May 2020, elections put an end to the domination of parliament by Bouterse's National Democratic Party. The originally Hindustani opposition Progressive Reform Party VHP (20 seats) and three other opposition parties agreed to form a new majority without the National Democratic Party. The leader of one of a smaller party (the ABOP) of the new majority is the former Jungle Commando leader, Brunswijk. The leader of the VHP became president in July 2020.

Protestants (about 24%) and Roman Catholics (about 22%) form a majority of the population, making the Christians the most important group. Hindu people account for about 23% and Muslims for about 14% of the population. The animist 'Winti' account for about 2% of the population.

Even after independence, Suriname maintained close economic and cultural ties to its former coloniser, the Netherlands. Many Surinamese people have relatives who live in the Netherlands. However, due to the political situation in Suriname, the Dutch government was reluctant to cooperate with the Suriname government. Consequently, the Dutch government suspended important development aid several times. Meanwhile, relations between the government of Suriname and the Netherlands have considerably deteriorated.

Suriname has border conflicts with neighbouring Guyana.

20.2 Legal Framework of Rights to Social Security

20.2.1 Constitutional Context

The current Constitution of Suriname dates from 1987 and has since been amended several times.

In article 4, it states that

> the concern of the State is aimed at:
>
> (...)
>
> b. a secured means of livelihood for the entire population;
>
> c. sufficient employment with the guarantee of freedom and justice;
>
> d. the sharing of everyone in economic, social and cultural development and progress;
>
> (...).

Article 6 enumerates the social objectives of the state:

The social objectives of the State shall aim at:

(...)

c. guaranteeing a government policy aimed at raising the standard of living and well-being of the society, based on social justice, and the integral and balanced development of State and society;

d. an equitable distribution of the national income, directed towards a fair distribution of well-being and wealth among all strata of the population;

e. a regional spread of public services and economic activities;

(...)

Article 24 states that "[t]he State shall take care of the creation of conditions in which an optimal satisfaction is attained of the basic needs for work, food, healthcare, education, energy, clothing and communication."

Chapter VI of the Constitution deals with social, cultural and economic rights and obligations. In this chapter, article 36 provides that:

1. Everyone has the right to health.
2. The State shall promote general health-care by a systematic improvement of living and working conditions and shall give information on the protection of health.

In Chapter VIII on the social system, we read in Article 50:

The policy in relation to social security for widows, orphans, the aged, the disabled and incapacitated workers shall be laid down by law.

Surinamese law belongs to the civil law group as it is strongly influenced by Dutch law.

20.2.2 Social Security Legislation and Structure

Social security in Suriname consists of both universal and professional schemes, all governed by specific statutes.

The AOV ('general old age provision') provides a flat rate pension from the age of 60.[4] The Law on General Pensions[5] provides an earnings-related old-age pension, a partner pension, an orphan pension and an invalidity pension. According to the Civil Servants Pension law of 1972, civil servants enjoy a separate arrangement, the 'civil servant pension scheme', including retirement pensions, early and deferred

---

[4]Wet Algemeen Oudedagsvoorzieningsfonds of 1981 as amended; http://www.dna.sr/wetgeving/surinaamse-wetten/geldende-teksten-tm-2005/wet-algemeen-oudedagsvoorzieningsfonds/.

[5]Wet Algemeen Pensioen of 2014. Accessed on: http://www.dna.sr/media/78060/SB_2014__no_113_Wet_Algemeen_Pensioen_2014.pdf.

pensions as well as invalidity pensions.[6] AOV and the general pension are independent from each other and can thus be cumulated.

The AKB (general child allowance)[7] is paid out for children under 18. No AKB allowance is paid when there is another child benefit paid (by the employer of the person in charge).

The National Basic Care Insurance Law[8] obliges all residents of Suriname to have a health insurance that covers a basic package of medical goods and services.

According to the (labour) Accident Law,[9] cash benefits must be paid to workers who are victims of a labour accident or their survivors. These benefits must be paid by the employers who can insure their liability with Surinamese banks or approved private insurance companies.

The AMZ or General Social Care Service provides material assistance to the poor. The material assistance may include, amongst other things, medical assistance not covered by the National Basic Care insurance nor by any other public financial assistance, financial assistance and a benefit for handicapped persons.

20.2.3 Enforcement of Constitutional and Statutory Rights

Decisions of the various social security administrations must first be appealed internally, e.g. to the General Pension Council or the Care Council.

Appeals against administratively final decisions in social security matters are heard by the ordinary civil judicature, the '*kantongerechten*' (magistrate courts), with appeals with the High Court of Justice of Suriname (Supreme Court).[10] However, social security litigation before the ordinary judicature is very exceptional.

In conformity with article 144 of the Constitution, a Constitutional Court was established in 2020 to review the constitutionality of statutes as well as their conformity with ratified international treaties. Appeals beyond the High Court are referred to the Caribbean Court of Justice, while human rights cases may be heard by the Inter-American Commission and Court on Human Rights.

---

[6]See: https://pensioenfondssuriname.org/.

[7]AKB-regeling 1973, G.B. 1973 No. 107, as amended. Accessed on: http://www.dna.sr/wetgeving/surinaamse-wetten/geldende-teksten-tm-2005/algemene-kinderbijslagregeling-1973/.

[8]Wet Nationale Basiszorgverzekering of 2014. Accessed on: http://www.dna.sr/media/76886/SB_2014__no_114_Wet_Nationale_Basiszorgverzekering.pdf.

[9]Ongevallenverzekering, G.B. 1947 n° 145, as amended.

[10]Art. 139 Constitution.

20.3 Population and the Personal Scope of the Social Security Schemes

20.3.1 General Data on the Population and Its Composition

Suriname's population was estimated at 610,000 in 2020, most of them concentrated on the northern coastal strip with the capital and largest city, Paramaribo. The remainder of the country is sparsely populated.

As a legacy of colonisation, the population of Suriname is among the most diverse in the world, spanning a multitude of ethnic, religious and linguistic groups. The original tribes inhabiting the country are still present, mainly in the interior of the country. They account for only about 4% of the population. Due to the slave trade in the early colonisation period, Afro-Surinamese people have populated the country; they account for over one third of the population. A distinction is made between Creole (mixed white and black) descendants of the African slaves who are mostly Christians (about 16%) and the Maroons, descendants of people of African origin who escaped slavery by taking refuge in the woods of the interior of Suriname and later moved to the cities (about 22%). Some Maroons adhere to animist religions. The Hindustani descend from people 'imported' from India as 'contract workers' after the abolition of slavery (1863); today they account for about 27% of the Surinamese population. In terms of religion, the Hindustani consist of both Muslims and Hindus. The Javanese (about 14%) are likewise descendants of contract workers, but this time coming from the former Dutch Indies (now Indonesia); they are mainly of Muslim faith. Other groups represent less than two percent of the population: Chinese, Europeans, Jews, Phoenicians and recently also a growing group of Brazilians. About 13% of the population considers itself of 'mixed' ethnicity. About half a million people of Surinamese descent live outside the country, about 350,000 of them in the Netherlands.

Suriname has a net migration rate of 0.5 migrants per thousand.

Whereas the official language of Suriname is Dutch, most people have another mother tongue, such as Sranang Tongo (of Creole origin, but now more widespread), Caribbean Hindustani or Javanese.

The labour force in Suriname was estimated at 144,000 persons in 2014, more than two thirds of them active in the services sector. Most of the people in the services sector work for public or semi-public administrations. In 2017, the unemployment rate was estimated at about 9%.

At the end of 2018, it was estimated that 19.8% of the population in Suriname lived in poverty;[11] some sources even stated that 70% of the population lived below the poverty line.[12] Poverty is most important in the rural areas of the interior of the

[11] Sobhie et al. (2015), p. 574.

[12] See: https://borgenproject.org/causes-of-poverty-in-suriname/.

country. Since 2015, income per capita has declined significantly. This places Suriname in the top three of poorest countries in South America.

20.3.2 Personal Scope of the Social Insurance and Social Assistance Schemes

As already mentioned, social security in Suriname consists of both universal and professional schemes, all governed by specific statutes.

The AOV covers all persons of Surinamese nationality living in Suriname, as well as persons of another nationality who have been continuously living in Suriname for at least 10 years and have been liable to pay contributions, i.e. those who have proceeds from enterprise, profession or employment and have not reached the age of 60.[13]

All Suriname residents who work, whether as employed or self-employed persons, are to affiliate with the General Pension Fund and pay contributions to it. To be entitled to a benefit, one must in principle have contributed for at least 5 years.

To qualify for AKB general child allowance the child must live in Suriname and the person in charge of the child must also be of Surinamese nationality and reside in Suriname.

The Basic Care insurance law obliges every resident in Suriname to have health insurance and to pay the basic health care premium. Employers must insure their employees and pay at least half of the premium. The basic health care services to be provided are established by the law. There are three private health care insurance companies active in Suriname as well as the State Health Foundation (SZF).

Every health care service provider is obliged to provide the services as mentioned in the law and must make an agreement about services and payment with the health care insurance companies.

Every employer or individual can choose between four insurers. Every insurer is legally obliged to accept applicants and cannot refuse the applicant based on medical condition, race, gender, age etc. Civil servants are insured with SZF, as are some people who are not able to pay the set premiums because they lack sufficient finances and for which the Government decided to pay the premium, such as:

- all children younger than 16 years and elderly of at least 60 years old, who otherwise would not be insured;
- all students up to 25 years, who otherwise would not be insured; and
- under strict conditions, some people with disabilities or prolonged sickness, unemployed persons and even self-employed persons who are not able to earn above the minimum wage can apply for premium subsidy.

---

[13]Wet Algemeen Oudedagsvoorzieningsfonds of 1981 as amended. Accessed on: http://www.dna.sr/wetgeving/surinaamse-wetten/geldende-teksten-tm-2005/wet-algemeen-oudedagsvoorzieningsfonds/.

The law sets a maximum premium for which the basic care insurance can be sold. However, as this amount was not duly adapted to the devaluation, the private insurance companies are not able to offer the basic care insurance at that price and offer basic care plus packages instead at a much higher price. Due to financial problems, the State Health Foundation is not always able to cover the health services established by the law, resulting in many out of pocket costs for the insured persons.[14] Although the basic health insurance is considered to cover the whole population, the Basic Care Administration estimates that about 90,000 people have no basic health insurance at all. A decree to sanction employers or persons failing to take out a basic health insurance has not been enacted.

Employed persons (but not self-employed, household workers or people working in a family context) qualify for cash benefits under the (labour) Accident Law.

The AMZ or General Social Care Service provides material assistance to the poor. This may include, amongst other things, free medical assistance, financial assistance and a benefit for handicapped persons.

20.4 Administration of Social Security

The Ministry of Social Affairs and Housing oversees social policy development and provides general supervision.

The AOV Fund in charge of paying out the AOV pension operates under the direct authority of the Sub-direction Administrative Services of the Ministry of Social Affairs and Housing. However, the Ministry of Finance is in charge of the collection of the AOV contributions.

The General Pension Council supervises the application of the General Pension Law. The General Pension Fund registers the affiliations, collects the contributions for the earnings-related general pensions, pays out the pensions and administers the investments of the General Pension Fund. Decisions taken by a pension fund or the General Pension Fund may be appealed with the General Pension Council. Both the members of the General Pension Council and the Board of the General Pension Fund are appointed by the *Onderraad Sociale-zekerheidsstelsel* i.e. the Sub-council of Ministers competent in social security matters.[15] The management of the General Pension Fund is appointed by the Board.

Civil servants have their own pension fund as well as their own health care insurer. The Pension Fund Suriname was established in 1973 and is in charge of

[14]Wet Algemene Ziektekostenverzekering, decreet van 19 november 1980 houdende machtiging tot oprichting van de Stichting Staatsziekenfonds. Accessed on: http://www.dna.sr/wetgeving/surinaamse-wetten/geldende-teksten-tm-2005/wet-algemene-ziektekostenverzekering/.

[15]Wet Algemeen Pensioen of 2014. Accessed on: http://www.dna.sr/media/78060/SB_2014__no_113_Wet_Algemeen_Pensioen_2014.pdf.

the civil servants' pensions.[16] The Foundation State Sickness Fund (SZF)[17] provides health insurance coverage to civil servants.[18]

Authorised private insurance companies and the Foundations State Sickness Fund (SZF) administer and provide health care insurance under the regulation and general supervision of the Basic Care Administration (*Uitvoeringsorgaan Basiszorg*). There is also a Care Council, advising the Government on the basic health care and hearing appeals against the decisions of the private health care insurers, the SZF and Basic Care Administration. Both the members of the Care Council and the Board of the Basic Care Administration are appointed by the *Onderraad Sociale-zekerheidsstelsel.* The management of the Basic Care Administration is appointed by the Board.

The latter operates under a Care Council, the members of which are appointed by the '*Onderraad'*. The Care Council hears appeals against the decisions of the private health care insurers and of the Basic Care Administration.

The Ministry of Labour provides general supervision of the Labour Accident Insurance.

Child benefits (AKB) are administered by the department of Social Provision Payments (AUSV) of the Ministry of Social Affairs and Housing.

The General Social Care Service operates material assistance to the poor and operates within the Sub-directorate of General Services of the Ministry of Social Affairs and Housing.

Procedures to apply for free medical assistance, financial social assistance benefits or a benefit for handicapped persons, differ somewhat, but always include the following features:

- Application for the assistance must be made in the 'neighbourhood offices' (*wijkkantoor*) of the Ministry of Social Affairs and Housing. The administration makes a yearly tour in the remote districts of Brokopondo and Sipaliwini to take in applications;
- A report is made by a social worker;
- The decision is made by the head of the district (administrator at the head of the administrative subdivision of Suriname); and
- Payment is effectuated by the 'neighbourhood offices' (or once a year at the occasion of the visit, in Brokopondo and Sipaliwini).

The districts of Brokopondo and Sipaliwini cover more than 80% of the territory of Suriname and are situated in the interior (country outside of the coastal strip).

[16]See: https://pensioenfondssuriname.org/.

[17]Wet Algemene Ziektekostenverzekering, decreet van 19 november 1980 houdende machtiging tot oprichting van de Stichting Staatsziekenfonds. Accessed on: http://www.dna.sr/wetgeving/surinaamse-wetten/geldende-teksten-tm-2005/wet-algemene-ziektekostenverzekering/.

[18]Wet Algemene Ziektekostenverzekering, decreet van 19 november 1980 houdende machtiging tot oprichting van de Stichting Staatsziekenfonds. Accessed on: http://www.dna.sr/wetgeving/surinaamse-wetten/geldende-teksten-tm-2005/wet-algemene-ziektekostenverzekering/.

The Surinamese Constitution explicitly mentions that the structure of the (decentralised) agencies of public administration must be organised in such a way to ensure proximity to the people in order to assure the participation of those concerned in the actual activities and to avoid undue bureaucracy.[19] Everyone also has the right to be informed by the public administration about the progress of cases under consideration in which they have a direct interest, and about final decisions regarding them personally.[20] Interested parties have the right to submit to the court for reassessment any final and enforceable act by public administration agencies, which is believed to be unlawful.[21]

20.5 Coordination

The Treaty between the Netherlands and Suriname on the export and enforcement of social security benefits, signed in Paramaribo on 17 August 17 2001,[22] aims to continue the payments of Dutch social security benefits to persons residing in Suriname, in exchange for allowing control and establishing administrative cooperation. The treaty is mentioned in Dutch governmental sources, but not in Surinamese sources.

Suriname, although member of CARICOM, is not part of the CARICOM social security agreement.

20.6 Additional Relevant Information

The most important environmental danger is flooding.

Suriname's economy is heavily reliant on the mining industry, with exports of oil and gold accounting for approximately 85% of exports and 27% of government revenues. This makes the country highly vulnerable to mineral price volatility. This was also illustrated by the closure of a major aluminium company in 2015, resulting in a considerable loss of public sector revenues and high unemployment. Since 2010 and subsequent years, the national currency has devaluated several times with double-digit figures, and inflation ran high, up to 55% in 2016. Since then, it has come down to 9%. As a consequence of high inflation, the purchasing power of the

---

[19] Art. 157 (1) Constitution.

[20] Art. 158 (1) Constitution.

[21] Art. 158 (2) Constitution.

[22] Het Verdrag tussen het Koninkrijk der Nederlanden en de Republiek Suriname inzake de export en handhaving van sociale-verzekeringsuitkeringen, getekend te Paramaribo op17-08-2001. Accessed on: https://wetten.overheid.nl/BWBV0001496/2002-11-01.

population has considerably diminished. This has also led to increased political and social unrest since 2016.

The country also has the issue of being a source, transit and destination country for human trafficking.

In the historical overview on the official website of the Government of Suriname, we can read that in the '00s public administrations were dominated by political parties. Partisanship and civil servants who appeared at the office at 07h00 and left shortly after to attend private business ('*zeven-even ambtenaren*') were recurrent concepts.[23] Corruption was present everywhere and under various forms, including civil servants who were only willing to deliver after receiving bribes. Some even considered corruption to be one of the major threats to social security.[24] There is no evidence that the situation has substantially changed since then, notwithstanding the declared intention of the President to wage a crusade against corruption.[25]

In the Executive Summary of the final report of UNDP's Corruption Risk Assessment for Suriname of 2017,[26] we read:

> Corruption is facilitated by poor legislation, inadequate institutional mechanisms, inefficient public expenditure management, limited transparency, conflicts of interest, and the abuse of influence and power. (...)
>
> The common features identified in institutions, sectors, and agencies as abetting corruption are:
> - A concentration of powers and weak or non-existent checks and balances.
> - Poor transparency surrounding executive decisions, combined with restricted access to information.
> - Unclear regulatory systems that allow for discretionary decision making.
> - Weak systems of oversight and enforcement.
> - Inconsistency in applying procedures and processes. [...]
>
> In Suriname, corruption is a systemic problem that is embedded in almost all structures, institutions, sectors, and transactions conducted among business organizations both domestic and foreign, as well as among citizens and the government.[27]

The fact that corruption is a major issue was also recognised by the president and the Parliament, which adopted a special Anti-corruption Law in 2017.[28]

[23]See: http://www.gov.sr/over-suriname/historie.aspx.

[24]See e.g.: https://www.waterkant.net/suriname/2013/05/01/sociaalzekerheidsstelsel-bedreigd-door-corruptie/?cn-reloaded=1; as well as: https://www.bearingpointcaribbean.com/en/government-news/vakbond-corruptie-bedreiging-voor-zekerheidsstelsel-in-suriname/.

[25]See: https://www.mo.be/reportage/suriname-de-erfenis-van-vijf-jaar-bouterse.

[26]See: https://info.undp.org/docs/pdc/Documents/SUR/CORRUPTION%20RISK%20ASSESSMENT%20FOR%20SURINAME%20_APRIL%2010_2017_SV_FINAL.pdf.

[27]*Ibidem*, p. 7.

[28]Wet van 24 september 2017, houdende regels inzake preventie en bestrijding van corruptie en instelling van een Anti-corruptie Commissie, alsmede wijziging van het Wetboek van Strafrecht en het Decreet Uitgifte Domein-grond (Anti-corruptiewet). Accessed on: http://www.dna.sr/media/257724/SB_2017_no_85_Anti_corruptiewet_1.pdf.

More specifically for social security, the gap between legal provisions on the universal coverage for a whole range of health services and the reality of out of the pocket payments for most health services is considered to be highly problematic. The way people are identified to qualify or not for social assistance is also experienced as highly discretionary and would require legislative regulation.

Websites

https://borgenproject.org/causes-of-poverty-in-suriname/
https://info.undp.org/docs/pdc/Documents/SUR/CORRUPTION%20RISK%20ASSESSMENT%20FOR%20SURINAME%20_APRIL%2010_2017_SV_FINAL.pdf
https://pensioenfondssuriname.org/
http://president.gov.sr/
www.bearingpointcaribbean.com/en/government-news/vakbond-corruptie bedreiging-voor-zekerheidsstelsel-in-suriname/
www.dna.sr/
www.gov.sr/
www.gov.sr/over-suriname/historie.aspx
www.mo.be/reportage/suriname-de-erfenis-van-vijf-jaar-bouterse
www.ucos.be/landenfiche-suriname/
www.waterkant.net/suriname/2013/05/01/sociaalzekerheidsstelsel-bedreigd-door-corruptie/?cn-reloaded=1
www.wdl.org/en/search/?countries=SR

References

Country Profiles (2020) International Social Security Association. https://www.issa.int/en_GB/country-profiles. Accessed 12 Feb 2020
Sobhie R, Deboosere P, Dekkers G (2015) Hoe arm is Suriname?. Acad J Suriname 6:574–591
World Factbook (2020) Central Intelligence Agency. https://www.cia.gov/the-world-factbook/countries/suriname. Accessed 12 Feb 2020

Chapter 21
Trinidad and Tobago

21.1 Context

The Republic of Trinidad and Tobago[1] is composed of two islands situated between the Caribbean Sea and the North Atlantic Ocean, north of Venezuela. A colony of the United Kingdom since the beginning of the nineteenth century, the country became independent in 1962 and adopted a republican form of government in 1976.

The republic follows the Westminster form of parliamentary democracy. The President, who is indirectly elected, performs a mainly representative function. Parliament consists of two houses: the Senate and the House of Representatives. The 41 members of the House of Representatives are directly elected in single-seat constituencies. The 31 members of the Senate are appointed by the ruling party (16), the president (9) or the opposition party (6). There are two main parties competing for the votes: the liberal-centrist People's National Movement (PNM) and the social-democratic United National Congress (UNC). With the island of Tobago being granted some self-rule, it has its own directly elected House of Assembly. The UNC gets the most support in Trinidad and from the Indian community, whereas the PNM is strongest on Tobago and with the people of African descent.

Various Protestant denominations accounted for about 32% of the population, Roman Catholics for about 22%, Hindus for about 18% and Muslims for 5% of the population in 2011.

Trinidad and Tobago remains a member of the Commonwealth and thus kept strong bonds with the United Kingdom, which is also expressed by maintaining the right of final appeal to the Privy Council in London.

Trinidad and Tobago is member of the Caribbean Community (CARICOM), which aspires to become an integrated economic union.

With special thanks to Ambassador Colin Connelly, the Ministry of Social Development and Family Services and the National Insurance Board of Trinidad and Tobago.

[1]For data and figures, see: Country Profiles (2020) and World Factbook (2020).

D. Pieters, *Social Security Law in Small Jurisdictions*, The World of Small States 8,
https://doi.org/10.1007/978-3-030-78247-4_21

21.2 Legal Framework of Rights to Social Security

21.2.1 Constitutional Context

The Constitution of Trinidad and Tobago does not contain a right to social security, but merely provides in sections 133 and 134 special protection for pensions and similar benefits to be granted to public officers in respect of their service in the public service.

Trinidad and Tobago follows the English common law tradition. It maintained the right of final appeal to the Judicial Committee of the Privy Council in London. Yet the legislative acts of Trinidad and Tobago may be reviewed upon their constitutionality by the Supreme Court of the Republic.

21.2.2 Social Security Legislation and Structure

Social security in Trinidad and Tobago consists of a contributory social insurance system, called the National Insurance System, and non-contributory Social Assistance Grants. The basic regulation of both dates back more than half a century: respectively the National Insurance Act, N°35/1971[2] and the Public Assistance Act, N°18/1951[3] (both as amended). The National Insurance Act was the product of expert advice from the International Labour Organisation and an extensive public consultation in Trinidad and Tobago.

There are also special benefits, especially pensions, for people in the public service, which we shall not discuss here.[4] We also leave aside the pension fund plans and other benefit schemes (such as medical costs benefits) established by employers for their employees.[5]

The National Insurance System delivers 23 different benefits, to be grouped in the following categories:

---

[2]See National Insurance Act, Chap. 32:01 of the Laws of Trinidad and Tobago.

[3]See Public Assistance Act, Chap. 32:03 of the Laws of Trinidad and Tobago.

[4]See the Pensions Act, Chap. 23:52; the Pensions Extension Act, Chap. 23:53 and the Widows' and Orphans' Pensions Act, Chap. 23:54 of the Laws of Trinidad and Tobago; persons in the service of the Government of Trinidad and Tobago not holding a pensionable office in the sense of the afore mentioned pension law, qualify for the Provident Fund, see Provident Fund Act, Chap. 23:57 of the Laws of Trinidad and Tobago.

[5]In 1980, the Trinidad and Tobago Insurance Act (Chap. 84:01) 5 was passed regulating private insurances, including privately administered occupational pension fund plans. The Central Bank of Trinidad and Tobago became the supervisor of the insurance sector in 2004, while the Trinidad and Tobago Board of Inland Revenue is the institution charged with the responsibility of approving specific pension plans. (See Robles and Vargas 2010, p.13).

- Sickness benefits;
- Maternity benefits, including a grant, an allowance and a special maternity grant;
- Invalidity benefits;
- Funeral grants;
- Retirement benefits, including a retirement pension and a retirement grant;
- Employment injury benefits, including an injury allowance, a medical expenses benefit, a disablement grant and a disablement pension;
- Employment injury death benefits, including a widow's pension, a widower's pension, a child's allowance, a dependent parent pension and a remarriage grant; and
- Survivors' benefits, including a widow's pension, a widower's pension, a remarriage grant, child's allowance, orphan's allowance and a dependent parent pension.

All claims and questions arising under or in connection with the National Insurance Act shall be determined by the National Insurance Board of Trinidad and Tobago (see further).

The health care system provides goods and services in kind through institutions and persons operating under the Regional Heath Authorities. Most services in the public health facilities are free.

The Social Assistance Grants consist of a (non-contributory) Senior Citizen' Pension (based on an Act N°15/1939, as amended),[6] Disability Assistance Grants and a Public Assistance Grant.[7] All these benefits are means-tested and target certain categories of persons in need with little or no means of support.

21.2.3 *Enforcement of Constitutional and Statutory Rights*

Appeals tribunals[8] hear appeals against decisions of the National Insurance Board of Trinidad and Tobago (NIBTT) on questions of fact. The appeals tribunals consist of an independent chair, one person nominated by the Government, one by business and one by labour, plus the Chief Medical Officer when a medical issue is involved. The law stipulates that persons nominated to serve on appeals tribunals should be selected equally from North Trinidad, South Trinidad, and Tobago. Over the last three years (mid 2017-mid 2020) in total 570 appeals were received, more than half of them relative to retirement benefit claims. Appeals against decisions of the NIBTT on questions of law or partly of law and partly of fact go to the High Court and from

[6]Senior Citizen' Pension Act, Chap. 32:02 Laws of Trinidad and Tobago.

[7]The latter two benefits are regulated by the Public Assistance Act and the Public Assistance Regulations, Chap. 32:03 Laws of Trinidad and Tobago. The recently introduced Disability Assistance Grant (Minor) is not based on a legislative act, but determined by policy of the Ministry of Social Development and Family Services of Trinidad and Tobago; we will not discuss this grant.

[8]National Insurance (Appeals) Regulations, Chap. 32:01 Laws of Trinidad and Tobago.

the High Court to the Court of Appeal. During last year (mid 2019-mid 2020) five legal actions against NIBTT were filed before the High Court.

Decisions of the Local Public Assistance Boards may be appealed to the Central Public Assistance Board and decisions of the latter may be appealed to the Minister of Social Development and Family Services. The decision of the Minister is subject to judicial review.

At the pinnacle of the judiciary of Trinidad and Tobago, is the Supreme Court. Beyond the Supreme Court, appeals can be filed with the Judicial Committee of the Privy Council in London. Below the Supreme Court, a Court of Appeal and a High Court are in operation in the republic.

21.3 Population and the Personal Scope of the Social Security Schemes

21.3.1 General Data on the Population and Its Composition

The population of the country is estimated at about 1,400,000 persons (2020),[9] sometimes called 'Trinbagogians'. Descendants of the slaves imported from Africa and descendants of the contract labourers from India constitute the main population groups; each group accounts for more than one third of the population.

The population of Trinidad is concentrated in the western half of the island, on Tobago in the southern half. More than half a million Trinidadians live in the capital, Port-of-Spain.

The labour force was estimated at about 630,000 (2018). The unemployment amounted to about 4% at that time. About one fifth of the working population is self-employed.[10]

Emigration from Trinidad and Tobago is important, resulting in a negative net migration rate of minus 5.4 per thousand. This result was achieved notwithstanding the inflow of over 18,000 Venezuelans in 2020.

Trinidad and Tobago is one of the most prosperous countries in the Caribbean. However, about one fifth of the population was considered to live below the poverty line in 2014.

[9]See: https://cso.gov.tt.

[10]https://cso.gov.tt.

21.3.2 *Personal Scope of the Social Insurance and Social Assistance Schemes*

All employed persons, as well as domestic workers,[11] casual agricultural workers[12] and unpaid apprentices should be registered as socially insured under the National Insurance System. Employment with a remuneration of less than 200 TT$[13] per week (2020) is considered uninsurable. Although section 2 of the National Insurance Act stipulates that an "employed person" is a paid apprentice, a self-employed person or anyone who is employed under a contract of service, registration under the National Insurance System has not yet commenced as far as self-employed persons are concerned. In other words, the self-employed are not insured under the National Insurance System. Employed persons who earn less than 200 TT$[14] per week, but previously made contributions to national insurance and continued in insurable employment, continue to participate in the National Insurance System. An insured person who is not liable to pay contributions because he/she is no longer an employed person, but who has not yet reached the age of sixty can continue to be insured on the basis of voluntary insurance. Persons in voluntary insurance only qualify for retirement benefits, survivors' benefits and funeral grants. An employed person who has not yet reached the age of 16 or who has reached the age of 65 shall not be insured against any contingency other than employment injury. In 2019, more than 420,000 persons contributed to the National Insurance System and more than 202,000 received a benefit from the National Insurance System.

The services of the public health system on the islands are in principle available to all.

Social Assistance Grants[15] are to be paid after a means test to certain categories of needy persons.

For the senior citizens' pension the applicant must:

- have been ordinarily resident in Trinidad and Tobago for 20 years preceding the application, except for periods of absence that do not exceed 5 years during the 20 years preceding the application. Periods of employment abroad are not counted as periods of absence if the recipient was employed in service of the Government of Trinidad and Tobago, or of a firm registered in the country or of a

[11]A domestic worker is a person employed other than for the purpose of a trade or business, who performs services for the comfort or convenience of a household or in or about a dwelling-house or such other premises occupied by or under the control of the employer. Maids, servants, chauffeurs, nannies etc. are as such considered domestic workers.

[12]A causal worker is a person who habitually engages in chance agricultural employment on the land of another, such employment not being based on any contract to employ that person.

[13]On 7 April 2020 this equals to 27 ¼ Euros.

[14]On 7 April 2020 this equals to 27 ¼ Euros.

[15]Public Assistance Act, art. 11A and Public Assistance Regulations art. 11 and 11A, Chap. 32:03 Laws of Trinidad and Tobago; Senior citizens' Pension Act art 4 and Senior Citizens' pension Regulations, section 17, Chap. 32:02 Laws of Trinidad and Tobago.

company incorporated in the country. Likewise, dependents of the persons employed abroad can benefit from this exception; or

- be a resident of Trinidad and Tobago and have lived in the republic for at least 50 (not necessarily consecutive) years.

For the Disability Assistance Grant the applicant must be a citizen or resident of Trinidad and Tobago and have been continuously resident in Trinidad and Tobago for 3 years preceding the date of application, except for periods of absence from the country that in total do not exceed 6 months during those 3 years. The Central Public Assistance Board may however approve an application for disability assistance of a person who has been absent for more than 6 months if this was for medical purposes. The Minister of Social Development and Family Services may decide to award the disability assistance to a person who has been continuously resident for 1 year (and not for 3 years).

To receive the periodic Public Assistance or the General Assistance Grant, no special requirements of past residence periods are set.

The public assistance benefit is suspended in case of temporary absence from the country for more than four months. After the return of the beneficiary, the payment of public assistance will resume and the person concerned is entitled to payment of public assistance for the period of suspension, but not for more than four months, except when need is established. The disability assistance is discontinued when the recipient is absent from Trinidad and Tobago for more than 1 year. The Senior Citizens' Pension law does not explicitly require the beneficiary to stay in the country. Section 16 of the Senior Citizens' Pension Regulation however stipulates that a beneficiary intending to leave Trinidad and Tobago for more than four months or returning to Trinidad and Tobago, has to notify the local public assistance board of the intended departure or return. The responsible Ministry has interpreted this stipulation to mean that no senior citizens' pension is to be paid to a person residing outside Trinidad and Tobago. This interpretation by the Ministry is however being contested both on the political arena and before the courts. In total about 146,000 persons received in September 2020 one of the social assistance benefits.

21.4 Administration of Social Security

The Minister of Finance provides general supervision of the National Insurance System. The National Insurance Board of Trinidad and Tobago (NIBTT)[16] operates and manages the National Insurance System. At the top of the NIBTT is a Board of Directors, which is set up as a tripartite body with equal representation by Government, Trade Unions and Business, plus an independent chair and the Executive Director. The Board acts in accordance with the general directions of the

[16] See: https://www.nibtt.net/.

Government given to it by the Minister of Finance, but is not subject to control or direction of any other person or authority in exercising and performing its functions.

Within NIBTT there are several specialised committees, such as the Investment Committee and the Audit, Risk and Compliance Committee. The NIBTT may invest assets that are not immediately needed through its Investment Committee. The Investment Committee consists of the Chairman of NIBTT, its Executive Director and CFO as well as three members nominated respectively by the Minister of Finance and the members of the Board nominated by Business and Labour.[17] The securities in which the funds of the NIBTT may be invested are extensively regulated in the First Schedule to the National Insurance Act.

The Ministry of Health is the national authority overseeing the entire health system in Trinidad and Tobago. It ensures that all organisations and institutions that produce health goods and services conform to certain standards. However, the responsibility for the actual provision of health care services was devolved to the Regional Health Authorities (RHAs).[18] RHAs are autonomous bodies that own and operate health facilities in their respective regions. There are five RHAs that deliver public health care services to the population: four regions in Trinidad and Tobago as one other region. The Tobago RHA falls under the purview of the Tobago House Assembly. The Ministry of Health takes up the challenge of providing tertiary care to the most vulnerable; to that effect it created the Children's Life Fund and the External Patient Programme. The Children's Life Fund is designed to provide financing for life-saving surgeries for children. The External Patient Programme funds essential surgeries that cannot be provided by the public health institutions. RHAs enter into a public-private partnership with private health institutions for dealing with certain diseases.[19]

The Social Welfare Division of the Ministry of Social Development and Family Services supervises the delivery of social assistance benefits. The actual operation of the social assistance schemes lies with the district based Local Public Assistance Boards. A Central Public Assistance Board is established to control, direct and assist the local boards in administering public assistance and to supervise all matters related to the granting of public assistance. Members of both the Central and Local Boards are nominated by the Minister of Social Development and Family

21.5 Coordination

Trinidad and Tobago is party to the CARICOM Agreement on Social Security (CASS) of 1996. CASS protects nationals of the member states who belong to the following groups of workers: workers in transnational enterprises, workers in

[17]National Insurance Act, arts. 23 and 24, Chap. 32:01 Laws of Trinidad and Tobago.

[18]Regional Health Authorities Act No. 5.

[19]See: http://www.health.gov.tt/sitepages/default.aspx?id=38.

international transport and on ships, workers in diplomatic missions, consulates and international organisations, self-employed workers and itinerant workers (i.e. working in more than one member state) as well as eventually their dependant family members. To be covered by CASS, the worker must move to work or have worked in two or more member states. CASS includes in its material scope only (contributory) pensions in case of invalidity, disablement, old-age and retirement, survivors' benefits and death benefits. CASS contains a non-discrimination on basis of nationality clause. CASS ensures that workers who have not made enough contributions to get an independent pension from their state's social security system, enjoy a totalisation with contributions in other member states. The worker then also enjoys an apportioned pension in the first state. CASS leaves untouched pensions that have been acquired solely on the basis of one member state's social security. Furthermore, CASS contains rules on posting of workers of international enterprises (in principle up to two years) and contains rules of assigning the competent country (or countries) for the other groups of workers.

Although many people of Trinidad and Tobago emigrate for work outside the Caribbean, Trinidad and Tobago has concluded only one bilateral social security coordination agreement, with Canada.[20] The agreement with Canada applies to contributory national insurance retirement, invalidity, survivors' and death benefits and the funeral grant. The agreement applies to persons, regardless of their nationality, who are socially insured in Canada or Trinidad and Tobago. The agreement contains provisions on the equality of treatment of each other's citizens, the export of benefits, the designation of the applicable legislation, the aggregation of periods of social insurance and administrative co-operation between the two countries. Interestingly, if a person is not entitled to the payment of a benefit based on the creditable periods under the legislation of both countries, totalised as stipulated in the agreement, that person's entitlement to the payment of that benefit will be determined by totalising these periods and creditable periods under the legislation of a third state with which both parties are bound by separate social security instruments, which provide for totalising of periods.

The national insurance (medical expenses) regulations stipulate that medical expenses incurred outside Trinidad and Tobago are payable only if the NIBTT is satisfied that the treatment required by the insured person (victim of a work accident) was not available locally and that with regard to all other circumstances of the case the insured person was justified in seeking care and treatment abroad.

The universal health care system that the Ministry of Health operates an External Patient Programme, which funds essential surgeries that cannot be provided by the public health institutions of Trinidad and Tobago. The Ministry may provide financial support for care abroad under this programme.[21]

[20]Agreement and Administrative Agreement on Social Security between the Government of Canada and the Government of the Republic of Trinidad and Tobago, Chap. 32:01 Laws of Trinidad and Tobago.

[21]See: http://www.health.gov.tt/sitepages/default.aspx?id=38.

21.6 Additional Relevant Information

Although the islands are not usually hit by hurricanes and tropical storms, they may occasionally pass by. In 1963, for instance, Tobago was struck by hurricane Flora, which caused enormous destruction to the island.

Oil and natural gas production lie at the basis of the prosperity of Trinidad and Tobago. They account for about 40% of the GDP and 80% of exports. The strong dependence on the energy sector makes the country very sensitive to fluctuations of oil and gas prices on the world market. The tourism sector is growing, mainly on Tobago. Tourism and the public service are the main employers in the republic.[22]

The country has a reputation concerning integrity issues; allegations of corruption have been made against successive governments. Legislation to protect the integrity of public service and to fight corruption is however abundant.

Websites

https://cso.gov.tt
www.health.gov.tt/sitepages/default.aspx?id=38
www.nibtt.net/

References

Country Profiles (2020) International Social Security Association. https://www.issa.int/en_GB/country-profiles. Accessed 12 Feb 2020

Robles C, Vargas LH (2010) Social protection systems in Latin America and the Caribbean. ECLAC/United Nations, Santiago de Chile, Trinidad and Tobago

World Factbook (2020) Central Intelligence Agency. https://www.cia.gov/the-world-factbook/countries/trinidadandtobago. Accessed 12 Feb 2020

[22]See Robles and Vargas (2010), pp. 9–11.

Chapter 22
Tonga

22.1 Context

Tonga[1] is a small[2] archipelagic kingdom situated in the South Pacific Ocean, consisting of over 170 islands of which about 40 are inhabited. The distances between the inhabited islands are considerable. The islands of what was then called 'The Friendly Islands' were united into a kingdom in 1845. In 1875, Tonga became a constitutional monarchy and from 1900 to 1970, Tonga functioned as a British protectorate.

Tonga is a constitutional monarchy, where the King and the nobility have retained more power than in ordinary parliamentary democracies. Only in 2010 did parliamentary elections put an end to a quasi-feudal rule. The monarchy is hereditary. The king is assisted by a Privy Council, an advisory organ that also has judicial and powers. The Privy Council advises the King on whether to veto an Act passed by Parliament; if the King refuses assent, the advice is being referenced.

The Prime Minister and Deputy Prime Minister are elected by the Legislative Assembly or Fale Alea, the unicameral Parliament. The Legislative Assembly consists of 17 members directly elected in single-seat constituencies and 9 members elected by and from among the 33 hereditary nobles of the five island groups of Tonga. In the last elections, one party, the Democratic Party (of democracy and human rights activists) won 14 of the 17 seats; they also provided the Prime Minister.

With special thanks to Ms Adi Talanaivini Mafi and Ms Milika Feaomoemanu Tuita for reviewing the report on Tonga.

[1]For data and figures, see: Country Profiles (2020) and World Factbook (2020).

[2]Only 747 km^2.

D. Pieters, *Social Security Law in Small Jurisdictions*, The World of Small States 8,
https://doi.org/10.1007/978-3-030-78247-4_22

Tonga has been labelled a "deeply conservative, Christian country".[3] Various Protestant denominations account for 64% of the population, Roman Catholics constitute about 14% and Mormons about 19% of the population.

Tonga is a member of the Commonwealth.

22.2 Legal Framework of Rights to Social Security

22.2.1 Constitutional Context

The Constitution of Tonga[4] does not contain any provisions concerning social security.

The legal system is of the English common law type.

22.2.2 Social Security Legislation and Structure

Social insurance, which takes the form of two superannuation arrangements, is regulated by the Retirement Fund Act[5] and the National Retirement Benefits Fund Act,[6] and their respective regulations.

We distinguish between two contributory, public superannuation funds: the Retirement Fund and the National Retirements Benefits Fund.

The Retirement Fund provides benefits to persons in the public service of the Government upon their retirement, ceasing service, death or total permanent disablement. The benefits can be paid in a lump sum or in instalments.

The National Retirements Benefits Fund covers the private sector (for membership see further) and provides benefits in respect of the retirement, permanent total disablement or the death of a member and does so from the individual accounts of the members in the form of instalments, a lump sum, or a combination of both. Early release of benefits is possible due to redundancy, on medical grounds, in case of migration overseas, or in case of financial hardship.[7] Moreover, the Fund pays a lump sum life insurance benefit to the compulsory member of the Fund who dies before retirement age. It is a no-loan scheme for both members and employers.

---

[3]See: https://www.bbc.com/news/world-asia-pacific-16197014.

[4]Cap. 01.01 Laws of Tonga.

[5]Retirement Fund Act, cap. 04.40 Laws of Tonga. We do not deal here with the pension arrangement for holders of a public office of the Pensions Act (Cap. 04.28 Laws of Tonga) as these only apply to officers in post before 1 July 1999, who were 50 years old and had at least 15 years of service at that moment.

[6]National retirement Benefits Fund Act, Cap. 04.42 Laws of Tonga.

[7]See: http://www.nrbf.to/index.php/about.

The health care system is governed by the Health Services Act[8] and related regulations. The Health Services (fees and charges) Regulations of 2000[9] provide an extensive list of medical fees and charges for services rendered by or on behalf of medical and dental officers of the public health system. The Minister of Health is competent to exempt persons from their payment or, on humanitarian grounds and upon recommendation of the CEO for Health, to waive the payment of the fees or charges for any person. Tonga has one national referral hospital, three community hospitals, 14 health centres and 34 reproductive and child health clinics. About 90% of health services are provided at hospitals. There are few specialists at the national referral hospital. Overseas referral schemes and visits of specialised medical teams from abroad cater to the growing needs for specialised care.[10]

The welfare schemes operate without a statutory framework and are mainly financed by foreign aid collected by a fundraising committee headed by the King's daughter.

Most important is the Social Welfare Scheme, which provides a monthly benefit to Tongans of at least 70 years of age. In the past, geographical remoteness and a culture of complacency caused births not to be registered in a timely fashion and sometimes not at all. As a consequence, some people face problems proving their age and thus qualifying for the welfare benefit for the elderly. Payments were originally made directly into bank accounts, but are now administered directly in cash.[11]

Since 2012, the Government has also been piloting a disability support scheme, including a cash benefit for the most severely disabled.[12]

After Cyclone Ian had devastated part of Tonga in early 2015, the Ministry of Agriculture, Fisheries and Forestry, together with UNDP, set up a 'post cyclone livelihoods recovery and cash for work project' in the affected locations. The project provided temporary cash for work income to disaster-affected families.[13] The project was terminated, but has received much attention. It is said to have impacted the vision of many Tongans on cash welfare benefits.[14]

[8]Health Services Act, Cap. 28.12 Laws of Tonga.

[9]Cap. 28.12.2 Laws of Tonga.

[10]TONGA–WHO Country Cooperation Strategy 2018–2022, p. 2. Accessed on: file:///C:/Users/u0018948/Downloads/WPRO-2017-DPM-023-ton-eng.pdf.

[11]Hobbs and Jackson (2016), p. 71. Accessed on: http://www.cashlearning.org/downloads/calp-pacific-scoping-study-web.pdf.

[12]Hobbs and Jackson (2016), p. 72. Accessed on: http://www.cashlearning.org/downloads/calp-pacific-scoping-study-web.pdf.

[13]Tonga. Making Social Protection More Responsive To natural disasters and Climate Change, The World Bank, 21 April 2015, p. 14. Accessed on: https://socialprotection.org/sites/default/files/publications_files/World%20Bank_SP_DRM_CCA_Tonga%20Case%20Study.pdf.

[14]Hobbs and Jackson (2016), pp. 65 and 71. Accessed on: http://www.cashlearning.org/downloads/calp-pacific-scoping-study-web.pdf. Authors report that "civil society and government were united in their view that cash and vouchers should be provided with the utmost care, so as to not damage

It may be observed here that faith-based organisations and NGOs that provide support to the needy receive annual grants from the Prime Minister's Office and from the Legislative Assembly.

Traditional community and church-based support provides important protection mechanisms. However, the erosion of money to be distributed due to natural disasters or economic recession, increasing urbanisation, and overseas migration, have gradually distanced people from the traditional community and church-based support. Nonetheless, traditional communities, churches and NGOs continue to play an important role in social service provision and support to people in need. In this respect, it is important to note that Tongans make considerable cash contributions to religious institutions and that churches provide support in the form of cash and vouchers during times of natural disasters and even supplement the social welfare pensions of their members.[15]

Some consider private overseas remittances to "remain the most important form of social protection in Tonga".[16] Remittances accounted for 31% of Gross Domestic Product and 82% of households benefitted from them in 2016.[17] Some see the remittances as 'easy money' that discourages young people from actively looking for work.[18]

22.2.3 *Enforcement of Constitutional and Statutory Rights*

Questions of fact regarding the Retirement Fund are determined by the Fund Board, and its determination is final and conclusive.[19] Decisions of the Board of the National Retirement benefits Fund can be appealed with the National Retirement Benefits Fund Appeal Board, the members of which are nominated by the Minister of Finance. These members are a chairperson who has at least 10 years of law

traditional self- and community-recovery approaches to rebuilding after emergencies, and to avoid fostering expectations for, and dependency on, relief assistance".

[15]Tonga. Making Social Protection More Responsive to Natural Disasters and Climate Change, World Bank, 21 April 2015, p. 20. Accessed on: https://socialprotection.org/sites/default/files/publications_files/World%20Bank_SP_DRM_CCA_Tonga%20Case%20Study.pdf; and Hobbs and Jackson (2016), pp. 27 and 72. Accessed on http://www.cashlearning.org/downloads/calp-pacific-scoping-study-web.pdf.

[16]Tonga. Making Social Protection More Responsive To natural disasters and Climate Change, The World Bank, 21 April 2015, p. 19. Accessed on: https://socialprotection.org/sites/default/files/publications_files/World%20Bank_SP_DRM_CCA_Tonga%20Case%20Study.pdf.

[17]Hobbs and Jackson (2016), p. 72. Accessed on: http://www.cashlearning.org/downloads/calp-pacific-scoping-study-web.pdf.

[18]Some interviewees quoted in Hobbs and Jackson (2016), pp. 82–83. Accessed on: http://www.cashlearning.org/downloads/calp-pacific-scoping-study-web.pdf.

[19]Retirement Fund Board Act, cap. 04.44 Laws of Tonga, section 9.

practice in Tonga, one member representative of the employees, and one member representative of the employers. Decisions made by the Appeal Board are final.

No appeal procedures seem to be established regarding the social welfare schemes. It appears that no further appeals with the ordinary judiciary are considered in social insurance or social assistance matters. The Court of Appeal is the highest jurisdiction in the country. Subordinate courts are the Supreme Court, Magistrates' Courts and land Courts.

22.3 Population and the Personal Scope of the Social Security Schemes

22.3.1 General Data on the Population and Its Composition

The population of Tonga was estimated at approximately 106,000 in 2020. Two-thirds of the population live on the island of Tongatapu, where the capital city Nuku'alofa is also situated. Nearly all citizens are of Tongan (Polynesian) ethnicity; most of them speak both English and Tongan.

The labour force was estimated at just under 34,000 in 2011, with an unemployment rate of 1.1%. Most people work in the services sector, including a large public sector and agriculture. Youth unemployment remains high: 11% in 2016, young people constituting half of the unemployed population.[20] The population living below the poverty line was estimated at 22.5% in 2010.

Tonga has a negative net migration rate of minus 17.9 migrants per thousand (2020). Data from 2004 tell us that about twice as many Tongans live abroad, compared to Tongans living in Tonga.[21] Another source mentions that in 2017 roughly half of the Tongans lived abroad.[22] Over 50,000 Tongans have permanently migrated to work abroad (2018). Seasonal workers from Tonga constitute the second largest group of low-skilled seasonal workers in Australia and New Zealand, with respectively about 2700 workers going to Australia and 1600 to New Zealand in 2017, working there in horticulture, viticulture and tourism.[23] There is also some seasonal work migration to the USA. The Tongan Government encourages seasonal

[20]United Nations Children's Fund, Situation Analysis of Children in Tonga, UNICEF, Suva, 2017, p. 83. Accessed on: https://www.unicef.org/pacificislands/media/1251/file/Situation-Analysis-of-Children-Tonga.pdf.

[21]Small and Dixon (2004), as quoted in United Nations Children's Fund, situation Analysis of Children in Tonga, UNICEF, Suva, 2017, p. 17. Accessed on: https://www.unicef.org/pacificislands/media/1251/file/Situation-Analysis-of-Children-Tonga.pdf.

[22]See: https://borgenproject.org/nine-facts-about-tonga-emigrants.

[23]See: http://documents.worldbank; or Hobbs and Jackson (2016), pp. 55–56. Accessed on: http://www.cashlearning.org/downloads/calp-pacific-scoping-study-web.pdfg/curated/pt/922451532395405180/text/Project-Information-Document-Integrated-Safeguards-Data-Sheet-Skills-and-Employment-for-Tongans-P161541.txt, 15.

work abroad and has created support services for migrant workers (processing their documentation and preparing for the overseas experience).[24]

22.3.2 *Personal Scope of the Social Insurance and Social Assistance Schemes*

Persons in the public service of the Government are members of the Retirement Fund. In 2019 approximately 5400 civil servants were member of the Retirement Fund.

All employees (of the private sector, churches etc.) are in principle required to be member of the National Retirement Benefits Fund. An employee is any person aged 15 years or older and below the retirement age, who works for an employer in Tonga under a contract of service or apprenticeship whether written or oral, expressed or implied, for remuneration. This includes a Tongan citizen employed under a contract of service entered into in Tonga as a master or member of the crew of any vessel, or as captain or member of the crew of any aircraft, whose owners have a place of business in Tonga.

Employers who set up a 'complying scheme', i.e. a retirement benefit scheme, before 1 July 2011, which provides legal entitlements that are equal to or better than those of the National Retirement Benefits Fund (excluding life insurance), and without rights to withdraw any part or the whole prior to the date of entitlement to benefit, are freed from contributing to the National Retirement Benefits Fund, and their employees are exempted from membership of the Fund.

Some categories of employees are exempted from membership:

- Domestic employees: these are persons employed in connection with the work of a private dwelling-house and not in connection with the trade, business or profession carried out by the employer in the dwelling-house. They can be employed as cook, house-worker, child's nurse, gardener, laundry worker, security officer, or a driver of a vehicle licensed for private use;
- Out-workers, meaning persons to whom articles are given to be made up, cleaned, washed, altered, ornamented, finished, repaired or adapted for sale in the person's own home or on other premises not under the control or management of the person who gave out the materials or articles;
- Casual workers, i.e. employees who have no ongoing expectation of permanent employment, and who have no fixed hours of work. They have an irregular pattern of working days and are paid at the end of each work period;
- Persons detained in a prison or mental hospital;
- Foreign diplomatic personnel; and

[24]Tonga. Making Social Protection More Responsive to Natural Disasters and Climate Change, World Bank, 21 April 2015, pp. 19–20. Accessed on: https://socialprotection.org/sites/default/files/publications_files/World%20Bank_SP_DRM_CCA_Tonga%20Case%20Study.pdf.

- Persons who are not Tongan citizens and contribute to a national statutory superannuation scheme in another country which provides equivalent or better benefits than those of the National Retirement Benefits Fund.

Moreover, the Minister of Finance may on recommendation of the Board exempt any other person or category.

Any person who is not compulsorily a member, including self-employed persons and citizens of Tonga living overseas, may contribute voluntarily on their own behalf or on behalf of another person.

The National Retirement Benefits Fund had about 12,800 members in 2018.[25]

The Medical Services Regulations of 1929 (as amended)[26] provide that it is the duty of each medical officer within his/her district to afford free medical and surgical aid to all Tongans in his/her district and to afford medical and surgical aid to all non-Tongans who may require his/her services for such remuneration as may be prescribed by the Cabinet.

The Government Social Welfare Scheme benefits Tongan citizens who permanently reside in Tonga and who are 70 years of age or older. They may no longer be in paid employment nor receive pensions or any other form of welfare support. In 2015 almost 4000 persons, i.e. about 60% of the persons estimated to be eligible, actually received the benefit.[27]

The disability benefit reached a little fewer than 600 persons that year.[28]

22.4 Administration of Social Security

The Retirement Fund and the National Retirement Benefits Fund are autonomous bodies operating under the political responsibility and control of the Minister of Finance.

The Retirement Fund is headed by a Retirement Fund Board consisting of the Prime Minister, the Minister of Finance and one other Cabinet Minister on the employers' side, and three members elected by the members (i.e. people in public

[25]See: http://www.nrbf.to/images/AnnualReport/Tonga-NRBF-Actuarial-Review-as-at-30-June-2018-1.pdf, p. 7.

[26]Cap. 28.12.1 Laws of Tonga.

[27]Tonga. Making Social Protection More Responsive To natural disasters and Climate Change, The World Bank, 21 April 2015, p. 17. Accessed on: https://socialprotection.org/sites/default/files/publications_files/World%20Bank_SP_DRM_CCA_Tonga%20Case%20Study.pdf; https://socialprotection.org/discover/programmes/social-welfare-scheme; and Hobbs and Jackson (2016), p. 27. Accessed on: http://www.cashlearning.org/downloads/calp-pacific scoping-study-web.pdf.

[28]Tonga. Making Social Protection More Responsive To natural disasters and Climate Change, The World Bank, 21 April 2015, p. vi. Accessed on: https://socialprotection.org/sites/default/files/publications_files/World%20Bank_SP_DRM_CCA_Tonga%20Case%20Study.pdf; and Hobbs and Jackson (2016), p. 71. Accessed on: http://www.cashlearning.org/downloads/calp-pacific-scoping-study-web.pdf.

service of the Government). The daily operations are managed by a Chief Executive Officer appointed by the Board with the consent of the Cabinet.[29]

The National Retirement Benefits Fund operates under the general direction and supervision of a Board of Directors. The Board advises and reports to the Minister of Finance; they manage the finances of the Fund as trustee. The Board collects the contributions and pays out the benefits. The Board devises investment strategies for investments of the Fund.

The Board of Directors consists of seven members appointed by the Minister of Finance:[30] one nominated by the current Chairman of the Board, and two nominated per sector of members of the Fund. Three sectors are distinguished: the Churches, the private businesses and the public enterprises and statutory bodies. Each sector determines the procedure for selecting its nominees. Each sector shall nominate an equal number of employers and employees.[31] The Board appoints the Chief Executive Officer.

The Board of the National Retirement Benefits Fund determines the investments of the Fund. In doing so, it may invest in other countries that meet the criteria for trustee management or retirement benefits funds. However, when undertaking overseas investments, the board requires approval from the National Reserve Bank of Tonga; such approval is given for periods of no less than 1 year.[32]

Public health services are under the authority of the Minister of Health. Within the Ministry of Health, daily operations are directed by the Chief Executive Officer for Health.

There is no ministry nor Minister for social affairs or the like. The Ministry of Internal Affairs has however created a Social Protection and Disabilities Division[33] in 2014, as well as an Overseas Employment Division. The Overseas Employment Division promotes seasonal work abroad.[34] The Social Protection and Disabilities Division aims at eliminating, reducing and minimising risks to marginalised and vulnerable people by designing, developing and implementing social policies, social programmes and protection mechanisms to safeguard the vulnerable population. As such, it is responsible for the social assistance programmes.[35] However, Social

[29]Retirement Fund Board Act, Cap.04.44 Laws of Tonga.

[30]National Retirement Benefits Fund (Appointment of Directors) Regulations, Cap. 04.42.3 Laws of Tonga.

[31]Apparently, this changes what was decided only 3 years earlier in the National Retirement benefits Scheme (Election) Regulations 2012 of 30th January 2012, which provided in elections to be held for the employee and employer representatives.

[32]National Retirement Benefits Fund Act, cap. 04.42 Laws of Tonga, section 12.

[33]It is reported that in 2015 this Division would consist of only Deputy Secretary and three other staff. Tonga. Making Social Protection More Responsive To natural disasters and Climate Change, The World Bank, 21 April 2015. Accessed on: https://socialprotection.org/sites/default/files/publications_files/World%20Bank_SP_DRM_CCA_Tonga%20Case%20Study.pdf.

[34]See: http://www.tongaworks.org/ and https://mia.gov.to/about/overseas-employment/.

[35]See: https://mia.gov.to/about/social-protection-and-vulnerables/.

Welfare Scheme benefits are administered (but not financed) by the National Retirement Benefits Fund.[36]

22.5 Coordination

Tonga has not concluded any bilateral or multilateral social security arrangements.

The National Retirement Benefits Fund Act provides some elements of coordination. According to section 62, postings not exceeding 12 months outside Tonga permit the retention of membership. Section 63 states that a person shall not be disqualified from receiving any benefit for any period during which that person is absent from Tonga.

There is no formal framework for the provision of health care abroad. Apparently, patients are referred for care abroad, i.e. to New Zealand, Australia, the USA (Hawaii) and Fiji, if they cannot be helped in Tonga and there are good chances of survival after treatment. Patients with private insurance or who are 65 years old or more are not eligible. Referral abroad is also refused if the condition can wait and be treated by a visiting medical specialist.[37] Bilateral agreements are in place with the New Zealand Medical Treatment Scheme (NZMTS); charitable organisations and faith-based organisations also play a role.[38]

22.6 Additional Relevant Information

The economy relies on agriculture (squash, vanilla beans, yam), fishery and tourism. Remittances from Tongans abroad are the largest source of foreign currency, followed by tourism.

The country is also highly dependent on official development assistance from overseas. Ongoing social protection (assistance) schemes as well as emergency response schemes (such as the cash-for-work) are overwhelmingly reliant on donor financing.[39] The main donors are Australia, the International Development Association, New Zealand and Japan.[40]

Pressures for democratic reform may create political turbulence in the future.

---

[36]See: http://www.nrbf.to/index.php/about.

[37]Boudville et al. (2019).

[38]Boudville et al. (2019).

[39]Hobbs and Jackson (2016), p. 56. Accessed on: http://www.cashlearning.org/downloads/calp-pacific-scoping-study-web.pdf.

[40]United Nations Children's Fund, situation Analysis of Children in Tonga, UNICEF, Suva, 2017, p. 19. Accessed on: https://www.unicef.org/pacificislands/media/1251/file/Situation-Analysis-of-Children-Tonga.pdf.

As summarised in a recent World Bank document:[41]

> Tonga is the second most exposed country in the world to natural hazard risks and faces the third highest level of disaster risk in the world, along with a high degree of vulnerability to climate change impacts. Its location, climate and topography render the country susceptible to many natural hazards. These include both climate-related hazards (e.g. cyclones, floods, drought, and storm surge) and geophysical hazards (e.g. earthquakes, tsunamis and volcanic eruptions). [. . .].
>
> Tonga is also highly vulnerable to climate change impacts. [. . .]. These changes are projected to negatively affect tourism, agricultural production, food security and health. This is likely to impact disproportionately on poor rural people.
>
> High concentrations of population in vulnerable coastal areas, population growth, urbanization, physical isolation and the socio-economic challenges associated with being a small island state are key contributors to increased vulnerability to the impacts of natural hazard events and climate change. People living in coastal areas are vulnerable both to sea level rise and increases in the intensity of tropical storms and storm surges. [. . .]
>
> Tonga's narrow economic base and heavy reliance on overseas remittances also put it at risk from external shocks. For example, the country was hard hit by the global economic slowdown of 2008, as well as food and fuel price shocks. Overseas remittances, on which many Tongan households depend, fell sharply. The effects of these shocks were compounded by the economic impacts of a tsunami in 2009 and multiple tropical cyclones between 2011-2014. [. . .]
>
> A sizeable number of Tongan households may be vulnerable to falling into hardship or poverty, even as a result of small shocks.[42]

In 2018, tropical cyclone Gita passed through two island groups of Tonga, causing enormous damages to housing and tourism, as well as significant losses in the agriculture and tourism sectors.

Websites

https://borgenproject.org/nine-facts-about-tonga-emigrants
http://documents.worldbank
https://mia.gov.to/about/overseas-employment/
https://mia.gov.to/about/social-protection-and-vulnerables/
https://socialprotection.org/discover/programmes/social-welfare-scheme
www.bbc.com/news/world-asia-pacific-16197014
www.nrbf.to/index.php/about

---

[41] Tonga. Making Social Protection More Responsive to Natural Disasters and Climate Change, World Bank, 21 April 2015, pp. iv–v. Accessed on: https://socialprotection.org/sites/default/files/publications_files/World%20Bank_SP_DRM_CCA_Tonga%20Case%20Study.pdf.

[42] For a disaster profile of Tonga, see also Hobbs and Jackson (2016), p. 68. Accessed on: http://www.cashlearning.org/downloads/calp-pacific-scoping-study-web.pdf.

www.nrbf.to/images/AnnualReport/Tonga-NRBF-Actuarial-Review-as-at-30-June-2018-1.pdf
www.tongaworks.org/

References

Boudville A, Irava W, Koafoa B (2019) Overseas medical referral priorities for Pacific Island Countries 2019 Pacific Update. University of the South Pacific, Suva, Fiji. Accessed on: http://devpolicy.org/2019-Pacific-Update/Day_1_Panel_3A_Andrea_Boudville.pdf

Country Profiles (2020) International Social Security Association. https://www.issa.int/en_GB/country-profiles. Accessed 12 Feb 2020

Hobbs C, Jackson R (2016) Cash transfer programming in the Pacific. A feasibility scoping study. CaLP. Accessed on: http://www.cashlearning.org/downloads/calp-pacific-scoping-study-web.pdf

Small C, Dixon D (2004) Tonga: migration and the homeland. Accessed on: http://www.migrationploicy.org/article.tonga-migration-and-homeland

The World Bank (2015) Tonga. Making social protection more responsive to natural disasters and climate change. Accessed on: https://socialprotection.org/sites/default/files/publications_files/World%20Bank_SP_DRM_CCA_Tonga%20Case%20Study.pdf

TONGA–WHO (2017) Country Cooperation Strategy 2018–2022. Accessed on: file:///C:/Users/u0018948/Downloads/WPRO-2017-DPM-023-ton-eng.pdf

United Nations Children's (2017) Fund, situation analysis of children in Tonga. UNICEF, Suva. Accessed on: https://www.unicef.org/pacificislands/media/1251/file/Situation-Analysis-of-Children-Tonga.pdf

World Factbook (2020) Central Intelligence Agency. https://www.cia.gov/the-world-factbook/countries/tonga. Accessed 12 Feb 2020

Part III
The Comparison: Facts and Recommendations

In the first chapter of this part we compare the social security (law) systems of the twenty small jurisdictions described in Part II. We come to comparative conclusions regarding the impact of the context, the originality of the social security approaches, the administration and personal scope of the social insurance and social assistance schemes, the impact of remoteness, immigration, emigration, and re-migration; remittances, health care abroad and the impact of economic and environmental shocks will also be dealt with. The impact of COVID-19 upon social security will also be addressed in this part. In the second chapter of this part we provide 21 recommendations that could be of use to the small jurisdcitions and their social security. They are built upon the knowledge gathered in the previous chapters.

Chapter 23
The Comparison

Following the uniform description of the social security and the social security law of twenty small states, we shall now elaborate on some conclusions that our comparison allows for. Let us recall that we are not interested here in the general issues these social security systems and their law are confronted with. Instead, we focus on the features, if any, that make the social security (law) of small jurisdictions special compared to the social security (law) of other nations. This will help us answer our main research question: do small jurisdictions present specific features regarding their social security and social security law? When we compare with what is usual in other states, we take our earlier studies as starting point.[1]

23.1 Political, Cultural and Constitutional Context

As established in our general background descriptions of the small states, political, religious or even ethnic tensions are sometimes important in the small jurisdictions. Yet these tensions do not substantively translate in specific approaches of social security (law). There is no clear link to be made between the political, religious or ethnic groups in power and the way social security is shaped and regulated. In fact, usually historical continuity seems to prevail, sometimes interrupted by economic or environmental shocks. In some rather homogeneous countries, such as Tonga or Bhutan, social security appears to be a 'modern' rival to more traditional forms of social protection, such as family, kinship or tribal solidarity. This leads to underdeveloped social security systems, but as such these cannot be seen as typical for small jurisdictions, but rather as a stage in the development of the concerned societies.

[1]Pieters (2006, 2019).

D. Pieters, *Social Security Law in Small Jurisdictions*, The World of Small States 8,
https://doi.org/10.1007/978-3-030-78247-4_23

Only very exceptionally has the religious context led to specific benefits, such as the aid in Maldives to perform one's first hajj.

Small jurisdictions reflect the worldwide variety in constitutional approaches to social security: in some of the constitutions no social security is mentioned, others contain a principle of social security or even an elaborate list of rights to social benefits. In some countries, a constitutional or other court is responsible for checking legislation for conformity with the constitutional precepts, in others this is not the case. As with larger states, it is not possible to establish a link between the quality of the social security system of the country and the extent to which social security has been dealt with in its constitution. Sometimes the constitution will limit the possibility of social security expanding, because it would clash with other values or institutions, such as family or the royal prerogative in the Bhutanese '*kidu*' system.

23.2 Conservatism and Absence of Originality

We were struck most by the importance of social security arrangements and legislation dating back to periods when the country was not independent or fully in control. To put it in differently, we observed the absence of originality in the social security (law) of the examined small jurisdictions. Of course, social security evolves and requires continuous legislative updating, but in most of the examined countries the basic social security structure and legislation of the country dated back to pre-independence and thus often 'colonial' legislation. This usually links these social security systems and their legislation rather strongly to the social security (law) of the former colonial powers of the concerned period. In other words, the social security structure and law of many of the examined states reflects a social security approach from more than half a century ago in European countries. Social security in Malta, Cyprus, Gibraltar, and Fiji continues to be strongly influenced by the social security in the United Kingdom of more than half a century ago. Social security (law) in Curaçao and Sint Maarten still very much dates from the time of the Netherlands Antilles. Only a few small jurisdictions made an effort after getting sovereignty over social affairs to create their own comprehensive social security legislation, notwithstanding that, even then, they often adopted social security approaches of former times. In the twenty-first century, important legislative work that restructured social security as a whole was performed in countries like Maldives, Seychelles, Suriname, Aruba, Bhutan, Iceland, the Faroe Islands and Greenland. Yet, the social security (law) of the latter three countries is still strongly influenced by Danish social security (law) and that of Suriname and Aruba by former Dutch law. In some cases, the influence was not so much that of a former colonial power, but that of the neighbouring state, such as with San Marino (Italy) and Liechtenstein (Switzerland).

In line with the above, most of the small jurisdictions examined maintain a plethora of different social insurance schemes and benefits, which are linked to traditional social security risks. In particular, the countries that have undergone

British influence have accumulated a whole range of different benefits: in Malta, Cyprus, Seychelles, Guyana, and Trinidad and Tobago we can count over 10 different benefits. Only very seldom can we identify 'original' social risks that do not correspond to the mainstream social risks. We already mentioned the financing of a first haj as an example, we could also mention the loss of income of fishermen due to the repairing of the ship in the Faroe Islands.

23.3 Administration

At a policy level, we usually do not encounter one single minister who is responsible for all social security, but mostly two to four ministers and ministerial departments. In most cases, the provision of health care and its social coverage is the responsibility of a minister of health, while other possible competent ministries refer to 'labour', 'social affairs', 'family', 'social development', 'well being' etc. Sometimes the minister of finance plays a role in the collection of social security contributions and/or the supervision of social insurance providers. This is all relatively in line with what we can also observe in larger countries. What is more specific is the sometimes strange competence combinations and denominations in small jurisdictions. For instance, we encounter ministers competent for social security combining this competence with tourism, environment, 'women', international business, 'society', housing, and other portfolio responsibilities.

The multitude of benefits contrasts with the relative unity in administration of social security schemes. In most small jurisdictions, the administration of the social insurance schemes has been allocated to one or very few distinct agencies or departments, usually fewer than the number of agencies in the European countries by which they were influenced. In this regard, we can observe increased efforts from many small jurisdictions to concentrate the administration of the social insurance schemes compared to that common in most larger states.

The administration of social assistance is usually managed by a ministerial department and/or local authorities. This seems to be in line with what can be observed in larger states. What is more remarkable is the relatively poor legislative framework that characterises social assistance in many small jurisdictions. In some small jurisdictions, the philosophy behind social assistance seems more like the poor-law philosophy of the beginning of the twentieth century than a reflection of modern social assistance thinking. The possibility for people to appeal negative social assistance decisions is less clear and less developed in some of the examined small jurisdictions.

Although many social security schemes (both social insurance and social assistance) are means tested, these means tests do not always appear to be 'state of the art', leaving room for quite some discretion to the administrators. This creates a risk of cronyism and abuse.

Many of the examined small jurisdictions seem to pay much attention to regulating the way social security funds are invested. Investment is of course also regulated in larger states, but it is striking that the power of investment decisions within the often limited body of social security legislation is extensively regulated. We could refer here to countries as diverse as Cyprus, San Marino, Tonga, Maldives, Seychelles, Guyana, Trinidad and Tobago, Grenada, Bhutan and Liechtenstein.

23.4 Personal Scope

Do we find specific features in the way in which the personal scopes of the social insurance and social assistance schemes are defined?

As far as social insurance schemes are concerned, we can see that nationality or citizenship[2] is usually not set as a condition for benefitting from the social coverage, with exceptions often relating to non-contributory social insurance schemes. Often the citizenship requirement is set aside when a condition of legal residence over a number of years is met. All this is in line with what can usually be found in larger states as well.

Health care in principle covers the entire population, but is sometimes restricted to its own citizens, such as in Fiji, Seychelles, Grenada or Bhutan.

More specific are the provisions we encounter in countries such as Tonga, Liechtenstein or San Marino, where citizenship opens access to voluntary affiliation to social security, and provisions such as those in Fiji or Maldives, where nationals of other states can more easily be freed from social insurance in the small jurisdiction.

We also observe that nationality or citizenship requirements are given a special significance in the context of the constitutional order of the small jurisdictions that lack full sovereignty: one is a Danish citizen and not a citizen of Greenland or the Faroes, one is a citizen of the Kingdom of the Netherlands and not a citizen of Aruba, Curaçao or Sint Maarten. Moreover, when citizenship requirements are set, one should keep in mind that international coordination agreements often result in citizens of the partner state(s) being treated as if they were the states' own citizens.

As is the case throughout the world, some social insurance schemes are primarily based on residence (so-called universal or general social insurance schemes), whereas others are based on the professional activity of the persons concerned (professional schemes). The small jurisdictions make no exception, as they mostly also reflect the pre-sovereignty approach. Of course, the social insurances of the small jurisdictions are no copy of these of their former 'masters', but we can generally state that countries like Iceland, Faroes and Greenland follow a Scandinavian model; Liechtenstein and San Marino a Bismarckian model. In line with the Netherlands, the other components of the Kingdom and Suriname combine universal and professional social insurances. It appears that the Beveridgean approach to social insurance, which is characteristic of the United Kingdom after World War II, is less

[2]Citizenship and nationality are used here as interchangeable concepts.

reflected in the social insurances of the Commonwealth small jurisdictions we studied, since in most of them the quality of being a social insured person is determined by one's professional activity.

Where professional activity is the key to social insurance, the small jurisdictions we studied often restrict this to formal employment in subordination to a private sector employer. Civil servants and military and police personnel are included or have even better social insurance arrangements of their own. The self-employed are sometimes included (such as in San Marino, Iceland and Faroes) and can sometimes join voluntarily (as in Tonga, Maldives, Seychelles and Liechtenstein). It is striking that in some small jurisdictions (such as Guyana or Grenada) the legal position of social insurance for self-employed persons remains unclear.

Rather exceptionally, some small jurisdictions will link social insurance to a minimum of hours worked (Gibraltar) or to a minimum income earned from work (Malta for the self-employed, Trinidad and Tobago), but again this does not appear to be very different from what we encounter in larger states.

Just as in larger countries, social insurance is seen as a right of everyone who works in some (wealthier) countries, whereas in other (poorer) countries it is in fact a privilege for those working for the public authorities and larger (often international) companies. In the latter countries, many, if not most, of the people work in the informal economy without professionally-based social insurance. It should be observed here that in most small jurisdictions we examined, the social insurance and the social assistance schemes operate completely independently from each other.

The social assistance schemes of the examined countries are sometimes general (only the need being relevant), whereas others are categorical (only covering needy elderly, needy children or needy one-parent families etc.). Compared to larger states, no striking differences can be noted, except perhaps the rather poor legislative framework in which some small jurisdictions' social assistance schemes operate. Sometimes it is even difficult to establish whether one is faced with a general or a categorical system, since the in principle general scheme is de facto restricted to certain categories of poor.

23.5 Remoteness

Although small jurisdictions are called 'small', they can stretch out over a large territory with some less accessible parts. 'Small' refers to the number of inhabitants. We can establish that in many 'small jurisdictions' the population may be concentrated in certain cities, but that some people also live in more remote locations, which are often more difficult to reach. This remoteness presents specific problems regarding the delivery of social security benefits, non-take-up as well as fraud, information about social security and so on. For the provision of health care, this means that secondary and tertiary health care may need to be sought hundreds of kilometers away and that the health care costs to be covered by social security may also include significant travel costs. We shall come back later to the issue of health care provided abroad, but already within the small jurisdiction, the remoteness of the health care provider often requires specific answers by social security.

Small jurisdictions often combine one or more local languages and a European language as official languages. As we have seen, legislation in many small jurisdictions dates back to the pre-sovereignty period and was only redacted in the European language. In some countries even today, legislation is written in the European official language and not in the local, although official language. We mention this here, since it is an important obstacle for people to understand the applicable social security law in these countries, and thus a hindrance for a proper implementation of the law. This state of affairs is worsened when the courts also prefer to work in the European, rather than in the local, language. This linguistic remoteness problem is most apparent when Dutch is used in Suriname and the Caribbean components of the Kingdom of the Netherlands, and to a lesser extent, when Danish is used in Iceland and the small jurisdictions of the Kingdom of Denmark. But also in the small jurisdictions of the Commonwealth, there may be a problem of linguistic remoteness between the official language and the language spoken by most people.

23.6 Immigration

Small jurisdictions are usually characterised by important immigration and/or emigration flows, with the exception of Bhutan, which was closed off from the world until relatively recently. Sometimes the net migration rates reach high values, but also when these values are very low, they may hide important immigration and emigration, which balance each other out, as is the case for Guyana. The importance of migrations calls for social security approaches adapted to this reality. We look first at immigration, then emigration.

Immigration is important in a number of small states. Net migration rates of 5 per thousand people and over can be found in Malta, Cyprus and San Marino. In the Maldives more than 40%, and in Seychelles more than a quarter of the workforce come from abroad (mainly from the Indian subcontinent). In Sint Maarten, Aruba and Curaçao respectively more than 70%, a third and a quarter of the residents were not born on the respective island. In other small jurisdictions, permanent immigration may be less important, but large numbers of workers may daily or weekly travel to the country from abroad to come and work in the small country. In Liechtenstein and Gibraltar more than half of the workforce consists of frontier workers. Yet, in other countries, we encounter a phenomenon of seasonal work, which brings workers into the small country for a number of months a year.

As a result, social insurances often insure important numbers of people who are not nationals and who often do not even reside permanently in the small jurisdiction. This means that social security designed by the legislator of a small jurisdiction is applied to people other than those who have voting rights in the country: this is a problem from a democratic point of view.[3]

> When in a democracy all residents decide upon who is to make the relevant policy decisions and social security is universal, both personal scopes overlap. This is however not the case in most countries. Political rights are often reserved to the persons who have citizenship, sometimes including even citizens living abroad. Social security is often organised on a professional basis and thus concerns a group far smaller than the entire population. [. . .] Decisions on social security issues will consequently be taken by (those representing) another group of persons, usually a larger group of people. [. . .]
>
> In some countries, the mismatch between the people socially insured and those taking part in the political elections may be even bigger than usual as a consequence of many foreigners living and working in the country or many workers living abroad. This is especially an issue for smaller democracies, such as the microstates Andorra, Monaco or San Marino.

Our study confirms these statements. We can however observe that, in order to cope with this imbalance, the administration boards and sometimes the appeals boards of many professional social insurance administrations consist of representatives of trade unions of workers and of business as well, thus providing some participatory rights to all workers and all employers, regardless of their nationality. This is the case in Fiji, Tonga, Aruba, Curaçao, Sint Maarten, Gibraltar, San Marino, Seychelles, Trinidad and Tobago, Grenada, Faroe Islands and Iceland. However, it should be observed that even such participation by the trade unions and business (or sometimes also other groups such as NGOs) is not a guarantee, as such, that the interests of foreigners will be fully taken into consideration, as this depends on the internal democracy of trade unions and organisations of employers. Moreover, even if such representatives of trade unions and employers' organisations are nominated, they are nearly always appointed by the national political authorities. Of course, to the extent that the workers are only in the country temporarily, as is the case for seasonal workers, their impact will be even more minute. We do not deal with the worse situation of illegal immigrants nor the sometimes important numbers of refugees here, which raises specific issues that are not specific to small jurisdictions, even though their impact may be particularly important when the problems need to be absorbed by a small population, as is the case in Guyana and Trinidad and Tobago, for instance.

It is interesting to observe that a specific category of immigrants, the so-called expats (who usually come from the richer Western countries, and often from the former colonial power), is sometimes dissociated from social insurance in the smaller jurisdiction. They are freed from participation in the social security arrangements of the small jurisdiction, often on the sole condition that they can show equivalent or better coverage of the social risks elsewhere. In doing so, those on higher incomes escape the solidarity systems in the country. This is somehow the

[3]We already made this observation in our article "Social Security and Democracy", which is to be published at the occasion of the centenary of the University of Ljubljana (2020).

case in Fiji, Tonga and Maldives. It may also be the consequence of setting citizenship as a condition for cover by social security arrangements.

It is in the context of immigration, be it the very temporary one of tourists, noteworthy that none of the small jurisdictions examined to associate tourists with the financing of social security, not even of health care in the small jurisdictions. These tourists may nevertheless have to rely upon it in a first phase of emergency need.

23.7 Emigration

Some of the small jurisdictions examined experience important emigration flows. Negative net migration rates of 5 per thousand and more are to be found in countries such as Trinidad and Tobago, Fiji, Maldives, Greenland and peaking to nearly 18 per thousand in Tonga! There are nearly as many Surinamese citizens living outside the country as within its borders. As was already observed, countries with lower negative net migration rates may also have important emigration figures, as these can be 'compensated' by high immigration rates.

High emigration figures also raise questions that social security schemes have to deal with. One is the question of the exportation of benefits acquired in the small jurisdiction; another is the maintenance of rights in course of acquisition. The way in which emigrants are welcomed back by the social security of the small jurisdiction also demands attention, as does the way in which remittances should be considered if we take a holistic social protection vision.

If one leaves the country, the question is raised: can the emigrant take social security benefits already acquired with him/her? This is what we call the question of the exportation of benefits. Another question is whether the rights he/she was building up, especially in pension or superannuation schemes, can be transferred to the country to which he/she emigrates or can be maintained for a future entitlement in the country of emigration. This is the question of transferability or maintenance of rights in course of acquisition. When the periods of insurance in the country of emigration can be taken into account in some way in the country of immigration, we can also speak of a principle of 'aggregation'.

Unlike in larger countries, which conclude international coordination treaties on these issues, exportation of benefits is often already governed by the national legislation of the small jurisdiction. This is probably due to the combination of an important migration volume and the absence of (m)any coordination agreements with the countries of emigration. It is however difficult to give a comprehensive picture of whether or not benefits can be exported, since even within a country the answer may be different from benefit to benefit. In general, one can say that non-contributory social insurance benefits and social assistance benefits cannot be exported, whereas contributory social insurance benefits, especially pensions and superannuation/provident fund benefits, have better chances of being exported. Sometimes exports may reach considerable heights: in Liechtenstein more than half of the AHV pensions are exported! Some countries will pay out a capital sum to persons who definitely leave the country after they have contributed to a pension or superannuation/provident fund arrangement, as is the case in Aruba, the Maldives (for foreigners) and the Seychelles ('emigration allowance').

23.8 Coordination

Aggregation of periods of social insurance, residence or work between the country of emigration and the country of immigration can obviously not be dealt with by the sole legislation of one state, but requires international agreements. Such aggregation also requires some form of similarity between the social security schemes, mostly pensions, that are to be coordinated. A more or less comprehensive coordination with export of benefits and some aggregation is achieved by regional coordination mechanisms, such as the European Economic Area/European Union coordination law, which benefits Iceland, Liechtenstein, Faroe Islands, Greenland and the EU member states Malta and Cyprus (the fate of Gibraltar remaining uncertain). Another example being the CARICOM agreement on social security benefiting Guyana, Trinidad and Tobago, and Grenada (but not CARICOM member Suriname, as the latter social insurance system is insufficiently similar to the others). An even stronger coordination links the Nordic countries, including the Faroe Islands, Greenland and Iceland.

It is striking that the countries participating in these regional arrangements are also the countries with the most bilateral agreements with other states. Canada seems to have been the most willing partner to conclude a bilateral social security agreement with small jurisdictions: it has coordination agreements that deal mainly with pensions with Iceland, Trinidad and Tobago, Grenada, Malta and Cyprus. The United States have concluded partial pension coordination agreements with Iceland and Liechtenstein; Australia with Malta and Cyprus. Switzerland concluded a bilateral agreement with Liechtenstein and expanded its bilateral treaty arrangements with Italy to the Sanmarinese social security. Moreover, Malta concluded bilateral agreements with New Zealand and Libya (the latter being a very limited agreement); Cyprus with Egypt, Québec, Serbia and Syria; San Marino with Italy and Belgium; Liechtenstein with Austria, Germany and Italy. The Netherlands concluded a very limited agreement to export Dutch social security benefits in exchange for the power to control the recipients living in these countries with Liechtenstein, Suriname and many other countries of the world.

Other than that, thirteen of the twenty small jurisdictions we studied did not conclude any bilateral agreements with other states. This can be partly explained by the lack of, or uncertainty around, competence to conclude such agreements. In small jurisdictions that are not fully sovereign, competence in social security may be allocated to the small jurisdiction, but as a rule competence in foreign affairs and thus the competence to conclude treaties and international agreements remains with the central power. This means that the United Kingdom, and not Gibraltar, is competent to make social security coordination agreements, and similarly the Kingdom of the Netherlands and not the countries Aruba, Curaçao and Sint Maarten. It is less clear whether the Kingdom of Denmark is still competent to make social security treaties on behalf of Greenland and the Faroe Islands, or whether the latter (alone or even together) can make such agreements on social security coordination. Unfortunately, it seems that if not the small jurisdictions but the entity competent for foreign affairs concludes social security arrangements, the small jurisdictions are excluded from the scope of these agreements or simply forgotten.

From our survey, we can see that the number of social security arrangements between small jurisdictions and the main countries of emigration remains very limited. A surprising finding is also that the United Kingdom apparently did not enter into bilateral social security agreements with the small Commonwealth countries, as many of its citizens have emigrated to Britain. Similarly, there are (nearly) no social security coordination agreements between the social security of the Netherlands (in Europe) and Aruba, Curaçao, Sint Maarten and Suriname, although many migrants in the Netherlands (in Europe) come from these countries. Also, the United States, another important immigration country, has only concluded very few agreements with small jurisdictions, and not even with those of major provenance of the immigrants.

23.9 Re-migration

Emigrants may and often do return to the country of origin. This may be after some years or after they have spent their active years abroad. If they are citizens of their country of origin, such a return is without any obstacle. But what about their social security rights built up abroad? Whether they can bring home social security benefits (pensions, other benefits) to which they are entitled on the basis of their work or residence abroad will, of course, first depend upon what the social security law of the country or countries to which they emigrated says about export of benefits. Some countries have no problem exporting opened entitlements, others require the beneficiaries to have their permanent residence in the country. There are no general rules in this respect; the only very general guideline is that countries will be more ready to export contributory benefits than non-contributory, but there are many exceptions. Of course, the small jurisdiction of return may have bi-or multilateral agreements on the subject, but as we have seen above, those social security coordination agreements are very limited in number.

Another issue is whether the re-migrants can rely upon the social security provisions in the small jurisdiction to which they returned. It is indeed true that many emigrants return after a number of (often less successful) years or after they have ended their active career. In general, one can assume that the re-migrants as citizens and residents of the small jurisdiction to which they returned will qualify for social assistance and possibly also for residence-based benefits if they fulfill the conditions. If a benefit is conditional not only on an active (current) residence, but also on a number of years of residence in the past, this may of course prevent the re-migrant from receiving the benefit concerned. What remains unclear is to what extent the small jurisdiction will know, and take account of, benefit payments from foreign social security systems when deciding upon benefit claims in the country of re-migration. It is also unclear whether workers are able to rejoin the social security system of the country of origin and take into account their past social insurance periods or contributions in the country of origin after they have emigrated and possibly after they have received a capital payment or emigration allowance at that occasion.

23.10 Remittances

When the small jurisdiction has many of its citizens living and working abroad, the money they send to their family members and friends back home, i.e. 'remittances', may be an important source of income for those who remained in the small jurisdiction, and indeed, for the small jurisdiction as such. Sometimes remittances reach very high amounts. This is especially the case for the Caribbean small jurisdictions we examined as well as for Suriname, Guyana, Tonga, Maldives and the Faroe Islands. Some believe that for Tonga remittances are the most important social protection provider in the country (and not the formal social security). We were struck by the fact that the social security law of the small jurisdictions we examined did not pay attention to the reality of the sometimes very important remittances. It even remains unclear whether the social assistance schemes and the means test of some social insurances take into account the money transferred by family members living abroad.

23.11 Health Care Abroad

All small jurisdictions are faced with not being able to provide all the necessary health care in the country, as the investment would be too costly for the number of potential patients. Social security agreements with other states may include provisions in this respect, as is the case for the countries bound to the EU coordination mechanism or the Nordic Convention. The bilateral, more comprehensive, social security coordination agreements usually do not deal with health care. Exceptionally small jurisdictions have concluded specific bilateral agreements on the topic; more often, the health care systems of the small jurisdictions have entered into agreements with the particular health authorities or hospitals to which many of their citizens go. This is the case for Gibraltar with NHS in England and the regional providers in Spain. San Marino has made agreements with the neighbouring regional health authorities of Italy, and Liechtenstein with the hospitals of the neighboring Swiss canton. Aruba, Curaçao, Sint Maarten, Tonga, Maldives, the Faroe Islands and Greenland also have agreements with health care providers abroad.

However, one must make a distinction between the existence or not of international agreements on the one hand, and the possibility for a social health care insured person to go abroad and receive health care, diagnostic examinations and so on and to have the related expenses compensated by the health (insurance) authority of the small jurisdiction on the other. Indeed, whether a patient is allowed to travel abroad to get the necessary health care or examinations and to have the (or some) related costs paid by the health (insurance) authority of the small jurisdiction depends upon the conditions established by the national law of the small jurisdiction. Many of the examined small jurisdictions have established detailed rules and procedures to that effect; these mostly include:

- the need of a referral by medical doctors/hospitals in the small jurisdiction;
- the absence of the possibility of having the examinations/treatment done in the small jurisdiction;
- the prospect of success in the long term;
- a previous ad hoc agreement with the health care provider abroad; and
- the specification of the costs borne by the small jurisdiction. These costs may include not only the health care, diagnostic etc. as such, but also the travel and stay of the patient plus possibly an accompanying person. It may also be that the costs to be compensated are limited to a maximum amount.

For the health care (insurance) authorities of a small jurisdiction, the amounts they pay for allowing patients to travel and get health care abroad, especially in countries with a higher standard of living, may constitute an important fraction of the total health care costs in the small jurisdiction. It may therefore be of interest to small jurisdictions to periodically invite foreign teams to come over and perform some medical examinations and treatments in the small jurisdiction, as is for instance the practice for certain health care interventions in Fiji and Tonga.

It may also be observed that if a large portion of the costs of the health care abroad still has to be paid by patients, the outcome of the payment by the health (insurance) authority of the (other) part of the costs will be an inversed redistribution: it will be the people who can afford to pay substantive amounts themselves who will get the support, whereas other poorer persons will simply not go abroad. Sometimes this effect will be countered by charitable organisations that help the poor to receive health care abroad, as is for instance the case in Tonga or Bhutan.

23.12 Integrity Issues

Most small jurisdictions we examined are confronted with integrity issues in one way or another, which also impact social security. As a consequence of corruption or cronyism, social security benefits do not reach the persons for whom they were intended (fraud and non-take-up), social security contributions may not be levied in a correct way, and means tests may not operate properly to identify the needy. On the one hand, social security law in a number of small jurisdictions acknowledged these problems and included provisions to maintain integrity, as well as created watch dog institutions and alarm bell procedures. On the other hand, the vagueness in the conditions set for some benefits, especially of the means-tested non-contributory and social assistance schemes, makes these benefits more easily a victim of integrity violations. The proximity of the social security administrations and the beneficiaries may also be a cause of problems. Whereas at the highest levels, the judiciary of many small jurisdictions has found the way to minimise the negative impact of proximity by including foreign judges in the decision making, no such mechanisms are used in social security decisions and social security litigation at a lower level. Integrity is recognised as an issue for the proper administration of social security in many small jurisdictions. It is, however, remarkable that little attention is paid to a lack of integrity in the legislation itself, by which we mean the use of the law (here social security law) to favour some people or enterprises over others. We are not only referring here to the possibilities in some small jurisdictions given to the Minister to waive some conditions (for instance, of previous residence) to obtain certain social security benefits, but also to the freeing from social insurance obligations for certain companies. As far as these exemptions are unmotivated and/or even discretionary, they may pose integrity problems. The structuring itself of social security may also raise questions when the outcome of the social protection system favours the rich over the poor, or some sections of society (elites, foreign companies, civil servants) over other comparable groups, and this without objective grounds to do so. The fact that in a number of the countries examined, formally employed workers only constitute a small portion of the real working population may not be typical for small jurisdictions (but rather related to developing and emerging economies), nevertheless, it contributes to the integrity problem of the small jurisdictions.

23.13 Economic and Environmental Shocks

Studies on small states, especially small island states, have repeatedly reported that the small jurisdictions often are especially sensitive to economic and environmental shocks. The twenty small jurisdictions we examined do not alter this picture. Many of them have suffered environmental disasters in the past such as hurricanes and earthquakes, and many of them are exposed to the dramatic possible consequences of global warming. Many small jurisdictions have a poorly diversified economy that is often built on volatile sectors, such as tourism. All these phenomena have already been described extensively. What was surprising, is that nearly all small jurisdictions we examined did not take these (real or potential) economic and environmental dangers into consideration when designing their social security systems. No special reserves were constituted for when an economic or environmental disaster might hit the country, the employment and thus also the financing of the social security schemes. Even if funded schemes are in place, the investment policy followed by most small jurisdictions prioritised investment in one's own economy, which is perfectly understandable, but contributes to the problems of social security when the national economy is the victim of external shocks. Special arrangements to meet the most urgent needs are often put in place when an environmental disaster occurred (and mostly only after it occurred), but are usually kept outside the formal social security system. Quite remarkable is the possibility of early withdrawal of sums from a provident fund account after a disaster, as provided for in Fiji: no solidarity is involved, because it is in fact the people's own money that is used to cover the costs caused by the disaster!

The Impact of the COVID-19 Pandemic on the Social Security of the Twenty Small Jurisdictions

In the course of writing this book, the COVID-19 pandemic spread across the entire globe. This also affected the small jurisdictions and their social security systems in various ways. Health systems were under heavy pressure. People were affected by the virus and needed medical treatment, in the worst cases, health care abroad. The borders of many countries were however closed. As a consequence of the lockdown measures imposed by governments, people lost their jobs and the economy slowed down as a whole. Small jurisdictions often suffered more than larger states because of their high vulnerability; this was and is especially the case for countries that are considerably dependent on tourism.

We do not intend to provide an exhaustive listing and description of the measures taken in each of the small jurisdictions being examined to counter the effects of the pandemic upon social security and the incomes of people in general. This would require another comprehensive study. We would simply like to report here upon the kinds of measures taken. We have left this description out of the country reports, as in many cases it is uncertain whether the measures taken during this pandemic are here to stay or will be limited to a few months.

We based our brief comparative description on the measures reported by the national social security administrations to the International Social Security Association and listed on their website on 15 June 2020,[4] i.e. 135 days or 4 ½ months after the World Health Organisation proclaimed the pandemic of global concern on 30 January 2020. Another important source was:

(continued)

[4]See: https://ww1.issa.int/coronavirus/country-measures, last accessed on June 17th, 2020.

U. Gentilini, M. Almenfi and P. Dale, 'Social protection and jobs responses to COVID-19: A real-time review of country measures', World Bank, dated 8 May 2020.[5] All twenty countries examined were reported to have taken special measures.

In countries such as Fiji, Liechtenstein, Malta, Seychelles and Tonga, the possibility of deferring the payment of social security contributions was instituted. In Seychelles, funds to cover additional expenses of existing social security schemes were raised.

New schemes or new benefits were created to compensate workers laid off as a consequence of the COVID-19 crisis; this was the case in Grenada, Maldives, Malta, Suriname and Tonga, amongst others. Workers were sometimes forced to stay at home and stop working because of lockdown, quarantine or other preventive measures, or simply because they were affected by the disease. In Trinidad and Tobago, a pandemic (paid) leave was introduced for these situations in favour of civil servants. In Cyprus, sickness benefit was now available for self-employed from the same day as it is for wage earners. In Malta, employers were compensated when they had to pay for the leave of their workers and a benefit was given to the disabled who, as a consequence of their condition, could not safely continue to work.

In many countries, measures were taken to provide income replacement for workers whose labour contract was maintained, but their working hours reduced (sometimes to nil) due to the reduction in the employer or the self-employed person's business. This was achieved by providing a benefit to the workers concerned in countries like Aruba, Cyprus, Iceland, Liechtenstein, Malta, and Trinidad and Tobago. In Fiji, the Government introduced a one-off payment benefiting the workers of the informal sector and financed a 21 days COVID-leave for wage earners on low income. In Aruba, Curaçao, Sint Maarten, Cyprus and Greenland, support was (also) given to the employers to maintain the employment of workers. Sometimes public intervention was even more direct, as for instance in Seychelles, where the state guaranteed the payment of salaries in the private sector for three months, or in Iceland, where the income of the self-employed was subsidised for three months up to a level of 80% of the average monthly income in 2019. The self-employed are now also eligible for financial support in Curaçao and in the Faroe Islands.

Due to the closure of schools in many countries, children could not attend school. When parents were working and had no possibility to do so from home, this posed a serious problem to the families involved. In response to this

(continued)

[5]See: http://documents1.worldbank.org/curated/en/448321588971503966/pdf/Social-Protection-and-Jobs-Responses-to-COVID-19-A-Real-Time-Review-of-Country-Measures-May-8-2020.pdf, last accessed on July 11th, 2020.

problem, an emergency child care service was put in place in Liechtenstein and a benefit compensating the worker was available in Malta and in the Faroe Islands; a special leave of absence for child care was introduced in Cyprus.

Furthermore, countries also took practical measures to avoid personal contacts and relax administrative procedures: for instance, patients in San Marino could now e-contact the health system for health care and in Trinidad and Tobago the periodic life certification duty for pensioners was suspended. A series of measures were also taken in Curaçao to limit the physical contact with the social security administration.

In Fiji and Iceland, provision was made to allow people access to their pension savings to cope with the COVID-19 crisis.

It may be remarkable that as a response to the COVID-19 crisis, some benefits were created or supplemented to the benefit of the poorest or the families without COVID-19 related conditions: this was the case, for instance, for the cash transfer (for three months) and family benefits in Trinidad and Tobago; also Curaçao and Suriname can be mentioned here, as well as the one-off special supplemental child benefit that was introduced in Iceland.

Websites

http://documents1.worldbank.org/curated/en/448321588971503966/pdf/Social-Protection-and-Jobs-Responses-to-COVID-19-A-Real-Time-Review-of-Country-Measures-May-8-2020.pdf

https://ww1.issa.int/coronavirus/country-measures

References

Pieters D (2006) Social security: an introduction to the basic principles. Alphen aan den Rijn, Kluwer Law International

Pieters D (2019) Navigating social security options. Palgrave-Macmillan, Springer Nature, Cham, 2019

Chapter 24
Twenty-One Recommendations

On the basis of the previous chapters, we provide 21 recommendations for the small jurisdictions and their social security (law).

In this last chapter, we would like to come to some concluding recommendations that could be of use to the small jurisdictions and their social security. These conclusions are built upon the knowledge gathered in the previous parts, but will also reflect some personal views of the author who has been dealing with social security (law) for more than 40 years. Let me repeat once more that it was not the intention to cover all the problems and issues that small jurisdictions and their social security may be confronted with, as we focus on those questions that are linked to the small nature of the jurisdictions. It goes without saying that they are also confronted with those issues that all other states face in relation to their social security (law). It is only to the extent that these universal issues present specific features in the context of a small country that we shall include them in our analysis.

It might have been 'safer' to present the concluding observations in a rather descriptive way, but I prefer to formulate them in the format of recommendations for the small jurisdictions. In doing so, I realise that this may seem somewhat imperative or even presumptuous. Moreover, as we pointed out from the very beginning, small jurisdictions are very diverse: there are rich and poor small states, they reflect different legal traditions, and have many other differences. Of course, the validity of each of the statements and recommendations put forward must be tested against the realities of each separate small jurisdiction. I hope, however, that putting forward clear statements and recommendations, be it general and thus generalising, may help the advancement of social security in the small jurisdictions.

D. Pieters, *Social Security Law in Small Jurisdictions*, The World of Small States 8,
https://doi.org/10.1007/978-3-030-78247-4_24

24.1 Define the Goals That Are Pursued by Social Security

In our introduction, we defined social security as the body of arrangements shaping the solidarity with people who face (the threat of) a lack of earnings (i.e. income from paid labour) or particular costs, and this in the case of recognised 'social risks'. Social security can take the form of social insurances or social assistance.[1] Furthermore, we restricted the scope of our comparative research in principle to cash transfers.

We also added that the goal of social security arrangements is twofold: combatting poverty or social exclusion, and providing income replacement or financial support in the case of certain eventualities, called 'social risks'. In Western countries with a long-standing social security tradition, this is still the approach of most social security systems, although we can observe that the goal of protection against poverty is overtaking the goal of income maintenance in some systems, the latter being pushed into private arrangements.[2] In many emerging economies with sometimes rather young social security systems, the question of the goals of social security, i.e. the paradigm of social security, seems less defined.[3] In these countries, social insurance schemes often seem to be merely privileges for the better-off workers, civil servants and military.

It is also important for the small jurisdictions to define the goal(s) they want to pursue with their social security schemes. These goals may differ from those pursued by the former colonising power half a century or more ago; they may also differ from the goals assigned to social security by international organisations that offer assistance. It is therefore very important for the small jurisdictions to raise and discuss the question: what do we want to achieve with our social insurance and social assistance schemes? Since we see that in a number of the small jurisdictions examined, social insurance arrangements are indeed reserved to the better-off workers, and lack redistributive solidarity, we need to face the question whether these deserve the appellation 'social'.

The reflection on the goals of social security will also allow the small jurisdictions to better position social security in the broader context of ways to protect and support people in general. Indeed, we have been able to observe that in a number of small jurisdictions, social security is still seen as a competitor, if not an enemy, of traditional informal protection systems, such as family, clan, or charity by the religious community. Social security is not an enemy of these informal protection systems, but rather means that the efforts of these systems are supported and complemented to make social protection a real right of each member of society, or if one prefers a less individualistic approach, to recognise the fundamental duty of each state, each jurisdiction to provide decent social protection to all its members, i.e. also to those on whom their families, clans, religious communities have turned

[1] Pieters (2006), pp. 1–8.

[2] See Schoukens and Pieters (2007).

[3] Pieters and Schoukens (2012).

their back. In a small jurisdiction that claims to be a democracy respecting human rights, this is essential In larger jurisdictions, people can often more easily 'disappear' in the anonymity of society and thus be less of a victim of ostracism of whatever kind. In small societies, it is the special task of the legislator to also care about outcasts of any kind. Moreover, let us not forget that phenomena such as a concentration of the population in the capital or a few cities, as well as immigration and emigration are common in many of the small jurisdictions we studied: these phenomena often make the operation of traditional informal protection mechanisms much more difficult.

Additionally, one must recognise that a state, even a small jurisdiction, has far more tools to organise (and impose) forms of solidarity than informal social protection mechanisms based merely on voluntary adhesion or tradition.

It is also only after defining the goals of social security, that one is able to establish whether the social security schemes are efficient and effective. If one wants to improve the social security system, it is necessary to know what a better social security system entails. In other words, one must be able to evaluate which means are better to reach the goals assigned to social security. It is only when we know the goal of our social security journey, that we can establish whether we are on the right path!

24.2 Make Social Security Address Your Own Reality of Today

Small jurisdictions have often acquired their autonomy after many years of struggle. The twenty examined jurisdictions now all have control over social security, i.e. one of the areas with the most impact on the daily lives of all inhabitants. It was therefore surprising to see that only a few of these small jurisdictions took the opportunity to use their competence to implement a social security system that best suited the needs of their own population. Instead, many continued with the social security structure, and often legislation, from before they took full control of their own destiny. Even in long-standing sovereign small states, social security arrangements were sometimes more of a copy of those of neighbouring states, rather than the product of their own reflection. We have seen in Part II that many authors refer to the great flexibility of small states compensating for the scale disadvantage, as well as to the proximity between citizens, political actors and administrations, which enables them to respond more swiftly to the challenges they are confronted with. Yet we do not encounter such flexibility and proximity effects when dealing with social security. Of course, the social security systems take some local realities into account, but in our opinion this is far less than could and should be the case. Solutions of half a century or more ago, developed in often completely different socio-economic settings, are not the best way to tackle the problems of poverty and maintenance of living standards in today's small jurisdictions: they could and should be more creative and come up with solutions adapted to their own realities. Why do we find many small jurisdictions hesitant to come up with original and adapted social security solutions? Why do many small jurisdictions stick to social security as they found it when acquiring sovereign competence in the matter? We believe that many reasons may play a role here.

First, it seems like a 'safe' approach to continue with the social security mechanisms that were found at the start of one's own competence. They were developed in the skilful and knowledgeable surroundings of the former colonial power. People have also become accustomed to this approach and everywhere in the world, one sees reluctance towards structural social security changes. Yet, one should realise that one of the aspirations of people who take control of their own destiny is to offer its members a better life, and here social security may play a crucial role. What is the value of independence to many, if there are no improvements in daily life? In other words, if a relatively small group of persons (by hypothesis less than one and a half million, and often much less) acquires or enjoys full control over its legislation for many years, that group is entitled to expect their legislator to offer them better possibilities to develop as a group and as individuals, and thus that their legislator makes suitable social security provisions.

Why is this not the case? The lack of human resources able to be creative probably plays a crucial role in this respect. We have seen that small jurisdictions struggle with a lack of human resources. Social security administrations of small jurisdictions must fulfil the same functions as the ones of larger states, yet with a restricted number of staff, many of them with no academic schooling. Training initiatives exist, but are difficult to reconcile with the needs of the daily operation of the administration.

Knowledge of social security is often concentrated in the administrations. This is logical, but the negative side is also that qualified criticism upon the operation of the (administration of the) social security schemes can probably not be expected from outside the administration. Within the administration, there may be people able to creatively reflect about what they are doing, but these reflections will often remain within the walls of the same administration. Ideas that would upset the administrative structure struggle to emerge in such a setting.

In larger states, trade unions, employers' organisations and especially political parties produce new ideas on how to optimally meet the social protection needs of the population. In parliaments, some members (of various parties) are expected to specialise in social affairs. Ministries competent in social affairs will have advisers who do not necessarily come from the administration. This is less, or not really, the case in small jurisdictions: here specialists in social security will often be concentrated in the administration and policy makers will have to rely on them. Sometimes there will be people working in the ministerial departments at a policy level who are not implied in the daily operation of the social security agencies. This is often not the case and there will be no one in between the direct surroundings of a minister and the institutions and agencies running the social security schemes.

Therefore, we very much advocate training initiatives that do not so much address technicalities of social security, but rather confront policy makers of all kinds, together with the leading staff of the existing administration with the basic challenges of social security and the various ways to address them. Such training then turns into a dialogue: once they know which roads to a better social security regime are available, policy makers and administrators could devise original solutions tailor-made for their social protection needs. More about training needs will follow later.

Copying foreign solutions or maintaining colonial legislation, whether it be occasionally or with own alterations, may seem to be the easier and cheaper way to exercise one's social security competence, but in the end this very often turns out to produce very complex, costly, but less efficient and effective social security solutions. It is noteworthy in this respect that many small jurisdictions have a plethora of different social security benefits, whereas a simpler social security structure with fewer different benefits could make administration simpler and cheaper, and, even more importantly, ensure that people know their social security rights better and thus that non-take-up is reduced. Complexity is indeed the enemy of good information, especially for the most vulnerable groups in society.

24.3 Listen to Advice, But Take Control

In line with the points we made earlier, it is important that local social policy makers and administrators receive proper, multidimensional training in the various options available to tackle the problems their societies are confronted with. This knowledge will probably have to be partially imported. In other words, it is likely that many small jurisdictions will not find the academic and other broad knowledge of social security (law, economics, policy and so on) within their own borders and thus will have to seek this knowledge elsewhere.

Many international and bilateral assistance and training schemes however do not have the desired broad and open vision. It is indeed logical that if an international organisation sets up a training program, it will do so to promote the own values and approaches. As such, there is nothing wrong with that, except when that one voice is the only to be heard in the small jurisdiction.

Take, for instance, the International Labour Organisation (ILO). This very valuable and open-minded organisation will, of course, promote its vision of social security as expressed in the ILO Convention n° 102 on minimum standards of social security. It is questionable whether such an approach is always the most adequate; does it make sense, for instance, for a small jurisdiction with a huge informal sector to set up an unemployment benefit (for only those who have lost a job in the formal sector)?

Other organisations such as the International Monetary Fund or the World Bank may provide training, information and assistance for reforming the social security in a country, but will do so in line with their own conception of (a capitalist) society. They will provide funds for supporting reform initiatives, but of course only if these reforms fit into their ideology.

Bilateral aid programs may provide training initiatives, information and assistance, but will often take the social security system of the aiding country as the example, or at least as the starting point. Experts being flown in will seldom present a variety of solutions, but will come up with one that is often coloured by the experience in the sending country.

A known problem of various foreign assistance, advice, and other programmes, is that foreign experts not only do not provide broad, non-coloured information on a variety of possible approaches, but that their knowledge of the social security of the concerned country and the reality behind it must be acquired at the start of their exercise. In other words, many international and bilateral assistance programs will start with taking inventory of what exists. In doing so, they rely on local administrators and possibly other social security experts who do not necessarily have the required general overview nor the independence or freedom of mind to provide adequate information, which is intelligible for the foreign experts. The starting point of the bilateral or multilateral assistance will thus often already be a coloured, if not biased, view of the assisted social security system. As stated above, we would like to promote another approach: foreign input should be broad and provide a variety of social security approaches to a number of identified real life problems. In the next stage, foreign and local social policy people, local administrators and possibly other local experts should enter into a dialogue, a debate to identify a better social security approach. Of course, it would probably require a different state of mind of many international and bilateral assistance institutions to take such an approach, which could lead to solutions that do not suit their interests or ideology.

It is, of course, easy to advocate such an open and broad dialogue-based approach, but the small jurisdiction will very often depend upon external funds to be able to carry out any possible social security reform. Therefore, if one wants the money, one will have to obey the 'advice' of the one providing the funds. However, the policy makers and administrators of the small jurisdiction which enters into such deals with international organisations or other states should at least be aware of the bias of the approach of the international experts and advisers. Moreover, let them be very cautious in accepting funds for reforming social security when these reforms need recurrent financing and the aid is only meant for introducing the reform. In other words, do not introduce new procedures, new benefits, or new schemes with non-recurrent aid, when the new procedures, benefits, and schemes need recurrent financing.

It may also be our own bias, but we believe that if foreign input is needed, the small jurisdiction may prefer to have unbiased information and advice, and this may more easily be found in the academic world than with foreign or international social security institutions or governments. Academics may also be more able to provide the broad spectrum of disciplinary, multidisciplinary and interdisciplinary knowledge required to offer a broad range of possible solutions to local issues. Such an academic approach could also be developed for more than one small jurisdiction (for instance, for all small jurisdictions of the same region of the world) and then rolled out in a dialogue with the local actors and experts in each small jurisdiction separately.

Foreign input also does not necessarily need to come from former colonial powers or other larger states. We would like to promote the idea that small jurisdictions (for instance, of the same region of the world) could co-operate in creating the necessary training and information tools to support their social security systems: as a single small jurisdiction they may not have the necessary academics and other independent experts, but together they may already come a long way in providing the broad and open-minded knowledge needed for their own social security development. In addition, let me add one perhaps less comfortable remark: do not limit yourself in regional cooperation to countries with a similar past, but look for countries with different backgrounds. To give concrete examples: do not limit cooperation to enhance broad knowledge to only Commonwealth countries of the Caribbean, or to only Nordic small jurisdictions in Europe.

24.4 Consider Social Security as a Whole

In many small jurisdictions today, a whole range of different social security benefits co-exist. Sometimes social cash transfers are even organised outside the competence of the ministers in charge of social security, e.g. directly by the Prime Minister. In nearly all small jurisdictions, more than one cabinet minister or ministerial department oversees social protection.

We would advise to look upon social security more as a whole and try to reduce the number of ministers and administrations dealing with social security benefits, as well as the number of different benefits that are operated. More about the number of ministers later. Let us now merely state that unity of political leadership in social security policy will make it easier to take into account the interaction between the various social security schemes and to avoid measures taken in one sector to have a spillover effect in another branch of social security. By having fewer different social security benefits, the administration would be able to make them better known to the public and thus to reach out more successfully, especially to the most vulnerable groups in the population.

It must be recognised that many small states have already realised a unifying movement as far as the administrations of social security are concerned. Unlike the examples from which they copied the benefits, many small jurisdictions have not copied the multitude of administrations corresponding to the various schemes, but have concentrated the administration in one or a few social insurance administrations and one social assistance administration.

Social assistance administration is usually kept apart from the social insurance administration, which is understandable, but it needs to be examined whether an economy of scale could not be created by administering social assistance schemes, also through larger social insurance agencies, rather than through ministerial departments, as is often the case. This is especially true for social insurance administrations that already operate means tests.

Here, however, we encounter another critical issue that is characteristic of not only many small jurisdictions, but perhaps also of special relevance to them: social insurances and social assistance schemes operate completely separately. Social insurances seem not to be interested in poverty alleviation, leaving that goal to social assistance. The persons covered by social insurance schemes, and those benefiting from social assistance, seem to belong to other groups of the population. However, if a country is to develop a comprehensive social security policy that takes the dual objective of social security seriously, it is important to build bridges between the social insurance schemes and social assistance. If a small jurisdiction wants to build a democratic society, it is important that broad sections of the population have an interest in a proper functioning of social security, both social insurance and social assistance.

It might be worth examining whether the development of social insurances, which are often reserved to the already better-off groups of workers, should not be accompanied more systematically by elements of solidarity with those excluded from the scope of these insurances, the weakest groups first. This does not, however, seem to be in line with the development of social insurance and social assistance in most of the small jurisdictions examined. Social insurances are rather inward-looking and finance themselves (be it often with public support), whereas the general budget has to cover the expenses of the social assistance arrangements.

Not only should one take a holistic view on social security, but one should also always keep in mind that social security is only one, be it very important, tool of social policy, and that under specific circumstances it might be better not to choose a social security option, but rather to go for other social policy tools, such as the development of certain public services.

24.5 Reflect on the Personal Scope of the Social Security Schemes

The number of their population defines small states: countries are called small jurisdictions if they have less than one and a half million inhabitants. Many of the small jurisdictions studied have even less than half a million inhabitants. Social security was defined here as the comprehensive body of schemes that shape solidarity with individuals who face (the threat of) either a lack of earnings or particular costs. It all boils down to a solidarity system between people. Hence, the great importance of determining the width of the solidarity circle(s). Who is supposed to contribute to the solidarity system, or putting it differently, who belongs to the personal scope of application in the collecting function of social security? On the other hand, who can enjoy the solidarity of social security once social risks have materialised, or in other words, who belongs to the scope of application *ratione personae* in the distributing function of social security? As a rule, one will of course try to merge both scopes of application in the best possible way.

In none of the small jurisdictions examined did the limited, even very limited, number of the population as such pose a problem for setting up their own social security arrangements. Only in the area of social health care do small states struggle with the impossibility of offering the same health services themselves, and thus social security must cover health care services abroad. For cash transfer benefits of social insurance and social assistance, the limited number of people does not pose problems, be it that local phenomena, such as migration, natural disasters or economic shocks may impact more small jurisdictions and their social security, than would be the case in larger states. Indeed, if there is an influx of many refugees, a hurricane or a collapse of tourism, it will only affect a section of the population and the territory of a larger state, whereas when these phenomena hit a small state the entire country may often be affected.

A general remark to be made regarding the personal scopes of social security schemes of some small jurisdiction relates to the fact that they are often unrelated to each other. It may be interesting to make the personal scope of the social insurance schemes common for all social risks and their related benefit schemes, in order to avoid adverse risk selection. Especially when some categories of people or workers are allowed to join social insurance schemes on a voluntary basis, it would be advisable to have them join all or none of the available schemes; otherwise one may end up with cherry-picking phenomena.

In general, we can say that in a number of small jurisdictions we studied, the personal scope of the social insurance schemes was not clearly defined: legal definitions of the personal scope suggest the coverage of all workers, whereas in reality only a fraction of them are covered. The situation of the self-employed and freelancers often also remains unclear. In most small jurisdictions, civil servants and the army enjoy a good social security protection, be it through their own schemes, or be it as part of the personal scope of the general or professional social insurance schemes.

The legal definitions of the people who are potential beneficiaries of the social health care system and of social assistance schemes are often vague, if not altogether lacking. Are foreigners included? Are temporary residents included? Here large margins of discretion are often left to the administration, national or local. A more consistent and precise definition by law of the personal scope of the social health care and social assistance schemes is therefore often advisable.

24.6 Take Care of the Democratic Consistency of Social Security

The small jurisdictions we studied all claim to be democracies. A democracy can be defined as a form of government of, for and by the people. We should add that democracy is not the same as the dictatorship of the majority, but that a state becomes really democratic if the rights of people and minorities are decently protected. In a representative democracy, all nationals, and exceptionally even all residents, participate in the decision-making process. Social security systems may be universal, basically covering all residents, or professionally organised, covering all wage earners or groups of self-employed, some civil servants etc. We have seen that in many small jurisdictions many people live and work without citizenship and thus without voting rights in the country. Moreover, many people living and working outside the small jurisdiction may have retained their political rights in the country of origin. Additionally, as a result of frontier work and seasonal work, many people who work and are therefore possibly socially insured in the country, may not participate in the political decision-making in the country in which they work and are socially insured in. In other words, more than in larger states, many small jurisdictions experience a mismatch between the personal scope of their social security schemes and the personal scope of political (voting) rights.

Here, two problematic features may appear: political decision-makers may exclude some people from their social security arrangements or may create a very privileged social security for other groups. As far as the exclusion of some groups is concerned, we will have to ask ourselves whether we are not confronted with unlawful discrimination, i.e. whether the political majority has a good justification for excluding these groups. As far as privileged social security arrangements are concerned, the question seems less legal and more political: why did a majority of political decision-makers in a democratic setting create privileged arrangements? At the end of the day, also here, the question is one inquiring for good reasons to have differential treatment.

How can we remedy the mismatch between social security and political decision-making? On the one hand, it is normal for the citizens of a country to define social policy and thus also the social security of their country through their representatives. On the other hand, it is normal for people who take part in social security schemes, especially contributory schemes, to have a say in how these are managed, and possibly also in how these schemes should cover the social risks involved.

We have seen that some small jurisdictions have tried to meet the latter aspirations by including representatives of the workforce (as well as of their employers) in the boards of the social insurance institutions as well as in the relative appeals boards. Through such representation of all workers (employers), foreign workers (employers) could also participate in decision-making. We make two remarks in this respect. Firstly, it remains to be seen whether the trade unions (business organisations) of the small jurisdictions also have (many) foreigners under their membership and whether these organisations take the opinions of their foreign members into account: it will very much depend on the local situation. Secondly, the participation rights given to trade unions and business are usually limited to participation in the administrative decisions or in litigation decisions, and do not include policy decisions that remain in the hands of the political deciders.

Let us further observe that non-citizen participation is often considered inappropriate for non-contributory benefit schemes, social health care schemes and social assistance schemes, the argument being that the foreign workers did not contribute to the financing of these social security arrangements. The argument however often lacks foundation, as these non-contributory health care and social assistance schemes are mostly budget-financed, thus financed out of (direct and indirect) taxes, many of which are also paid by foreign workers.

A possible solution could be the establishment of advisory social security policy committees, elected by all socially-insured persons, whether they are citizens or not. At least in this way, the sometimes important, groups of non-citizens covered by social security could make their voices heard with the (national) social security policy makers.

24.7 Deal in a Fair Way with Frontier and Seasonal Workers

It is not only in relation with the democratic quality of social security frontier workers and seasonal workers deserve our special attention. It is important to also substantively consider their special situation when designing social security.

By definition, a frontier worker does not live in the (small jurisdiction) in which he works; he/she crosses the border to work in the small jurisdiction. Mostly, the frontier worker will be insured in the recipient country, just like the other workers, be it that residence-based benefits might be refused to him/her. Coordination agreements may lift this disadvantage. In addition, the social health care requires adapted rules, as the frontier worker will normally go to health care providers in the country in which he/she lives; yet it may be that the worker also wants or needs to address the health care services of the small jurisdiction in which he/she works. These situations may get good solutions, but coordination agreements with the neighbouring countries will be needed. Which country is responsible for unemployment benefits and labour mediation when a frontier worker loses his/her job? Again, solutions are possible if one can agree on them between the recipient small jurisdiction and the neighbour state from which the worker comes. We see that many small jurisdictions with a considerable number of frontier workers have indeed concluded agreements with the countries from which their frontier workers come, but one must realise that small jurisdictions will often find themselves in weaker positions when having to negotiate with the (large) neighbour state.

If the frontier worker is socially insured in the country in which he/she works, the important issue remains that he/she should be able to receive the corresponding benefits, although he/she does not reside in the country. Usually this export of benefits is not problematic as such, as no country is so cynical to accept that the frontier workers are included in a contributory social insurance arrangement, but refuse the benefit because the frontier worker stays outside the country. What can be an issue here, is the cost of the money transfer to the country of residence. Especially when there are small recurrent benefits, the money transfer (bank) costs may be disproportionate.

Frontier workers may work for lengthy periods in the small jurisdiction; this will not be the case for seasonal workers, as they will come for the season and go back home when the season is over. Of course, they may return the following year, but this is not certain and depends on their availability and the employer's willingness to hire them again. All this makes the relation between the recipient (small jurisdiction) and the country the seasonal workers come from more problematic. Moreover, whereas frontier workers come by definition from the neighbouring state(s), seasonal workers may come from a range of other countries, and it may be more problematic to conclude agreements with all of these. Seasonal workers come to work for a limited number of months: how should we define their social security rights? Should they be entitled to short-term benefits (sickness pay; unemployment benefit; family allowances)? It is not self-evident. Should they participate in pension schemes? This may seem easier, but the risk is that the social security system of the recipient state ends up with many dormant participants and beneficiaries of pensions, the amounts of which are less than the administrative costs they bring with them. It is therefore no wonder that many small jurisdictions that receive seasonal workers (e.g. in the tourism sector) leave them out of their social security schemes. The problem is however that many of these workers will end up without any social security at all.

24.8 Reconsider Advantages of Expats and Foreigners; Co-involve Tourists

It is remarkable how many social insurance schemes are 'accommodating' to expatriates and other foreigners coming to work in the country. These expats and foreigners are often freed from social insurance contribution when they demonstrate that they have an equivalent coverage elsewhere (this may even be privately). As a result, these often very well-earning foreigners are excluded from the solidarity system in the country. Often, they will also benefit from beneficial tax treatments. We do not hold this situation to be fair.

We have seen that many small jurisdictions 'inherited' social security regulations from former colonial times. Consequently, provisions were also maintained to exclude the colonial (public and private sector) workers from insurance schemes of the colony: these persons were of course to be socially insured in the 'motherland'. This exclusion was not altered after gaining sovereignty in social affairs, but was extended to all foreign or expat workers.

Another factor that may have played a role, is that large (often multinational) companies operating in small jurisdictions often have a disproportionate power and influence on local decision makers. Indeed, when a factory employing, for instance, five thousand workers closes down in a large state, this may create a serious problem for the local community, but for the state and the social security system as such, the problem is manageable. When the same occurs in a small jurisdiction with an active population of one hundred thousand persons, the situation is different. Hence the power of larger enterprises in small jurisdictions. Some of those larger, multinational enterprises will be able to have their officers (CEO, CFO, etc.), if not all staff coming from abroad, excluded from social security obligations in the small jurisdiction.

Since social security is not only a question of private interests, but also involves an element of solidarity, we are of the opinion that there are no good reasons for excluding people from social insurance duties because they come from abroad and/or hold another nationality. In order to avoid double contribution payments, i.e. in the country of origin and in the small jurisdiction, it may be appropriate to negotiate a coordination agreement with the state of origin, possibly freeing the concerned (posted) workers from insurance in the country in which they work. However, in such a case, there is reciprocity and it creates an interest with the larger state to enter into coordination agreements with the small jurisdiction, allowing the latter to also put elements in their favour on the table.

In most of the small jurisdictions, the tourist sector is an important sector of economic activity. No matter how small the number of residents of many small jurisdictions may be, they often get many more tourists visiting them every year. Tourism also employs many people, not least seasonal workers and foreign work-force, who often escape social security in the small jurisdiction. Yet tourists enjoy the country, the work of people there and possibly even (emergency) health care in the country. We therefore advise the co-involvement of tourists and the tourist industry in the financing of social security. From a solidarity perspective, there is no reason that tourists should not contribute. From a practical point of view, very modest social security levies per day of stay in the country may make an enormous difference to the financing of social security in the small jurisdiction and may allow workers in the tourism sector who are not (decently) socially insured to get an adequate social protection.

The co-involvement of tourists is also possible, not by levying the contribution from the tourists directly, but by making the tourist industry pay a contribution per day per guest.

One may reject the idea of co-involving tourists in the financing of social security by arguing that this would be detrimental to the tourist industry and thus cost much more than it would bring in. The competitive argument certainly plays a role here: if tourists like to go to small states, they may easily switch one small jurisdiction with another; a big cruise ship may, for instance, rather board one island state than the other. We therefore would invite small jurisdictions to make agreements amongst each other—and of course larger states could join in—in order to introduce a similar social security levy upon tourists in their countries.

Co-involving tourists in the financing of the social security of small jurisdictions (with many tourists) may seem like a bold idea, but perhaps it makes more sense than having many rich tourists staying in a country where social security depends on the lifeline of foreign or international funds, which may be stopped at any moment.

It may also be possible to earmark levies on tourists for some specific tourism-related expenditures, such as maintaining a good health care system in the small jurisdiction or as contribution to a social fund to cope with environmental disasters.

This may better 'sell' the idea of tourist levies, but the fundamental reasons for co-involving tourists in the financing of the social security schemes remain the same.

24.9 Pursue a Coherent Vision on the Social (Security) Responsibility Towards Emigrants

Some small jurisdictions have large numbers of citizens living abroad. They (or their parents) emigrated in search of work or a better life; often they send money back home to family and in this way maintain an important bond with the country from which they emigrated. Many of them also continue to identify themselves in the country of emigration as belonging to the country they emigrated from. The small jurisdictions from which they come often have a keen interest in these nationals who emigrated, as they may return to the country and bring along the skills, knowledge and experience they gathered in the country they emigrated to. When these emigrants finish their professional life, they may also want to return to the country of origin and enjoy the last part of their lives there.

The governments of the small jurisdictions need to develop a vision on how to deal with the phenomenon of emigration. Do they want to encourage it (for instance, to get in more remittances and thus foreign currency) or rather discourage it (in order to stop brain and brawn drain)? Once people have emigrated, how can the country deal with remittances? Should the cultural and even political bonds between the country of origin and its citizens abroad be strengthened by state? Is there a special responsibility, also a financial responsibility, towards citizens who emigrate, get into trouble and eventually want to return? Should emigrated workers be given incentives to return to the country of origin to work there? Should emigrated workers who have terminated their professional career be incentivised to return to the country of origin?

The answer to all these questions should be reflected in social security legislation. Depending upon these answers, national legislation should facilitate the export of rights in course of acquisition or not; the payment of an emigration capital could be considered; remittances could be included in means testing; voluntary continuation of social insurance in the country of origin should be made possible or barred.

Unfortunately, we find that in most small jurisdictions, social security lacks a clear vision on how to deal with persons who emigrate and eventually return later. This is partially due to the fact that the respective governments did not establish a clear position towards emigration as such; partially it is also due to the fact that the social security systems never established a consistent and comprehensive approach to the issues mentioned. Some benefits may be exported, others are transformed in capital or simply lost when leaving the country. Some countries make provisions in their social security to provide citizens who return to the country with some (non-contributory or social assistance) benefits, others do not. Even within one country, the approach may differ from one scheme to another, sometimes without apparent reason.

We therefore call upon the governments and social (security) policy deciders in the small jurisdictions to develop a clear vision upon the emigration of their citizens and their possible return, and to introduce social security measures corresponding to the choices they make. In other words, there is no single right approach, but what small jurisdictions should do is reconsider the way their social security systems deal with emigrants and possibly returning emigrants.

Another recommendation we would like to make to the small jurisdictions is to seek coordination agreements with the states to which many of their citizens have emigrated, to ensure that their citizens may return to their country of origin and maintain their entitlements to social security benefits from the country they emigrated to. In other words, to provide the export of social security benefits to the small jurisdiction. It is striking to see that many small jurisdictions do not have such agreements with the major countries where their citizens emigrated. This can be the result of unwillingness of the countries to which the citizens emigrated; it can also be the result of a lack of interest, if not a resistance against such coordination from the part of the social security institutions of the small jurisdiction. There is more about this issue further in our 18th recommendation.

The countries to which citizens of the small states emigrated may also have an indirect interest in accepting the exportation of their benefits. When the benefits cannot be exported, especially the pensions and other benefits of non-active migrants, it will force the latter to stay in the country they emigrated to, possibly creating social expenditures there (e.g. in the health care system). In addition, not allowing the exportation of social security benefits to the country of origin, acquired by working and contributing in the country to which the citizens of the small jurisdiction emigrated, may also encourage migrant workers to prefer to work in an undeclared way in the country they emigrated to: why would they work in a declared way and pay social security contributions if they intend to go back home once and cannot take their social security entitlements with them?

A last aspect of the social security of small states and the need to develop a coherent and consistent vision on emigration relates to the question of whether the small jurisdiction should offer the possibility to voluntarily join social insurance to citizens who leave the country. In doing so, their return to the country may be facilitated and it brings in additional funds for the country of emigration. However, it may also encourage the citizens of the small jurisdiction who work in the country they emigrated to, not to declare their work nor join the social security in the latter country, as they should do. For the recipient countries, it increases the danger of moonlighting and/or increases the chances of abusing citizens of small jurisdictions as cheap workforce (with poor social protection at home).

24.10 Unify the Political Responsibility for Social Security

In any country, the administrative hierarchy of social security will usually be headed by a minister who is politically responsible. This may be the minister of social security, welfare or social affairs. However, the highest responsibility in terms of administration is regularly spread over more than one government member: in addition to the minister of social affairs, there can be a public health minister who is in charge of the health care system and/or a minister of employment who is in charge of the social protection in case of unemployment. Exceptionally, the ministers responsible for certain areas of activities will also be responsible for the social protection of people working in those areas. Concretely, this may mean, for instance, that the minister of the interior may be responsible for the social security of policemen. This may result in many ministers having some responsibility for social security.

For the execution of their competence in the social security administration, ministers can rely on ministerial departments staffed by specialised civil servants.

The minister's competence in the field of social security usually implies the drafting and supervision of policies, as well as the preservation of the common interest. He/she can also be bestowed with a number of legislative competences.

All this is true in general and also applies to small jurisdictions, be it with some specific features.

First of all, we usually see more than one, even more than two or three ministers dealing with social security schemes in the small jurisdiction, but these ministers are also often in charge of completely different departments, such as tourism, or economic development. In some countries even the Prime Minister will be responsible for some schemes. All this means that the responsible ministers may not always allocate the necessary attention and staff to social security, as social security competes with other policy areas also within their competence. This may be problematic and result in administrations or agencies in charge of the schemes factually taking over policy responsibility.

The multiplicity of ministers responsible for different social security schemes will also not facilitate a consistent and comprehensive vision of social security and its role in social protection as a whole. It will rather be conducive of every minister developing their own vision and own approach at best. Comprehensive social security reforms become rather problematic in this case.

The fact that many ministers oversee various aspects of social protection does not necessarily lead to, but may facilitate, the use of social security schemes and benefits to service the political, if not clan, interests of the ministers in charge. Unity in social policy responsibilities at the highest level may therefore strengthen political responsibility and thus support integrity standards in social security. When political responsibilities in social affairs are scattered, integrity violations have better chances of succeeding.

24.11 Overcome the Geographical, Linguistic and Digital Literacy Remoteness Between Social Security and the Persons It Protects

Small jurisdictions are small in terms of their population. Often this is associated with proximity between the administration and the people. Yet we find that in a substantial number of small jurisdictions one faces problems of remoteness. This remoteness may be linguistic or physical.

In some small jurisdictions, the official language is not the language spoken by most of the population. Moreover, even if an official language is also shared by many citizens of the country, legislation may be in another (official or not) language, mostly the language of the previous colonial power. We have seen that in several small jurisdictions, sometimes entire pieces of legislation from before autonomy continue to regulate social security schemes. Yet in social security it is of vital importance that people understand the rules: not only the lawyers and the elites, but all people, the most vulnerable sections of the population first. Social security and especially social assistance are there to protect them. Social security benefits will often need to be applied for. Again, it is crucial to know about one's rights and duties regarding social security in order to avoid the phenomena of non-take-up and fraud. If the law on social security is in a language that is not shared by most of the population, or even inaccessible by significant, less educated sections of the population, we face a serious problem. If litigation on social security is conducted in an unintelligible language, the chances that the persons involved will be satisfied by the decisions decrease.

There are, of course, tools to overcome some of the handicaps related to language: interpreters and translators (or their IT substitutes) may play a role. Social security institutions may, and indeed often do, provide through all kinds of channels information in the language(s) spoken by the population, even if these languages are not official in the country. Yet, when it comes to dealing with an application, establishing a duty or litigation, the linguistic remoteness may re-emerge. We therefore plead for social security legislation, both statutes and regulatory texts, to be drafted in the official language(s) shared by large sections of the population. Translations into the other (often European) language can then be made (and not the reverse). Perhaps the lawyers practising in the country and even more, the 'flown in' lawyers from outside, as well as foreign advisers, may not be happy with such an approach, but at least in social security, their 'privilege' must yield for the interest of the community and its solidarity system, social security. And to be clear: social security is so near to (the needs of) the daily life of the citizens that it is perfectly possible to formulate social security legislation in any language; and would one contend that this is not possible, there will be something wrong with the social security scheme rather than with the language.

Two more remarks on linguistic remoteness. We see that in many small states, social security administrations have introduced all kinds of IT-supported tools, apps and so on to apply for benefits via the web, fulfilling administrative duties, paying contributions or paying benefits. This is good and we find that the small jurisdictions do not lag behind in this respect compared to larger states. However, it is important to keep in mind that in many small jurisdictions you may indeed have large portions of people with the needed digital literacy, but there are often also groups of people who have stayed behind. When these groups also live in geographically more remote areas, social security administration faces a problem it must take seriously.

The second remark concerns the many migrant workers who may be working in the small jurisdiction. Their language may not be a (official) language of the small jurisdiction, yet it is important that social security law is also to be properly applied in respect of these foreign workers, and thus able to provide at least basic information about their rights and duties in their own language.

So much for the issue of linguistic remoteness. There may also be a problem of physical or geographical remoteness. Small states may be small in terms of their population, but as we have seen, many small jurisdictions cover a large territory or stretch over many hundreds of kilometres. In some small states, parts of the country may be very remote from the centre and/or difficult to access. Again, this poses problems for the proper administration of social security in these places, where often already underprivileged communities live. In order for the social security system to be a tool of social inclusion, special attention and thus adequate additional means will have to be spent to reach out to these communities. Treating them equally compared to other parts of the country may often not be sufficient, and social security administrations will have to find creative ways to ensure that also in the remote locations people are protected by social security. Of course, traditional or informal solidarity mechanisms may be stronger in these remote areas, but this is not an excuse for social security administrations not to protect every citizen in an equal way.

Finally, let us observe that geographical remoteness and to a certain extent, linguistic remoteness poses special problems to the social health care system. When health care services are to be provided, these should be available to the entire (covered) population. Yet health care services, especially hospitals and specialised hospitals, cannot be present everywhere. It is then important to have a system of various tiers of health services. We do find this stratification indeed in most small states. Very specialised diagnosis and treatment is often sought abroad; more about this issue will follow hereafter. But even with health care that can be provided within the small jurisdiction, geographical remoteness may cause patients having to undertake a long and/or difficult journey to get to the hospital able to help them. It is important here that the health care system also includes transportation (costs) in its coverage. Moreover, it will often be desirable not only from the perspective of the patient, but also from the health care to be provided itself, that the patient is accompanied by a family member, friend or his local health officer. It is advisable under the circumstances to also cover the transportation (costs) of the accompanying person. In addition, the problem of linguistic remoteness deserves special attention when we talk about health care: when patients have to travel (even inside) the country to get the adequate diagnosis or treatment, they may end up in another linguistic environment. This phenomenon may even be strengthened when foreign medical specialists are employed in the reference hospitals. Good communication between patient and medical staff is essential to the success of any health care diagnosis or treatment. Therefore, the service of medically trained translators may have to be integrated into the operation of the central reference hospitals. These translators should have enough knowledge of the local languages and dialects spoken especially in the more remote parts of the country. Whereas larger states may also be confronted with the problem of linguistic distance between patient and health care provider, the challenge of dealing with the issue is especially important for small states that stretch over many hundreds of kilometres and/or have remote, less accessible local communities.

24.12 Provide the People Designing and Managing Social Security with the Right Knowledge

Training needs are often suggested in relation to the social security (administration) of small jurisdictions. Indeed, small jurisdictions have to fulfil the same tasks as larger states, but have fewer people to perform all these tasks. Moreover, domestic (higher) education in areas relevant to social security is often absent in the small state, which causes people with a foreign education or training to be given the responsibility of building and operating the social security system of the small jurisdiction.

There may be a tendency with the social security administrations of the small jurisdictions and their staff to emphasise the training needs for certain technical issues they are confronted with. International and foreign assistance programmes may also be tempted to prioritise technical training of social security administration staff members, for instance in sophisticated IT applications for social security. This may be very appealing to the trainees involved, but is this the right training and knowledge that is needed?

Earlier we advocated that training initiatives should not so much address technicalities of social security, but rather confront policy makers of all kinds in collaboration with the existing administration's leading staff with the basic challenges of social security and the various ways to address them. Such training would lead to a dialogue: knowing what roads to a better social security are available, policy makers and administrators could then develop original solutions tailor-made for their social protection needs. We also already warned about information, advice and training biased by foreign interests and preconceptions.

The training should also be multidisciplinary and interdisciplinary: all too often, also in small jurisdictions, there is no interaction between lawyers, economists, and social policy people. Solutions brought forward by economists hardly consider social policy consequences and neglect a decent legal translation. Social policy experts and even social law makers find solutions in which the economic impact has not even been considered. Good training in a multidisciplinary and interdisciplinary manner for all persons involved in social security at a certain level, which does not provide only one way to go, but a variety of solutions to be discussed with the local players, seems to be of the utmost importance. Then one will truly be able to realise that improving the social protection of people should not be seen exclusively as a burden to the economic development of the country, but that social and economic development may go and should go hand in hand.

Of course, some technical skills and knowledge will sometimes be needed in the small jurisdiction, and one will need to look outside the own organisation to provide that knowledge, skills or training of the own staff. However, it is important that the need emerges from the operation of the social security system itself and does not originate from what is in favour elsewhere. An example: a popular issue in many countries is the development of an app for contact between the people and their social security administration. When developing such an app, the small jurisdiction first has to ask: do enough people have the needed smartphones and the like? Does it bring any improvement to our concrete operations? Only when these questions are answered affirmatively, and even better, when these questions have emerged from the experience from the own needs, does it make sense to try and introduce the necessary knowledge, skills and related training. One more condition needs to be fulfilled though: there must be reasonable expectations that there will also be means to effectively introduce the app and to maintain its functioning. In other words, it makes no sense to train people for all kinds of new techniques, if the latter are too costly, or if the obstacles for effective introduction would be too important in any case. In this regard, we would especially like to warn against all kinds of (often well-intentioned) aid and training programmes with the aim of introducing and even financing the introduction of new techniques, mechanisms etc. when there are no funds reasonably foreseeable to support these in the long run, i.e. when the aid programme stops.

As we already indicated, small states' social security administrations will not have all the highly specialised skills available and will have to look for them elsewhere. We now make some remarks in this respect.

Firstly, it may be better to not look immediately to foreign social security administrations for help, as other administrations and private companies inside the country may also have the necessary knowledge. The advantage of using this domestic knowledge is that the translation of the new techniques or the application of new skills in social security will be realised in dialogue between social security and the other national company or administration; and thus not more or less dictated from outside the country.

Secondly, a strong argument is to be made for social security administrations of small jurisdictions to make agreements with each other (perhaps best on a regional level) in order to pool highly specialised expertise. This could be achieved by setting up common systems or by funding common training institutions, or simply by sharing the services of one highly specialised expert between different small states' social security administrations.

Finally, we would also like to stress the need for a specialised and at the same time very general training need: ensure that those who make the law, the members of government, parliament and the political parties, understand the main issues and challenges of social security. In essence, the content of the training of these persons, most of them not specialists at all, should be general. Yet at the same time such training should be highly specialised in the sense that the training should be designed for this particular group and should start with a helicopter view of social security and its present day challenges. The training should also be very concentrated in time, as these persons are by definition short in time and do not deal exclusively with social security. Such training is possibly also best organised at academic institutions, the reach of which spans over various small jurisdictions of the region. Also providing this specialised, though general, training to politicians of various, comparable, small jurisdictions, could possibly provide added value, if at least followed-up by a national reflection in each state afterwards.

24.13 Reconsider the Amount and the Processes of Means Testing

The social security of many countries, large and small, operates means tests (income tests, property tests) in order to determine who is in need of the benefit and thus should get the benefit and who is not in need and should thus not get the benefit. This seems logical if the (main) purpose of the social security arrangement is to fight poverty. International funding institutions, such as the World Bank, have even set up sophisticated tools to operate means tests. Some small jurisdictions have also been helped to introduce these.

However, operating means tests is costly in itself and creates quite some administrative workload. Small jurisdictions especially should ask themselves whether the (administrative) cost of operating means tests outweighs its benefits. In other words, if the purpose is poverty alleviation, is the reduction of poverty better achieved with a means-tested than with an appropriate non-means-tested scheme? We believe that when this question is seriously examined, many means tests could be cut and replaced with other benefits that are better suited. An example may be useful: many jurisdictions have a scheme that provides family benefits only to families who pass a means test. The cost of operating this means test may be high and its trustworthiness limited; one could replace such family benefits by providing all families with vouchers with which they can buy child-related goods and services within a certain time period. This may seem less 'modern', but may be more efficient in meeting the needs of the poorest sections, whereas the richer families may decide simply not to use the vouchers. One can also consider making the non-means-tested child benefit part of taxable income: again, this may mean that the poorest will benefit (most) from the benefit in the end and this without operating a means test.

Means tests are often designed within the context of Western rather individualistic societies. If they have to operate in a different context, where informal solidarity mechanisms are important, this may be problematic. We have seen that in many small jurisdictions, family and clan solidarity, as well as remittances from abroad, play an important role in the social protection of people. We have also seen that social security is not the enemy of these forms of solidarity but complements it and cares for whoever does not enjoy forms of informal solidarity. If this is all true, how should we deal with the income (in money, but also often goods and services) generated by the informal solidarity when operating means tests? How should we deal with gifts from charitable organisations? How should we deal with remittances? Not taking them into account would falsify the picture of who is in need and who is not; taking them into account would discourage these forms of informal solidarity, gifts and remittances. It is very difficult to overcome this contradiction and therefore it is also interesting to explore ways to avoid operating a means test. We shall come back to the issue of how to deal with remittances at a later stage, as this is of particular interest to many small jurisdictions.

Means testing benefits has been popular in certain, mostly Anglo-Saxon, literature on social security over the recent decades. Sometimes it may indeed make sense to operate means tests, but one must realise the limits of such a technique: we have already noted the administrative burden it implies as well as its difficult relation with informal solidarity mechanisms, gifts and remittances. Let us add one more element: to operate a means test, one must have a fairly good view of the incomes (out of work and otherwise) of people. Moreover, incomes are very often thought of in terms of money incomes, yet these preconditions may not be met by many small jurisdictions: informal work may be important, non-monetary sources of income may be important too (especially in rural areas). Under such circumstances, how can we be sure that the means test really identifies the persons most in need? Again, to reach out to the most underprivileged, other methods may be better used: universal cash benefits (to be included in the taxable income of the middle and high-income classes), subventions to the prices of certain goods or in kind provision of certain essential goods (food, shelter, etc.) and services (schools, health care). In other words, the issue of means testing social security benefits reminds us of the fact that social security is only one tool of social protection and that other social policy tools may occasionally be more effective and efficient.

24.14 Develop the Legal Framework of Social Assistance

Social assistance schemes are aimed at providing the neediest people with recurrent or occasional aid to meet the necessities of life and in that way allow them to have a dignified existence. As such, social assistance schemes will generally operate means testing mechanisms. We will not return to what we said previously on the matter. We would rather like to start our discussion on social assistance by insisting on the development of a full-fledged legal framework for providing social assistance. We have indeed seen that in many small jurisdictions, the legislation on social assistance is far less developed than the social insurance legislation. The administration of social assistance is often managed by a ministerial department, combining this task with other action areas. Sometimes a whole variety of social assistance schemes co-exist, with responsibilities occasionally even spread over various ministerial departments. All this means that the social protection schemes for the poor often end up being poor social protection schemes. This should not be the case and a start in remedying this would be the drafting of statutes and regulations clearly establishing who is in charge, coordinating the various benefits in a consistent way, clearly defining their personal scope and the conditions of entitlement to social assistance, and providing trustworthy, easily accessible and independent tribunals for decisions in case of disputes.

In a modern society, social assistance is as good a right of the people who qualify for it, as is social insurance. The times when poor people just had to be grateful that they received some assistance are over: they are now entitled to social assistance and they are entitled to it, not because the local or central administrators have conceded them a favour, but because it is the law. Although this also holds true for the social assistance schemes of small jurisdictions, the way social assistance is perceived may still differ in many of them, due to the proximity between administration and citizen. Some administrators of social assistance, especially locally, may still present social assistance as some benefit they personally arranged for the beneficiary, who in turn should be grateful to him/her. It is clear that we are confronted with an integrity issue here, but let us point out that this integrity issue could already be tackled by clear and better social assistance legislation.

24.15 Pay Attention Not Creating Expectations that Cannot Be Upheld

Social security is about providing security against the social risks, i.e. taking steps now to make the future more secure. This time dimension is essential to the concept of social security and appears most clearly in the pension schemes, but is not absent in e.g. social health care schemes or unemployment benefit schemes. In the latter, we take measures now for when we (or others) become in need of health care, become reliant on long-term care or become unemployed. Obviously, pensions show the time dimension most clearly: whether in repartition-based or funded schemes, social security pension schemes guarantee an income in a number of years from now. Pension arrangements put in place today will only show their full impact two, three, four decades later, when pensions will start to be fully determined by the new rules. This time dimension of various decades is in sharp contrast with the time dimension shown by democratic decision-making. Leading figures in parliament or government, those who really make the policy decisions, will seldom be in that position longer than 10 years in today's democracies. Politicians are confronted with elections every 2–5 years.

Small jurisdictions often have social security schemes, including pension schemes, which have been put in place relatively recently. This raises a first danger, as these schemes, especially the funded ones, will in the early years take in considerable amounts of money not to be spent on people who have acquired already (full) entitlements to benefits. There is a risk that in such cases the competent social security administrations may avail themselves of buildings, equipment, salaries etc. above their real financial possibilities. Even more important is the danger that when creating new schemes, benefits or conditions, which are more favourable to the socially insured, especially in the area of pensions, legislators create future entitlements that they know, or should know, will not be able to be maintained at the moment they are to be paid.

In other words, it is very tempting for politicians to make promises regarding benefits in the future, the bill for which will be passed on to the politicians of 10, 20 or more years later. When many Western European countries' social security systems, especially pension schemes, were confronted with major financial problems since the '70s, it was often blamed on external factors such as the oil crisis, demographic decline and so on, whereas we believe that it (also) had much to do with the 'maturation' of arrangements, especially pensions created in the period after WW II that were far too generous, but the bill for which was only presented in full since the '70s. For many small jurisdictions, the time frame may be shifted slightly: they will get the effect of unreasonably generous legislation, especially on pensions, only two, three or four decades after their introduction; for many of them, this means that it may already be a pressing problem or soon will be.

At the same time, these findings should be a warning to future social security legislators not to create expectations that cannot be honoured in the future. This, of course, requires honest politicians who want to know what is going to happen if this or that expectation is created. However, we believe that it is often not so much a question of honesty, but rather of the capability to have a complete view, hence the importance of providing politicians and policy makers in charge with a specialised, very general training in social security, as we explained above. We should however also widen the perspective and encourage persons responsible for social security to take care of adequate information, if not training, of trade unions, journalists and other opinion makers on the broad issues and challenges of social security. Especially in small jurisdictions, where the proximity between politicians, opinion makers and the public is important, good information and possibly training on the 'ins' and 'outs' of social security is crucial to avoid foolish promises and Santa Claus social security legislation, followed after some period of time by disillusion and loss of trust in social security and in politicians, journalists and other opinion makers.

24.16 Take a Multifaceted View on Investment Policy

When a country finances social insurance schemes on a funded (capitalisation) basis, but also when social security schemes based on repartition collect more contributions than immediately needed, the issue arises of how to invest the funds that are at disposal. Many countries and also small jurisdictions have therefore developed a policy on the investment of social security funds. This policy may be in the province of the concerned social security institutions, belong to the competence of the concerned minister(s) or be the product of a cooperation procedure between the political and the administrative level. However, small jurisdictions and their social security administrations may not always have themselves the right expertise to develop such investment policies. Deciding how to invest social security funds is also a rather complex matter, much more complicated than the already difficult issue for a private person of how to invest his/her savings. Indeed, many interests may be involved in the investment decision and in small jurisdictions, the proximity between the various actors and the interests they stand for may make it all even more difficult.

It must be stressed from the outset that developing an investment policy is not primarily a question of financial skills and specialised expertise. These are very important, but it should come after some basic decisions have been made on a general policy level. It is not clear whether this sequence is always followed in small jurisdictions, where investment policy decisions may be more easily shifted to the professional investors (in and outside) the country, who were called in for their technical skills and expertise.

What are these main policy decisions?

Firstly, one has to decide what purpose to pursue with the investment: is it only about having a maximal return upon investment, the best interest upon the money invested? Alternatively, should one use the investment to finance local social infrastructure (hospitals, nursing homes, kindergarten, housing)? Or should the investment stimulate the national economy and the diversification of the local economy?

Secondly, one has to decide upon the rigidity or not of the investment: should the invested funds be inaccessible (including by government) or should the investment be easily liquidated for the funds to be used quickly for more pressing needs (for instance, to address the consequences of a natural disaster)?

The decision whether or not to keep the funds inside the country or not is also difficult. Investment opportunities within the small jurisdiction will often be limited. This fact may be seen as an argument both in favour and against investment abroad. Since there are few possibilities to invest at home and the available means are limited, it can plead for the use of the money available for domestic investment. On the other hand, investment abroad may provide better opportunities and makes the invested funds less dependent on local events (such as natural disasters or the collapse of the main national industry) and thus better protects the later social security entitlements.

Deciding upon its purpose, the rigidity and the location of the investment are primarily social policy decisions, but of course, these decisions need to be fed by more technical input about the pros and cons of the various options, about the investment objects and so forth. This is where investment experts come in, as well as for the management of the investments of course. As said, small jurisdictions and more specifically their social security administrations will often lack this expertise: acquiring a very small number of own experts by definition will often be too costly and does not necessarily guarantee objectivity. Sometimes other national institutions (such as the central bank) will have the necessary expertise and arrangements can be made with them; however, the danger of them 'taking over' the entire investment policy is often real in such cases. The (social security administration of the) small jurisdiction may prefer to outsource the technicalities (if not more) of their investment policy to specialised, often multinational, investment agencies. This might guarantee more objectivity, but should not entail that the policy decisions are sourced out to them.

Again, we could call upon the small jurisdictions in this respect to establish more cooperation mechanisms: if it is difficult to hire one or more investment specialists for each national social security administration, why not set up non-profit expertise centres, duly staffed and with a good know-how to service a number of small jurisdictions (of the region or even world-wide)? Such cooperative investment centres of expertise would probably be best suited to respect the fundamental policy issues taken by each administration whilst providing them first with objective information and good service in the management of the funds.

24.17 Take Integrity Issues Seriously

Many small jurisdictions appear to struggle with integrity issues. Many of them have also developed policies that target respect for integrity on all levels of government. Legislation is in place to fight corruption and cronyism. It would lead us too far to discuss all integrity problems and measures taken to confront them here. It goes without saying that social security, an area where important sums of money circulate, cannot escape the more general integrity problems. What we would like to focus on here are the specific social security measures that can be put in place to counter and reduce integrity problems.

It all starts with qualitative legislation, easily accessible and understandable to the people involved (and not only the lawyers and administrators). If legislation no longer matches the reality of today, if the legislation leaves many questions open and is vague or extremely complex, this is the best recipe for allowing people to (ab)use (of) this legislation for their own profit and not for the general interest.

It is also necessary to avoid creating too many areas in which the minister, the administration, a local authority or other decisionmakers are allowed to take discretionary measures, in other words, in which they can freely decide whether to grant the benefit. This danger is especially present in social assistance, but also emerges when, for instance, the minister can free certain employers from social insurance at his or her own discretion. The operation of certain evaluation methods (within the framework of more sophisticated means tests or not), which leaves much freedom to the one conducting the evaluation, also entails the danger of unequal assessments, if not outright favouritism.

Another important link in the integrity chain, is that there are accessible, independent appeal possibilities against adverse administrative social security decisions. In many small jurisdictions there is the possibility of going to the courts of the ordinary judiciary, but this will often be costly. If one is dissatisfied with a decision concerning social security benefits or contributions, one will mostly have to address first administration-linked appeals boards, if not the deciding administration itself. The appeals boards will sometimes be composed of panels with representatives of the trade unions and business, which may provide some more assurance of an independent evaluation. The use of external lawyers, even from outside the country, which is not uncommon for the judiciary in the small jurisdictions, is something the appeals boards do not know, but may have to be considered in the future. Proximity between members of the appeal boards and the parties in litigation may endanger the fairness of the decision-making and even constitute an integrity risk.

It may also be advisable, especially in small jurisdictions, to have specialised independent social security inspection services, which are not linked to the social security administrations and invigilate the right application of the social security legislation, both in favour of the administration and in favour of socially protected persons. Social inspections very often function within administrations and only control people the administration suspects to defraud the system by not paying the due contributions or by receiving benefits to which they are not entitled. Fraud that is not identified by the administration first, will usually not be detected. In other words, if the administration (or some of its officers) are too favourable to some employers or some beneficiaries and provide them with advantages they are not entitled to, neither the administration (or its officers) nor the beneficiary will complain and the social inspection will not be activated. It is therefore important to have a social security inspection that operates outside the relevant social security administration.

24.18 Make Suitable Coordination Agreements with Main Migration Countries

We have seen that nearly all small jurisdictions we examined experience significant immigration and/or emigration. It is therefore important to arrange measures for situations in which the migrant is confronted with the social security system of the small jurisdiction and that of the state of emigration or immigration. To a certain extent, this can and is dealt with by national legislation: the national social security law may, for instance, determine which of its benefits are to be paid out when the beneficiary is abroad, and which benefits are not to be exported. Yet in most cases, good solutions, both in favour of the migrant workers and the concerned administrations, require social security coordination agreements between the states concerned, i.e. in our case between the small jurisdiction and the states to which its citizens emigrate and/or the states from which people come to live or work in the small jurisdiction.

Social security coordination agreements may be multilateral, such as those established by the EU coordination regulations in Europe or the CARICOM social security agreement in the Caribbean, or they may be bilateral, *in casu* between the small jurisdiction and the country of major migration.

We have seen that a country like Canada has been willing to conclude coordination agreements (mainly dealing with pensions) with many small jurisdictions. However, it is fair to say that many large countries to which citizens of small jurisdictions migrated have not been ready to enter into social security agreements with the small jurisdictions. Especially if the other country is the former colonial power (as for instance the United Kingdom or the European Netherlands), this does not reflect a fair treatment by the dominant power. Of course, small jurisdictions do not have the tools to pressure larger states to conclude social security coordination agreements with them. The contrary is much more true: if larger states enter into (often partial) bilateral agreements with small jurisdictions, they more or less impose their conditions or even simply pursue their own interests. Yet we have seen that small jurisdictions may occasionally have some instruments not to force, but to encourage larger states to enter into coordination agreements. We refer here to the already discussed privileges to expats or the mechanisms by which the small jurisdiction may support or rather counteract moonlighting by its citizens in the larger state.

However, fairness also commands us to point at the fact that people who know about social security in small jurisdictions, and these are often concentrated in the administrations, may sometimes not insist upon making coordination agreements either. Indeed, an agreement on the export of benefits may be very beneficial for the workers returning to their home country, and thus to the small jurisdiction as such, but may not benefit the social security of the small jurisdiction directly. Even the contrary may be true, as such an export of benefit agreements will be reciprocal and might force the social security systems of the small jurisdiction to export benefits which they have not hitherto exported. However, it is self-evident that having international agreements that provide export of benefits is far more beneficial to the citizens and the general interest of the small jurisdiction than it would cost to its social security to export some more of its benefits. Moreover, social security, and especially the non-contributory and social assistance schemes of the small jurisdiction, would benefit from returning emigrants who receive foreign benefits, as these could be included in the means tests of the non-contributory or social assistance arrangements. In other words, more foreign benefits being exported to the small jurisdiction will enable the latter's social security to pay out fewer benefits to these returnees.

Another handicap that small jurisdictions may experience (corresponding to reality or not) is that they do not feel skilled enough to make appropriate social security coordination agreements, especially when they are confronted with large states with an entire team of experienced social security experts. Moreover, operating coordination agreements, especially if they are rather comprehensive and complex, is not an easy task for a small jurisdiction and its social security administration. We therefore dare to suggest that small jurisdictions jointly try to develop a model agreement of social security coordination, not as complicated as the ones proposed by, for instance, the International Labour Organisation, but taking into account the interests specific to small jurisdictions. Such a simplified model bilateral agreement could contain:

- a prohibition of discrimination on grounds of nationality between citizens of the contracting parties of the coordination instrument;
- an allocation as to which state(s) is/are competent for the social security of persons whose social security situation contains cross-border elements; in other words, solving conflicts of law between the diverse national rules concerning the scope of application of the social security systems;
- the payment of social security benefits in the other countries bound by the coordination instrument, i.e. the export of social security benefits or 'maintenance of acquired rights' and provisions to limit the cost of the money transfer; and
- the exchange of all relevant information between the social security administrations of the concerned countries.

Provisions on health care provided to each other's citizens could be added; however, we reserve this topic for discussion hereafter. Provisions on health care could be included in a simplified agreement, but could perhaps be better dealt with in separate agreements.

We would not include questions of aggregation or maintenance of rights in course of acquisition in a simplified bilateral social security agreement, as experience (e.g. of the EU mechanism and the CARICOM agreement) shows that these pose quite complex issues for the social security administrations.

Once such a simplified model bilateral social security agreement had been drafted, the small jurisdictions would find themselves in a better negotiating position towards the larger states they would have to agree with. The specific bilateral agreements could then, of course, depart from the model or deal with more elements, but the starting point would at least be more equilibrated.

Finally, we have to address an issue regarding non-sovereign small jurisdictions. In such jurisdictions, social security may be the full competence of the legislature and other national institutions, but the power to conclude international agreements remains with the 'motherland' or whatever name is given to the higher level. This automatically raises the question: what about international (*in casu* coordination) agreements that exclusively deal with the social security of the small jurisdiction? Is it within the competence of the small jurisdiction (as a competence implied in the social security competence) or is it within the competence of the level competent for concluding international agreements? Moreover, what if the latter neglects to conclude such agreements on behalf of the small jurisdiction or does not include them in negotiations of agreements between the higher level and third countries? It is important that these questions be given clear answers, which take into account the own interests of the small jurisdiction.

24.19 Regulate Health Care Abroad and Avoid Inverse Redistribution

An issue all small jurisdictions are confronted with is that they cannot provide their citizens with all the necessary medical diagnostics and treatments, as the health infrastructure in the small jurisdiction may be good, but will obviously not include highly specialised staff and equipment in all areas of health care. Since the small state is defined as a country with a limited population of less than one and a half million and often much less, medical science and health economics tell us that such a population is not sufficient to have enough patients to enable highly specialised care, both in terms of staff and equipment. Thus, all small jurisdictions will have to either limit their social health care coverage to care at home (which is only exceptionally the case) or send patients for diagnostics and/or treatment abroad when this health care cannot be provided at home.

Some small jurisdictions seem to have regulated health care abroad in detail, establishing amongst others:

- whether it is required that the care cannot be provided in the country at all, or whether it is sufficient that it is not suitable for the patient to have (to wait for) the diagnostic or treatment in the country;
- how the decision to refer the patient for health care abroad should be made, by whom and with which appeal possibilities;
- what to do in case of urgent care abroad;
- whether the patient has a full or limited choice of where to go abroad, or whether the patient has to go to the health care provider abroad that has been assigned to him/her by his health authority/social security administration;
- whether the chances of success in the (middle) long term (recovery, life) of the patient after health care provided abroad need to be considered;
- whether the chances for the patient to resume professional activity after health care provided abroad need to be taken into account;
- how and to what level the costs of the diagnostic and treatment abroad will be compensated by the social health care scheme of the small jurisdiction; and
- whether the non-medical costs related to receiving health care abroad will be covered: the costs of the travel and stay of the patient and his/her potential accompanying persons (family members, medical doctor etc.).

Other small jurisdictions do not have clear legislation on the matter, so much is left to the discretion of who makes the decision to refer the patient to health care abroad. We believe this is not good and can lead to integrity problems; we therefore strongly recommend regulating this matter in detail, minimising space for discretionary evaluation and personal appreciation. This may lead to harsh negative decisions in some cases, but especially in small jurisdictions characterised with a high degree of proximity between various actors, this seems to be absolutely necessary when the health care abroad is financed by public money in one way or another.

A related issue we would like to draw attention to in respect of arrangements to cover health care abroad, concerns the costs that are left with the patient, i.e. the costs of the health care abroad that are not taken over by the social health care system of the small jurisdiction. It is indeed not difficult to understand that the small jurisdiction wants to limit the costs when sending a patient abroad, as such highly specialised or elaborate treatment abroad may take up a very considerable portion of the entire national budget for health care. So often not all costs are compensated, or they are only compensated up to a certain limit. The real costs are not taken into account, but fixed sums per for example pathology and corresponding therapy are set. The costs of travel and stay, especially of accompanying persons, will often not be covered etc. The problem is that, to the extent that not all real costs are reimbursed and the patient will thus have to bear part of the costs him/herself, a reverse redistribution effect may be the result: the intervention of the social health care system to refer a patient to care abroad and partially pay for it, will benefit wealthier patients more, as they will be able to pay for the costs not covered. Poor patients will have to desist from receiving care abroad, as they cannot pay for the costs not covered. Such phenomena can be perceived in some small jurisdictions we have studied. We would therefore urge the policy makers to reflect carefully on the matter and to include as much of the real costs as possible when allowing persons for health care abroad with coverage by the social health care system, to limit the coverage to the essential real costs and eventually to decide not to cover certain health care services or goods at all.

In some countries social health care systems refer patients to charitable institutions and the like in order to cover the non-compensated real costs of care abroad, or to early withdrawals from their pension or provident fund. Although these complementary sources of financing may provide practical solutions, they should not be considered a suitable answer: charitable support is always discretionary and depends on factors beyond the patient's control, whereas forcing the patient to 'eat' his pension before getting the necessary health care abroad does not seem in line with the goals pursued by social security.

Patients may be allowed to receive health care abroad and these costs (fully or partially) are compensated without any previous contact between the social health care system and the concerned health care provider abroad. It is however preferable that the (social health care system of the) small jurisdiction makes prior agreements with the government, the health care authorities and/or the health care providers (hospitals, medical doctors) abroad. In this way, the costs can be better evaluated and the practical arrangements of stay and travel are more easily made. We can only recommend that small jurisdictions promote such previous agreements. Such agreements may also extend to other aspects, such as sending specialised health care teams into small jurisdictions to provide health care services that cannot be offered on a continued basis and/or by local health care providers.

24.20 Make Social Security Aware of Remittances

Many small jurisdictions have larger groups of their citizens emigrating to other countries to make a living there, possibly with the idea of returning to the country after completion of their professional career, or simply after a number of years of working abroad. The bonds with family (and friends) staying in the small jurisdictions remain strong and social pressure upon them is considerable, so they more or less regularly send a portion of what they earn to their relatives back home. Remittances are therefore important in quite a number of small jurisdictions, and in some they are even considered as an important source of informal social protection for the family members who have stayed in the small jurisdiction. We do not evaluate the positive or negative aspects related to the importance of remittances, but we were rather surprised to find that social security arrangements were silent on remittances. Yet we believe there is a good case to make in favour of building some bridges between the phenomenon of remittances and the formal social security.

To begin, we must address the question of whether remittances are to be considered when establishing the needs of people: should they be included in the means test? In addition, if so, how can we know how important they are and who benefits from them? If not, how can we prevent families and persons well bestowed by their emigrated relative to still also get state support, whereas poorer families and persons without such a relative would not receive it? We already discussed the problems related to means testing in detail, but these are very much noticeable here.

We have also already raised the question of what the responsibility should be, including the financial responsibility, of the small jurisdictions towards citizens who return after years of emigration, possibly in poor health, without a job or after having finished their active career. Here we believe that the solution may partially consist of assigning a certain percentage of the money sent as remittances to the funding of social security rights upon return to the country. This may possibly imply better control on the remittances. It could be promoted by setting up cheap or even free channels to transfer the money and by freeing remittances from means test, provided that they transit in the official way and thus are submitted to the social security levy. This approach would also reflect a certain logic: the remittance is money the emigrated worker does not need at that moment and is not saved, but transferred back home; there it benefits family members. Perhaps the latter will take care of the returning emigrant, but perhaps not. In case the family bond only worked in one direction, the state should not take the full impact on its shoulders, but it is good that part of the remittance is put on the account of the emigrated person for when he/she returns.

How to deal with the funds accumulated via the levy on remittances is, of course, something to be determined in function of the entire set-up of the social security in the concerned small jurisdiction: it may open entitlements in existing schemes or lead to the creation of new schemes.

24.21 Make Social Security Prepared to Absorb Temporarily Contained Economic and Environmental Shocks

We have seen that nearly all examined small jurisdictions have been, and may in the future be, exposed to environmental calamities and economic shocks. This is, of course, a broader issue than only a social security matter. Yet social security can play a role as a stabilising factor in case of such a crisis. However, it should be emphasised that such a stabilising effect can only be maintained for a limited period of time. Social security is far too much dependent upon the work and the incomes generated in the country. When the environmental or economic shocks undermine employment and income creation in the country for a longer period of time, social security financing is bound to get in deep waters, and will not be able to continue this stabilising effect. For some months, though, social security may bridge periods of income setbacks. It can be very important at that moment, but social security cannot have this effect over a longer period.

Some people have advocated the establishment of reserve funds to cope with environmental or even economic shocks outside the context of social security; exceptionally it was also suggested to create such reserve funds within the social security system. We are not convinced that this would be the most appropriate approach, at least not within social security. As we have seen, environmental shocks tend to hit the entire small jurisdiction and the whole or large parts of its economy: it is the country as a whole that suffers a hurricane or is threatened by the consequences of global warming etc. In order to absorb the consequences of possible future environmental shocks, huge amounts of money would have to be reserved and thus immobilised, and this in countries often still building up their infrastructure, improving the living conditions, attracting investors, and associated activities. Moreover, in case of major disasters, social security may then use the funds reserved for the payment of benefits to people without employment—and that would be positive—but the pressing needs would probably be much more to reconstruct housing and roads, ensure that the country gets working again, etc. Also, in order to absorb future major economic shocks, the reserves to be accumulated would be so enormous that they would already now outbalance social security. In addition, other measures seem more appropriate to prevent and eventually absorb long-lasting economic depressions, such as diversifying one's economy or trade partners.

While we do not advocate the establishment of special reserves in social security to cope with prolonged environmental or economic crisis periods, and we believe that the ordinary social security system could absorb the environmental and economic shock waves for a limited number of months, we would recommend that the social security systems of small jurisdictions reflect on how to proceed in case of temporary setback periods and how to adjust the system in place in case environmental or economic problems last over a longer period of time. Reflecting on these questions, making a blueprint of how to handle both temporary and longer lasting periods of trouble, getting commitments of support (by the state or others) will be easier when there is no immediate need nor a pressing reality. Eventually, in case of temporary or lasting crisis, the social security arrangements could even be embedded in legislation to come into effect only when these emergency periods would emerge.

References

Pieters D (2006) Social security: an introduction to the basic principles. Kluwer Law International, Alphen aan den Rijn

Pieters D, Schoukens P (2012) Social security in the BRIC countries. IBM Center for the BRIC Countries, Washington

Schoukens P, Pieters D (2007) Social security quo vadis? Interviews with social security administrations CEOs in 15 Western European countries. IBM Global Social Segment - IBM Corporation, New York

Chapter 25
Epilogue

Both small jurisdictions and social security have been the object of academic attention in the past, but the social security of small jurisdictions has rarely been systematically explored. This book seeks to fill this gap, concentrating on the research questions: how is social security (law) impacted by the smallness of the jurisdictions? Are small jurisdictions confronted with specific problems and challenges, and if so, how should they deal with these?

After setting out the conceptual framework, we first examined the current literature on small jurisdictions. This allowed us to identify some features that appeared to be directly relevant to social security in such countries, such as the impact of economic and environmental shocks, scale disadvantages, the importance of migration and the proximity between citizens and administration.

In the main part of this book, we screened twenty selected small jurisdictions according to a uniform pattern. First, we provided context and the legal framework of the rights to social security (constitutional context and social security legislation and structure), after which we dealt with the population of the small jurisdiction and the personal scope of its social security schemes. The administration of social security and the coordination arrangements applicable to the small jurisdiction were also discussed.

The information gathered allowed us to identify some common features of the social security (law) of the small jurisdictions in the next part of the book, based on the comparison of the 20 countries examined. Some of these common features appear to be directly related to the smallness of the jurisdictions, such as the need to unify the administration of the various social security schemes as much as possible, the importance of immigration and/or emigration and the difficulties, both in terms of capacity and power, to conclude balanced social security coordination agreements with major emigration and/or immigration countries, and the need to provide health care abroad. In this context, it may also be observed that the mere fact that the social security schemes of the small jurisdictions by definition cover only a small number of persons did not, as such, pose serious problems. Some other common features of the social security (law) of the small jurisdictions are related

D. Pieters, *Social Security Law in Small Jurisdictions*, The World of Small States 8,
https://doi.org/10.1007/978-3-030-78247-4_25

to characteristics shared by many small states, although there is no necessary link between these characteristics and the smallness of the jurisdiction. As examples we can mention the challenge of reaching out to very small communities in remote areas, the gap between the language of social security law and the language spoken by most people, and most importantly, the impact that economic and environmental shocks may have, not in the least on the tourism sector that is so important in many small states. The latter was also dramatically illustrated by the impact the COVID-19 pandemic had on (the social security of) most small states. Furthermore, we were struck by the fact that the prevalent political, ideological or religious factors were less determinative factors for the shape of social security of the small jurisdiction than the legacy of the former dominant power. In fact, much of the still valid social security law of many small jurisdictions dates back to a time when the country had not yet acquired its full autonomy.

We did not want to restrict ourselves to the role of mere observer and therefore, in the last part of the book, we presented 21 recommendations for small jurisdictions and their social security (law), focusing on the problems and challenges specific to small jurisdictions or at least experienced by most of them, in contrast to most larger states. Most of these recommendations revolve around the following five poles:

- If the small jurisdiction is proud of its autonomy, it should make full use of it to create a tailor-made social security that fits its own population today; hence it should reflect on what goals it wants to achieve with its social security system.
- Simple, understandable and clear legislation should define the rights and duties under the social insurance and social assistance schemes; exceptions and discretionary powers should be avoided. Means testing should be limited as much as possible.
- Considering the goals pursued by the state, the social security system should define the rights and duties of migrants, frontier workers and seasonal workers; tourists and expats should also contribute to the financing of social security.
- Cooperation between small states is the best way to overcome the limitations related to smallness. It can be achieved by combining expertise and establishing common information and training strategies on the fundamentals of social security. Cooperation will also allow for more balanced coordination agreements with other states, including the former colonising power.
- Support for health care abroad, integrity issues and the responsibilities for investment policy decisions should be given the necessary attention.

This book only compared twenty small jurisdictions, but we believe that they were selected in such a way that many other small jurisdictions may also find the information and conclusions provided by this book useful. If some of the recommendations in the last part of the book can help advance social security in some small jurisdictions, I will be satisfied. In the meanwhile, the Small Jurisdictions Research Group of KU Leuven and I will continue to be at the service of all small jurisdictions and their social security. May this book be the start of a fruitful cooperation with and also between (the social security systems of) small jurisdictions, to the benefit of the people who live there, the most vulnerable first.

The manufacturer's authorised representative in the EU is Springer Nature Customer Service Centre GmbH, Europaplatz 3, 69115 Heidelberg, Germany. If you have any concerns regarding our products, please contact ProductSafety@springernature.com

Printed and bound by CPI Group (UK) Ltd, Croydon, CR0 4YY
30/09/2026
02225704-0011